CW01647126

MILTON AND THE BURDI

Throughout his writings, Milton, deeply engaged in political and theological controversy, sought to clear a space for human freedom in a world ruled by an omniscient and omnipotent deity. *Paradise Lost* and *Samson Agonistes*, as well as other works by Milton in verse and prose, explore the problematical aspects of a universe ruled by an Old Testament God of wrath, demanding obedience, who allows his creatures the freedom to be 'authors' of their own fate. *Milton and the Burden of Freedom* examines the contradictions inherent in Milton's religious, political and ethical beliefs as expressed in his poems, prose writings and the treatise *De Doctrina Christiana.* Milton, whose writings are rooted in the Reformed tradition while challenging Calvinist orthodoxy, is both radical and conservative. Warren Chernaik traces the evolution of Milton's attitude towards freedom, servitude and virtue during a century of political upheaval and disappointed hopes.

WARREN CHERNAIK is Emeritus Professor of English, University of London. He was the founding Director of the Institute of English Studies (IES), University of London, and is now a Senior Research Fellow of IES. He is the author of *The Myth of Rome in Shakespeare and His Contemporaries* (2011), *The Cambridge Introduction to Shakespeare's History Plays* (2007), a study of *The Merchant of Venice* (2005), *Sexual Freedom in Restoration Literature* (1995), *The Poet's Time: Politics and Religion in the Work of Andrew Marvell* (1983) and essays on such authors as Marvell, Milton, Shakespeare, Jonson, Herbert, Traherne, Rochester, Pepys and Behn, as well as co-editing books on topics as diverse as detective fiction, changes in copyright law and Andrew Marvell.

MILTON AND THE BURDEN OF FREEDOM

WARREN CHERNAIK

University of London

CAMBRIDGE
UNIVERSITY PRESS

CAMBRIDGE
UNIVERSITY PRESS

University Printing House, Cambridge CB2 8BS, United Kingdom

One Liberty Plaza, 20th Floor, New York, NY 10006, USA

477 Williamstown Road, Port Melbourne, VIC 3207, Australia

314-321, 3rd Floor, Plot 3, Splendor Forum, Jasola District Centre, New Delhi - 110025, India

79 Anson Road, #06-04/06, Singapore 079906

Cambridge University Press is part of the University of Cambridge.

It furthers the University's mission by disseminating knowledge in the pursuit of education, learning and research at the highest international levels of excellence.

www.cambridge.org
Information on this title: www.cambridge.org/9781316607114

First published 2017
First paperback edition 2019

A catalogue record for this publication is available from the British Library

ISBN 978-1-107-15318-9 Hardback
ISBN 978-1-316-60711-4 Paperback

In memory of Stella Purce Revard

Contents

Acknowledgements

Any book of literary criticism or scholarship is part of a continuing dialogue, one voice in a conversation. Stella Revard has been a friend since, many years ago, we were students at Yale in Louis Martz's seminar in Poetic Traditions of the Renaissance, and I have learned an immense amount from her in our conversations about Milton, the classical tradition and, her particular love, opera. I also owe a continuing debt to Tom Corns, from whom I have learned more than from any other Milton scholar, though we have sometimes disagreed, and he has given me the opportunity to give papers on Milton and his contemporaries at the British Milton Seminar and elsewhere. His detailed comments as a reader for Cambridge University Press have been extremely helpful to me in revision, as have the comments of a second, anonymous reader. Judith Chernaik, as a novelist and a student of English and European Romanticism, as well as a discerning editor and critic, has provided an invaluable perspective at every stage in the composition of this book. Achsah Guibbory, Neil Forsyth, N. H. Keeble and Peter Medine have read drafts of several chapters and have given me helpful advice in revising the book. Other friends and colleagues who have helped me in formulating and clarifying my ideas on Milton and his age include Paul Stevens, Sharon Achinstein, Martin Dzelzainis, David Loewenstein, Quentin Skinner, Nicholas Tyacke, Laura Knoppers, Karen Edwards, Joseph Shub, Nicholas von Maltzahn, John Coffey, Carter Revard, Gordon Campbell, Janet Clare, H. Neville Davies, Tom Cain, Kevin Killeen and Nicholas McDowell. Sarah Stanton of Cambridge University Press has been encouraging and supportive throughout. I am grateful to Sarah Starkey for overseeing the later stages of production. An earlier version of Chapter 6 was published by the University of Toronto Press in *Early Modern Nationalism and Milton's England*, edited by David Loewenstein and Paul Stevens (2008), copyright University of Toronto Press Incorporated. I am grateful to Manchester University Press for permission to publish a revised version of the essay

'Choosing a Captain Back for Egypt: Milton and the Restoration', in *From Revolution to Restoration*, edited by Janet Clare (forthcoming, 2016), in Chapter 8, and passages from the essay 'Christian Liberty in Marvell and Milton', from *Freedom and the English Revolution*, edited by R. C. Richardson and G. M. Ridden (Manchester University Press, 1986), in Chapter 2. Revised versions of passages in 'Biblical Republicanism', *Prose Studies*, 23 (2000), 147–60; 'Civil Liberty in Milton, the Levellers and Winstanley', *Prose Studies*, 22 (1999), 101–20; 'Tragic Freedom in *Samson Agonistes*', *The European Legacy*, 17 (April 2012), 197–211; and '*Areopagitica:* The Known Rules of Antient Liberty', *The European Legacy*, 17 (2012), 317–31, appear in several chapters, and once more I am grateful to the publishers for permission to use these extracts. I owe particular thanks to Tom Corns, Hugh Adlington, Sarah Knight and Tony Crawley for giving me the opportunity to try out early versions of several chapters at the British Milton Seminar in 2011, 2014 and 2015, the International Milton Symposium in 2009 and 2015 and a conference on Images of Monarchy in 2013. The staff of the Rare Book Room at the British Library (where most of the book was written, in longhand drafts to be revised afterwards) and the University of London Library at Senate House have been helpful at all times.

INTRODUCTION

Free to Fall
Milton and the Old Testament God

I

Milton and the Burden of Freedom examines the contradictions inherent in the religious, political and ethical beliefs of Milton, as expressed in his poems, prose writings and the treatise *De Doctrina Christiana.* Like his fellow seventeenth-century radicals John Goodwin and Richard Overton, Milton can be considered a post-Calvinist, rooted in the Reformed tradition yet challenging Calvinist orthodoxy. Milton's political views, like his religious beliefs, are radical in some respects, conservative in others. Milton is a biblical republican as well as a classical republican, and, as with many of his contemporaries, secular arguments in his polemical writings are buttressed with citations from scripture and Reformed theologians. As *Paradise Regained* and *Samson Agonistes* show, the relationship between the biblical and classical sides of Milton is complex and problematical, and the two cannot always be harmonized as easily as they are in such poems as *Lycidas.*

Though in *De Doctrina Christiana* and *Paradise Lost* Milton dissents from the standard tenets of Calvinism in his anti-Trinitarianism and his rejection of Calvinist doctrines of predestination and the utter extinction of free will after the Fall, there remains a residue of Calvinist belief even in those passages where he sets forth his own independent position. This is illustrated in a passage in *Paradise Lost*, Book III, in which God explains to his Son that even after Adam and Eve have succumbed to temptation, 'Man shall not quite be lost, but sav'd who will, / Yet not of will in him, but grace in me' (*PL*, III.173–4). The idea that man cannot achieve salvation through his own efforts, but only through the freely offered grace of God is standard Calvinist doctrine, with which Milton entirely concurs.[1] But the lines that follow are flatly self-contradictory, and seem to waver between a Calvinist assertion that there are some privileged mortals who are, without any regard to merit, predestined for salvation, and the claim that there is another group of mortals, not specially chosen for election or damnation, who have been given the chance to earn salvation by repenting their sins.

> Some I have chosen of peculiar grace
> Elect above the rest; so is my will:
> The rest shall hear me call, and oft be warnd
> Thir sinful state, and to appease betimes
> Th'incensed Deitie, while offerd grace
> Invites; for I will cleer thir senses dark,
> What may suffice, and soft'n stonie hearts
> To pray, repent, and bring obedience due.
> (*PL*, III.183–90)[2]

Like the Dutch Remonstrants, followers of the theologian Arminius, and his fellow Puritan radical John Goodwin, Milton redefines predestination and election as conditional on faith, rather than an arbitrary assertion of the divine will, by which some are chosen and others irretrievably damned: 'Predestination and election are not particular but only general: that is, they belong to all who believe in their hearts and persist in their belief' (*De Doctrina*, I.iv/*CPW*, VI.176).[3] Yet even in the key passage of theodicy in *Paradise Lost*, bringing out how, with the guidance of the inner 'Umpire *Conscience*', postlapsarian mankind is able 'once more' to 'stand / On even ground against his mortal foe', the emphasis is on God's power: man must learn how feeble he is, and how dependent upon the all-seeing deity:

> By me upheld, that he may know how frail
> His fall'n condition is, and to me ow
> All his deliverance, and to none but me.
> (*PL*, III.178–82, 194–5)

A. S. P. Woodhouse in *Puritanism and Liberty* has suggested that within the Puritan tradition, a desire for liberty (defined explicitly as Christian liberty) frequently comes into conflict with 'a passionate zeal for positive reform . . . in the interests of righteousness', even if it involves a degree of coercion.[4] Both Luther and Calvin believed in a clear distinction between spiritual and civil liberty: 'in civil policy, obedience to the Law must be severely required':

> There are in man, so to speak, two worlds, over which different kings and different laws have authority. Through this distinction it comes about that we are not to misapply to the political order the gospel teaching on spiritual

> freedom . . . as if [men] were released from all bodily servitude because they are free according to the spirit.[5]

Milton, in contrast, defines Christian liberty in terms of freedom from slavery, making no distinction in this respect between civil and spiritual liberty. In the *Second Defence*, he speaks of 'three varieties of liberty without which civilized life is scarcely possible, namely ecclesiastical liberty, domestic or personal liberty, and civil liberty'.[6] In *De Doctrina*, citing as proof-texts a series of New Testament passages contrasting 'the yoke of slavery' and liberation from bondage, he asserts, 'Christian Liberty means that Christ our liberator frees us from the slavery of sin and thus from the rule of the law and of men, as if we were emancipated slaves'.[7]

In *De Doctrina* as in such works as *A Treatise of Civil Power* (1659), Milton argues a position characteristic of radical Protestantism, going far beyond the orthodox Calvinist doctrine: that the entire Mosaic Law, both moral and ceremonial, has been abolished by the coming of Christ and the promulgation of the Gospel, with 'the new dispensation of the Covenant of Grace'.[8] *De Doctrina* I.xxvi presents the Mosaic Law of the Old Testament as 'a written code, consisting of many stipulations and intended for the Israelites alone', an 'elementary, childish and servile discipline', which, for Christian believers, has been supplanted. The Gospel, he says in the next chapter, 'much more excellent and perfect than the Law', 'has been written in the hearts of believers', promising 'eternal life to all men of all nations who believe in the revealed Christ'.[9] Milton held similar views as early as 1641, in *The Reason of Church-Government*: 'God is no more a judge under the sentence of the Law, nor as it were a schoolmaister of perishable rites, but a more indulgent father'. The Law, an 'imperfect and obscure institution', he argues, 'could not give rules to the compleat and glorious ministration of the Gospell', and is appropriate for 'a Childe' not yet attaining maturity (*CPW*, I.837). In *A Treatise of Civil Power*, arguing against the power of the magistrate to regulate religious worship, Milton made a similar distinction between 'inward perswasion', appropriate to the individual conscience, and outward force:

> The state of religion under the gospel is far differing from what it was under the law: then was the state of rigor, childhood, bondage and works, to all which force was not unbefitting; now is the state of grace, manhood, freedom and faith; to all which belongs willingness and reason, not force . . . As if God of his special grace in the gospel had to this end freed us from his own commandments in these things, that our freedom should subject us to a more greevous yoke, the commandments of men. (*CPW*, VII.259, 263)

By this argument, the promptings of conscience must be seen as sovereign, overriding 'the commandments of men', rulers who falsely claim to be God's representatives on earth.

As we will see, Milton's view of the relationship between Gospel and Law was not always consistent, and he argued a position in the divorce tracts different from that in *De Doctrina* and *A Treatise of Civil Power*.[10] But he was consistent, both before and after the Restoration, in his desire to 'advance the cause of real and substantial liberty; which must be sought, not without, but within', and in using similar arguments in defence of spiritual, domestic, and political liberty.[11] Milton was notorious, both in his own time and afterwards, for his arguments in favour of tyrannicide, and for extending the principle of consent from the political to the domestic sphere. In *The Doctrine and Discipline of Divorce*, he writes:

> He who marries, intends as little to conspire his own ruine, as he that swears Allegiance; and as a whole people is in proportion to an ill Government, so is one man to an ill mariage. If they against any authority, Cov'nant, or Statute, may, by the sovereign edict of charity, save not only their lives, but honest liberties from unworthy bondage, as well may he against any private Cov'nant, which he never enter'd to his mischief, redeem himself from unsupportable disturbances to honest peace and just contentment.[12]

In *Tetrachordon*, Milton argues that the remedy of divorce, freeing oneself by legal means from 'unworthy bondage', is made necessary under the fallen state, at a time when 'the sons of men grew violent & injurious': 'while man and woman were both perfet each to other, there needed no divorce'. The parallel between domestic and political servitude is developed further in a passage where Milton suggests that an erroneous choice should not doom men to endless suffering: '[God] suffer'd divorce as well as mariage, our imperfet and degenerat condition of necessity requiring this law among the rest, as a remedy against intolerable wrong and servitude above the patience of man to beare'.[13]

In *The Tenure of Kings and Magistrates*, Milton argued a position that was no less radical and that laid him open to attack as one 'that by his will would shake off his Governours as he doth his Wives'. Answers to Milton's writings on kingship treat him as a dangerous 'Libertine', one who sought '*to pull down Monarchy, and set up Anarchy*', just as, in his tractate on divorce, 'the bonds of marriage are let loose to inordinate lust'.[14] The radical nature of Milton's version of the theory of popular sovereignty is evident in the title page of *Tenure*, in the reference to 'any, who have the

Power, to call into account a Tyrant, or wicked King', and in the following bold statement:

> It follows lastly, that since the King or Magistrate holds his autoritie of the people, both originaly and naturally for their good in the first place, and not his own, then may the people as oft as they shall judge it for the best, either choose him or reject him, retaine him or depose him though no Tyrant, meerly by the liberty and right of free born Men, to be govern'd as seems to them best.[15]

Here Milton goes well beyond the position argued by Calvinists and in the Reformed tradition generally, and indeed, beyond the Huguenot tract *Vindiciae contra Tyrannos*, a classic statement of the right of resistance to tyrants. In the 'constitutionalist' position argued by Martin Bucer, John Knox, and the author of *Vindiciae*, the right of resistance against a ruler who had abused his power was limited to 'inferior magistrates'.[16] According to *Vindiciae*, 'private persons . . . have no power, they have no publik command, nor any calling to unsheath the sword of authority'. The author of this tract argues that the ultimate sovereignty rests with the people, but defines 'the people' as 'those who hold authority from the people . . . to represent the whole body of the people'.[17] Milton, in contrast, interprets the doctrine of popular consent in a way that unequivocally gives to the body of the people the right to depose their rulers whenever it suits them to do so, or, alternatively, to choose to retain them. The people set kings on their thrones and can topple them from their thrones, even if the ruler is 'no Tyrant'. With sovereignty on temporary loan to those holding power, the people are able at their discretion 'to reassume it to themselves . . . or to dispose of it by any alteration, as they shall judge most conducing to the public good' (*Tenure*, *CPW*, III.212).

In the second edition of *Tenure*, Milton reinforces his secular republican arguments with several pages of testimony from 'true Ministers of the Protestant doctrine . . . famous and religious men, who first reformd the Church' – Luther, Zwingli, Calvin, Martin Bucer, the Marian exile Christopher Goodman. On the title page of the 1650 edition he claims that these extracts from 'the best & learnedest among Protestant Divines' concur in 'asserting the position of this book'. But these 'Testimonies' draw back from the radical position Milton had initially maintained: 'And indeed I find it generally the cleere and positive determination of them all . . . who have writt'n on this argument; that to do justice on a lawless King, is to a private man unlawful, to an inferior Magistrate lawfull'.[18]

There are two arguments advanced by Milton in *Tenure*: that tyrants forfeit their right to rule by abusing the power they have been granted, and, more boldly, that all free men have 'in themselves the power to remove, or to abolish any governour supreme or subordinat', or else must be considered 'no better than slaves or vassals'.[19] But even if the two lines of argument (both common in republican discourse) can be seen as complementary, Milton's imprecision in defining 'the people' is troubling, and reveals problematical aspects of his ideology.

Sir Robert Filmer, author of *Patriarcha* and a hostile critic, in *Observations on Mr Milton upon Salmasius*, is scathing in his comments on the shifting meanings of 'the people' in Milton's polemics against kingship. In the *Defence*, in which 'the People of England' are central to the Latin title (*Pro Populo Anglicano Defensio*), Milton at one point defines 'the people' as 'the sounder and better part only', and in *Tenure*, in a passage quoted by Filmer, he writes:

> But who in particular is a Tyrant cannot be determin'd in a general discours, otherwise then by supposition; his particular charge, and the sufficient proof of it must determin that: which I leave to Magistrates, at least to the uprighter sort of them, and of the people, though in number less than many, in whom faction least have prevaild above the Law of nature and right reason, to judge as they find cause.[20]

The argument in *Tenure*, stated on the title page, is that 'the ordinary Magistrate', i.e. the legally constituted Parliament, has 'neglected, or deny'd' to fulfil its responsibilities in deposing a king who has abused his power, and that therefore the power reverts to 'the people' to call a tyrant to account.[21] In the *Defence*, Milton explicitly defends both Pride's Purge, the expulsion of members from the Parliament who were reluctant to proceed against the king, and the trial and execution of the king, as the acts of a 'sound' or healthier 'part' (*pars potior et sanior*, in the Latin text). Answering Salmasius, Milton argues not only that a 'part' can act on behalf of the whole, but that a virtuous minority has the right to override a majority complicit with injustice:

> 'Did the people', you say, 'do violence to the commoners of the lower house, putting some to flight, and so on?' I say it was the people; for why should I not say that the action of the better, the sound part of the Parliament, in which resides the real power of the people, was the act of the people? If a majority in Parliament prefer enslavement and putting the commonwealth up for sale, is it not right for a minority to prevent it if they can and preserve their freedom?[22]

Filmer comments critically on both of these passages: if 'the people' can be defined in terms of virtue or soundness, how can we know who they are?

> Nay, J[ohn] M[ilton] will not allow the major part of the representers to be the people, but 'the sounder and better part only' of them and in right down terms he tells us, to determine who is a tyrant he leaves 'to magistrates, at least to the uprighter sort of them, and of the people'. . . If the 'sounder, the better, and the uprighter' have the power of the people, how shall we know, or who shall judge who they be?[23]

In a later passage, Filmer returns to the attack, arguing not only that Milton is inconsistent in his use of the term 'people', but that his arguments, nominally in defence of liberty, in fact restrict liberty, justifying the use of force. He cites several passages where Milton speaks of a minority as a 'sounder part'.

> If it be demanded what is meant by this word people? 1. Sometimes it is *populus universus* [the whole people], and then every child must have his consent asked, which is impossible. Sometimes it is *pars major* [the greater part], and sometimes it is *pars potior et sanior* [the better and sounder part] . . .
>
> But it seems the major part will not carry it, nor be allowed except they be the 'better part and the sounder part'. We are told 'the sounder part implored the help of the army when it saw itself and the commonwealth betrayed', and that the 'soldiers judged better than the great council, and by arms saved the commonwealth, which the great council had almost damned by their votes'.[24]

Filmer continues, with biting irony:

> Here we see what the people is – to wit, 'the sounder part of which the army is the judge'. Thus upon the matter the soldiers are the people – which being so, we may discern where the liberty of the people lieth . . . A miserable liberty, which is only to choose to whom we will give our liberty, which we may not keep. (*Observations*, p. 203)

Several of Milton's political allies in and around 1649 had literally argued that 'the soldiers are the people', gaining de-facto legitimacy for their actions on the grounds that they were acting for the public good, filling a political vacuum. John Goodwin in 1648 justified Pride's Purge on exactly these grounds in a pamphlet ominously titled *Right and Might Well Met*. The Parliament, Goodwin argued, by abusing its power, had lost its legitimacy, and the Army was acting as the people's deputies in expelling those members of Parliament who sought accommodation with the king.

> If we measure the lawfulness of Parliamentary Judicature by the call of the people thereunto, the Army hath every whit as lawfull a constitution to judge who are enemies to the peace and safety of the Kingdome, as the Parliament it self hath. Nor doth it at all argue any illegality in their judgements about the Parliament men, that they had not the express consent of the people therein.[25]

According to William Sedgwick in *A Second View of the Army Remonstrance* (1649), 'This Army are truly the *people of England*, and have the nature and power of the *whole* in them'.[26] Goodwin's title suggests a damaging weakness in this version of contract theory, by its too easy identification of might with right: any body of armed men can justify their actions by declaring themselves unacknowledged legislators.

In a passage in *The Readie and Easie Way* (1660) that has troubled twentieth-century Milton scholars, Milton, having become deeply distrustful of 'the noise and shouting of a rude multitude' whom he considers full of 'prejudice and impatience' and ignorant of 'thir own good both religious and civil', goes so far as to urge compulsion on those who differ from his opinion of 'the main end of government'.

> Is it just or reasonable, that most voices against the main end of government should enslave the less number that would be free? More just it is doubtless, if it com to force, that a less number compell a greater to retain, which can be no wrong to them, thir libertie, than that a greater number for the pleasure of thir baseness, compell a less most injuriously to be thir fellow slaves. They who seek nothing but thir own just libertie, have alwaies right to winn it and to keep it, when ever they have power, be the voices never so numerous that oppose it.[27]

This argument for the forcible rule of the enlightened minority over the unregenerate majority, added in the second edition of *The Readie and Easie Way*, is consistent with passages in *Tenure* and *Defence* justifying the actions of a Parliamentary minority acting as 'the sounder part' of the whole. *The Readie and Easie Way* in its second edition includes several passages defending these acts of 'the best affected . . . and best principl'd of the people', who 'stood not numbring on which side were most voices in Parlament, but on which side appeerd to them most reason, most safetie' (*CPW*, VII.414). Milton's proposed 'free commonwealth' in *The Readie and Easie Way* is extremely remote from egalitarian democracy, with a severely limited franchise and power vested in a perpetual Senate of 'ablest men' chosen by this limited electorate, with its members, once elected, to hold office until death (*CPW*, VII.432–4). Several twentieth-century critics have commented on the discrepancy between this 'repressive programme', with its appeal to 'naked force', and the ringing phrases about liberty and the hopes of revolutionary England as a 'towardly and pregnant soile', on the verge of transformation into 'a Nation of Prophets, of Sages, and of Worthies' in *Areopagitica*.[28]

As theorists of republicanism have pointed out, the republican tradition, both in its Roman antecedents and in the Renaissance, has an inherent bias toward aristocracy rather than democracy. The 'politics of virtue' is a recurrent theme among republicans, and is particularly prominent in Milton. Milton's proposals for models of government in *The Readie and Easie Way*, while they reject any aristocracy of birth or landed property, envisage 'an aristocracy of civil and . . . religious virtue', rather like the Guardians in Plato's *Republic*.[29] The idea of the virtuous minority or saving remnant, an aristocracy of the godly, with its origins in the Old Testament, can be seen as 'the political counterpart of the harsh Puritan belief in the duty and privilege of the righteous to impose the divine will on the unregenerate mass'.[30]

Woodhouse and Barker, historicist critics of an earlier generation, have argued that though Milton and other radical Protestants such as Goodwin disagreed with orthodox Calvinist tenets in many respects, Milton expressed himself consistently 'in terms of the doctrines fundamental to Puritanism'. Central to these beliefs and 'constant amongst all the Puritan groups' was the idea of the 'holy community', set aside from a potentially defiling sinful world. Puritanism, according to Woodhouse, 'means a determined and varied effort to create the holy community and to meet, with different degrees or compromise and adjustment, the problem of its conflict with the world'.[31] The paradox of Christian liberty, as Woodhouse has argued, is that it is simultaneously liberating and exclusionary: 'the very fact of grounding one's appeal on *Christian* liberty restricts the direct benefits of that appeal to the regenerate: Christian liberty freed you *for*, not *from*, the service of God'.[32]

The religious doctrines set forth in *De Doctrina* and in such pamphlets as *Considerations Touching the Likeliest Means to Remove Hirelings Out of the Church* (hereafter, *Hirelings*) and *A Treatise of Civil Power* are in many ways those associated with Congregationalism or Independency: a suspicion of the very idea of a national church as of compulsion in religious matters, a belief in 'free consent'.

> The Christian church is universal; not ti'd to nation, dioces or parish, but consisting of many particular churches complete in themselves; gatherd, not by compulsion or the accident of dwelling nigh together, but by free consent chusing both thir particular church and thir church-officers.[33]

The emphasis on universality, an invisible church existing 'in the hearts of believers' and not 'subject to spatial considerations', is characteristically Miltonic, where the idea that a church is 'gatherd' rather than tied to a particular diocese is central to Congregationalism. According to Geoffrey Nuttall, the principle of separation 'from the Ignorant the Vile and the Profane', 'a separation . . . of the clean from the unclean', is a guiding tenet of the more radical varieties of Puritanism, coexisting with an insistence on 'every man's own voluntary consent' to church membership.[34] Where Milton in *Areopagitica* emphasized the need to accept 'brotherly dissimilitudes', as against 'a grosse conforming stupidity, a stark and dead congealment of *wood and hay and stubble*, forced and frozen together', his political ally and fellow Puritan Arminian Goodwin was militant in the way he sought to implement the ideal of a gathered church. In 1648, he was expelled from his London church after refusing to administer the sacrament to anyone but 'the godly', and his gathered church, which after 1645 initially met in his own house, admitted covenanted members both inside and outside parish boundaries.[35]

Though Milton argued in *De Doctrina* and elsewhere that the Mosaic Law of the Old Testament had been supplanted by the Gospel, the deity of *Paradise Lost* and *Samson Agonistes* is in many respects an Old Testament God. The idea of election, like the idea of the chosen people, depends upon an act of exclusion: 'identity is purchased at the expense of the Other'. In God's covenant with Abraham, the gift of land and of eventual prosperity is conditional on obedience, and on the rejection of other gods, other nations, as unclean: 'On that day, the Lord made a covenant with Abram and said, "To your descendants I give this land, from the river of Egypt to the great river, the Euphrates – the land of the Kenites, Kenizzites, Kadmonites, Hittites, Perizzites, Rephaim, Amorites, Canaanites, Girgasbites and Jebusites." '[36] What is extraordinary about this passage is the catalogue of all the nations, each worshipping its own false gods, already occupying this land. After Abraham has shown his obedience by offering to sacrifice his son Isaac, Yahweh goes on to say, 'And your descendants shall possess the gates of their enemies and by your descendants shall all the nations of the earth bless themselves – because you obeyed my voice'.[37] The book of Leviticus sets forth a number of detailed regulations by which believing Israelites can testify to Yahweh that 'you are his people':

> I am the Lord your God, who have separated you from the peoples. You shall therefore make a distinction between the clean beast and the unclean . . . You shall be holy to me; for I the Lord am holy, and have separated you from the peoples, that you should be mine.[38]

Though such dietary prohibitions may well, as Milton says in *De Doctrina*, be 'intended for the Israelites alone', embodying 'a curse for the disobedient' (*CPW*, VI.517), nevertheless, when the Hebrew and Christian Bibles are set side by side, the continuities outweigh the discontinuities. Again and again throughout human history, divine sanctions will be cited for acts of expropriation, in which communities outside the pale are defined 'in such a way as to justify our possession of what belongs to them'.[39]

A recurrent metaphor in the Old Testament is 'whoring after false gods', suggesting a jealous deity who deplores the sexual infidelity of his weak-willed followers, and again and again needs to 'show them who was master . . . so that they will always fear me'.[40] Though in the theology of *Paradise Lost*, as in *De Doctrina*, 'imposition of strict Laws', worship based on 'servil fear', is contrasted with 'free / Acceptance of large Grace' (*PL*, XII.304–5), the God of *Paradise Lost* is pre-eminently a God of wrath. The word 'wrath' occurs twenty-six times in *Paradise Lost*, mostly in connection with Satan ('infinite wrauth, and infinite despaire', in IV.74), but also, memorably, in Adam's anguished soliloquy in Book X:

> For though the Lord of all be infinite,
> Is his wrauth also? Be it, man is not so,
> But mortal doom'd. How can he exercise
> Wrath without end on Man whom Death must end? . . .
> Will he draw out,
> For angers sake, finite to infinite
> To punish man, to satisfie his rigour
> Satisfi'd never[?].
>
> (*PL*, X.794–7, 801–4)

Where George Herbert's God, even when he shows himself to be a 'Lord of power, / Killing and quick'ning, bringing down to hell / And up to heaven in an hour', is always a 'Lord of love', extending a hand of friendly communion even to 'unkind, ungrateful' man, Milton's God seldom relaxes his sternness towards his creatures.[41]

Though Milton, like Calvin, rejects any anthropomorphic conception of a God who is 'far beyond man's imagination, let alone his understanding', so that, according to *De Doctrina*, 'the ascription of human feelings to God' is inappropriate, Milton's deity, like the God of the Old Testament, is frequently represented as grieving, raging, giving vent to his power to destroy.

> And it repented the Lord that he had made man on the earth, and it grieved him at his heart.

> Furthermore the Lord spake unto me, saying, I have seen this people, and, behold, it is a stiff-necked people: Let me alone, that I may destroy them, and blot out their name from under heaven.[42]

One emotion Milton's God frequently is represented as expressing, Michael Lieb has argued, is hate. In *PL*, Book VI, the War in Heaven, the Son, invested with the Father's awesome power, says 'Whom thou hat'st, I hate, and can put on / Thy terrors, as I put thy mildness on': 'So spake the Son, and into terrour chang'd / His count'nance too severe to be behold / And full of wrauth bent on his Enemies' (*PL*, VI.734–5, 824–6).[43]

The emotion of hate, in passages anathematizing one's opponents as God's enemies, is prominent in Milton's anti-prelatical pamphlets: 'whom thou hat'st, I hate'. In *An Apology*, Milton invokes the 'fiery Chariot' of 'the invincible warriour Zeale', which with 'high autoritie and indignation' can confute 'perverse and fraudulent seducers', as it 'drives over the heads of Scarlet Prelats . . . brusing their stiff necks under his flaming wheels'. This 'bitter and irefull' voice Milton associates with 'the true Prophets of old'.[44] One particularly strong instance of Milton's fiery zeal is the peroration of his first anti-prelatical pamphlet, *Of Reformation in England*, expressing a desire to obliterate his opponents, consigning them to eternal perdition, while, in contrast, 'the *Hymns*, and *Halleluiahs* of *Saints*' shall resound in heavenly chorus in praise of the righteous.

> But they . . . shall be thrown downe eternally into the *darkest* and *deepest Gulfe* of HELL, where under the *despightfull controule*, the trample and spurne of all the other *Damned*, that in the anguish of their *Torture* shall have no other ease then to exercise a *Raving* and *Bestiall Tyranny* over them as their *Slaves* and *Negro's*, they shall remaine in that plight for ever, the *basest*, the *lowermost*, the *most dejected*, most *underfoot* and *downe-trodden Vassals* of *Perdition*.[45]

Here, as he piles on the punishment, Milton is exulting in the pain he can inflict on the prostrate bodies of his imagined vanquished adversaries.

In the last two books of *Paradise Lost*, where the Archangel Michael instructs Adam, showing him some of the consequences of the Fall, the emphasis throughout is on God the judge, the inexorable course of punishment handed out to transgressors. The recurrent conflict in Milton's writings between what can be called 'authoritarian' and 'liberal' perspectives is particularly marked in Books XI and XII. The deity made manifest in the two concluding books of the poem is an arbitrary, punitive God not unlike the fierce, unyielding God of Calvinist ideology, directly intervening in human affairs. Such passages leave little scope for human agency. In Michael's grim narrative of postlapsarian history, sinful man is, more often than not, the passive recipient of punishment by an incensed God, provoked from time to time 'to raise them enemies', while at other times the all-powerful deity 'relents', deciding to 'remit his Ire'. This is a deity who, under the Old Law, can accurately be described as ruling by 'servil fear'.[46]

Some Milton scholars, claiming that Milton after 1660 turns away from politics, in pursuit of a 'paradise within', see the Restoration of Charles II as marking a clear divide between the early and later Milton. In *Milton and the Burden of Freedom*, in contrast, I argue that in certain fundamental respects, Milton is unchanged as he responds to differing circumstances.[47] *Paradise Lost* and *Samson Agonistes*, as well as other works by Milton, early and late, explore the problematical aspects of a universe ruled by an all-powerful God of wrath, demanding obedience, who allows his creatures the freedom to be 'authors' of their own fate. In the chapters that follow, I examine some of the unresolved tensions in Milton's writings, as he grapples with the implications of the worship of an Old Testament deity 'whose jealousie brooks no corrival'.[48]

II

Though Milton in works written at different times was alert to particular audiences and immediate historical contexts, there is an underlying consistency in his ethical, religious, and political beliefs during most of his career. The evidence for Milton's doctrinal allegiances during his residence at Cambridge between 1625 and 1632 is inconclusive.[49] In *The Reason of Church-Government* (1641), he describes himself as having been 'Church-outed by the Prelats', deflected from an original plan to enter the ministry in 'the church, to whose service, by the intentions of my parents and friends I was destin'd of a child, and in mine own resolutions'. The remarks on the 'tyranny' that had 'invaded the Church' are in keeping with the attacks on Laudian prelates in the other anti-prelatical tracts of the 1640s and with his bitter reflections in *Lycidas* (1637) on 'our corrupted Clergy then in their height', neglecting their pastoral duties and spreading 'foul contagion'.[50]

Milton characteristically sees the poetic calling as akin to a religious calling, a response to God's command. In his *Letter to a Friend*, written at the age of twenty-four in 1632, Milton alludes to 'that command in the gospell set out by the terrible seasing of him that hid the talent' and to a second parable, in which 'the maister of the vinyard came to give each one his hire', in passages which, full of tortured self-castigation, present his career up to that point as a failure to perform the tasks allotted him by his 'great task Master'. The letter, possibly addressed to Thomas Young, his former tutor, encloses Milton's sonnet 7, 'How soon hath time', and can serve as a commentary on that poem.

> Besides that in sundry other respects I must acknowledge me to profitt by you when ever wee meet, you are often to me . . . as a good watch man to admonish that the howres of the night passe on (for so I call my life as yet obscure, & unserviceable to mankind) & that the day wth me is at hand wherin Christ commands all to Labour while there is light.[51]

In *Ad Patrem* and in *The Reason of Church-Government*, Milton associates 'labour and intense study (which I take to be my portion in this life)' with his choice of the vocation of poet, but in the *Letter to a Friend*, in contrast, 'too much love of Learning' is presented as an 'emptie & fantastick chase of shadows', producing nothing but endless frustration and guilt at being 'unable to doe that wch all mortals most aspire to'.[52]

Milton's Latin elegy on the death of Lancelot Andrewes, Bishop of Winchester, written in 1626 at the age of seventeen, has been claimed as evidence for Laudian sympathies in the early Milton, though the poem remains wholly within the conventions of its genre. The praise of the venerable Andrewes, ascended into Heaven and surrounded by applauding angels, does not imply any ideological allegiances; as Stella Revard has suggested, the poem can be considered a 'meditation on death as the universal human end'.[53] Milton's Latin poem addressed to Thomas Young, written in the following year, on the other hand, is charged with feeling, and suggests not only the ties of friendship but spiritual affinities. Young, then living in Hamburg, is addressed as an exile, 'alone and helpless in a strange land', surrounded by wars and rumours of wars, and the poem presents him as 'expelled from England for his Puritan faith', a victim of the ingratitude of a 'cruel parent', his homeland:

> Et, tibi quam patrii non exhibuere penates
>   Sede peregrinâ quaeris egena opem.
> [The livelihood your home failed to provide you,
>   You seek, impoverished, in a foreign place.]

The poem compares Young to the prophet Elijah, fleeing the wicked King Ahab, and to Odysseus, who, after a series of misfortunes, can look forward to seeing his homeland once more.[54]

In Chapter 1, 'Milton's Post-Calvinist Theology', I argue that from the mid-1630s to the end of Milton's career, a clear trajectory can be discerned in his religious beliefs and allegiances. Like Young, and like the political and religious radical John Goodwin, as well as the more moderate Puritan controversialist Richard Baxter, Milton can be described as post-Calvinist in his theology. Again and again, Milton expresses a kinship with 'the rest of the *Churches* abroad', 'our firmest, & faithfullest neighbours abroad', 'all Protestant Princes, and Commonwealths', arguing that the English should come 'to *unity* with our neighbour Reformed sister Churches, which with the blessing of *peace* and *pure doctrine* have now long time flourish'd'.[55] Petty differences that distinguish 'one visible congregation from another, though it be not in fundamentals', he says in *Areopagitica*, are insignificant, merely 'brotherly dissimilitudes'.[56] Reform, he argues, must be a continuous progress, never degenerating into 'a gross conforming stupidity, a stark and dead congealment'.

> We boast our light; but if we look not wisely on the Sun it self, it smites us into darknes . . . No, if other things as great in the Church, and in the rule of life both economical and politicall, be not lookt into and reform'd, we have looked so long upon the blaze that *Zuinglius* and *Calvin* have beacon'd up to us, that we are stark blind. (*Areopagitica*, *CPW*, II.550, 564)

Milton's starting point in his theological speculation, then, is the commonly held doctrine of Reformed Protestantism. But in a series of stages he works out an independent position, which departs in many ways from Calvinist orthodoxy. A similar process can be observed in the development of Milton's political views, as, in response to differing contexts and audiences he wishes to persuade, he moves in less than a decade from the statement in *Of Reformation in England* that 'there is no Civill Goverment that hath beene known, no not the *Spartan*, not the *Roman* . . . more divinely and harmoniously tun'd, more equally ballanc'd as it were by the hand and seale of Justice, then is the Common-wealth of *England*', under a limited monarchy, to the utter rejection of monarchy in *Tenure* as a system of government which makes 'the subject no better than the Kings slave, his chattell, or his possession that may be bought and sould'.[57]

Though Milton's disagreements with standard Reformed theology are most fully set forth in *De Doctrina*, similar views find expression not only in *Paradise Lost*, *Paradise Regained*, and *Samson Agonistes*, works published after the restoration of the Stuart monarchy in 1660, but in many of his works written earlier, in very different circumstances.

Throughout his writings, Milton sought to clear a space for human freedom in a world ruled by an omnipotent and omniscient deity. In Chapter 2, '"Providence Thir Guide": Providence in Milton', I examine how Milton invokes the idea of providence and its secret workings in times of tribulation and uncertainty, often associating it with the concept of 'trial', a situation that presents both a danger and an opportunity. Many of such passages in Milton's poems and prose, responding to very different historical contexts, raise questions as often as they suggest possible consolation or assurance. 'Does God exact day-labour, light deny'd?' (Sonnet 19, 7). Does an exacting, jealous deity set us tasks to perform, and then deny us the means by which we can perform them, punishing us for our inadequacies? This chapter explores the complex interrelationship of ideas of providence and freedom in Milton and in some of his contemporaries.

The idea of virtue under trial, I argue in Chapter 3, is as central to Milton's *Mask Presented at Ludlow-Castle* as it is to *Areopagitica* and the divorce tracts: 'For God sure esteems the growth and compleating of one virtuous person, more then the restraint of one vitious' (*Areopagitica*, *CPW*, II.528). Where the Ludlow Masque focuses on the temptations facing such an aspiring 'true Servant' of virtue in the 'perplex't paths' of life (*A Mask*, 10, 37), the divorce tracts concern themselves with the problems confronting one who, exercising free choice, has chosen wrongly, with painful consequences. The persistent use of the masculine pronoun in phrases such as 'trusts him with the gift of reason to be his own chooser' (*Areopagitica*, *CPW*, II.514) suggests one problematical element in Milton's ideology: these works, like *Paradise Lost*, are in some respects radical and egalitarian, and in others authoritarian, imbued with notions of male superiority. If *Doctrine and Discipline* and *Tetrachordon* tend to define the virtuous subject as an injured male, in other ways the arguments from consent that Milton deploys in these works anticipate the radical stance of *Tenure*: with subject and ruler as with parties bound by a marriage contract, 'there is no power above their own consent to hinder them from unjoyning' (*Doctrine and Discipline*, *CPW*, II.328), when the bonds prove oppressive.

The next two chapters examine Milton's political prose of the 1640s and 1650s in its historical context. Chapter 4, 'Classical and Biblical Republicanism', treats the relationship between the scriptural or theological and the classical, secular elements in political writings by Milton and others during this period. In the pamphlet wars of the seventeenth century, the arguments for calling kings to account were at least as much theological as secular or contractarian. Chapter 4 considers the relationship, often uneasy, between the traditions of classical republicanism and Puritan theology in the writings of Milton and some of his contemporaries. In Chapter 5, 'Victory's Crest: Milton, the English People, and Cromwell', once again comparing writings by Milton and others, the central figure is Oliver Cromwell, seen by Milton's fellow republicans as potential liberator or potential tyrant. Where republicans such as Richard Overton and Edward Sexby, former allies of Cromwell, saw his accession to power as a new tyranny, Milton in *Second Defence* praises the Lord Protector as the patron of liberty, servant of the commonwealth. The defence of liberty, as Milton presents it here, is beset with uncertainties, and he warns both Cromwell and his fellow countrymen that liberty is conditional on virtue, on conquering the tyrant within: 'Peace itself will be by far your hardest war, and what you thought liberty will prove to be your servitude' (*CPW*, iv.i.683).

The problematical relationship between politics and theology is once again a central concern in Chapter 6, 'Monarchy and Servitude: The Politics of *Paradise Lost*'. Where to some twentieth-century critics there is a clean break between pre-Restoration and post-Restoration Milton, others find thematic links and continuities in Milton's political and ethical views as expressed in works written before and after 1660. Critics of varying persuasions have been troubled by the evident similarities between a number of Satan's speeches in Books i, ii, and v and Milton's own earlier attacks on monarchy and defences of liberty, and by authoritarian aspects of divine monarchical rule. Where Abdiel in Book v and Adam in dialogue with Michael in Book xii draw a distinction between earthly and heavenly monarchy – 'Man over men / He made not Lord, such title to himself / Reserving, human left from human free' (*PL*, xii.69–71) – the romantic Satanists Blake and Shelley and their follower William Empson seek to overturn that distinction, challenging the ideology underlying the poem. What is at stake in the confrontation between Satan and Abdiel, as in two key scenes in Book ix, the separation scene, with its dialogue between Adam and Eve, and the temptation of Eve by Satan, is the unstable balance between two positive values, freedom and obedience. In a universe where only God the Father is allowed omniscience, the power to foresee the future, free choice is presented as hedged round with uncertainties. Those in a position of partial ignorance, who are forced to choose, must accept the consequences that will inevitably follow. Though the theological and ethical stance central to *Paradise Lost* is essentially that set forth in *Areopagitica*, two decades earlier – 'We ourselves esteem not of that obedience, or love, or gift, which is of force: God therefore left him free' (*CPW*, II.57) – the politics of *Paradise Lost* are strongly influenced by its historical context, in Restoration England, and the chastening of hopes after the failure of the English Revolution. The political question in Books X–XII is how to endure, how to maintain one's allegiance to beleaguered 'Truth' and the obligations of sovereign conscience, under the limitations imposed by a hostile environment.

In Chapter 7, 'God's Just Yoke: Power and Justice in *Paradise Lost*', I consider two key terms in Milton's poem, 'power' (and the related term 'strength') and 'justice' (with the related terms 'just', 'judge', and 'judgement'). Justice in *Paradise Lost* always refers to divine justice, which in the poem is presented as strict, punitive, retributive. God's justice, in judging his fallible creatures, is regularly associated with obedience, submission to God's overwhelming power: as a chastened Adam tells Michael in Book XI, 'I yield it just . . . and submit' (*PL*, XI.526). God the Father is pre-eminently a God of power: the term appears seventy-nine times in *Paradise Lost*, and the associated terms 'strength', 'stronger', 'strongest' seventy-eight times. For Satan, strength and power are purely material considerations, measurable in terms of more troops or better weapons. Abdiel, in his confrontation with Satan, presents a very different view of power, as including a moral dimension, and Milton's authorial comment on the action of the war in Heaven in Book VI takes much the same stance: 'For strength from Truth divided and from Just, / Illaudable, naught merits but dispraise' (VI.381–2).

If God's justice is at times presented as both incomprehensible and impervious to challenge, the use of the parallel terms 'just and right' in several passages suggests that in humans, 'just' is a moral term, suggesting a capacity, a possible way to behave. What distinguishes the rare 'just man' from the unjust is free moral choice: here Milton firmly rejects the Calvinist doctrine that God has singled out from eternity certain individuals for salvation, regardless of merit, condemning all the rest. In Book III and elsewhere in the poem, Milton is consistent in his anti-Trinitarianism, presenting the Son as separate from and subordinate to the Father. Again and again in *Paradise Lost*, the Father is associated with severe, uncompromising justice, and the Son with compassion, forgiveness, the free embrace of suffering. The hints in Book VII of a more gentle Father, rather than one ruling by fear, complicate the distinction between an Old Testament God of wrath and a Son willing to stand up as advocate for man. But in Books XI and XII, the treatment of postlapsarian history is overwhelmingly bleak: Adam is educated into a world of 'paine' (x.964), though not without hope that 'sorrow unfeign'd. and humiliation meek' might allow the deity to 'relent, and turn from his displeasure' toward his fallen creatures (x.1092–3), allowing them a second chance.

Chapter 8, '"Tyrannie Must Be": Milton and the Restoration', examines the complex relationship between two major poems published in a single volume in 1671, *Paradise Regained* and *Samson Agonistes.* These two poems, published at a dark time for Dissenters and republicans, both concern themselves with the problems and temptations facing those who seek to serve God in a hostile, unjust society. When in *Paradise Regained,* Satan tempts Jesus by reminding him of the prophecy that 'to a Kingdom thou art born, ordain'd / To sit upon thy Father *David's* Throne', Jesus answers that 'all things are best fulfill'd in their due time'. An implication of such a passage, in the context of Restoration England, a time when, in Milton's view, the unjust flourished and the just faced 'tribulations, injuries . . . / Contempts, and scorns', is that any deliverance from oppression may be long delayed.[58] Jesus in his combat with the tempter Satan in the wilderness can serve as a model for the conscientious yet troubled believer, faced with what Milton's friend Andrew Marvell calls 'the batt'ries of alluring sense' and persevering in resolute defiance.[59]

Samson Agonistes is a tragedy that begins with imprisonment, apparent helplessness, despair, and ends in the violent death of its hero, surrounded by a heap of 'slaughter'd foes' (*Samson Agonistes,* 1067), in what may be seen as a fantasy of revenge by the oppressed on their oppressors. Ethically and politically, *Samson Agonistes* is entirely consistent with Milton's earlier writings, in advancing arguments for resistance against an unjust ruler or conqueror, with fidelity to God outweighing any secular political obligations. Here as in many of his other works in verse and prose, Milton suggests a fear of freedom, a preference for 'Bondage with ease' over the pains and uncertainties of 'strenuous Liberty' as an explanation for why tyrants thrive, propped up by 'the inward vicious rule' by which most men, 'slaves within doors', govern themselves.[60] The universe of *Samson Agonistes* is ruled by a demanding, implacable God who allows his creatures freedom of choice, subjecting them to repeated tests, in which they may stand or fall, with the possibility held out of a 'final pardon' (1171) for those who repent. What is particularly troubling about *Samson Agonistes* is the violence of the tragic ending, in which Samson, agent of a fierce and jealous God remorselessly punishing any who defy his awesome power, virtually wipes out the Philistine nation, condemning them as idolators who do not deserve to live. Like the Archangel Michael's claim in *Paradise Lost,*

Book XII, that 'Tyrannie must be' in the fallen world as punishment for those who fail to meet God's exacting standards, the closing moments of *Samson Agonistes* illustrate the most problematical elements of Milton's theology and ethics and of the Old Testament God who looms behind Milton's writings.

1

Milton's Post-Calvinist Theology

The association of Milton with Puritanism, evident in the titles of Woodhouse's *Puritanism and Liberty* (1938) and Barker's *Milton and the Puritan Dilemma* (1942), as well as in Sharon Achinstein's *Literature and Dissent in Milton's England* (2003), has recently come under attack. Catherine Gimelli Martin, in *Milton among the Puritans* (2010), devotes over 300 pages to 'argue that, contrary to long-standing assumptions still widely held in the academic community, Milton was not a Puritan'. Instead, Milton's 'outlook is basically secular and rationalist' rather than being 'spiritual or theological', and his prose writings represent a 'mainline reformist position'. Martin's Milton is a Baconian, a liberal humanist, akin to the Latitudinarians and deists of the later seventeenth century and eighteenth century.[1] Where Martin's book received mixed reviews in its determined attempt 'to create a "moderate" shorn of Puritan fierceness', *John Milton: Life, Work, and Thought*, by Gordon Campbell and Thomas N. Corns (2008), a biography acclaimed as 'a magnificent achievement' by reviewers, is no less revisionist in its approach. As several reviewers point out, the principal 'paradigm-shifting' reassessment in this biography's approach is its treatment of Milton's early career. The early Milton, Campbell and Corns argue, rather than being an incipient radical, taking up 'a reformist and oppositional stance' on many issues, was attracted to English sacramental and ceremonial Arminianism. Before he wrote *Lycidas*, with its strong attack on the 'corrupted Clergy then in their height', Campbell and Corns claim, Milton can be considered a Laudian conservative.[2] They cite evidence that indicates that Milton's father and his tutors at Cambridge might have sympathized with Laudian ceremonialism, and find similar doctrinal leanings in a number of his poems, including his elegy on Lancelot Andrewes. Milton's *Mask Presented at Ludlow-Castle*, often described as a 'Puritan masque', they interpret as 'the most complex and thorough expression of Laudian Arminianism and Laudian style within the Milton oeuvre'.[3]

C. S. Lewis, writing in 1942, has no doubts about Milton's theological allegiances in *Paradise Lost:* 'As far as doctrine goes, the poem is overwhelmingly Christian. Except in a few isolated passages, it is not even specifically Protestant or Puritan. It gives the great central tradition . . . one which all Christendom in all lands and ages can accept.' Lewis, like Douglas Bush in the Oxford *English Literature in the Earlier Seventeenth Century* (1962), sees Milton as an orthodox Christian humanist, minimizing any doctrinal heterodoxy as well as any contamination by Puritanism: 'Heretical elements exist in it, but are only discoverable by search: any criticism which forces them into the foreground is mistaken, and ignores the fact that this poem was accepted as orthodox by many generations of acute readers well grounded in theology.'[4] Bush agrees: 'There is in *Paradise Lost* (as in the whole body of Milton's poetry) very little that is specifically Puritan.' *Paradise Lost* is 'simply a poem of traditional Christianity, Catholic as well as Protestant'. In Bush's account, Milton is homogenized to fit in with 'the orthodox tradition of Renaissance humanism' or 'all Christian humanists from Petrarch to Matthew Arnold': 'To speak briefly, as we must, of Milton's theological thought is to recognize his essential orthodoxy and to slight particular heresies (heresies which he derived from the Bible).'[5]

Though C. A. Patrides in *Milton and the Christian Tradition* (1966) concedes that *Paradise Lost* is 'a Christian *Protestant* poem', the only doctrinal distinctions Patrides recognizes are those that are not likely to be 'palatable to Catholic readers'. As Patrides' title suggests, there is for him essentially one Christian tradition, within which Milton fits comfortably: 'However much one interpretation happened to vary from the next, Protestants were agreed that original sin . . . must be accepted as "a maine principle of the Christian faith". Milton's exposition of that principle in *De Doctrina Christiana* has, accordingly, no surprises for us.'[6] Phrases like 'a commonplace of Christian thought' and a 'common tenet of the Renaissance' recur constantly. In quoting the problematic lines in *Paradise Lost*, Book III, 'Some I have chosen of peculiar grace, / Elect above the rest' (*PL*, III.183–4), Patrides comments that Milton, eschewing the 'absurdities' of theological controversy, 'trod the safer road of Protestant tradition, whose essence he finally expressed in the Father's statement in *Paradise Lost*'. Predestination, Patrides tells us, is a 'common belief' which 'all Christians share', 'a truth which none questions'.[7] Patrides devotes more attention than Lewis to *De Doctrina*, but downplays aspects of that treatise and of *Paradise Lost*, which Milton describes as 'at odds with certain conventional opinions': 'The relevant passages in the epic keep entirely within the

Christian tradition; none, I think, can reasonably be located on its periphery.'[8] In this book as in the essays by Patrides and William B. Hunter collected in *Bright Essence* (1971), there is a consistent attempt to acquit Milton of the charge of a heretical anti-Trinitarianism or Arianism, as well as cleansing his writings of any engagement with doctrines that might appear radical or unorthodox.[9]

The essays in *Bright Essence* by Hunter and Patrides, originally published in scholarly journals between 1958 and 1969, are a concerted attack on the claim, advanced by Maurice Kelley and others, that in *De Doctrina* and *Paradise Lost*, Milton expressed views on the Trinity similar to Arian doctrines condemned as heretical in the Nicene Creed. There are several strands to their argument: that Milton's position is not anti-Trinitarian or Arian, but a perfectly respectable 'subordinationism'; that Milton's position cannot properly be called 'Arian' because Milton in *De Doctrina* differs from Arius in certain important respects, especially in his doctrine of creation and in presenting the Son as of the same substance as the Father; and that there are significant differences between the theology of *De Doctrina* and that to be found in *Paradise Lost*. According to Patrides, 'in *Paradise Lost* the unity of the Godhead is not impaired; for the most part, indeed, Milton does not seem to distinguish between the Father and the Son'.[10] In *Visitation Unimplor'd*, Hunter goes a step further and argues that *De Doctrina* is not by Milton. Here again there is the claim that Milton, who has too readily been 'characterized as a Puritan', is a traditional, orthodox Christian: 'When we dismiss the critical accretions from the canon that derive from the treatise, a new understanding of the man and his work emerges . . . In this new light Milton stands closer to the great traditions of Christianity, being no longer associated with a merely eccentric fringe.'[11] Hunter dismisses any parallels between *De Doctrina* and Milton's canonical writings, as claimed by Kelley, Lewalski, and others, and denies that 'the heterodox view of the Son of God' in *De Doctrina* is present in *Paradise Lost:* before the manuscript of *De Doctrina* was discovered, 'generations of readers' considered the poem orthodox in its theology. Hunter constructs an imaginary narrative in which the manuscript was compiled by a former student of Milton, probably living in Continental Europe, and eventually ended up in Milton's possession, where it was mistakenly assumed to be by him.[12]

Hunter's challenge to Milton's authorship of *De Doctrina* occasioned considerable controversy among Milton scholars, and a research group under the chairmanship of Corns was set up to examine Hunter's claims, which were first set forth in 1991. The preliminary findings of this research group were published as 'The Provenance of *De Doctrina Christiana*' in *Milton Quarterly* in 1997, and a final, revised version as *Milton and the Manuscript of* De Doctrina Christiana (2007). Their conclusion is that '*De Doctrina Christiana* rightfully belongs in the Milton canon', in terms of its provenance, its Latin style, and its 'powerful argumentation'.[13] In the final report as in the earlier draft, Corns and his colleagues argue that *De Doctrina* is unfinished, that the process of composition may suggest, in some passages, 'a Miltonic appropriation of other texts into his own', and that much of the treatise is 'substantially in accord with the mainstream of Protestant thinking'. : 'To be the author of a systematic theology is to absorb into one's own work the writing of others and to make it one's own by changing key arguments . . . Milton, like his fellow systematizers, overwhelmingly agrees with received opinion but occasionally champions a minority or a personal opinion.'[14]

In his recent book *Milton's Theology of Freedom* (2006), Benjamin Myers has said, 'We can understand Milton's theological achievement only when we situate his thought within the context of the theological traditions to which he was indebted, especially the traditions of post-Reformation Protestantism.' Myers argues that the sharp division between scholars who portray Milton as a 'spokesperson for orthodoxy' and those who characterize Milton as heterodox or radical in his theology can be attributed to the individual critic's *a priori* notions of what Milton is like: the critic then singles out aspects of *Paradise Lost* or *De Doctrina* that fit this template, ignoring others. Myers' study, in contrast, argues that *Paradise Lost* 'draws on and appropriates orthodox and heterodox traditions alike', and seeks to examine ways in which 'various aspects of the poem's theology exhibit continuity and discontinuity with post-Reformation theological discourses'.[15]

Milton and the Burden of Freedom follows a similar approach. Milton's theology takes as its starting point the theology of Reformed Protestantism, from which he works out an independent position, differing in some important respects from Calvinist orthodoxy. In *De Doctrina*, he writes from within 'the citadel of reformed religion', claiming that everything in the work was 'drawn from the sacred scriptures alone', needing to be 'measured with greater strictness against the yardstick of the Bible, and reformed with greater care'.[16] What is heterodox in *De Doctrina*, far from deserving the 'invidious title' of heresy, Milton argues in his prefatory Epistle, is the result of a project of Reform, in the collaborative aim of 'restoring religion to something of its pure original state'. His emphasis on 'searching after truth', the need 'that men should be free not only to sift and winnow any doctrine, but also openly to give their opinion of it and even to write about it', recalls similar arguments in *Areopagitica*:

> Where there is much desire to learn, there of necessity will be much arguing, much writing, many opinions: for opinion in good men is but knowledge in the making. Under these fantastic terrors of sect and schism, we wrong the earnest and zealous thirst after knowledge and understanding which God hath stirr'd up in this City.[17]

When Milton in his prose pamphlets uses the term 'Puritan', he generally recognizes its origin as an insult, while at the same time asserting his affinity with those who have been 'branded with the name of *Puritans*':

> We must not think it strange if his best Disciples in the reformation, as at first by your tribe they were call'd Lollards and Hussites, so now by you be term'd Puritans, and Brownists. But my hope is that the people of England will not suffer themselves to be juggl'd thus out of their faith and religion by a mist of names cast before their eyes.

Barker uses the broad term Puritanism 'to signify all those who wished to purify the Church in accordance with directions divinely revealed, either in Scripture or by the Holy Spirit'.[18] The emphasis on 'the inward testimony of the Spirit' and 'the outward testimony' of scripture are hallmarks of Reformed Protestantism, as is the belief, central to Milton as to Bunyan, that 'every man shall bear his own burden'. As Milton says in *A Treatise of Civil Power*, drawing radical conclusions from these general principles:

> It cannot be deni'd, being the main foundation of our protestant religion, that we of these ages [have] no other divine rule or autoritie from without us warrantable to one another as a common ground but the holy scripture, and no other within us but the illumination of the Holy Spirit . . . It follows cleerly, that no man or body of men in these times can be the infallible judges or determiners in matters of religion to any other mens consciences but thir own . . . If then we count it so ignorant and irreligious in the papist to think himself dischargd in Gods account, beleeving only as the church beleevs, how much greater condemnation will it be to the protestant his condemner, to think himself justified, beleeving only as the state beleevs.[19]

There is no single Puritan tradition, and Puritans, led by a desire to change, to reform, to improve, disagree widely with one another as to the extent to which 'a compleate *Reform*' (*CPW*, 1.529) in the church and in the state has been or can be carried out. Though neither in theology, ecclesiology, nor views of the role of the state in religious matters was there any consensus among those who could be considered Puritans or Reformed Protestants, dissatisfaction with 'an established church which retained government by bishops and a liturgy still modelled on that of Rome', as well as dissatisfaction with the political arrangements then currently prevailing, were principles shared by the differing factions that could generally be classified as Puritan during the 1640s.[20] Imagery of 'strenuous', unrelenting spiritual warfare was habitual among Puritans. 'Our faith and knowledge', Milton argued in *Areopagitica*, 'thrives by exercise, as well as our limbs and complexion': 'Truth is compar'd in Scripture to a streaming fountain; if her waters flow not in a perpetuall progression, they sick'n into a muddy pool of conformity and tradition.'[21]

In compiling his doctrinal treatise, the 'examples' Milton followed in collecting materials and in the early stages of composition were the systematic treatises of William Ames (Amesius) and John Wolleb (Wollebius), both of which were entirely orthodox in their Calvinist theology. As Maurice Kelley has shown, in passage after passage Milton in his Latin text takes the Wollebius *Compendius Theologiae Christianae* (1626) as a model or template and either echoes, expands on, or conscientiously departs from Wolleb's text. This is especially the case in Book II, a relatively conventional treatment of virtues and duties:

> Sobrietas est temperantia ab immodico cibo et potu (Milton)
>
> Sobrietas est temperantia a superfluo cibo & potu (Wolleb)[22]

Similarly, in the treatment of Justification in Book I, where in several passages Milton carefully distinguishes his position both from 'the Papists' and from those who, unlike 'our theologians', 'contend that we are not justified by faith alone', at one point he follows Wolleb almost exactly.

> Pontificiis aeque absurdum videtur nos aliena iustitia iustos fieri, ac siquis alterius doctrina doctus diceretur: sed dispar est exemplorum ratio, cum homo homini non perinde sit coniunctus, ac fidelis Christo capiti suo. (Milton)
>
> Pontificiis aeque absurdum videtur, nos aliena justitia justos fieri, ac si quis alterius doctrina doctus diceretur. Sed dispar est exemplorum ratio, cum homo homini non perinde unitus sit, ut fidelis Christi tanquam Capito suo. (Wolleb)[23]

The most extensive departures from Calvinist orthodoxy in *De Doctrina* are in Book I, Chapter iv, 'Of Predestination', and Chapter v, 'Of the Son of God', the longest of the chapters in the treatise, which includes its own preface defending his dissent from 'the received opinion': 'I see no reason why anyone who calls himself a Protestant or a member of the Reformed Church, and who acknowledges the same rule of faith as myself, could be offended with me', 'especially because I am not imposing any command on anyone, but merely proposing what I think more credible'.[24]

The historian Nicholas Tyacke, in his influential study *Anti-Calvinists* (1987) and his earlier 'Puritanism, Arminianism and Counter-Revolution' (1973), has argued that in the reigns of Elizabeth I and James I 'the characteristic theology of English Protestantism was Calvinist'. According to Tyacke and to Patrick Collinson, England during this period 'was doctrinally a part of Calvinist Europe'. This is reflected in the Thirty-Nine Articles, in the Paul's Cross sermons between 1570 and 1628, and in the proposed Lambeth Articles of 1595, all of which endorse strict Calvinist views of predestination and reprobation.

> God from all eternity predestinated some to Life, and reprobated some to Death.
>
> Predestination to life is the everlasting purpose of God, whereby (before the foundations of the world were laid) he hath constantly decreed by his counsel, secret to us, to deliver from curse and damnation those whom he has chosen in Christ out of mankind.[25]

The ascendancy of Archbishop William Laud in the 1620s represented a sharp break from this Reformed Protestant consensus, after which 'Calvinist teaching was proscribed, and a novel ceremonialism and sacramentalism introduced', policies and practices that by 1640 proved deeply divisive. Though the term 'Arminian' was often, at the time and later, applied to these 'novel and destabilizing' doctrines, Peter Lake has argued that the term 'Laudianism' brings out its political and ideological dimensions more accurately. Laud and his followers, whose primary interest was 'in ritual and the condition of the visible institutional church', things which the Archbishop sought to regulate in detail, had little common ground with the Dutch Arminians.[26] In this study, I will generally reserve the term 'Arminian' for doctrines advanced by the Dutch theologian Jacobus Arminius and his followers, as distinguished from 'Laudian' ritual and doctrines, which can accurately be described as 'anti-Calvinist'.

Milton's first anti-Episcopal pamphlet, *Of Reformation . . . in England: And the Causes That Hitherto Hath Hindered It* (1641), presents a similar narrative, though in a much more combative way. The progress of Reform in England, once promising (as 'the first that should set up a Standard for the recovery of *lost Truth*, and blow the first *Evangelick Trumpet* to the *Nations*'), has been 'but a short blaze soon dampt and stifl'd', to the extent that 'as yet we are amongst the last' to embrace Reform 'in *Uniforme Consent* to the rest of the *Churches* abroad'.[27] Those responsible for this interruption, Milton says, are the Laudians, a 'Tyrannicall crew and Corporation of Impostors' who, like equivalent figures in earlier ages, find 'a pious pretext . . . ready at hand to cover their insatiate desires' for secular power. Milton's emphasis in this pamphlet is entirely on 'the courses they tooke' rather than on 'the opinions they held' (*CPW*, 1.537, 590). His main charge against his adversaries, conveyed with powerful persuasive force through recurrent metaphors, is carnality: worshipping 'two Gods . . . *Mammon* and their Belly', ambitious clerical politicians like Laud, lacking a true understanding of 'spirituall things', are unable to break free from enslavement to the body, 'bolstering, and supporting their inward rottenes by a carnal, and outward strength'.[28] Though in many passages he attacks the Laudian imposition of 'Ceremonies thrust purposely upon the groaning Church' (*CPW*, 1.545), the word 'Arminian', omnipresent in the pamphlet wars of this period (EEBO lists 1, 125 hits in 265 texts between 1640 and 1660), is absent from Milton's attack on Laud and his followers in *Of Reformation.* Milton's stance throughout this tract is that of an orthodox Calvinist, doctrinally consistent with 'the reformed Churches beyond the seas' (*CPW*, 1.609).[29] There is no trace here of the heterodox views Milton expressed later in *De Doctrina* and elsewhere: the extended prayer in the peroration (*CPW*, 1.613–14) is explicitly Trinitarian.

Laud and his followers were bitterly anti-Calvinist, treating Calvinists both in England and Continental Europe as part of a conspiracy to undermine order and discipline in the church and in the state. As Samuel Brooke wrote in a letter to Laud in 1630:

> I daresay, that their doctrine of predestination is the root of all Puritanism, and Puritanism the root of all rebellious and disobedient intractableness in Parliament, etc. and of all schism and sauciness in the country, nay in the Church itself . . . They, I say, that hold the same opinions, cry out now the Church of England, and will have the Church of England to be theirs.[30]

To Peter Heylyn, Laudian diehard, ardent royalist, and author of a hagiographical biography of Laud, *Cyprianus Anglicanus* (1668), arguing a consistent line from the 1630s to the 1660s, Calvinism was seen as 'a body of destructive ideas – destructive of worship and true doctrine but also of good order in church and state – and as the force that could drive the country to civil war'. In country after country, Heylyn argued, 'the infusion of Calvinist doctrine' led to insurrection.[31]

In contrast to the Laudians, Milton, like the Dutch protestant Jacobus Arminius, the French theologian Moses Amyraut, the Cambridge divine John Preston, the radical Congregationalist minister John Goodwin, the moderate Puritan theologian Richard Baxter, and General Baptists such as Thomas Helwys, John Murton and Thomas Lambe, can best be described as post-Calvinist.[32] Amyraut, head of the Saumur school and described as 'the most influential Reformed theologian of the seventeenth century', argued that in doctrinal points that 'disputed orthodox Calvinist teaching' he was closer to the teachings of Calvin than his opponents and represented the true Reformed tradition. At the Synod of Dort, at which the followers of Arminius presented views very like those developed in Milton's *De Doctrina*, both sides spoke as members of the Dutch Reformed Church. As Tyacke points out, the 'Arminianism' of Laud and his followers has 'an additional, sacramental dimension' that differentiates it from Dutch Arminianism, which comes from within the Reformed tradition.[33] Thomas Young, Milton's tutor, 'best of Teachers' and the recipient of verse and prose letters by the young Milton, was, like John Preston, a 'moderate' or 'conformable' Puritan in the late 1620s and 1630s, and later was part of a group of anti-Laudian clergy writing under the acronym Smectymuus. For Young, and conforming Calvinists like him, 'a desire for further reform' in the church was compatible with remaining 'integrated and loyal members of the Church of England'.[34] Preston, though an orthodox Calvinist in many respects, questioned the doctrine of double predestination, arguing like Milton that God's 'primarie intent' was not to display his wrath in damnation, but 'was to show mercy to all creatures, to men and angels both'.[35]

John Goodwin, attacked by his Presbyterian enemies as 'a monstrous Sectary, a compound of Socinianisme, Arminianisme, Libertinisme, Antinomianisme, Independency, Popery', the 'Patron of Heresy and Shame of Divinity' for propagating 'detestable and damnable' heresies, nevertheless considered himself, in his theological writings, to be firmly within the Reformed tradition. His writings, he claimed, advanced 'such Notions concerning the Nature of God, and his Attributes and Perfections, which I finde generally subscribed with the Names and Pens of all that is called *Orthodox* amongst us'.[36] Until the late 1640s, Goodwin accepted the orthodox Calvinist doctrine of unconditional predestination, but gradually, like Milton, he came to believe in universal atonement and freedom of the will. As he writes in the preface to his treatise *Redemption Redeemed* (1651), 'If the opinions commended by me for Truth in the work in hand be *Arminian;* certain I am that the ancient Fathers and Writers of the *Christian* Church were generally *Arminian:* yea and that *Calvin* himself, had many fits and pangs of *Arminianism.*'[37] For Goodwin, a defender of free inquiry and a resolute opponent of tyranny in all its forms, politics and theology intersect, as he compares proponents of absolutist political doctrines with those who would deny that 'the wills of men are left free by God', allowing them to make 'their owne proper and free election of what they act'.[38]

In Richard Overton the Leveller, even more radical than Goodwin or Milton in his political views, again there is a close connection between politics and religion. Overton was a General Baptist, holding doctrinal views that were 'Arminian and undoubtedly puritan', defining election in terms of faith in Christ, and thus allowing the possibility of salvation to repentant sinners.[39] Overton's clandestine press in 1645, the year that it printed several pamphlets by Overton and William Walwyn defending freedom of conscience, published *The Fountaine of Free Grace Opened* by Thomas Lambe, a General Baptist minister with a large following in London. This pamphlet sets forth a version of election differing from orthodox Calvinism, arguing that 'God admonishes all men everywhere to repent' and that 'he that doth truly believe, that Christ . . . has suffered for his sins, cannot but believe, that his sins are pardoned'.[40] Overton in *Mans Mortalitie* (1644), with characteristic acerbic wit, strongly attacks any doctrine that would make God the author of sin, suggesting that such doctrines imply a 'malignant' or tyrannous deity:

> And so Gods immediate hand is the cause of all sin, that man had better been without this soul; for it must needs be some damnable wicked spirit, or some Devil that God puts into him . . . This is as if a man should break his horses legs and then knock out his brains for halting.[41]

In *Mans Mortalitie*, Overton, radical in his religious as in his political views, argues a heterodox position that he shares with Milton: mortalism, or soul-sleeping, the belief that after death, body and soul die together, to be revived at the Day of Judgement. Overton's aim is to prove 'both Theologically and Philosophically, that whole Man (as a *rationall Creature*) is a compound wholly mortall, contrary to that common distinction of Soule and Body'.[42] Monist theories of this kind, which reject 'the common view that the soul is separate and can exist outside the body' and that 'the soul is exempt from death', were condemned as 'erroneous opinion' by Calvin. Milton argues the mortalist case in *De Doctrina*, claiming that differing views on this topic 'can be debated without detriment to faith or devotion', in terms very similar to Overton's treatise, which he is likely to have known.[43]

Aside from mortalism, the principal doctrines in *De Doctrina* that can be considered departures from 'the received opinion' in Reformed theology are Milton's anti-Trinitarianism and his dissent from Calvinist doctrines of predestination, election, and reprobation. On these topics, Kelley's introduction and detailed notes in *CPW*, VI, remain a reliable guide, and with minor modifications, Kelley's general position is followed in more recent accounts by Michael Bauman in *Milton's Arianism* (1987), by John Rumrich and Stephen Fallon in *Milton and Heresy* (1998) and by Benjamin Myers in *Milton's Theology of Freedom* (2006).[44] Another unorthodox view 'at odds with . . . conventional opinions' in *De Doctrina* is the argument that polygamy is 'a true marriage' sanctioned by scripture. Though there is no parallel here with *Paradise Lost*, the treatment of marriage and divorce in the same chapter of *De Doctrina* is, as we will see, close to that argued in Milton's divorce tracts.[45]

In *De Doctrina*, Book I, Chapter V, 'Of the Son of God', Milton argues 'that the doctrine of the Trinity, as accepted at present, could not be proved from any passage of scripture'.[46] Scornful of 'the sheer vacuity of the orthodox view', and arguing for the need 'to be disentangled from the windings of controversy', that obscure 'the simple truth' by the 'glosses of metaphysicians', Milton consistently upholds anti-Trinitarian views of the deity in *De Doctrina*, and this conception of the relationship of Father and Son is reflected in *Paradise Lost* and *Paradise Regained*.[47] Like Calvin and other Reformed theologians, he sees the Son as in his nature double, human and divine, 'both God and man' (*CPW*, VI.424), and as a mediator, who takes on human flesh to redeem fallen man. But he differs from the Calvinists in consistently seeing the Son as distinct from and inferior or subordinate to the Father.

> He could not have been a mediator, nor could he have been sent by and obedient to God, unless he was by nature less than God . . . the Father.
>
> Now generation produces something that is and exists apart from the generator, Therefore God cannot generate a God equal to himself, because he is by definition one and infinite.[48]

The relationship between Father and 'his Anointed Son' in *Paradise Lost* is clearly indicated in several passages:

> Effulgence of my Glorie, Son belov'd,
> Son in whose face invisible is beheld
> Visibly, what by Deitie I am,
> And in whose hand what by Decree I doe.
> (*PL*, VI.680–3)

> Begotten Son, Divine Similitude,
> In whose conspicuous count'nance, without cloud
> Made visible, th'Almighty Father shines.
> Whom else no Creature can behold . . .
> Hee Heav'n of Heavens and all the Powers therein
> By thee created, and by thee threw down
> Th'aspiring Dominations.
>
> (*PL*, III.384–7, 390–2)

As Milton says in *De Doctrina*, '*God was made manifest in the flesh*, that is, in his Son, his image: in any other way he is invisible' (*CPW*, VI.244).[49] When, in Book VI, the Son is entrusted with the task of overthrowing Satan and his forces, or when in Book X he is sent down to judge Adam and Eve, with his Father's power 'transferr'd' (*PL*, X.678) and made manifest in him, he is acting, in a purely 'voluntarie' capacity, as the agent of his Father's power: 'Father Eternal, thine is to decree, / Mine both in Heav'n amd Earth to do thy will / Supream' (*PL*, X.61, 68–70). The action of both *Paradise Lost* and *Paradise Regained* is dependent on anti-Trinitarianism, in presenting a son who does not share his father's omniscience and can act freely, with no privileged foreknowledge affecting his choice of action.

The term 'Arianism' is often applied to Milton's anti-Trinitarianism, though he disagrees with the doctrines of Arius in some respects, especially in arguing that the Son was created by the Father not *ex nihilo* but out of his own substance. Arianism, defined and anathematized as a heresy at the Council of Nice, has always been condemned, by orthodox Protestants and Catholics alike, as 'damnable' and dangerous. Calvin considered Arius a 'man of wiles' full of 'impiety' and 'hatred' in blasphemously attacking 'the purity of the faith'. In the 1640s, the anti-Trinitarian Paul Best was threatened with hanging, and both he and John Bidle were imprisoned for advancing similar views, with their books burnt.[50] Though attempts have been made to sanitise Milton's theological views, claiming him for one or another version of orthodoxy, a whiff of brimstone has always hung around Milton's epic poem. Well before the publication of *De Doctrina* in 1825, *Paradise Lost* was accused of 'heresy and impiety' by orthodox critics. Defoe in his *History of the Devil* (1726) singles out as unjustified 'poetic license' Milton's invention of the exaltation of the Son in Book V, by which Satan, full of 'envy against the Son of God . . . thought himself impair'd' (*PL*, V.603–7), as the cause of Satan's revolt. What Maurice Kelley sees as a 'theological fiction' that 'furnishes Satan with a concrete reason for his resentment', Defoe in the eighteenth century characterises as an 'invented scheme' that 'jostles religion and shocks our faith'.

> The design is well laid; it only wants two trifles, called truth and history . . . The plot is wrong . . . because contradicted by the Scripture account, according to which Christ was declared in heaven, not then, but from eternity . . . So that Mr. Milton is not orthodox in this part, but lays an avowed foundation for the corrupt doctrine of Arius, which says, there was a time when Christ was not the Son of God.[51]

As with his radical Arminianism, Milton started out adhering to orthodox Calvinist beliefs and only gradually came to adopt the anti-Trinitarian doctrines evident in *Paradise Lost* and *De Doctrina.* In 'On the Morning of Christ's Nativity' (1629), he speaks of 'Trinal Unity' (11), and in *Of Reformation* (1641) he evokes 'one *Tri-personall* Godhead'.[52] The chapter 'Of the Son of God' in *De Doctrina* is the only one with a separate preface, and there he argues that the anti-Trinitarian views he presents, though differing from 'the currently accepted doctrine', are 'deducible from the text of scripture' and are 'more credible' than the orthodox view: 'For I take it upon myself to refute, wherever necessary, not scriptural authority which is inviolate, but human interpretation. That is my right, and indeed my duty as a human being' (*CPW*, VI.202–3).

Though, as Dennis Danielson and Maurice Kelley have shown, Milton's treatment of free will and predestination in *Paradise Lost* and *De Doctrina* closely resembles the position argued by Arminius and his followers in the Dutch Reformed Church, Milton never calls himself an Arminian.[53] To do so in the highly charged atmosphere of the 1640s would be the equivalent of calling oneself a Stalinist in the period of the Cold War. The many references to 'Popery and Arminianism' (corruptions of, tyranny of, gangrene of) in pamphlets of the time are in most cases battle cries, rather than examinations of Arminian doctrine. Milton's own references to Arminius tend to be respectful, while distancing himself from doctrines attributed to Arminius. In *Areopagitica* (1644), arguing against licensing restrictions as applied to 'books of controversie in Religion', Milton treats 'the acute and distinct' Arminius as subject to error, but as one whose writings 'cannot be suppress without the fall of learning, and of all ability in disputation'.[54] In *Doctrine and Discipline* (1643), Milton clearly identifies himself as a Calvinist, in distinguishing what 'we' believe from 'that sect' of Arminians:

> The Jesuits, and that sect amongst us which is named of *Arminius*, are wont to charge us of making God the author of sinne . . . because we hold that he hath decreed some to damnation, and consequently to sinne, say they . . . Yet considering the perfection wherin man was created, and might have stood, no decree necessitating his free will . . . they might, methinks be perswaded to absolve both God and us. (*CPW*, II.293)

In this passage, 'us' in 'charge us', like 'we' in 'we hold', means orthodox Calvinists (who were frequently accused of making God the author of sin), while 'that sect amongst us' could refer either to English Arminianism or to disputes within 'the Reformed churches generally'. The association of 'the Jesuits' with Arminians might suggest that Milton is speaking here of English or Laudian Arminians.[55] But the view of predestination and free will in this passage, though presented as consistent with the teachings of Calvin, in many ways is close to Milton's later position. Milton consistently argued that God's decree of predestination or election in no way impeded the free will of Adam, Eve, or their descendants, and that to 'have stood', resisting temptation, was in their 'owne power' (*CPW*, II.293). Here as in *Paradise Lost* and *De Doctrina*, Milton explicitly disavows the claim of necessity as overriding free will. The cause of the Fall and of man's continuation in sin, rejecting the opportunity for repentance, Milton says later in this passage in *Doctrine and Discipline*, is 'that mans own freewill self corrupted is the adequate and sufficient caus of his disobedience' (*CPW*, II.294).

Calvin's doctrine of double predestination, to reprobation as well as election, was controversial, questioned by some Reformed theologians. In this passage in *Doctrine and Discipline*, where Milton denies that Calvinist doctrines of predestination make God 'the author of sinne', he has moved part way towards his later position, expressed in *Paradise Lost* and *De Doctrina*, denying any divine decree of predestination to reprobation. 'The cause of reprobation, which is followed by punishment, must, if it is to be just, be man's sin alone, not God's will' (*CPW*, VI.195). If the sinner, deaf to the entreaties of God and his 'Umpire *Conscience*', goes on defiantly to 'greater sinne', that is the fault of the unrepentant sinner.

> God . . . excludes no man from the way of repentance and eternal salvation, unless that man has continued to reject and despise the offer of grace, and of grace sufficient for salvation, until it is too late . . . This reprobation lies not so much in God's will as in their own obstinate minds . . . resulting from their refusal to repent while they have an opportunity.

Or, as Milton puts it, in a speech by God the Father, in *Paradise Lost*: 'This my long sufferance and my day of grace / They who neglect and scorn, shall never taste; / But hard be hard'nd, blind be blinded more.'[56]

In *De Doctrina*, Milton explains that the sinner's responsibility for his own fate is in no way incompatible with God's providence: 'Even in sin . . .

we see God's providence at work . . . God, who is the supreme governor of the whole universe, may urge on a criminal though he is in no sense the cause of his crime', hardening the heart of those bent on sin (*De Doctrina*, I.viii, *CPW*, VI.331–3). In arguing that 'just as election is founded and established upon faith, so reprobation is rescinded by repentance' (*CPW*, VI.191), the later Milton was entering controversial territory doctrinally, and yet there was no agreed consensus on these matters among Reformed theologians.[57]

At the Synod of Dort in 1618–19, the Remonstrants or Arminians challenged Calvinist orthodoxy, and their five Articles of Remonstrance were condemned as heretical.[58] The Calvinist 'five points', all of which were closely followed by the Westminster Confession in 1646, are:

1 Total depravity
2 Unconditional election
3 Limited atonement
4 Irresistible grace
5 Perseverance of the saints.

The Arminian Articles of Remonstrance rejected the doctrines of unconditional election and limited atonement, and here Milton adapted the position of Arminius and his followers. Christ 'died for all men and for every man', not simply for the elect, and election, rather than being an arbitrary assertion of the divine will, is conditional on faith. According to Milton in *De Doctrina*, 'Predestination and election are not particular but only general: that is, they belong to all who believe in their hearts and persist in their belief. Peter is not predestined or elected as Peter or John as John, but each only insofar as he believes and persists in his belief.'[59] As Maurice Kelley has argued, the redefinition of predestination and election as conditional – that 'Salvation or Damnation is destin'd to no Man, but either as he believes, or does not believe in Jesus Christ' – is central to *Paradise Lost* and *De Doctrina*.[60]

The chapter on predestination in *De Doctrina* is largely devoted to arguing, with many scriptural citations, this unconventional view of election as conditional on faith. Milton rejects 'false theories about preterition from eternity', the supralapsarian doctrine that election preceded the creation and the fall of man, and was in no way dependent upon man's sin, and argues against 'the abandonment of the non-elect' (*CPW*, VI.174). Predestination is defined by Milton and by the Dutch Remonstrants as a decree by which God 'had mercy on the human race, although it was going to fall of its own accord' and therefore 'predestined to eternal salvation . . . those who would in the future believe and continue in the faith' (*CPW*, VI.166).[61] As Kelley paraphrases Miltonic doctrine, 'the elect are those who of their own accord use their restored freedom of the will to obey God's call and persist in righteousness'. God's grace is a necessary but not sufficient cause for man's salvation, since man must respond to the offered grace, exercising freedom of choice.

> Man shall not quite be lost, but sav'd who will,
> But not of will in him, but grace in me
> Freely voutsaft; once more I will renew
> His lapsed powers, though forfeit and enthrall'd
> By sin to foul exorbitant desires.[62]

Unlike strict Calvinists, Milton and the Remonstrants believed that 'God made his decrees conditional . . . for the very purpose of allowing free causes to put into effect that freedom which he himself gave them' (*CPW*, VI.160): man's free will was not obliterated after the Fall.[63] The Remonstrant principle of resistible grace and the possibility of backsliding, 'turning away from the holy doctrine which was delivered them' and 'forsaking' the true path, are closely related to the Miltonic belief in free will. Strict Calvinist doctrine rendered man entirely passive. For Wolleb, for example, who believed that the grace of God was 'absolutely irresistible', 'those who attribute to unredeemed man either a free will or powers by which he might do good . . . are seeking a house in ashes'.[64] Free will in a universe ruled by God's providence, for Milton and the Dutch Arminians, allowed for the possibility of choosing wrongly, and yet having a second chance.

Though Milton disliked the term 'original sin', to some extent he and the Remonstrants shared the Calvinist belief in the depravity of fallen man. According to Calvin, 'The mind of man has been so completely estranged from God's righteousness that it conceives, desires, and undertakes, only that which is impious, perverted, foul, impure, and infamous.'[65] The first of the Calvinist 'five points' states that 'all people are conceived in sin and are born children of wrath, unfit for any good, inclined to evil, dead in their sins, and slaves to sin', and goes on to say that 'without the grace of the regenerating Holy Spirit they are neither willing nor able to return to God, to reform their distorted nature, or even to dispose themselves to seek reform'.[66] The equivalent Article of Remonstrance follows the same bipartite pattern, but with a change in emphasis: here 'saving grace' is mentioned at the outset, and there is an equal balance between fallen man and regenerate man, freed from captivity.

> That man has not saving grace of himself, nor of the energy of his free will, inasmuch as he, in the state of apostacy and sin, can of and by himself neither think, will, nor do any thing that is truly good (such as saving faith eminently is); but that it is needful that he be born again of God in Christ, through his Holy Spirit, and renewed in understanding, inclination, or will, and all his powers, in order that he may rightly understand, think, will, and effect what is truly good.[67]

In *Paradise Lost*, where postlapsarian man, even though 'enthrall'd / By sin', is allowed the opportunity to 'stand / On even ground' once again, confronting 'his mortal foe', a repeated, insistent emphasis in Milton's theodicy, as stated by God the Father in Book III, is on the role of the deity in gratuitously extending grace to his 'frail' creature: 'I will renew', 'upheld by me', 'by me upheld', 'by none but me' (*PL*, III.175–82). In the Son's response to 'that word which clos'd / Thy sovran sentence, that Man should find grace', though he praises his Father as judge and embodiment of justice, 'who art Judg / Of all things made, and judgest onely right', the theology may be essentially the same, but here grace is associated not with God's power but with love and forgiveness, freely flowing (*PL*, III.144–5, 154–5).

> And shall not grace find means, that finds her way,
> The speediest of thy winged messengers,
> To visit all thy creatures, and to all
> Comes unprevented, unimplor'd unsought.
> (*PL*, III.228–31)

Man, 'once dead in sins and lost', the Son goes on to say, cannot on his own initiative 'seek' that grace: grace is a gift not dependent on man's own efforts (*PL*, III.231–2). Yet, according to Milton and to Remonstrant theology, grace is available even to sinners, if they respond to the opportunity freely offered them. Grace, paradoxically, is open to those who repent, yet entirely dependent on a God whose sovereign power is absolute over his creatures. This heavenly monarch, according to Milton's sonnet on his blindness, commands 'thousands' of winged messengers who 'speed' to do 'his bidding', while letting his servants know that 'God doth not need / Either man's work or his own gifts'.[68] Donne expresses a similar paradox in one of his Holy Sonnets, in speaking of grace: 'Yet grace, if thou repent, thou canst not lack; / But who shall give you that grace to begin?'[69] Even the impulse towards repentance, allowing access to God's free grace, is dependent upon the prior gift of grace allowing one to repent. As we shall see in later chapters, there are problematical elements in Milton's presentation of a God who, alone in the universe, is absolutely free, with creatures torn between the desire to be free and the recognition that every move they make is in some sense in accordance with a pre-existing script.

2

'Providence Thir Guide'

Providence in Milton

I

Paradise Lost begins and ends with Providence. Milton's aim, he tells us, is to assert or demonstrate 'Eternal Providence' and show to his readers that the 'wayes of God' are just (*PL*, I.25–6). In the poem's concluding lines, after the 'hastning' Angel has led Adam and Eve away from their former home in Paradise, now irretrievably closed to them, they are now 'solitarie', deprived of the familiar intercourse of angels and deity.

> Some natural tears they dropp'd, but wip'd them soon;
> The World was all before them, where to choose
> Thir place of rest, and Providence thir guide.
> They hand in hand with wandring steps and slow,
> Through Eden took thir solitarie way.
> (*PL*, XII.637, 645–9)

It is open to question in what way providence can be said to be the guide of the fallen Adam and Eve. In Milton's *Mask Presented at Ludlow-Castle*, written thirty-odd years earlier, the Attendant Spirit describes himself as a guardian angel, sent down to look after one of the few mortals 'that by due steps aspire / To lay their just hands on that Golden Key / That ope's the Palace of Eternity' (*A Mask*, 12–15). In the closing lines, the Attendant Spirit suggests that in some circumstances a heavenly guide could not only act as mentor but actively intervene, providing material assistance to the virtuous undergoing trial:

> Mortals that would follow me,
> Love vertue, she alone is free,
> She can teach ye how to clime
> Higher then the Spheary chime;
> Or if Vertue feeble were,
> Heav'n it self would stoop to her.
> (*A Mask*, 1018–23)

But this kind of angelic intervention is explicitly precluded by the conditions of Adam and Eve's exclusion from Paradise, and the word 'choose' suggests that what is left to them, even in their fallen state, is an element of choice – in the terms of *Areopagitica*, 'When God gave him reason, he gave him freedom to choose, for reason is but choosing; he had bin else a mere artificiall *Adam*, such an *Adam* as he is in the motions.'[1] What is at issue in this passage from *Areopagitica* is whether Adam's transgression is compatible with divine providence: did an omnipotent deity allow Adam to fall, did he compel or cause Adam's fall, should he have prevented Adam's fall? As the Son asks the Father in dialogue in Book III,

> Should Man finally be lost, should Man
> Thy creature late so lov'd . . .
> or wilt thou thy self
> Abolish thy Creation, and unmake . . .
> what for thy glorie thou hast made?
> (*PL*, III.150–1, 162–4).

Or, if God is omnipotent, omniscient, and benevolent, is the test a genuine one, or is it one in which the outcome is known in advance, predestined? The passage in *Areopagitica* assumes that the biblical narrative, or reflections on it, may well give rise to such questions: 'Many there be that complain of divin Providence for suffering *Adam* to transgresse' (*CPW*, II.527).

Calvin's view of providence allowed no scope for human freedom of action: all things are predetermined, to the extent that postlapsarian humans are no better than automata:

> God presides over individual acts, as they call them, so as to move men, like rods, in whatever way he pleases, to guide their plans, to direct their efforts; and, in a word, to regulate their determinations, in order to inform us that everything depends on his providence.[2]

According to Calvin, 'it is certain that not a drop of rain falls without the express command of God'.

> We hold that God is the disposer and ruler of all things, – that from the remotest eternity, according to his own wisdom, he decreed what he was to do, and now by his power executes what he decreed. Hence we maintain that, by his providence, not heaven and earth and inanimate creatures only, but also the counsels and wills of men are so governed as to move exactly in the course which he has destined.[3]

In *De Doctrina*, Milton makes the conventional distinction between 'ordinary' or general providence and 'extraordinary' providence, defining the first of these (in a vocabulary very close to that used by the strict Calvinist Ames) as 'that by which he maintains and preserves that constant and ordered system of causes which was established by him in the beginning'.[4] Milton associates ordinary providence with 'what is commonly . . . called Nature'. Though Milton, like Calvin, is careful to say that the secondary operations of nature are not autonomous, rejecting the idea of a watchmaker God who set his universe in motion and then left it to its own devices, he nevertheless restricts the moments when God actively intervenes, suspending ordinary natural processes, to the 'extraordinary', or 'what we call a miracle'. 'The extraordinary providence of God is that by which he produces some effect outside the normal order of nature or gives to some chosen person the power of producing this effect . . . The purpose of miracles is to demonstrate divine power and strengthen our faith.'[5]

Calvin, in contrast, links providence with predestination, which he sees as individual or 'special' rather than as ordinary or general. God directs all human actions according to his own ends, by exercising his overwhelming power over the acts of his creatures. Anyone foolish enough to claim that postlapsarian man has 'a free choice of good and evil' makes the grave error of making 'man the partner of God'.

> The world is governed by God, not only because he maintains the order of nature appointed by him, but because he takes a special charge of every one of his works . . . Hence we infer, not only that the general providence of God, continuing the order of nature, extends over the creatures, but that by his wonderful counsel they are adapted to a certain and special purpose.[6]

Before their fall, according to Calvin, Adam and Eve possessed free will, but 'those who, while they profess to be the disciples of Christ, still seek for free-will in man, notwithstanding of his being lost and drowned in spiritual destruction, labour under manifold delusion'. In Adam's descendants, freedom of the will is utterly extinguished by the 'hereditary taint' that is their legacy from him (*Institutes*, 1.169–70).

Dissenting from Calvinist orthodoxy as well as the divine right theories of Salmasius, Milton throughout his writing upheld a view of providence that allowed a space for human freedom. The conception of an iron necessity that rendered all human action futile and made all talk of moral choice superfluous, a necessity that, in the words of Milton's friend Andrew Marvell, 'was pre-eternal to all things, and exercised dominion not only over all humane things, but over *Jupiter* himself and the rest of the Deities and drove the great Iron nail thorough the Axle-tree of Nature' was antipathetic to him.[7] In *De Doctrina*, Milton advanced a number of arguments against 'a Universal Dictatorship of Necessity over God and Man', claiming that 'from the concept of freedom . . . all idea of necessity must be removed': 'It would be much more unworthy of God to announce that man is free but really deprive him of freedom; and freedom is destroyed or at least obscured if we admit any such sophistical concept of necessity.'[8] Ventriloquizing through God the Father, Milton makes much the same point in *Paradise Lost*, Book III: forced obedience renders freedom empty and 'useless'.

> What pleasure I from such obedience paid,
> When Will and Reason (Reason also is choice)
> Useless and Vain, of freedom both despoild,
> Made passive both, had servd necessitie,
> Not me.
>
> (*PL*, III.107–11)

In *Paradise Lost* and in *De Doctrina*, Milton distinguishes between prescience or foreknowledge, consistent with God's omniscience, and any form of determinism, maintaining that for Adam and Eve (and by inference, for their descendants) there was no sense in which 'predestination overruld / Thir will': 'If I foreknew, / Foreknowledge had no influence on their fault, / Which had no less prov'd certain unforeknown' (*PL*, III.114–19). Though later critics have found the distinction in some ways puzzling, especially as set forth in Book III by a God who seems to be justifying himself against charges of being unfair in setting a test that he knows Adam and Eve will fail, Milton is one of a number of seventeenth-century writers who argue that God is in no way the author of sin, as, they claim, the doctrines of strict Calvinists imply. As Milton says in *De Doctrina*, 'Shall we say that God's providence or foreknowledge imposes any necessity upon them? Certainly not: no more than if some human being possessed the same foresight.'[9] The Presbyterian moderate John Howe, author of *The Reasonableness of God's Prescience of the Sins of Men* (1677), similarly argues, 'his prescience, no way, imposing on them a *necessity* to transgress. For they do it not because he foresaw it, but he only foreknew it because they would do so'.[10]

A recurrent theme in Milton is that the ways of providence, however little they correspond to our desires and preferences, cannot finally be challenged: freedom is possible once we recognize God's sovereignty. The relationship between the workings of providence and individual choice, human preferences and what it pleases God to bring to fruition is central to Milton's early Sonnet 7, 'How soon hath Time' (1631–2). Milton habitually uses the first person, in passages often considered autobiographical, to explore ethical problems which are of direct concern to him and at the same time universal: the 'I' is both individual and representative.

> How soon hath Time the suttle theef of youth,
>   Stoln on his wing my three and twentith yeer!
>   My hasting dayes flie on with full career,
>   But my late spring no bud or blossom shew'th.
> Perhaps my semblance might deceive the truth,
>   That I to manhood am arriv'd so near,
>   And inward ripenes doth much less appear,
>   That som more timely-happy spirits indu'th.
>
> (Sonnet 7, 1–8)[11]

The lines powerfully convey a sense of inward frustration and dissatisfaction conveyed by outward signs. Anger and resentment here are fuelled by the comparison with the 'more timely-happy spirits', time's favoured children crowned with early success, as well as by the sense of alienation from normal patterns of growth and ripening. Yet the terms of the eventual consolation are already apparent in the evocation of these normal patterns of the natural world and emphasis on 'semblance', the possibility that the speaker's perception of reality, however strongly felt and expressed, might be self-deceived, myopic.

> Yet be it less or more, or soon or slow,
>   It shall be still in strictest measure eev'n,
>   To that same lot, however mean, or high,
> Toward which Time leads me, and the will of Heav'n;
>   All is, if I have grace to use it so,
>   As ever in my great task Master's eye.
>
> (9–14)

The sudden shift in perspective is stunning: the pagan conception of time hastening on to oblivion, time the deceiver, a capricious and cynical joker, is supplanted by a slow, sure providential procession in which the god of time is enlisted in the angelic hierarchy as the servant of a just and benevolent God. 'What in me is dark' is suddenly illumined, 'what is low' (*PL*, 1.22–3) raised and supported. Milton's choice of language in the sestet, bald, dignified, chastened, largely unmetaphorical, reflects the change in perspective, and helps to involve the reader in the internal debate.

The theology of the closing lines, like that in *De Doctrina* nearly three decades later, is Arminian, yet within the overall framework of Puritan belief. God's grace is freely vouchsafed, but God's will is sovereign and incomprehensible; man cannot merit salvation by his works, demanding admission to Heaven, and must submit himself to God's will, whatever it may be. And yet man can *use* his time, is granted the opportunity to take advantage of the offered grace and perform whatever tasks are set him by his invisible master.[12] The *Letter to a Friend*, in which, in its initial context, the poem is embedded, is a tissue of scriptural allusions, all of which involve a powerful, enigmatic master and his problematic demands. The sonnet's final line, like the letter, alludes to the parable of the master of the vineyard (Matthew 20:1–16), which in Milton's troubled letter is given an optimistic reading. 'Beeing late', he argues in the *Letter to a Friend*, is not always disadvantageous, since 'those that were latest lost nothing when the maister of the vinyard came to give each one his hire'.[13] Other scriptural allusions in the letter suggest punishment rather than reward, the fear of being found wanting like an 'unprofitable servant', in the parable of the wise and foolish virgins (Matthew 25:1–13) and the parable of the talents (Matthew 25:14–30). The implication in Sonnet 7 as in each of these New Testament parables is that every natural object may hold within it the seeds of an unanticipated test: 'Watch therefore, for ye know neither the day nor the hour wherein the Son of man cometh.'[14] As Milton says in *Areopagitica*, seeking to justify the ways of a provident God:

> Wherefore did he creat passions within us, pleasures round about us, but that these rightly temper'd are the very ingredients of vertu? . . . This justifies the high providence of God, who though he command us temperance, justice, continence, yet powrs out before us ev'n to a profuseness all desirable things, and gives us minds that can wander beyond all limit and satiety. (*Areopagitica*, *CPW*, II.527–8)

In Sonnet 7 and in *Paradise Lost*, Milton dissents from the orthodox Reformed doctrine that fallen man, 'dead in sin', is entirely passive before God, whose offer of grace, 'absolutely irresistible', is open only to a specially chosen body of the elect. For Milton as for Arminius and the Dutch Remonstrants, 'the initial influence of prevenient grace is only a *necessary* condition for conversion; while for Reformed orthodoxy, the initial influence of grace is a *sufficient* condition for conversion'.[15] The repentance of Adam and Eve at the end of Book X is described as wholly spontaneous, 'sent from hearts contrite, in sign / Of sorrow unfeign'd', and at the same time is the result of God's 'implanted Grace in Man':

> Thus they in lowliest plight repentant stood
> Praying, for from the Mercie-seat above
> Prevenient Grace descending had remov'd
> The stonie from their hearts, and made new flesh
> Regenerate grow instead.
>
> (*PL*, X.1103–4; XI.1–5, 23)

II

To Milton as to many of his contemporaries, the hand of providence could be found in times of trial and uncertainty, giving a pattern to apparent chaos, illuminating each moment in the lives of the faithful: 'But even the faithful are sometimes insufficiently aware of all these methods of divine providence, until they examine the subject more deeply and become better informed about the word of God' (*De Doctrina*, I.viii, *CPW*, VI.339). With characteristic rhetoric, full of scriptural echoes, Cromwell, in a letter of 1650, attributed the victories of the New Model Army in Ireland to the God he and his soldiers served.

> Truly our work is neither from our brains nor from our courage or strength, but that we follow the Lord who goeth before, and gather what he scattereth, so that all may appear to be from him . . . What can we say to these things? If God be for us, who can be against us?[16]

Claims of divine intervention in battle were common during the 1640s and 1650s. Victories by the New Model Army were again and again acclaimed as evidence of 'the hand of God' humbling their enemies. God, one Puritan minister exclaimed, 'hath stepped out of heaven . . . to judge his adversaries', and, according to a proclamation of 1649, 'the great God of battle, by a continued series of providences and wonders', had 'determined very much in favour of the parliament'.[17] Cromwell often cited 'the great hand of God' in his victories: 'even our enemies', he said in 1653, had to admit 'that God himself was certainly engaged against them, or else they should never have been disappointed in every engagement'.[18] In *Eikonoklastes* (1650), Milton treats claims of this kind with considerable scepticism: his objections against royalist rhetoric can, of course, be applied to his own side equally well.

> Most men are too apt, and commonly the worst of men, so to interpret and expound the judgements of God, and all other events of providence or chance, as makes most to the justifying of their own cause, though never so evill; and attribute all to the particular favour of God towards them.[19]

In another passage in *Eikonoklastes*, where Milton is seeking to refute particular statements in *Eikon Basilike*, he inveighs against 'fals' claims in the king's partisan version of recent history, 'as if the very manuscript of Gods judgements had bin deliverd to his custody', but again the point he is making has more general application.

> Dispensing oft'n to his own bad deeds and successes the testimony of Divine favour, and to the good deeds and successes of other men, Divine

> wrath and vengeance. But to counterfet the hand of God is the boldest of all Forgery: And he, who without warrant but his own fantastic surmise, takes upon him perpetually to unfold the secret and unsearchable Mysteries of high Providence, is likely for the most part to mistake and slander them. (*CPW*, III.564)

In *An Apology* (1642), Milton makes the same kind of assertion that he criticizes in his royalist or Presbyterian antagonists a few years later: not simply arguing from success, attributing 'Divine favour' to his own side, but finding God to have actively intervened to bring about a particular result – what might be classified as 'extraordinary providence' as a gift to his chosen servants.

> And whereas at other times we count it ample honour when God voutsafes to make men the instrument and subordinate worker of his gracious will, such acceptation have their prayers found with him, that to them he hath bin pleas'd to make himselfe the agent, and immediat performer of their desires; dissolving their difficulties when they are thought inexplicable, cutting out wayes for them where no passage could be seene; as who is there so regardlesse of Divine providence, that from late occurrences will not confesse. If therefore it be so high a grace when men are preferr'd to be but the inferior officers of good things from God, what is it when God himselfe condescends, and workes with his owne hands to fulfill the requests of men . . . Not that we should think they are at the end of their glorious progresse, but that they will go on to follow his Almighty leading, who seems to have thus cov'nanted with them, that if the will and the endeavour shall be theirs, the performance and the perfeting shall be his. (*An Apology*, *CPW*, I.927–8)

In this passage, the insistence that certain phenomena can be interpreted in only one manner ('who is there . . . that from late occurrences will not confesse') is an appeal to the reader of a rather bullying kind to accept just such an interpretation and embrace the Parliamentary cause the author is defending. The claim that God has not only allowed men to be his instruments and 'inferior officers' but descended to earth to perform miracles at the 'request' of mortals is the kind of hubristic statement Milton frequently attacks in his opponents. By arguing from success, Milton comes perilously close to the identification of earthly power with divine power that he argues against in many of his tracts, as in *Samson Agonistes* and *Paradise Regained*.

Theologically, his argument in *An Apology* is that the 'testimonies' he adduces are evidence of a covenant, like the covenant with Abraham, by which God has chosen the English, as he had chosen the descendants of Abraham, as 'one peculiar Nation . . . select / From all the rest' (*PL*, XII.111–12). The idea that England has been 'chosen before any other' nation as herald of Reformation 'to all Christendom' is a recurrent theme in Milton's prose writings of the 1640s, in *Of Reformation in England*, *Areopagitica*, and *Doctrine and Discipline:*

> Why else was this Nation chos'n before any other, that out of her as out of *Sion* should be proclam'd and sounded forth the first tidings and trumpet of Reformation to all *Europ?* (*Areopagitica*, *CPW*, II.552)

> How it should come to passe that *England* having had this *grace* and *honour* from God to bee the first that should set up a Standard for the recovery of *lost Truth*, and blow the first *Evangelick Trumpet* to the *Nations*, holding up, as from a Hill, the new Lampe of *saving light* to all Christendome . . . (*Of Reformation*, *CPW*, I.515)

> Who but *Alcuin* and *Wicklef* our Country men open'd the eyes of *Europe*, the one in arts, the other in Religion. Let not England forget her precedence of teaching nations how to live. (*Doctrine and Discipline*, *CPW*, II.231–2)[20]

As a number of these passages, including the one from *An Apology*, make clear, the covenant or supposed national election, like the covenant of grace to the individual believer, is for Milton conditional: man must recognize, accept, and take advantage of the opportunity of the offered grace. His language in the passage from *An Apology* therefore is conditional, with 'if' occurring three times and 'as if' once. In every one of the passages quoted above, the words not only suggest that man needs to live up to his part of the bargain, but that he may well fail to do so. What is required of man, a free agent endowed with Christian liberty, is 'will and endeavour' ('Though but endevourd with sincere intent', *PL*, III.192), but neither may be forthcoming. The passage in *Of Reformation*, part of which is quoted above, contrasts hope of what 'should have been followed with more happy successe' with disappointment, a failure to realize this great promise, so that England, rather than being among the leaders of the Reformation, is now 'amongst the last' (*Of Reformation*, *CPW*, I.526). In the peroration of the *Second Defence* (1654), the possibility of failure is brought out even more fully, in a passage that combines exhortation with warning:

> If after such brave deeds you ignobly fail, if you do aught unworthy of yourselves, be sure that posterity will speak out and pass judgment . . . It will be a source of grief that to such great undertakings, such great virtues, perseverance was lacking.[21]

After the Restoration, when Milton and his fellow republicans had to live with the consequences of the English people having chosen 'a captain back for Egypt', Milton tried to reconcile this sense of having been abandoned by God with faith in the providential direction of all events, even the worst. Patience is defined in *De Doctrina* as 'the virtue which shows itself when we peacefully accept God's promises, supported by confidence in the divine providence, power and goodness: also where we bear any evils that we have to bear calmly, as things which our supreme Father has sent for our good'.[22] In *Samson Agonistes*, when Samson, in the depths of despair, longs for 'speedy death', the Chorus, urging on him 'the bearing well of all calamities', is unable to provide consolation, and finds the hand of 'contrarious . . . providence' in the 'causeless suffring' even of the virtuous: 'Just or unjust, alike seem miserable, / For oft alike, both come to evil end.' In lines of unrelieved bleakness, Milton recalls the fate of the regicides, his former associates, men like Sir Henry Vane and John Cook, savagely punished in the 1660s by the 'unjust tribunals', hanged and disembowelled while still alive, and their heads mounted on poles in public display, 'thir carcasses / To dogs and fowls a prey'.[23]

And yet the belief that all things, however difficult to bear, were directed by a providential deity whose ways were beyond human understanding, could be a source of solace in adversity. In domestic life, the sudden death of a beloved child or unexpected reverses like crop failure, fire, or drought were throughout this period seen as the acts of God, 'working by causes . . . that we knowe not': 'Whensoever misery or plague happeneth to man, it cometh not by chaunce or fortune, or by a course of nature, as vain worldly men imagine, but by the assured providence of God.'[24] When the diarist Ralph Josselin lost 'a pretious child . . . to us a bundle of sweet ointment', he reflected 'shee is not mine, but the Lords . . . Lord I rejoyce I had such a present for thee'.[25] Sir Thomas Fairfax, deploring the execution of Charles I but unwilling to break openly with Cromwell and his other associates in the New Model Army, after withdrawing from political life in 1650, wrote the following lines in his commonplace book:

> Oh Lett that Day from time be blotted quitt
> And let beleefe of't in next Age be waved
> In deeper silence th'Act Concealed might
> Soe that the King-doms Credit might be save'd
> But if the Power devine permitted this
> His Will's the Law and we must acquiesce.[26]

A more rueful, less anguished version of the felt need to submit, however reluctantly, to the lot assigned by providence is Richard Cromwell's comment on his fall from power in 1659: 'having I hope, in some degree learned rather to reverence and submit to the hand of god than to be unquiet under it', he had no choice but to accept 'the late providences' that had deprived him of power. 'Though I could not be active in making a change in the government of these nations: yet, through the goodness of God, I can acquiesce in it, being made.'[27]

Faith in providence as a bulwark against despair in dark times is a dominant theme in *A Voyce from the Watch-Tower*, the account by Milton's fellow republican Edmund Ludlow of the years 1660–2, when, in fear of his life at the hands of the triumphant royalists, he avoided capture and went into exile.[28] Whatever happened, however painful and humiliating, 'was done by the wide disposing hand of God, without whose providence not a sparrow falls to the ground, much less the blood of any of his pretious saints and witnesses'. Those who 'desire to live godly in the land' may be suffering now, but 'when in the furnace they are melted into one lamp, they shall come forth as refined gold': 'But it's the Lord's pleasure they should take this turne in the wildernesse, and that man may not have whereof to boast. Hee seemes to take the rod into his owne hand to correct them for their disobedience.'[29] In many passages in Ludlow's account of his tribulations, a faith in God's multiple 'providences' goes hand in hand with prudence, self-preservation: 'But seeing it was the will of the Lord we should be under such governours, I thought it my duty to use all the prudence I could for the keeping myselfe out of their hands' (Ludlow, *Voyce*, p. 182).

In an extended passage, Ludlow contrasts the great promises held forth with the failure of revolutionary hopes. Like Milton, he sees a defect of 'wisedom' as primary cause of an inability to achieve the 'prize' put 'into our hands', a sense that his countrymen, faced with an unparalleled opportunity, proved unworthy.

> The Lord hath appeared in our dayes to doe great things, such as our fathers had not seene, nor eares scarse heard of. He raysed up the poore, foolish, unexperienced and weake ones of the earth, to confound the rich, the wise, and the mighty thereof, speaking clearely, as well by his providence as his word . . . But so it was, that having through the assistance of the Lord subdued all those enemyes who publiquely opposed the liberty due to us as men and Christians, our enemyes began to be those of our owne howse; amongst whom the lust of power and domination prevayling. (Ludlow, *Voyce*, p. 307)

Since Ludlow steadfastly opposed the Cromwellian Protectorate as well as the return of Charles II, his condemnation of backsliders and open enemies of revolutionary transformation is even stronger than Milton's, but, like the post-Restoration Milton and Milton's Samson, he treats the state of bondage not only as deeply disturbing but as raising serious ethical problems. It is not always easy to reconcile 'the consideration of prudence' with the obligations of 'duty and conscience'. On the one hand, prudence suggests we should be content with 'submitting to, or at least not opposing, those in whom the Lord by his providence declares the power to be, who . . . it may be are not so righteous and just as were to be wisshed' (Ludlow, *Voyce*, p. 309). And yet when that power is manifestly unjust, it can be acutely painful to be 'under a persecuting and AntiChristian power, who for the setting up of carnall policy would roote out the forme of godlyness itselfe'.

> The Lord therefore unite us in his feare, that by suffering we may be fitted for the doing of his will, and give us wisedome to know when to goe forward and when to stand still, that by making hast we may not strengthen the hand of the enemy, nor by standing still neglect the opportunity he puts into our hands, but that, being on our Watch Tower, and living by faith, we may see our duty so plainly, that when the Lord's tyme is come we may up and be doing, and the Lord may appear to be with us and to owne us. (pp. 309–10)

III

When Milton uses the word 'providence' in his poems or prose writings, he frequently, as in the Lady's words in the Ludlow Masque, presents providence as a guide, while asserting human freedom to withstand 'trial': 'Eie me blest Providence, and square my triall / To my proportion'd strength' (*A Mask*, 329–30). Satan, in contrast, speaks of resisting God's providence, asserting his own freedom to defy his powerful enemy:

> If then his Providence
> Out of our evil seek to bring forth good,
> Our labour must be to pervert that end,
> And out of good still to find means of evil.
> (*PL*, 1.162–5)

The lesson Adam learns at the end of his encounter with the Archangel Michael after the Fall is exactly the opposite: unquestioning obedience to whatever providence will allot him. This is one of the few passages in Milton in which providence is not coupled with freedom of choice:

Henceforth I learne, that to obey is best,
And love with feare the onely God, to walk
As in his presence, ever to observe
His providence, and on him sole depend . . .
Taught this by his example whom I now
Acknowledge my Redeemer ever blest.
(*PL*, XII.561–5, 573–4)

In *Paradise Regained*, when the disciples express their fears and doubts after the apparent disappearance of their leader ('For whither is he gone, what accident / Hath rapt him from us?'), they invoke providence in an attempt to allay these fears: God, they claim, cannot mock their hopes, though the insistent verbs 'fail', 'withdraw', 'mock', and 'snatch' suggest doubts that threaten to drown the hope of redress:

Let us be glad of this, and all our fears
Lay on his Providence; he will not fail
Nor will withdraw him now, nor will recall,
Mock us with his blest sight, then snatch him hence,
Soon we shall see our hope, our joy return.[30]

The Son twice invokes providence in answering Satan, both times in stating that the ways of providence, hidden from man, will be revealed 'in due time'. Satan's reign over 'Idolatrous' man is a temporary one, consistent with the will of a just deity.

For God hath justly giv'n the Nations up
To thy Delusions; justly, since they fell
Idolatrous, but when his purpose is
Among them to declare his Providence
To thee not known, whence hast thou then thy truth.
(*PR*, I.442–6)

In a second passage, the Son contrasts the idolatry of the Israelites, fallen off from the worship of 'the God of their fore-fathers', with the covenant with Abraham, the memory of which may, if providence permits, bring about their repentance and the fulfilment of what has been promised under this covenant. In this passage, Milton is counselling against impatience, murmuring against God, suggesting that in times of trial, 'waiting on God', for whom past, present, and future are one, is the best course to follow.

Yet he at length, time to himself best known,
Remembring *Abraham* by some wond'rous call
May bring them back repentant and sincere,

And at their passing cleave the *Assyrian* flood,
While to their native land with joy they hast,
As the Red Sea and *Jordan* once he cleft,
When to the promis'd land thir Fathers pass'd;
To his due time and providence I leave them.
(*PR*, III.422, 433–40)[31]

In a letter to Leonard Philaras written in 1654, similar in the circumstances described to Milton's Sonnet 19 on his blindness, the poet finds consolation in 'the guidance', even in affliction, of a God who 'provides for me' and 'leads me throughout life'. In this letter, the tone is one of quiet resignation and acceptance, with no sense of anguish or rebellion against the state of 'ever-during dark' into which he has been plunged. Indeed, 'the cheerful ways of men', rather than being something from which the poet has been 'cut off', as in the invocation of *Paradise Lost*, Book III, are presented here as providing respite, in the frequent 'visits of friends'.[32] In this letter, the 'murmur' of discontent directed at a deity who seems inexplicably to hand out punishments to those who wish to serve him is almost wholly silenced.

> I prepare and resign myself as if the case were quite incurable, and I often reflect that since many days of darkness are destined to everyone, as the wise man warns, mine thus far, by the signal kindness of Providence, between leisure and study, and the voices and visits of friends, are much more mild than those lethal ones . . . Why should one not . . . find comfort in believing that he cannot see by the eyes alone, but by the guidance and wisdom of God. Indeed while He himself looks out for me . . . and leads me throughout life, surely, since it has pleased Him, I shall be pleased to grant my eyes a holiday.[33]

A number of passages in Milton's prose present the ways of providence as secret or hidden, inaccessible to man's limited reason. A passage from *Eikonoklastes*, quoted earlier, speaks of 'the secret and unsearchable Mysteries of high Providence', and 'the secret providence of God' and 'the same secret providence' are invoked in *Hirelings*.[34] In *Doctrine and Discipline*, Milton contrasts 'the hidden wayes' of God's providence, 'high and secret past finding out', with the Law of God as revealed in scripture, available to human understanding.[35] Two passages in *Hirelings* (1659) contrast limited human capacity and understanding with the secret workings of providence, presented here as benevolent, expressing mercy towards God's feeble and confused creatures. In one passage, where Milton is arguing against the idea of a professional clergy motivated by material considerations, demanding payment for their services, he argues that 'faithful and stedfast' Christians do not need state-appointed ministers in order to serve their master: God will provide. 'And so exhorted to continue faithful and stedfast, they may securely be committed to the providence of God and the guidance of his holy spirit, till God may offer som opportunitie to visit them again and to confirm them' (*Hirelings*, *CPW*, VII.304). Another passage from *Hirelings*, in the prefatory address to the restored Rump Parliament, again presents the ways of providence as beyond human comprehension. Like several other passages in Milton's poems and prose writings, it contrasts a period of darkness, with hopes deferred or denied, even for those who seek to serve God, with the promise of a new dawn. Once again the emphasis is on the need for man to grasp the opportunity offered: providence allows a space for man's freedom, setting new tests. What interests me here is not whether the praise of the Rump Parliament as 'the authors and best patrons of religious and civil libertie' is justified, or what Milton could possibly mean by 'a short and scandalous night of interruption'(*CPW*, VII.274), but what the passage says about providential direction in a time of uncertainty.[36] Here Milton is addressing Parliament, praising its 'magnanimous councels', in the hope of predisposing it to look sympathetically at his proposals for religious reform: 'The care and tuition of whose peace and safety, after a short but scandalous night of interruption, is now again by a new dawning of Gods miraculous providence among us, revolvd upon your shoulders' (*Hirelings*, *CPW*, VII.274).

In *The Readie and Easie Way* (1660), Milton invokes providence not in hopes of delivery from hardships suffered in the recent past, but in a desperate attempt to avoid a bleak future, a threatened new age of darkness. Here Milton speaks with the voice of a biblical prophet crying in the wilderness, warning that the God by whose providence the English people have been liberated from slavery may no longer listen to them, if they willingly resume their servitude under the Stuart monarchs.

> Us if he shall hear now, how much less will he hear when we cry heerafter, who once deliverd by him from a king, and not without wondrous acts of his providence, insensible and unworthie of those high mercies, are returning precipitantly, if he withold us not, back to the captivitie from whence he freed us. (*Readie and Easie Way*, *CPW*, VII.450)

A choral ode in *Samson Agonistes* counselling patience in affliction, discussed earlier, presents the ways of providence as incomprehensible, as God hands out rewards and punishments, 'causeless suffring', through the 'short course' of human life, seemingly without regard to individual merit. Even with those, like Samson, 'with gifts and graces eminently adorn'd / To some great work, thy glory', God, with his 'contrarious' hand, 'throw'st them lower then thou didst exalt them high'.[37] This is probably the darkest of all the references to providence in Milton's writing, presenting the ways of providence not simply as beyond human understanding but as arbitrary, akin to 'the blind Fury with th'abhorred shears' in *Lycidas*, which can in a moment sever 'the thin-spun life', without redress (*Lycidas*, 75–6).

In several passages in *Doctrine and Discipline* (1643–4), Milton presents a view of providence much more consolatory, while warning against the temptation to blame God or 'complain of divin Providence', because of one's limited perspective, blinded by consciousness of one's suffering as unmerited or unfair. Melancholy or despair, a feeling that one is trapped as a result of an erroneous choice, 'bound fast to an uncomplying discord of nature', reduced to an imprisonment from which there appears to be no escape, can lead, Milton says, to the 'temptation' to lose faith in God.[38] The term 'bondage' recurs again and again in Milton's divorce tracts, his other prose writings, and *Samson Agonistes*.[39] When one 'sees . . . that his bondage is now inevitable' and can 'know no remedy' against a continuing misfortune, and 'perceives the just expectance of his mind defeated', then:

> Though he be almost the strongest Christian, he will be ready to dispair in vertue, and mutin against divine providence: and this doubtles is the reason of those lapses and that melancholy despair which we see in many wedded persons, though they understand it not.[40]

A few pages later, commenting on how an unhappy marriage, 'without any true love and contentment', can cause someone to 'languish and fade away beneath the waight of an immeasurable grief and discouragement', Milton again points out that the temptation of murmuring or rebelling against God under such circumstances is hard to resist. Though Samson cannot be said to be 'without fault', the language here anticipates Samson's anguished self-condemnation at the memory of his 'servitude', 'base' and 'ignominious', as the 'Bond-slave' of the deceitful Dalila.

> Such a disturbance especially as both assaults our faith and trust in Gods providence, and ends, if there be not a miracle of vertue on either side, not onely in bitternes and wrath, the canker of devotion, but in a desperate and vitious carelesnes, when he sees himself without fault of his train'd by a deceitful bait into a snare of misery.[41]

Towards the end of *Doctrine and Discipline*, Milton, in a direct address to readers who might have experienced a similar experience of 'unworthy bondage' that may have tempted them to rail against 'the providence of heaven', goes on to suggest a possible remedy. 'The ways of God' are not unjust, and allow fallible humans the possibility not simply of bearing up under misfortune but of throwing off the burden under which they suffer.

> If any therfore who shall hap to read this discours, hath bin through misadventure ill ingag'd in this contracted evill heer complain'd of, and finds the fits and workings of a high impatience frequently upon him . . . let him not op'n his lips against the providence of heav'n, or tax the waies of God and his divine Truth; for they are equal, easy, and not burdensome. (*CPW*, II.342)

Milton argues in this passage and throughout the tract that the legal bond of marriage, like 'all other cov'nants and vowes', may legitimately, under certain circumstances, be 'broken for the good of man', adducing a number of biblical proof-texts to support the argument that 'the general and supreme rule of charitie' should take precedence over a 'stony rigor' (*CPW*, II.238, 275, 277). Milton's terminology in such passages is often implicitly political, in stating theological and ethical principles applicable in other contexts ('not to canonise marriage either as a tyrannesse or a goddesse over the enfranchiz'd life and soul of man') [*CPW*, II.277]. God enfranchises man, rather than locking him into a prison. Milton says of the ways of God (whose yoke is easy and his burden light):

> Nor do they ever crosse the just and reasonable desires of men, nor involve this our portion of mortal life, into a necessity of sadnes and malecontent, by Laws commanding over the unreducible *antipathies* of nature, sooner or later found: but allow us to remedy and shake off these evills into which human error hath led us through the middest of our best intentions; and to support our incident extremities by that authentick precept of sovran charity. (*CPW*, II.342–3)

As with Adam and Eve, or as with Samson, 'human error', in Milton's view, is never irreparable.

Though the circumstances differ, the question these passages from *Doctrine and Discipline* ask is essentially that expressed in Milton's two sonnets on his blindness. In the tract, the phrase 'to make men the day-labourers of their own afflictions' (*CPW*, II.342) comes immediately before the words just quoted. In each of these sonnets, the affliction of loss of sight, the constant awareness of being plunged into darkness and the frustration of hopes that follows from this impairment tempt the poet to challenge God and his ways: 'Doth God exact day-labour, light deny'd?' (Sonnet 19, 7). Does God set us a task and then prevent us from accomplishing it? The two sonnets differ in the way they seek to answer these questions, suggesting ways to 'bear up' under God's 'milde yoak'. In both poems, 'patience', or the conviction that even when one is 'bereft of light' God can serve as a 'guide', provides a consolation, allowing one to be 'content though blind'.

> Yet I argue not
> Against heavns hand or will, nor bate a jot
> Of heart or hope; but still bear up and steer
> Right onward.[42]

In the sonnet to Milton's friend Cyriack Skinner, 'what supports' the blind poet is 'conscience', the conviction that he has been allotted and has performed a 'noble task', that of 'libertyes defence' (Sonnet 22, 9–11). In the other sonnet, there is no sense of a job well done, a successful 'use' of the talent (as in the biblical parable) handed to him by God to invest or employ wisely. Instead, the blind poet learns that God will not reward men according to their works or deserts, but that the ways of providence are ultimately beyond his comprehension: 'God does not need / Either man's work or his own gifts'. All God's creatures can do is 'waite', expecting a call that may never come.[43]

One of the other poems in the collection *Justa Edouardo King* (1638), which includes *Lycidas*, begins with the lines:

> No Death! I'le not examine Gods decrees,
> Nor question providence, in chiding thee:
> Discreet Religion bids us t'admire
> The wayes of Providence, and not enquire.[44]

But this is precisely what *Lycidas* does. Where the other poems in the collection largely devote themselves to praising the dead Edward King, with occasional conceits about salt tears and death by water, Milton uses the occasion to raise a number of painful and troubling questions. Since Tillyard in 1930, it has been a critical commonplace that *Lycidas* is a poem about Milton himself, and, more generally, about the inability to control one's fate, 'the seeming profitlessness of the dedicated life and the seeming deficiency of divine justice' exemplified by this particular sudden death.[45] The poem's tribute to a fellow poet is presented as a propitiatory offering, in anticipation of the same fate befalling Milton himself.

> He must not flote upon his watry bier
> Unwept, and welter to the parching wind,
> Without the meed of some melodious tear . . .
> So may some gentle Muse
> With lucky words favour my destin'd Urn.
>
> (*Lycidas*, 12–14, 19–20)

For its first 164 lines, the poem, far from expressing confidence in a benevolent, nurturing providence, pours out a series of anguished questions, in apparent turmoil.[46] Repeatedly, hopes of consolation, possibilities of escaping from a prevailing darkness, are shown to be inadequate, instances of 'false surmise', faced with the humbling fact of early death, extinction of promise. 'For so, to interpose a little ease, / Let our frail thoughts dally with false surmise' (152–3).

The most powerful of these grim eruptions, challenging any sense of divine justice, is the account of the violent death of Orpheus, a mythical figure exemplifying both the magical transformative power of poetry and its ultimate failure to overcome the hostile forces, with their bestial 'hideous roar', jealous of it and intent on its destruction.

> What could the Muse her self that *Orpheus* bore,
> The Muse her self, for her inchanting son
> Whom Universal nature did lament,
> When by the rout that made the hideous roar,
> His goary visage down the stream was sent,
> Down the swift *Hebrus* to the *Lesbian* shore.
> (59–63)

Two passages, often described as digressions, carry much of the burden of questioning in the poem, and both end with a partial, enigmatic answer, akin to the words of 'Patience' in Milton's sonnet on his blindness. Poets hope for lasting fame – Milton speaks elsewhere of 'an inward prompting which now grew daily upon me, that by labour and intense study (which I take to be my portion in this life), joyn'd with the strong propensity of nature, I might perhaps leave something so written to aftertimes, as they should not willingly let it die'.[47] Is it worth it, after all, to devote 'uncessant care' to one's calling as poet/shepherd, in endless 'laborious dayes', when our hopes are likely to be arbitrarily cut short by 'the blind *Fury* with th'abhorred shears'? The reply, in the voice of a Christianized Phoebus, is that earthly fame is evanescent and meaningless and that one can look forward to eventual judgement 'in Heav'n', when 'all-judging *Jove*' will hand out rewards and punishment.[48]

A second digressive interruption, differing markedly in its angry, explosive tone from the rest of the poem, is described, misleadingly, in a headnote in the 1645 edition, as a passage which 'by occasion fortels the ruine of our corrupted Clergy, then in their height' (*Lycidas*, headnote, p. 74). Until the mysterious last lines, the passage, rather than foretelling their downfall, bitterly laments the apparent triumph, at least for the present, of the powers of darkness, flourishing in their pride and doing immeasurable damage. Except for maintaining the decorum of pastoral metaphors, the rhetoric here is closely akin to that in Milton's anti-prelatical pamphlets several years later: selfish, bloated clergy blind to all but 'their bellies sake', enemies of 'the worthy', as they spread 'foul contagion' by their malign influence: 'The hungry Sheep look up and are not fed' (*Lycidas*, 114, 118, 125, 127). The closing lines in this passage promise some kind of retribution, a severe judgement, but in terms so opaque that no one has ever been able to give a satisfactory explanation what the 'two-handed engine' that 'stands ready to smite' could mean.[49]

In the final section of the poem, the consolation appropriate to the genre and the occasion is provided, with imagery that, throughout lines 165–85, is consistently Christian. The movement from grief to consolation is a conventional pattern in pastoral elegy, and the poem's redemptive conclusion is foreshadowed earlier, in suggestions that there is a realm beyond the natural processes exemplified by 'the rathe Primrose that forsaken dies . . . / With Cowslips wan that hang the pensive hed', mourning their own transience as well as the dead youth (142, 147). Like the sun that sinks out of sight each night, to rise the next morning, or like the resurrected Christ, 'one greater Man' whose sacrifice on the behalf of fallible humans makes it possible to 'restore us, and regain the blissful Seat' (*PL*, 1.4–5), Lycidas, we are assured, is 'not dead' (*Lycidas*, 166), but risen into heavenly bliss. If the vision of the 'haples youth' denied the customary burial rites, stripped to his bare bones 'under the whelming tides' and subjected to the capricious elements 'at the bottom of the monstrous world', is the poem's bleakest moment, immediately after this we are told, three times, to 'weep no more' (154–8, 164–5, 182). As in Milton's sonnet on his blindness, the sense of a providential order, assuaging doubts, is restored by the end of the poem. But the balance of contrasting elements is different in *Lycidas* from Sonnet 19, in which the relationship of divine master and servant is present from the beginning and the reply of 'patience' follows swiftly, linking octave and sestet, 'to prevent' despair and rebellion (Sonnet 19, 8–9). Here the questioning is incessant, taking up all but the final thirty lines: in powerful moments that keep erupting throughout *Lycidas*, these doubts are never silenced, and the epilogue in Heaven cannot counteract the poem's overwhelming concern with uncertainty and potential unfulfilled.[50]

In the works discussed in this chapter, written in varying circumstances over a period of nearly forty years, certain recurrent patterns can be discerned. Milton does not equate providence with predestination, the belief that all human activities are under the unsleeping control of a deity who has programmed all possible contingencies in an individual life in an unalterable script. Providence for Milton is 'general' rather than 'special', with a detailed plan worked out in advance for each individual. No individual, not even the Son of God in *Paradise Regained*, is able to foresee a clouded future.[51] The Lady in the Ludlow Masque has a free choice that cannot be alienated except by a conscious act on her part; the same is true of Adam and Eve, and was true of Satan before his fall, and of Abdiel before and after he learns of Satan's rebellion: all are formed free, 'and free they must remain, / Till they enthrall themselves' (*PL*, III.124–5). As we will see in Chapter 6, many readers of *Paradise Lost* have been puzzled by the paradoxical combination of an all-powerful and all-seeing deity who chooses to allow a freedom to his creatures under conditions he has set them. But Milton is consistent in his early poems, his prose pamphlets of the 1640s and 1650s, and his great works in verse published after 1660 in presenting the events of an individual life or a nation as a series of opportunities which may be grasped or missed, tests set by a 'task Master' whose ways are not always easy to understand.

In these writings, Milton almost never depicts God as actively intervening in human affairs, working 'with his own hands to fulfil the requests of men' or directly punishing them, through his 'special providence', for their sins.[52] Rather than showing the miraculous acts of divine providence in protecting God's favourites (as, for example, in the parting of the Red Sea to allow the Israelites to pass through unscathed, while drowning the Egyptians immediately afterwards), Milton most often presents a 'confidence in the divine providence' as providing hope in difficult circumstances, giving us strength to 'bear any evils that we have to bear'.[53] In the letter to Philaras, as in the two sonnets on his blindness, works with direct autobiographical significance, the affliction is the loss of sight, and each of them gives expression to the need to 'prepare and resign myself', accept the ordeal allotted by 'heavns hand or will', however painful it may be.[54] Where the letter to Philaras is calmly resigned in tone, the two sonnets bring out the pain of loss, the sense of being cut off from ordinary human activities, the fear of being cast out by one's divine master as an 'unprofitable servant', in what Milton's Samson describes despairingly as 'total Eclipse / Without all hope of day': 'Nor to thir idle orbs doth sight appear / Of Sun or Moon or Starre throughout the year, / Or man or woman.'[55]

What is most characteristic of Milton's treatment of providence is the element of conflict, the strongly conveyed desire to 'murmur' or 'argue' against God, succumbing to the temptation, as he puts it in the divorce tracts, to lose faith in God, overwhelmed by despair, and 'mutin against divine providence'.[56] In the sonnet to Cyriack Skinner, 'what supports me', Milton says, is 'conscience': here the 'guide', rather than external, a mentor providing counsel or support, is an inward one, the 'Umpire *Conscience*' implanted by God in the descendants of Adam and Eve. 'This thought might lead me through the worlds vain mask / Content though blind, had I no better guide.'[57] But the gift of conscience, in creatures limited in their power and awareness, can only allow for the possibility of choosing, rather than in any sense dictating choice. As Milton warns his fellow Englishmen in *A Readie and Easie Way*, those who are 'insensible and unworthie' of 'the wondrous acts of his providence', the 'honour wonn or deliverances voutsaf'd from heaven' in the past, and neglect the opportunities offered to them, deserve the punishment they have willed on themselves (*CPW*, VII.422, 450).

3

The Unpolluted Temple of the Mind
Virtue on Trial

I

Milton's *Mask Presented at Ludlow-Castle* and his divorce tracts, though they differ markedly in genre and in circumstances of composition, have in common a concern with virtue under trial. In the masque, first performed in 1634, and the pamphlets, published a decade later, as in *Areopagitica* (1644), the idea of trial 'in the field of this World' is associated with the possibility of being misled or deceived, since good and evil are 'involv'd and interwoven . . . in so many cunning resemblances hardly to be discern'd'. In a fallen world, any apparent innocence is compromised, threatened by its very nature: 'Assuredly we bring not innocence into the world, we bring impurity much rather; that which purifies us is triall, and triall is by what is contrary.'[1] The Ludlow Masque, *Doctrine and Discipline*, and *Tetrachordon* are works which in some respects are radical and egalitarian, in some respects authoritarian and repressive. Their ambivalence, with apparent contradictions often unresolved, is, I would argue, characteristic of Milton and of the theological and ethical tradition in which he writes.

A Mask Presented at Ludlow-Castle, like *Lycidas*, exhibits Milton's characteristic mixture of radicalism and conservatism. *A Mask*, performed 'before the Right Honorable, John Earle of Bridgewater . . . Lord President of Wales, And one of His Majesties most honorable Privie Counsell', is an aristocratic entertainment, with a considerable element of flattery, conventional in masques, directed at its patron.[2] In *Poems of Mr. John Milton* (1645), the *Mask* is buttressed by a dedication by Henry Lawes to the heir-apparent, the masque's Elder Brother (praising his 'Noble Family' and the 'fair Hopes, and rare Endowments of your much-promising Youth'), and a letter to Milton by Sir Henry Wotton about the 'dainty peece of entertainment' Milton has sent him.[3] Like *Lycidas*, the *Mask* is the work of a traditionalist and humanist, and is full of classical allusions: '*Joves Court*' in the opening line, shortly followed by Neptune and his 'tributary gods', and, in the Attendant Spirit's closing speech, the gardens of Hesperus, the Graces, the Hours, Venus and Adonis, Cupid and 'his dear *Psyche*' (1, 18–24, 981–1011).

In *A Mask*, the figures from classical mythology frequently have a Christian colouring, so that, for example, 'the starry threshold of *Joves* Court' is clearly identified with the Christian Heaven, while, on another level of topical allegory, the lesser deities under Neptune, exercising their 'severall government' over different provinces, include 'a noble Peer of mickle trust, and power', the Lord President of Wales, the Earl of Bridgewater (*A Mask*, 1–11, 18–34). In *Lycidas*, Neptune, Apollo, the Muses, and the blind Furies walk hand in hand with St Peter, and 'all judging *Jove*, / As he pronounces lastly on each deed' (*Lycidas*, 82–3), is transparently an image of the Day of Judgement. The classical and Renaissance pastoral tradition, as handed down to Milton, allowed room for both topical compliment and religious allegory, and the masque as a form also could rise to allegorical presentation of virtues and vices, while flattering rich and powerful noblemen and monarchs. But Milton's *Mask* is unusual in its sustained seriousness, the length of its speeches, and the relative absence of spectacular scenery, gorgeous costumes, and the opportunity for the aristocratic masquers (including the Egerton children in *Tempe Restored* in 1632) to display their expensive finery in dances and tableaux. In Jonson's *Pleasure Reconciled to Virtue* (1618), the figure of Comus is a jolly, unthreatening comic spirit of excess, bloated with food and wine, whose opening lines are 'Room, room, make room for the bouncing belly, / First father of sauce, and deviser of jelly', as he leads his revellers in an anti-masque. In the central action, Hercules, an 'active friend of virtue', easily overcomes 'the voluptuous Comus', and a second anti-masque of pygmies demonstrates that 'virtue's seat' is the Court of James I.[4] Aurelian Townshend's masque *Tempe Restored*, in which the enchantments of Circe are dissolved without effort, explains that 'in Heroic Virtue is figured the King's Majesty, who therein as far transcends common men as they are above beasts'.[5] Milton's *Mask*, in contrast, shows that virtue and pleasure can never be reconciled.

What is most radical about the Ludlow Masque is not its criticism of court culture in the Lady's scornful remarks about 'that which lewdly-pamper'd Luxury / Now heaps upon som few with vast excess' (770–1): it is Milton's decision to make a young woman (Alice Egerton, fifteen years old) the embodiment of 'Heroic Virtue'.[6] Virtue, defined here and elsewhere by Milton as the ability to 'apprehend and consider vice with all her baits and seeming pleasures, and yet abstain, and yet distinguish, and yet prefer that which is truly better', is, as he presents it in this work, independent of gender. The example he gives from Spenser, 'a better teacher then *Scotus* or *Aquinas*', to illustrate 'true temperance', is Sir Guyon, who is able 'to see and know, and yet abstain', when faced with the temptations of the Cave of Mammon and the Bower of Bliss.[7] In the climactic episode of *The Faerie Queene*, Book II, the 'faire Witch' and her temptations are female and the resolved soul, stoutly resisting temptation, is male.

> There, whence that Musick seemed heard to bee,
> Was the faire Witch her selfe now solacing,
> With a new Lover, whom through sorceree
> And witchcraft, she from farre did thither bring:
> There she had him now layd a slumbering,
> In secret shade, after long wanton joyes:
> Whilst round about them pleasauntly did sing
> Many faire Ladies, and lascivious boyes,
> That ever mixt their song with light licentious toyes.[8]

In Marvell's *Dialogue, between The Resolved Soul, and Created Pleasure*, a capsule version of the central action of Milton's masque, the warrior soul is, with his allegorical sword and helmet, implicitly male, and the temptations are, like those facing Sir Guyon in the Bower of Bliss, either female or, like the 'lascivious boyes' or knights that have abandoned their shields in Spenser, unmanly, effeminized.

> *Pleasure*
> All this fair, and soft, and sweet,
> Which scatteringly doth shine,
> Shall within one beauty meet,
> And she be only thine.[9]

Though the Elder Brother, using imagery of warfare, characterizes the hidden strength of 'sacred . . . chastity' as 'clad in compleat steel', the analogy is not with knights in armour but with Diana and her followers, 'like a quiver'd Nymph with arrows keen'. The danger to his young sister, rather than falling short of the principles of knighthood, is sexual pollution, rape, the loss of virginity at the hands of a predatory male who might 'dare to soyl her Virgin purity' (*A Mask*, 418–27).

In presenting exemplary virtue, a 'single soul' able to fend off 'The batt'ries of alluring sense', in the form of a young woman – and not an overtly allegorical figure, but a masquer playing herself, Alice

Egerton – Milton's masque is, in some respects at least, egalitarian.[10] Where, in a notorious passage in *Paradise Lost*, Milton, in line with misogynist tradition, presents woman as by her nature inferior to man, and subject to a domestic form of 'Absolute rule', here virtue under trial can, indifferently, take on masculine or feminine form. Probably no passage in Milton has met with more commentary, mostly hostile or troubled, than these lines:

> Whence true autoritie in men, though both
> Not equal, as thir sex not equal seemd;
> For contemplation hee and valour formd,
> For softness shee and sweet attractive Grace,
> Hee for God only, shee for God in him.
> (*PL*, IV.295–9, 301)

As James Turner and Mary Nyquist have argued, there is an irreconcilable contradiction at the heart of Milton's ideology, evident in *Paradise Lost* and his divorce tracts, as well as in *A Mask* – at some times smugly patriarchal and sexist, at other times egalitarian.[11] The uneasy coexistence of two incompatible positions – man and woman as equal, or woman as inferior, a subject to or a supplement to man – can be traced to the account of the creation in Genesis, which on the one hand presents 'male and female' as created together and on the other presents man as the prior creation and woman as a kind of afterthought. The contradiction is apparent in Raphael's account of the creation in *Paradise Lost*, VII, paraphrasing Genesis 1:26 and 27, with its switch from singular noun to plural pronoun.

> Let us make now Man in our image, Man
> In our similitude, and let them rule
> Over the Fish and Fowle of Sea and Aire,
> Beast of the Field, and over all the Earth.
> (*PL*, VII.519–23)[12]

Though, as one seventeenth-century Puritan minister put it, 'soules have no sexes', and though the Lady in Milton's masque, as true warfaring Christian, is the representative and champion not of 'any specific, isolated virtue' but of virtue in all its forms, nevertheless in *A Mask*, the Lady is explicitly identified with one particular virtue, chastity. According to the Elder Brother:

> So dear to Heav'n is Saintly chastity
> That when a soul is found sincerely so,
> A thousand liveried Angels lacky her,

Driving far off each thing of sin and guilt,
And in cleer dream, and solemn vision
Tell her of things that no gross ear can hear.
(*A Mask*, 453–8)[13]

In a later passage, the Elder Brother, trying to counteract his brother's fears at the terrible dangers facing 'th'unarmed weakness of one Virgin / Alone, and helpless', presents the power protecting his sister as 'virtue', in the war of good against evil, pitted against one another in recurrent 'trial'.

Virtue may be assail'd, but never hurt,
Surpriz'd by unjust force, but not enthrall'd,
Yea even that which mischief meant most harm,
Shall in the happy trial prove most glory.
But evil on it self shall back recoyl,
And mix no more with goodness.
(581–2, 589–94)

These lines describe virtue both as an intrinsic quality in the virtuous individual, acting as autonomous moral agent, or, as in the first passage above, as an external protection, warding off the influence of evil enchanters, 'sin and guilt', as incompatible with impregnable 'goodness'.

Throughout *A Mask*, the terms 'chastity' and 'virginity' are used interchangeably. As the speeches of the two brothers (one of them eleven years old and the other nine) consistently indicate, both the Lady and her siblings are innocents, inexperienced in the ways of the world. For all their careful nurture at the hands of their music master Henry Lawes and other mentors, each of them is 'but a youngling in the contemplation of evill', and indeed the naivety of the two brothers ('How charming is divine Philosophy!') gives rise to occasional comic touches in the masque.[14] In performance, with the lines declaimed in the piping voices of two young boys, the exchange between the two brothers may lose some of its seriousness. The text in the Bridgewater manuscript, indicating what was performed at Ludlow Castle in 1634, is 115 lines shorter than the published 1637 and 1645 text, and the cuts make the work seem more like an ordinary masque, a 'dainty peece of entertainment'. Nevertheless, the emphasis on trial and temptation, on 'vice with all its baits and seeming pleasures', is as pronounced in the shorter as in the longer version.[15] The particular virtue thought to be appropriate to young, marriageable women in the dominant ideology of Milton's day (and in succeeding centuries as well) is remaining a virgin until marriage, not lessening one's exchange value as property passed on from father to husband. As a horrified Leonato says in *Much Ado about Nothing*, instantly condemning his innocent daughter as an adulteress, damaged goods – a 'rotten orange', in Claudio's savage verbal assault on her:

> O, she is fallen
> Into a pit of ink that the wide sea
> Hath drops too few to wash her clean again,
> And salt too little which may season give
> To her foul-tainted flesh.[16]

Images of pollution, of the felt need to avoid contamination in the 'pig-sty' of quotidian life, abound in Milton's writings. The Elder Brother's speech, quoted above, like a number of passages in *Paradise Lost*, suggests the possibility of a soul becoming defiled or imbruted, descending into 'bestial slime', or, conversely, being refined so that it is transformed to a bodiless purity, 'made immortal':

> But when lust
> By unchaste looks, loose gestures, and foul talk,
> But most by leud and lavish acts of sin,
> Lets in defilement to the inward parts,
> The soul grows clotted by contagion,
> Imbodies, and imbrutes, till she quite loose
> The divine property of her first being.
> (*A Mask*, 463–9)

In similar terms, Satan, who has gradually been losing his celestial brightness, bitterly laments his 'foul descent', from an angel among angels to the 'indignitie' of becoming 'incarnate' in a brute beast:

> O foul descent! That I who erst contended
> With Gods to sit the highest, am now constraind
> Into a Beast, and mixt with bestial slime,
> This essence to incarnate and imbrute.
> (*PL*, IX.154, 163–6)

Throughout Milton's poems and prose, a Pauline or Platonic dualism, with a marked distrust of anything corporeal as a potential source of 'contagion', clashes with a monism suggesting not so much an irreconcilable opposition as a continuum, an ultimate harmony, of spirit and matter.[17] As Raphael tells Adam in Book V, humans may, becoming 'more refin'd, more spiritous, and pure', eventually ascend the ladder of creation and turn into angels:

> Time may come when men
> With Angels may participate, and find
> No inconvenient Diet, nor too light Fare;

And from these corporal nutriments perhaps
Your bodies may at last turn all to Spirit,
Improv'd by tract of time.

(*PL*, v.475, 493–8)

The Elder Brother, in slightly different terms, sees the possibility of upward ascent not as a distant prospect, a magical transformation, but as something that is likely to happen to those who remain 'unpolluted' and have the advantage of familiar intercourse with angelic messengers:

Till oft convers with heav'nly habitants
Begin to cast a beam on th'outward shape,
The unpolluted temple of the mind,
And turns it by degrees to the souls essence,
Till all be made immortal.

(*A Mask*, 459–63)

In a lengthy autobiographical digression in *An Apology*, where Milton is defending himself against defamatory charges that in his youth he frequented bordellos, he at one point presents himself as a male equivalent of the Lady in his Masque, rejecting one offered cup and preferring another. Chastity, which he couples here with love, is one 'whose charming cup is only vertue which she bears in her hand to those who are worthy. The rest are cheated with a thick intoxicating poison which a certaine Sorceresse the abuser of loves name carries about.'[18] However valuable chastity in a woman is, Milton says, chastity in a male (who he says in a sexist aside, is 'the perfeter sex') is even better:

> If unchastity in a woman whom Saint *Paul* termes the glory of man, be such a scandall and dishonour, then certainly in a man who is both the image and glory of God, it must, though commonly not so thought, be much more deflouring and dishonourable. In that he sins both against his owne body which is the perfeter sex, and his own glory which is in the woman, and that which is worst, against the image and glory of God which is in himselfe. (*An Apology*, *CPW*, I.892)

After Fielding's *Joseph Andrews*, it is difficult to see male chastity as anything but comic, and, indeed, Fielding in that novel as in *Shamela* is satirizing the ideology of virginity as a jewel to be preserved, in order to increase its material value, puncturing the hypocrisy underlying a pattern of belief prevalent in his day. But Milton is entirely serious in his praise of 'those chaste and high mysteries', identifying abstention from sexual dalliance with the arduous task of equipping oneself for the demanding vocation of poet, the 'high rewards' only accessible to 'those who were not defil'd with women'. Though he allows in this passage for the possibility of married chastity ('for mariage must not be call'd a defilement'), here, as in *A Mask*, chastity is seen as virginity, keeping clear of the contaminating influence of potential seducers.[19] In his Latin Elegy 6, addressed in 1629 (the year of the Nativity Ode) to his close friend Charles Diodati, Milton argues that for the budding poet, it is a necessary part of his preparation to keep aloof from the pleasures of the flesh, avoiding impurity:

> Stet prope fagineo pellucida lympha catillo,
> Sobriaque è pura pocula fonte bibat.
> Additur huic scelerisque vacans, & casta juventus,
> Et rigidi mores, & sine labe manus.
>
> [Let water stand nearby in a beechwood bowl;
> let him drink sober cups from a pure spring.
> And add to this a youth spent chaste and free of crimes –
> unbending morals, a hand undefiled.[20]]

In *An Apology*, Milton first identifies chastity with the pleasures of reading about 'the deeds of Knighthood' in romance, in the company of 'the Laureat fraternity of Poets', and then with the composition of poetry, ready to 'write well hereafter in laudable things'. A knight in romance is a defender of chastity, but a poet, whose calling is even higher than knighthood, must himself embody chastity.

> There I read it in the oath of every Knight, that he should defend to the expence of his best blood, or of his life, if it so befell him, the honour and chastity of Virgin or Matron. From whence I learnt what a noble vertue chastity sure must be. (*An Apology*, *CPW*, 1.890–1)

Milton, defensively pointing out his own 'reserv'dnesse of naturall disposition, and morall discipline' and 'a certain nicenesse of nature, an honest haughtinesse, and self-esteeme' of 'what I might be', sees an instinctive aversion to baseness, keeping one 'still above those low descents of minde', as essential to the high calling of poetry. A true poet, retaining his virgin purity of mind, will be 'in disdain' of 'incontinences', whenever he encounters them.[21] This can be interpreted as an overinsistence on an impossible purity, a claim of being somehow sinless in a fallen world, or as an attempt, as with the Younger Brother, to escape from an overwhelming fear of violation:

> But beauty like the fair Hesperian Tree
> Laden with blooming gold had need the guard
> Of dragon watch with unenchanted eye,
> To save her blossoms, and defend her fruit

From the rich hand of bold Incontinence.
You may as well spread out the unsun'd heaps
Of Misers treasure by an out-laws den,
And tell me it is safe.[22]

The element of choice, of resisting temptation or succumbing to it, is as central to *A Mask* as it is to *Areopagitica* or *Samson Agonistes*. Rather than characterizing the world as one in which the 'Sin-worn' inhabitants are 'confin'd', unable to escape from the prison of the flesh, *A Mask* from the outset distinguishes those who, refusing to 'perceive their foul disfigurement', are content in their 'brutish form' to 'roule with pleasure in a sensual sty', from the few 'true Servants' who are able to see more clearly (7–10, 16, 69–76). Both the Lady and the Elder Brother contrast the threatening or enclosing 'single darknes' and its 'black usurping mists' with the light that virtue, shining inward, can give in adversity. 'These thoughts may startle well, but not astound / The vertuous mind, that ever walks attended / By a strong siding champion Conscience'.[23] The Elder Brother, reassuring his anxious sibling that 'He who has light within his own cleer brest / May sit i'th center, and enjoy bright day', says of his sister, well schooled 'in vertues book': 'Vertue could see to do what vertue would / By her own radiant light, though Sun and Moon / Were in the flat Sea sunk' (367, 373–5, 381–2). These two passages raise a question as to how autonomous, in the action of Milton's masque, the inner light of 'Conscience', described in Book III of *Paradise Lost* as an 'Umpire' implanted within (*PL*, III.194–5), actually is. The Lady's lines are ambiguous, describing 'the vertuous mind' both as exercising independent choice and as under the protection of an invisible chivalric champion, walking by its side. As she says a moment later:

I see ye visibly, and now believe
That he, the Supreme good, t'whom all things ill
Were but as slavish officers of vengeance,
Would send a glistering Guardian if need were
To keep my life and honour unassail'd.
(216–20)[24]

Though the Attendant Spirit describes his role as acting for the 'defence, and guard' of those who are specially 'favour'd of high *Jove*' and 'might suffer perill' – 'I shoot from Heav'n to give him safe convey' (40–2, 78, 81) – his active interventions are in fact limited. He serves as mentor to the two brothers, warning them (and the audience of the masque) of the dangers in 'this hideous Wood', and saying that he has been unable, 'harrow'd with grief and fear', to protect 'the aidless innocent Lady' from 'the deadly snare' of the sorcerer Comus (520, 565–7, 573–4). In the guise of the shepherd Thyrsis, he accompanies them in the attempt to rescue the Lady from 'the might of hellish charms', telling them of a magical herb Haemony, that would allow them to resist the spells of Comus. When the two brothers, though they drive Comus and his followers away, fail to break the spell and 'let the false enchanter scape', the disguised Thyrsis tells them of 'som other means I have that may be used' (613, 814, 821). He then summons Sabrina, the dominant figure in the later part of the action.

In the masque, the Attendant Spirit serves as a kind of master of ceremonies, opening and closing the action, singing (and, as Lawes, composing) all but two of the songs and having more lines to speak than any other performer, and introducing the dancing at the end as the Egerton children are presented to their parents. In terms of Milton's theology of Arminian puritanism, the Attendant Spirit serves a similar function to the Archangel Raphael in *Paradise Lost*, Book v, sent as emissary to one who has been 'left to his own free Will . . . yet mutable', to deliver a warning and 'tell him withall / His danger, and from whom', while conversing 'as friend with friend' (*PL*, v.229–30, 236–9). The Lady is shown to be able to resist Comus' temptation, refute his arguments, even though initially she fails to see through the pretended 'honest offer'd courtesie' of his disguise as 'gentle Shepherd' (271, 322). But she is unable to free herself from the enchanter's spell, remaining within his power, 'in stony fetters fixt, and motionless' (819). Only Sabrina is able to free her, and, indeed, in the latter part of the action the Lady's role is unusually passive, as one acted upon rather than displaying agency – in theological terms, the recipient of grace, rather than meriting heavenly reward because of demonstrated virtue, justified by works.

In her dialogue with Comus in his 'stately Palace', though physically under restraint, the Lady is able to hold her own, unyielding in her stance. As Milton argues in *Areopagitica*, optimistically, one should not 'misdoubt' the strength of Truth, when put to the test: 'Let her and Falshood grapple; who ever knew Truth put to the wors in a free and open encounter.'[25] The Lady's first lines in this scene state a principle of conduct that, under differing circumstances, has empowered resistance to those who would place fetters on free conscience, imprisoning or outlawing dissenters, from Milton's contemporary Lovelace to Thoreau or Mandelstam: 'Thou canst not touch the freedom of my minde / With all thy charms, although this corporal rinde / Thou haste immanacl'd, while Heav'n sees good' (*A Mask*, 663–5). The qualification 'while Heav'n sees good', with its suggestion of the all-seeing eye of providence, differentiates this passage from

Osip Mandelstam's defiance of Stalin, which suggests that the poet's words (thoughts, given poetic expression) will outlive the dictators and prison guards:

> You took away all the oceans and all the room.
> You gave me my shoe-size in earth with bars around it.
> What did it get you? Nowhere.
> You left me my lips, and they shape words, even in silence.[26]

Earlier, the Lady's 'credulous innocence' has led her to be deceived by the plausible 'visor'd falshood' of the disguised Comus, but now she has arguments to counter his 'many baits, and guileful spells', though others before her, 'unwary', have been taken in by the 'seeming pleasures' spread out before them.[27]

As many critics have noted, the lines spoken by Comus in this scene contain some of the most impressive poetry in *A Mask*, and may offer a temptation for the reader as well as for the Lady. The sensuous richness of Comus' language in the temptation scene is certainly more attractive and emotionally persuasive than the bare austerity of the Lady's 'I had not thought to have unlockt my lips / In this unhallow'd air' – 'the lean and sallow Abstinence' Comus dislikes (756–7).[28] At Comus' first appearance in the masque, though Milton's stage direction presents Comus' troupe as making 'a riotous and unruly noise' (*Complete Shorter Poems*, p. 91), the enchanter's own language, in tripping tetrameters reminiscent of *L'Allegro*, aligns him and his followers with an orderly dance of benign nature, as well as with the world of faerie. Anyone looking on would be tempted to join in the dance:

> Meanwhile, welcome Joy, and Feast,
> Midnight shout, and revelry,
> Tipsie dance, and Jollity . . .
> We that are of purer fire
> Imitate the Starry Quire,
> Who in their nightly watchfull Sphears,
> Lead in swift round the Months and Years . . .
> And on the Tawny Sands and Shelves,
> Trip the pert Fairies and the dapper Elves.
> (102–4, 111–14, 117–18)

Leah Marcus is one of several critics who have pointed out the disparity between 'the hateful vision' the audience have been warned they are about to see and the attractiveness they encounter: is this really 'foul disfigurement'?[29] In the temptation scene, as in this invitation to the dance,

Comus' argument, sensitive to the beauties of the natural world, is that nature and its riches are there to be enjoyed.

> Wherefore did Nature powre her bounties forth
> With such a full and unwithdrawing hand,
> Covering the earth with odours, fruits, and flocks,
> Thronging the seas with spawn innumerable,
> But all to please, and sate the curious taste?
> And set to work millions of spinning Worms,
> That in their green shops weave the smooth-hair'd silk
> To deck her Sons.
>
> (*A Mask*, 709–17)

The Lady's answer, both in the Bridgewater manuscript and in the longer published version of *A Mask*, makes a case for Temperance. Nature is not, as Comus has suggested in this speech, lawless, ready to overflow in its 'fertility' – 'The Sea o'erfraught would swell, & th'unsought diamonds / Would so emblaze the forhead of the Deep, / And so bestudd with Stars' – but contained, governed by 'sober laws' (732–4, 766–7). Using the Lady as a spokesperson for his own ethical and political views, Milton in this passage goes on to mount a critique of the Caroline court and its values, and, in particular, the lavish display of wealth associated with the masque as a spectacle. Passages like this, answering Comus' praise of beauty on show 'in courts, at feasts, and high solemnities', have led critics to describe the Ludlow Masque as a 'puritan masque' or a 'reformed masque', calling into question the ideology underlying the masque as a form. Certainly, the egalitarianism of this passage, suggesting a kind of primitive Christian socialism, is striking:

> If every just man that now pines with want
> Had but a moderate and beseeming share
> Of that which lewdly pamper'd Luxury
> Now heaps upon som few with vast excess,
> Natures full blessing would be well dispenc't
> In unsuperfluous eeven proportion,
> And she no whit encomber'd with her store.
>
> (746, 768–74)[30]

The temptation scene in the Bridgewater and Trinity manuscripts is substantially shorter than in the 1637/1645 version of *A Mask*, and the additional material, both for the tempter and for the Lady in her answer, significantly changes the emphasis of the poem. Up to now, the point at issue, as with Sir Guyon in *The Fairie Queene*, has been temperance, self-control, as against indulgence or excess, what the Lady calls the 'sober . . . dictate of spare Temperance' (*A Mask*, 766–7). In the expanded version,

Comus then goes on, in smoothly persuasive lines, to set forth the standard arguments of *carpe diem* in so many Renaissance poems, reminding his addressee, as Marvell does in 'To his Coy Mistress', Waller in 'Go, Lovely Rose', and Herrick in 'To the Virgins to Make Much of Time', that beauty lasts only a moment.

> List Lady be not coy, and be not cosen'd
> With that same vaunted name Virginity.
> Beauty is nature's coyn, must not be hoorded,
> But must be currant, and the good thereof
> Consists of mutual and partak'n bliss . . .
> If you let slip time, like a neglected rose
> It withers on the stalk with languish't head.
>
> (737–44)[31]

The later part of the Lady's answer to Comus, and Comus' admission that she has bested him in the exchange – 'I feel that I do fear / Her words set off by some superior power' – are absent both in the Trinity and Bridgewater versions of this scene (*A Mask*, 800–1). The Lady's extended tribute to chastity, treating it as a 'sublime notion' that Comus, in his unworthiness, is unable to comprehend, is one of the two passages in praise of this virtue in *A Mask*. Here she speaks of the power that the 'pure cause' of chastity would have to unleash a 'flame of sacred vehemence', as something that is held in abeyance, though these words alone are enough to unsettle her adversary (794–5).

> To him that dares
> Arm his profane tongue with contemptuous words
> Against the Sun-clad power of Chastity,
> Fain would I somthing say, but to what end?
> Thou hast not Eare, nor Soul to apprehend
> The sublime notion, and high mystery
> That must be utter'd to unfold the sage
> And serious doctrine of Virginity.
>
> (780–7)

With these lines, the direction of the Lady's and Milton's argument changes, no longer defending temperance, but abstinence, unyielding resistance against a force that would compel, and suggesting that the danger the virtuous Lady faces is rape, rather than a life of pleasure. With virginity, preserved against temptation or lost, as with the unspotted soul faced by a pollution it finds unbearable, there can be no half-way measures. As Kerrigan points out, 'A faithful, hopeful, charitable, wise, prudent, courageous, patient, or temperate Lady could not have her virtue snatched away by force . . . The one taint of the flesh subject to absolute denial is sexuality.'[32]

The intervention of Sabrina, herself a violated virgin who has undergone an Ovidian metamorphosis into a river goddess and can be called on 'to aid a Virgin, such as was her self', has been interpreted in different ways. Evidently there is some theological element: Sabrina's role in the masque clearly indicates that neither the Lady nor her Brothers are able to break the spell that has 'insnared' the Lady (885–6, 909). In an influential reading, Woodhouse has identified Sabrina as an allegorical representation of the realm of grace, whereas the other characters, good or bad, remain within the realm of nature: her intervention, sprinkling drops of water to release the Lady from her enchantment, is an allegorical representation of 'a renewed infusion of divine grace', akin in standard Christian symbolism 'to the sacrament of baptism'. In another essay, elaborating the distinction between the realms of nature and grace, Woodhouse associates the Attendant Spirit with Providence, as 'its minister and almost its symbol'.[33] Corns, in his essay 'Milton before *Lycidas*' and in the Campbell and Corns biography of Milton, carries the identification of Sabrina with the operations of divine grace a step further, arguing that the passage, with its 'powerful element of ceremonialism', is in its implicit theology closer to Laudianism than to orthodox Protestant doctrine. Unconvincingly, Sabrina is turned into a representation of 'external agencies', the church and clergy, helping out on the pathway to salvation, and *A Mask* becomes 'the most complex and thorough expression of Laudian ceremonialism and Laudian style within the Milton oeuvre'.[34]

But Sabrina, whatever her role may be in the poem's implicit theology, is also a tutelary nature goddess, the spirit of place, associated with a particular landscape, the 'brimmed waves' of the river Severn, bringing a blessing on the surrounding land, a representative of British tradition ('Sprung of old *Anchises* line'), and the companion of a large number of goddesses and nymphs in the service of the sea-god Neptune (*A Mask*, 923–4). Sabrina is invoked in song, the atmosphere in which she lives. In the Bridgewater manuscript, nearly all of the text in the later part of the masque, starting with the Attendant Spirit's song 'Sabrina faire', is set to music. The ceremonial ritual with which Sabrina is associated is as much the spirit of the 'tuneful and well-measur'd Song', poetry in alliance with music, praised in Milton's sonnet to Lawes, as it is evocative of a realm of heavenly grace distinct from nature.[35]

Milton's masque ends, conventionally, with dances for the company of masquers, as the Attendant Spirit presents the three children of Lord

Bridgewater to their parents, celebrating their victory after being 'tri'd' during their journey: 'To triumph in victorious dance / O're sensual Folly, and Intemperance' (970, 974–5). The Attendant Spirit's closing lines speak not of chastity, but more generally of 'vertue', and, indeed, the lines in praise of the happy couples Venus and Adonis (cured of his wound) and Cupid and Psyche suggest that virginity as an ideal has receded into the background. As a female guardian, with magical powers exercised to help beleaguered virtue rather than entrap it, Sabrina, metamorphosed from a victimized young woman to a benevolent force of nature, illustrates the transformative process that the final lines suggest will be possible for those who persist in the pursuit of virtue:

> Mortals that would follow me,
> Love vertue, she alone is free,
> She can teach ye how to clime
> Higher then the Spheary chime;
> Of if Vertue feeble were,
> Heav'n it self would stoop to her.
> (1018–23)

II

In Milton's divorce tracts, beleaguered virtue is not independent of gender, but almost exclusively male. Though the title page of *Doctrine and Discipline* speaks of a true doctrine being 'Restor'd to the good of both Sexes', there is little emphasis on reciprocity in Milton's tract (*CPW*, II.221). It is the man who is wronged, enslaved, condemned to a life of misery, or, like Samson, seduced by a temptress and made to suffer as a consequence of his own erroneous choice.

> For all the warinesse can be us'd, it may yet befall a discreet man to be mistak'n in his choice . . . The soberest and best govern'd men are lest practiz'd in these affairs; and who knows not that the bashfull mutenes of a virgin may oft-times hide all the unlivelines & naturall sloth which is really unfit for conversation . . . Many who have spent their youth chastly, are in some things not so quick-sighted, while they hast too eagerly to light the nuptiall torch . . . When as the sober man honouring the appearance of modestie, and hoping well of every sociall vertue under that veile, may easily chance to meet, if not with a body impenetrable, yet often with a minde to all other due conversation inaccessible, and to all the more estimable and superior purposes of matrimony uselesse and almost liveles; and what a solace, what a fit help such a consort would be through the whole life of a man, is lesse paine to conjecture then to have experience. (*CPW*, II.249–50)

Annabel Patterson is one of several critics who have read Milton's divorce tracts as disguised autobiography, claiming that they 'turn private domestic embarrassment into public polemic'.[36] Though Milton may be generalizing from his own experience with Mary Powell, the passage resonates with familiar Miltonic themes, in its emphasis on choice, temptation, the need for 'wariness', and the painful consequences that may follow when one chooses wrongly. What is particularly striking about this passage is the way he presents the unwary young man entering into a disastrous marriage as blameless: innocent, chaste, sober and discreet, yet, with no Attendant Spirit by his side to instruct him, misled by false appearances.

In this tract as in the Ludlow Masque, there is a recurrent emphasis on chastity, sexual purity, and the danger of pollution. Several passages in *Doctrine and Discipline* seem to show a loathing of the flesh, treating sexual desire as demeaning, bestial. When Milton refers to 'the perpetuall and ceaseles duties of a husband', the primary reference is to the sexual act, seen as 'a brutish congresse', without pleasure, undertaken as a burdensome labour or penance: 'To grind in the mill of an undelighted and servil copulation, must be the only forc't work of a Christian mariage, oftimes with such a yokefellow, from whom both love and peace, both nature and Religion mourns to be separated.'[37]

The term 'servile' echoes throughout this tract: the unhappily married man, forced to grind in the mill of joyless copulation, is like the blinded Samson, reduced to a humiliating servitude, 'eyeless in Gaza, at the Mill with slaves' (*Samson Agonistes*, 41). In another passage, with an even more disturbing metaphor, sex without 'love and amity' becomes monstrous, akin to necrophilia. Here the idea of slavery, loss of autonomy or surrender of an initial freedom, is made shockingly literal as a grotesque imprisonment within the flesh, the body as all-powerful tyrant and the soul as helpless victim.

> But that can never be where no correspondence is of the minde; nay instead of beeing one flesh, they will be rather two carkesses chain'd unnaturally together; or as it may happ'n, a living soule bound to a dead corps, a punishment too like that inflicted by the tyrant *Mezentius;* so little worthy to be receav'd as that remedy of lonelines which God meant us.
> (*CPW*, II.326–7)

In *Doctrine and Discipline*, Milton urges Parliament, in the cause of liberty, to liberalize the laws regulating marriage and divorce, under which adultery, sexual impotence, and desertion were the only legitimate excuses for the termination of a marriage. In this tract and in *Tetrachordon* and *De Doctrina* I.x, Milton cites Genesis 2:18 as central to his argument: 'And the

Lord God said, It is not good that the man should be alone: I will make him a help meet for him.' Commenting on the words 'help meet' and 'one flesh' in Genesis 2:24, Milton argues that a true marriage is a union of minds:

> Since wee know it is not the joyning of another body will remove lonelines, but the uniting of another compliable mind; and that it is no blessing but a torment, nay a base and brutish condition to be one flesh, unlesse where nature can in some measure fix a unity of disposition . . . Only then, when the minds are fitly dispos'd and enabl'd to maintain a cherfull conversation, to the solace and love of each other, according as God intended and promis'd in the very first foundation of matrimony, *I will make him a help meet for him.*[38]

He summarizes his argument in *De Doctrina*, I.x, claiming that his position, far from being a radical one, strongly attacked by his opponents as dangerously immoral, is one that 'everyone' accepts: 'Who is so base and swinish as to deny that this is so?'[39] In sonnet 12, 'On the detraction which follow'd upon my writing certain treatises', Milton employs a similar rhetoric in dismissing his 'barbarous' detractors as no better than 'Owles and Cuckoes, Asses, Apes and Doggs'. His own view of 'the prime end of marriage', he claims, is eminently reasonable.

> But the prime end and form of marriage is not the bed, but conjugal love and mutual assistance in life: nearly everyone admits that this is so. For the prime end and form of marriage can only be what is mentioned in the original institution, and mention is made there of pleasant companionship (a thing which ceases to exist if someone is left by himself), and of the mutual assistance of a married couple (a thing which only thrives when there is love). No mention is made of the bed or of procreation, which can take place even where there is hatred.[40]

The ideal of a companionate marriage, a 'fellowship' of two individuals 'fit to participate / All rational delight', is central to *Paradise Lost*, though there the praise of 'wedded Love' is not accompanied by a revulsion against its physical expression. In the relationship of the unfallen Adam and Eve, 'love is integrated with sexuality', far more than in traditional accounts of prelapsarian innocence: 'Farr be it, that I should write thee sin or blame, / Or think thee unbefitting holiest place'.[41] Though Raphael warns Adam against subjection to 'carnal pleasure' – 'in loving thou dost well, in passion not' – Adam's answer to Raphael defines love as the manifestation, in daily actions, of 'Union of Mind, or in us both one Soule', and the actions of the body are presented in the poem as fully harmonious with such a 'Union of Mind'.[42]

To Milton, as in the Reformed tradition generally, marriage was not a sacrament, but a contractual agreement: both the initial compact and its dissolution must in his view depend upon the free choice of the individuals involved. The power of the magistrate, Milton consistently argued, does not extend to compulsion over the inviolable conscience: as the Lady says, defying her captor, 'Thou canst not touch the freedom of my minde' (*A Mask*, 664).

> To interpose a jurisdictive power upon the inward and irremediable disposition of man, to command love and *sympathy*, to forbid dislike against the guiltles instinct of nature, is not within the province of any law to reach.

Feelings, 'the innocent affections of nature', cannot be compelled, and forcible constraint by 'the iron manacles and fetters of Law' often defeats its own end.[43] Though Milton refers to 'the will and consent of both parties' (*CPW*, II.344) as necessary for marriage or divorce, his account of marital unhappiness tends to be one-sided, with a 'guiltles' victim forced to endure the consequences of an erroneous choice.

There are very few passages in Milton's divorce tracts where he allows for the possibility that the unhappy partner in an ill-suited couple might be a woman and not a man. In *De Doctrina*, commenting on the Mosaic Law under which a 'wife is allowed to leave her husband if he is harsh and inhuman', Milton speaks of the need for a 'just, equitable and humane' legal remedy to be available 'to rescue the wretched wives' from enslavement to tyrannous husbands:

> But that a woman who is not loved but . . . neglected, a woman who is loathed and hated, should, in obedience to the harshest of laws, be kept beneath the yoke of a crushing slavery (for that is what marriage is without love), by a man who has no love or liking for her, that is a hardship harder than any divorce. (*De Doctrina*, I.x, *CPW*, VI.374–5)

More frequently, Milton associates the 'injury' in a marriage, 'not to be belov'd . . . to be slighted . . . to be contended with in house-rule who should be the head', with men denied the superior status they deserve. 'Who can be ignorant that woman was created for man, and not man for woman?' (*Doctrine and Discipline, CPW*, II.324). An extended commentary on Genesis 1:27 in *Tetrachordon* exposes the contradictions in Milton's ideology, as spiritual equality, with men and women alike as 'the redeem'd of Christ', clashes with masculine supremacy. The passage begins and ends with inequality, categorizing women from the moment of Eve's creation as 'an inferiour sexe', and citing St Paul to prove that the woman differs from the man as not being 'primarily and immediatly the image of God'

(*CPW*, II.589, 591). But then, in the middle of a long paragraph, several concessions enter in. A husband should not treat 'a creature so like him' as a mere 'servant'. Some women are more wise and virtuous than some men: 'Not but that particular exceptions may have place, if she exceed her husband in prudence and dexterity, and he contentedly yeeld, for then a superior and more naturall law comes in, that the wiser should govern the lesse wise, whether male or female' (*CPW*, II.589). The passage ends with a reassertion of masculine domination, as Milton criticizes a woman whose 'wilfulnes or inability to be a wife frustrates the occasionall end of her creation', citing the male partner's 'naturall birthright' of 'freedom' and 'that indeleble character of priority which God crown'd him with'.[44]

Tetrachordon includes several other passages which allow that a woman may be the injured party in an unhappy marriage. Commenting on Deuteronomy 24:1, while on the one hand characterizing woman as by nature the 'less worthy' sex, created for man, Milton concedes that the dictates of the Mosaic Law apply to aggrieved wives as well as husbands: 'Although ther bee nothing in the plain words of this Law, that seems to regard the afflictions of a wife, how great so ever, yet Expositors determin, and doubtless determin rightly, that God was not uncompassionate to them also in the framing of this Law.'[45] Several other passages in this tract, in commenting on 'male and female created he them' and 'one flesh' in Genesis 1:27–8, use a rhetorical formula that implies a degree of parity between men and women, rather than insisting on male superiority:

> to enthrall husband or wife to duties or to sufferings, unworthy and unbeseeming the image of God in them.
>
> . . . unworthy and unseemly for a man to do or suffer in wedlock; and the like proportionally may be found for women.
>
> A bad wife is a help for the devil, and the like may be said of a bad husband.[46]

Milton's extended commentary on Deuteronomy 24:1, while it presents 'bondage' as 'unmanly', sees 'the duties of mariage' as 'mutual' and reciprocal: women no less than men deserve something better than oppressive servitude.

> The Law is to tender the liberty and human dignity of them that live under the Law, whether it be the mans right above the woman, or the womans just appeal against wrong, and servitude. But the duties of marriage contain in them the duty of benevolence, which to do by compulsion against the Soul, where ther can bee neither peace, nor joy, nor love, but an enthrallment to one who either cannot, or will not bee mutual in the godliest and the civilest ends of that society, is the ignoblest, and the lowest slavery that a human shape can bee put to. (*Tetrachordon*, *CPW*, II.625–6)

Here as elsewhere in Milton, a commitment to freedom against any form of 'compulsion' and a detestation of a humiliating condition of slavery clashes with a belief in a natural hierarchy, in which man the master ought to treat his wife and other servants with respect and 'benevolence'. The tyranny with which Milton is primarily concerned here and throughout the divorce tracts is not that of abused wives, but husbands who find themselves trapped in a relationship they find 'actively hateful, and injurious' (*CPW*, II.622) as a result of an erroneous choice.

In *Tetrachordon* and in *Doctrine and Discipline*, Milton attempts to explain away the conflict between the prohibition of divorce in the teachings of Jesus and the liberal treatment of divorce under the Mosaic Law. In Matthew 5:31–2, the Sermon on the Mount, Jesus challenges the assumptions behind Deuteronomy 24:1–2, allowing a man to divorce his wife when 'he has found some uncleanness in her', as he does in Matthew 5:38 in contesting 'an eye for an eye, and a tooth for a tooth'. Uncharacteristically, the Gospel, in its treatment of divorce, as Milton points out, is more strict and rigorous than the Mosaic Law.

> It hath been said, Whosoever shall put away his wife, let him give her a bill of divorcement. But I say to you, That whosoever shall put away his wife, saving for the cause of fornication, causeth her to commit adultery; and whosoever shall marry her that is divorced committeth adultery. (Matthew 5:31–2)

Milton's usual position, maintained in *De Doctrina* and in *A Treatise of Civil Power*, is that the Mosaic Law has been utterly superseded by the Gospel. Neither the ceremonial law (covering such things as circumcision and the forbidding of certain foods as unclean) nor the moral law of the Old Testament remains valid for believing Christians. He differs in this respect from the orthodox Calvinist position that 'no Christian man whatsoever is free from the obedience of the Commandments called Moral'.[47]

In *De Doctrina* and in the divorce tracts, Milton consistently maintains that 'the end, and the fulfilling of every command is charity': 'Thus anyone with any sense interprets the precepts of Christ in the sermon on the mount not in a literal way but in a way that is in keeping with the spirit of charity.'[48] On the grounds that the teachings of Jesus should not be made the excuse for 'new severities' (*Tetrachordon*, *CPW*, II.636), Milton argues that in this particular case the Mosaic Law remains in force, and should form the basis of statute law, allowing divorce under certain circumstances. Only in Paradise before the Fall was marriage 'an indissoluble bond'. A remedy, in accordance with 'the infinit enlargement of charity', must be available for those trapped in 'the perpetuall squabbles and the slavish pounding-mill of unhappy marriage':

> But when man had fallen, [God] granted by the law of nature and by the Mosaic law, which Christ did not contradict, that it should of necessity be subject to dissolution. In this he intended to prevent the innocent from being exposed to perpetual injury at the hands of the wicked.[49]

As the term 'injury' may suggest, Milton in this passage in *De Doctrina* moves from the unchanging law of nature to the civil law, and the possibility of redress of grievances or protection of the innocent. 'Injury' (*injuria)* as a legal term means 'an invasion of another's rights', 'an actionable wrong'. In other passages in *De Doctrina,* Milton associates injury with the possibility of 'recompence', as he sees 'not to be belov'd & yet retain'd' or 'not to be able to love' as the heaping up of injury, and argues that while 'a meer separation' cannot be 'an injury to the divorc't', it is the province of law to 'take care that the conditions of divorce be not injurious'.[50] Marriage is a contract between two parties, and should be treated like any other contract, when one of the two parties fails to fulfil the stipulated conditions. 'In the same way practically every treaty or contract is meant to be permanent and indissoluble when it is made, but it is immediately nullified if either party breaks his word' (*CPW*, VI.379). The political implications of Milton's treatment of marriage as a civil contract rather than as a sacrament are made clear in the preface to the second edition of *Doctrine and Discipline* (1644), addressed to Parliament: the husband trapped in an unhappy marriage is like the subject languishing under tyranny, and should have the same remedy available to him.

> As a whole people is in proportion to an ill Government, so is one man to an ill marriage. If they against any authority, Covnant, or Statute, may by the soveraign edict of charity, save not only their lives, but honest liberties from unworthy bondage, as well may he against any private Covnant, which hee never enter'd to his mischief, redeem himself from unsupportable disturbances to honest peace, and just contentment . . . For no effect of tyranny can sit more heavy on the Common-wealth, then this houshold unhappines on the family.[51]

The analogy between the marriage bond and the hypothetical contract between ruler and subject was more frequently used to argue that such a bond could not be dissolved: once consent is given, it could not be withdrawn. So, for example, to the royalist Henry Ferne in 1643, the right of resistance by subjects was a doctrine no less pernicious than the belief that 'in Matrimony (for the King is also . . . wedded to the kingdom by a Ring at his Coronation) the parties should agree, upon such and such neglect of duties, to part a sunder'.[52] Milton's divorce tracts were greeted by a storm of protest, largely by orthodox Presbyterian heresy-hunters such as Thomas Edwards, Ephraim Pagitt and Robert Baillie, accusing him of having 'pleaded for a full liberty for any man to put away his wife, when ever he pleaseth, without any fault in her at all, but for any dislike or dyspathy of humour'.[53] Herbert Palmer, a more moderate Presbyterian, in a sermon preached before Parliament on 13 August 1644, at a time when the Westminster Assembly was debating whether marriage should be considered 'merely civil' or 'the covenant of God', singled out Milton for particular opprobrium. *Doctrine and Discipline* was 'a *wicked booke* . . . abroad and *uncensured*, though *deserving to be burnt*, whose Author hath been so *impudent* as to . . . *dedicate it to your selves*'.[54] After the publication of *Tenure* in 1649, hostile critics explicitly linked Milton's political views and his treatment of the 'Nuptiall knot', as advocating a 'Bill of plain Divorce', regardless of possible consequences, in both cases :

> There is lately come forth a Booke of *John Meltons* (a Libertine that thinketh his Wife a Manacle, and his very Garters to be Shackles and Fetters to him: one that (after the Independent fashion) will be tied by no obligation to God or Man) wherein he undertaketh to prove, *That it is lawfull for any that have power to call to account, Depose, and put to death wicked Kings and Tyrants.*[55]

The idea that marriage is a contract or covenant, which can be revoked when one of the parties fails to fulfil the agreed conditions, is introduced near the beginning of *Doctrine and Discipline*:

> For all sense and equity reclaimes, that any Law or Cov'nant how solemn or strait soever, either between God and man, or man and man, though of Gods joyning, should bind against a prime and principall scope of its own institution, and of both or either party cov'nanting; neither can it be of force to ingage a blameles creature to his own perpetuall sorrow, mistak'n for his expected solace. (*CPW*, II.245)

Here as elsewhere in the divorce tracts, the injured party is presented as 'blameless', suffering as a result of a 'mistake' – as Milton says a few sentences later, 'so noble a creature as man . . . shut up incurably under a worse evill by an easy mistake' (*CPW*, II.247). The implication in both these passages, with their appeal to common sense and to the legal principle of equity or fairness, is that a remedy should be available in such cases, without at this point specifying what that remedy might be.

In *Tetrachordon*, commenting on Deuteronomy 24:1–2, Milton states a general ethical and political principle, applicable to marriage and to all laws and ordinances, civil or religious: once again, the individual concerned is without fault, and the situation he endures is presented as being forced upon him.

> Secondly, It is unjust that any Ordinance ordain'd to the good and comfort of man, where that end is missing, without his fault, should be forc't upon him to an unsufferable misery and discomfort, if not commonly ruin. All Ordinances are establisht in thir end; the end of Law is the vertu, is the righteousnes of Law. And therefore him wee count an ill Expounder who urges Law against the intention therof. The general end of every Ordinance, of every severest, of every divinest, eevn of Sabbath is the good of man, yea his temporal good not excluded. (*CPW*, II.623)

The political version of this principle, not explicitly stated here but central to the argument of *Tenure* and *Defence*, is 'the common good', the good of the people, *salus populi*.[56] In this chapter of *Tetrachordon*, Milton goes on, citing the principle of equity once again, to argue that no covenant can be binding 'without redress', when it contradicts the very end for which it was instituted. Equity, defined in the *Oxford English Dictionary* (citing instances from the late sixteenth century) as 'the recourse to general principles of justice (*naturalis aequitas)* to correct or supplement the ordinary law', is associated by Milton with the spirit rather than letter of the law, as applied either to the Mosaic Law or civil law.

> Thirdly, as no Ordinance, so no Covnant, no not between God and man, much less between man and man, beeing as all are, intended to the good of both parties, can hold to the deluding or making miserable of them both. For equity is understood in every Covnant, eevn between enemies, though the terms bee not exprest. If equity therfore made it, extremity may dissolve it. (*Tetrachordon*, *CPW*, II.624)

In arguing against the conventional view that covenants by their nature must be honoured, even to our disadvantage, Milton states a general principle which in later tracts he applies to the contract of allegiance to a ruler: 'But faith they say must bee kept in Covnant, though to our dammage. I answer, that only holds true, where the other side performs, which failing, hee is no longer bound.'[57]

In *Tenure*, *Eikonoklastes* and the *Defence*, Milton makes precisely this point, drawing radical conclusions from it. The authority exercised by a monarch, rather than being divinely inspired, is held contractually or in trust: it 'was by the People first giv'n to him conditionally, in Law and under Law, and under Oath also for the Kingdoms good, and not otherwise' (*Eikonoklastes*, *CPW*, III.593). In *Tenure*, Milton grounds the right of resistance on a contractual basis, again citing the common good as a principle governing both the formation and dissolution of governments. Since a 'King or Magistrate holds his autoritie of the people, both originaly and naturally for their good in the first place, and not his own', then the people from whom he has received this power have the right to 'choose him or reject him, retain him or depose him' as they see fit (*Tenure*, *CPW*, III.206). As Barker points out, the analogy between the marriage contract and the contract between ruler and subject was used to justify both resistance and tyrannicide in the mid-1640s and in 1649. As 'the very bond and knot of marriage' can be broken by adultery by one of the partners, so 'the King breaking his covenant with the people in proving a tyrant' is justly punished.[58] Even Presbyterians such as Samuel Rutherford agreed that in a 'mutual contract made upon certain conditions . . . if the conditions be not fulfilled the party injured is loosed from the contract'.[59] Thus, Milton's strong statements in *Tenure* and *Defence* can be seen as closely linked to the arguments he developed in the divorce tracts, drawing more radical conclusions from the general principle than some of his contemporaries were willing to accept:

> Certainly, if no people in their right wits ever gave power over themselves either to a king or to any magistrates for any other purpose than the common good of all, there can be no reason why, for exactly the inverse purpose, to prevent the utter ruin of them all, they may not take back again the power they gave.[60]

In *Tetrachordon* and *Doctrine and Discipline*, Milton says that the essential element in a marriage contract is consent, and that if that element, not only in entering into the marriage, but in its continuation, is lacking, then the marriage has no validity. When that consent is brought about through 'error', Milton claims, it is no longer a true marriage, and the contract bringing it about no longer holds.

> This brings in the parties consent; until which be, the mariage hath no true beeing. When I say *consent*, I mean not error, for error is not properly consent: And why should not consent be heer understood with equity and good to either part, as in all other freindly covnants, and not be strain'd and cruelly urg'd to the mischeif and destruction of both? (*Tetrachordon*, *CPW*, II.612)

In *Doctrine and Discipline*, with another political analogy, he goes so far as to say that if the key element of consent is absent, then the marriage is in effect dissolved, and the injured husband retains the right, like the right of the people in delegating their power in trust to a sovereign, to reclaim the freedom he still retains even though he may have temporarily alienated it under a formal agreement.

> The rest whom either disproportion or deadnes of spirit, or somthing distastfull & avers in the immutable bent of nature renders uncongenial, error may have joyn'd; but God never joyn'd against the meaning of his own ordinance. And if he joynd them not, then is there is no power above their own consent to hinder them from unjoyning; when they cannot reap the soberest ends of beeing together in any tolerable sort. (*Doctrine and Discipline*, *CPW*, II.328)

In the next chapter, we will see how Milton employs similar arguments from consent in justifying resistance to legally constituted authority, citing precedents from scripture and history. 'Unjoyning' in this case means the dissolution of the contract binding subject and sovereign. If kings who abuse their power can be called to account like any other miscreants, Milton claims, this will 'teach lawless Kings, and all who so much adore them, that not mortal man, or his imperious will, but Justice is the only true sovran and supreme Majesty upon earth' (*Tenure*, *CPW*, III.237).

4

Classical and Biblical Republicanism
Milton and Some Contemporaries

Hobbes, in a passage frequently cited by twentieth-century critics, complained that 'the reading of the books of policy, and histories of the ancient Greeks, and Romans' had encouraged subversive doctrines: 'From the reading, I say, of such books, men have undertaken to kill their kings, because the Greek and Latin writers, in their books, and discourses of policy, made it lawful, and laudable, for any man to do so; provided, before he do it, he call him tyrant'.[1] In a similar fashion, he held that the reading and interpretation of the Bible, in its readily available vernacular versions or in its original languages, unless strictly controlled by the state, was prejudicial to monarchy. A major 'cause of our late mischief', licentious interpretation of verses in scripture, was 'likely to lead men to Sedition', teaching men 'that they may lawfully Rebell'.[2] In the pamphlet wars of the seventeenth century, the arguments for calling kings to account were at least as much theological as secular.

Appeals to nature and reason, chains of deduction, point-by-point refutation of an opponent's arguments are in pamphlets of this period again and again buttressed by citations from scripture and Reformed theologians, in the text or as marginal glosses. Thus, Milton, in the second edition of *Tenure* (1650), adds six and a half pages consisting (he tells his readers on the title page) of 'many Testimonies . . . out of the best & learnedest among Protestant divines' – Luther, Calvin, Zwingli, Martin Bucer, and other authorities – in support of his proposition 'that it is Lawfull . . . for any who have the Power, to call to account a Tyrant, or wicked KING, and after due conviction, to depose, and put him to death' (*CPW*, III.189). A striking example of parallel lines of argument, one secular and one theological, can be found in an official document published 'for more publique satisfaction' in December 1648 to justify the forthcoming trial of the King, *An Abridgement of the late Remonstrance of the Army. With some Marginal Attestations, for the better Understanding, Remembrance and Judgement of the PEOPLE.* Here practical arguments attuned to present circumstances, seeking to demonstrate that Charles I, as 'Author and contriver of an unjust Warre', has by a breach of trust forfeited the allegiance of his subjects, 'absolving the people of the bonds betweene him and them', take up the body of the text, while extended marginal glosses, nearly as long as the primary text, keep up a constant barrage of scriptural citation, finding typological precedent for contemporary history in the history of the Jews.[3] In *Vindiciae contra Tyrannos* (1579), often considered 'secular' in the theory of resistance it argues, the original Latin text is full of marginal references to scripture – a total of 249 from the Old Testament (222) and New Testament (27), as compared to 55 to Roman law. 'The text is dominated at every point by references to God's law, not Roman law.'[4]

The favourite biblical proof-text for the proponents of divine right and non-resistance was Romans 13:1 and 2: 'Let every soul be subject unto the higher powers. For there is no power but of God: the powers that be are ordained of God. Whosoever therefore resisteth the power, resisteth the ordinance of God, and they that resist shall receive to themselves damnation.' The passage plays a central role in *A Homily against Disobedience and Wilful Rebellion* (1570), and is regularly cited by absolutist theorists such as Salmasius, Filmer, Henry Ferne, and Marvell's antagonist Samuel Parker (who was particularly inept in choosing Nero and Caligula as instances of the supreme power which must at all times be obeyed). Those who, like Milton, disputed the identification of earthly and divine authority, presented rival interpretations of Romans 13:1–2 that allowed space for resistance to legally constituted authority.

In *Scripture and Reason Pleaded for Defensive Armes* (1643) by 'divers Reverend and Learned Divines', including Herbert Palmer, a detailed refutation of arguments for non-resistance based on Romans 13:2 is accompanied by copious references to scripture and interpretations of biblical texts. As the title page states, 'The Scriptures alleadged are fully satisfied. The rationall Discourses are weighed in the ballance of right reason.' The formula, repeated over and over again, for defining a tyrant is one who 'is bent to subvert Religion, Lawes and Liberties'.[5] In this pamphlet, biblical examples of justified resistance to a legitimate ruler abusing his power include David resisting Saul and the three virtuous men, Shadrach, Meshack, and Abednego, thrown by Nebuchadnezzar into the fiery furnace and preserved by God. Other arguments, citing 'right reason' and common sense, include the analogous right of 'the naturall body' to 'defend it selfe . . . against the natuall malignity of any disease' and, in the body politic, 'the generall and maine fundamentall Law of all States, to save the whole from ruine and subversion . . . when the Prince will not discharge his trust'.[6] John Goodwin's *Anti-Cavalierisme* (1642), arguing that obedience to God must take precedence over obedience to any earthly power, cites as complementary guides to behaviour 'the veriest Law of God, and the common light of nature'. Here again his appeal to his readers is twofold: on the one hand, 'the defence of your Lives, your Liberties, your Estates, your Houses, your Wives, your Children, your Brethren', and on the other, 'you are exhorted to stand up in defence of the true Protestant Religion, for the name and honour of your God, your Ordinances, and . . . for the safe conveyance of that great treasure of the Gospel over unto your posterities that are yet unborne'.[7] Biblical citations, extending over ten pages, include Jonah, Lot's sons in Sodom, David and Saul, the punishment of Ahab, the prophet Elisha, and Solomon, with 1 Samuel, warnings by God about the consequences of having a king in Israel, set against Romans 13:1–2 and 1 Peter 2:13, the proof-texts most frequently cited by proponents of non-resistance.

Milton's most extensive treatment of Romans 13 occurs in the *Defence of the English People*, where he is specifically directing his arguments against Salmasius' claim that by scriptural authority kings 'could with impunity do as they pleased' (*Defence*, *CPW*, IV.i.371). Like the author of *Vindiciae contra Tyrannos*, a Huguenot tract originally published in 1579, and like the Marian exile Christopher Goodman, one of the 'true Protestant divines' Milton quotes in the second edition of *Tenure*, Milton argues that obedience is properly due only to those who in the words of Romans 13:3 (reinterpreted with considerable latitude) 'do that which is good' (*Tenure*, *CPW*, III.251; *Defence*, *CPW*, IV.i.385). Wicked kings, in effect, depose themselves. 'When Magistrates cease to do thir Duty', says Goodman, as quoted in *Tenure*, 'the people are as it were without Magistrates' (*CPW*, III.250). In *Defence*, Milton uses arguments similar to those advanced by John Goodwin and others in 1642–3, though in this work he is not only arguing for taking up arms against Charles I but justifying tyrannicide.

> Without magistrates and civil government there can be no state or human society or life itself. But whatever power or magistrate acts in the contrary manner is not truly ordained of God, and therefore we are not obliged or instructed to obey such a power or magistrate, nor debarred from wise opposition, inasmuch as we shall not be resisting the power or the magistrate here favorably depicted, but a cut-purse, a tyrant, and a foe; and if he must be termed magistrate simply because he has power and may seem appointed by God for our punishment, then by such reasoning the devil himself will be a magistrate.[8]

The boldest statement of republican principles in *Tenure*, a clarion call to revolutionary action, is expressed entirely in secular terms, as an appeal to 'plain reason'. Milton derives the right of 'the people' – or as he puts it on the title page, 'any, who have the Power' – to call their ruler to account, and 'as oft as they shall judge it for the best, either choose him or reject him, retaine him or depose him', from the general principle of popular sovereignty.[9] As he says earlier in this tract, citing '*Aristotle*, and the best of Political writers', as providing precedent:

> The power of Kings and Magistrates is nothing else, but what is only derivative, transferr'd and committed to them in trust from the People, to the Common good of them all, in whom the power yet remaines fundamentally, and cannot be tak'n from them, without a violation of their natural birthright. (*CPW*, III.202)

This fundamental birthright, described in the later passage, in characteristically republican terms, as 'the liberty and right of free born Men, to be govern'd as seems to them best' (*CPW*, III.206), is presented by Milton as inalienable: under his version of contract theory, the sovereign people may temporarily lend power to their rulers, but can always take it back. One indication of how radical Milton's position here is, more than in such classics of republican political theory as *Vindiciae contra Tyrannos*, always careful to distinguish good kings from tyrants, is that Milton at times elides the distinction, saying that the people have the right to choose and depose their governor, 'though no Tyrant', as a consequence of the gift of free choice.[10] Yet immediately after this bold statement, Milton adds several pages of biblical exegesis to show that the propositions he had advanced can be 'made good also by Scripture'. Here as elsewhere in *Tenure*, Milton's perspective is never wholly secular, since he draws his historical examples from 'all Stories Heathen and Christian', citing Euripides, Livy, and the Code of Justinian side by side with Deuteronomy and the Psalms (*CPW*, III.201, 206–12). In setting forth his initial premise that 'all men naturally were borne free', he locates the origin of government in the fall of man – a very different version of the state of nature from that suggested by Hobbes two years later in *Leviathan* (though Hobbes was sufficiently of his age to devote twelve chapters of biblical exegesis as underpinning for his deductive arguments).[11]

Classical and biblical examples, drawing on the history of Rome or Athens and the history of the Jews, are frequently deployed side by side in the writings of classical republicans. In *The Commonwealth of Oceana* (1656), James Harrington contrasts 'the ancient prudence', the 'principles of a commonwealth' he considers worth imitating, with the modern doctrines of reason of state, serving private interests, which he associates with Hobbes. The example Harrington discusses most fully is 'the commonwealth of Israel', with its separation of powers between 'the senate, the people, and the magistracy', following this account with a shorter discussion (to be treated 'more at large hereafter' in later sections of the tract) of the commonwealths of Athens, Sparta, Carthage, and Rome, all based on similar principles of tripartite division of powers.[12] In one short passage, he draws his examples, in rapid succession, from Elijah, John the Baptist, Alcibiades, Dionysius the Areopagite, and Cicero (pp. 39–40). When Milton advances arguments in *The Readie and Easie Way* (1660) for a perpetual senate, a grand council in whom 'the sovereignty, not transferrd, but delegated only, and as it were deposited', would reside, he adds a caveat: 'least this which I affirme, be thought my single opinion, I shall add sufficient testimonie'. Though the specific form of government for which Milton is arguing differs from Harrington's, the ancient precedents are the same:

> Therefor among the *Jews*, the supreme councel of seaventie, call'd the *Sanhedrim*, founded by *Moses*, in *Athens* that of *Areopagus*, in *Sparta* that of the Ancients, in *Rome* the Senat, consisted of members chosen for term of life; and by that means remaind as it were still the same for generations.[13]

The classical republican Marchamont Nedham, thoroughly secular in his approach, in arguing the case against monarchical government in *The Excellencie of a Free-State* (1656) and in *Mercurius Politicus* in 1651–2, often lists a series of historical examples to support his propositions. For example, to prove that 'the Government of a Free State is less Luxurious, than Kings or Grandees', Nedham's 'Instances' are drawn from 'the State of *Athens*' and Rome 'in the days of *Tarquin*, dissolved into Debauchery', and to illustrate other benefits of republican government he cites Athens, Sparta, Carthage, Rome, and, among modern states, Venice and the Dutch republic.[14] On several occasions, his list of instances, as with Harrington and Milton, includes examples from the Old and New Testament as well as from ancient and recent history. So, in arguing against the modern doctrine of 'Reason of State':

> It was *Reason of State*, made *Pharoah* hold the *Israelites* in bondage . . . It was *Reason of State*, that made *Saul* to spare *Agag*, and plot the ruine of *David* . . . It was *Reason of State*, that made *Jeroboam* to set up Calves in *Dan* and *Bethel* . . . It was *Reason of State*, that moved *Herod* to endeavour the destruction of Christ, as soon as he was born . . . It was *Reason of State*,

> that was pleaded in behalf of *Borgia*, to justifie all his Villanies, in wading through so much bloud and mischief to a Principality in *Italy* . . . It made *Richard* the Third in *England*, to butcher his own Nephew; for which, vengeance pursued him.[15]

In *The Case of the Commonwealth, Stated* (1650), Nedham similarly cites authorities 'both Sacred and Civill', including 'the History of the Kings of *Israel*' and 'the *Romans*' in support of his arguments.[16]

A particularly interesting example by Nedham is a passage justifying tyrannicide, very close in its arguments to Milton's *Defence*, which was included in *Mercurius Politicus*, 92, 3–11 March 1652, but omitted for prudential reasons from *Excellencie* in 1656. The passage has sometimes been attributed to Milton, who was closely associated with Nedham at this time, but parallels with Nedham's other writings and consistency in tone and arguments with the rest of *Mercurius Politicus* conclusively prove Nedham's authorship. Here examples from scripture and 'Profane stories (both old and new)' are treated as equivalent, showing 'that tis no new thing for Kings to be deprived, or punish't with death for their crimes in government':

> We read of Amon, King of Judah, that was slain by a part of the people, Because he walked not in the way of the Lord . . . In like maner we read, that the whole People tooke Amaziah King of Judah, and put him to death for his Idolatry; which seems to have been don by judiciall process, in a full Assembly of the People, and speaks much to the honor of those who have had the courage to imitate so Heroick an Act of Justice . . .
>
> Romulus the first King of Rome, was for his Tyranny cut in pieces by the Senate; and Tarquin (their last King) with his whole Family was cashiered, the Government changed, by the same power, and upon the same occasion.[17]

John Goodwin's *The Obstructors of Justice* (1649), a tract supporting the trial and execution of Charles I, which was condemned and publicly burnt in 1660 along with Milton's *Eikonoklastes* and *Defence*, frequently cites Milton's *Tenure*, published three months earlier. Of Goodwin's eighteen references to 'Tenure of Kings and Magistrates by J. M.', some with page references in the margin (at one point, he refers to Milton's tract as a 'sermon'), at least twelve are to historical and scriptural precedents for justified regicide, 'some pieces published of late, in which presidents of this kind, are to be seen as plentifull, as *silver*, or *Cedars* were in Jerusalem in the days of *Solomon*'. These include 'the *Romans*', 'the State of *Holland*', and a number of examples from the Old Testament: 'The fact of *Ehud* in killing *Eglon*, and so of *Jehu* in slaying *Jehoram* . . . with much more to this purpose, which I leave to the Readers perusal in the discourse it self.'[18] In *Tenure*, Milton sets forth a series of historical examples, classical and biblical, to show 'what the people lawfully may do, as against a common pest, and destroyer of mankinde'.

> The *Greeks* and *Romans*, as their prime Authors witness, held it not onely lawfull, but a glorious and Heroic deed, rewarded publicly with Statues and Garlands, to kill an infamous Tyrant at any time without tryal . . .
>
> Among the Jews, this custom of tyrant-killing was not unusual. First *Ehud*, a man whom God had raysd to deliver Israel from *Eglon* King of *Moab* . . . on just principles, such as were then and ever held allowable, to deal so by a Tyrant that could no otherwise be dealt with. Neither did *Samuel* though a Profet, with his own hand abstain from *Agag* . . . And whereas Jehu had special command to slay *Jehoram* a successive and hereditary Tyrant, it seems not the less imitable for that.

To Milton, as to Goodwin and Nedham, such instances of tyrannicide were 'imitable', providing precedents to show that it 'hath been held . . . through all Ages' that wicked kings can be called to account by their subjects.[19]

'The known rules of antient libertie', as Milton presents them in *Areopagitica* and in a sonnet defending himself against attacks on his divorce tracts as immoral and 'wicked . . . deserving to be burnt', are both classical and biblical. From its outset, in which Milton characterizes his opponents as 'barbarous', enemies of learning, and those he is addressing as 'civill and gentle', receptive to 'the study of wisdome and eloquence', Milton in *Areopagitica* invokes a living European tradition, 'the old and elegant humanity of Greece' and Rome.[20] The vocabulary of *Areopagitica* is full of echoes of republican discourse, with terms like 'tyranny', 'slavery', 'yoke', 'servile', 'thraldom', and 'true liberty': 'We can grow ignorant again, brutish, formall, and slavish, as ye found us; but you then must first become that which ye cannot be, oppressive, arbitrary, and tyrannous, as they were from whom ye have free'd us' (*CPW*, II.559).

At no point in classical antiquity, Milton claims, was an attempt made by those in authority to prohibit the publication of books: 'in Athens where Books and Wits were ever busier then in any other part of *Greece*', in the more 'unbookish' Sparta, or among the Romans, not only in the relatively austere republic, but even at a time when 'we shall meet with little else but tyranny in the Roman empire' (*CPW*, II.494, 496, 499–500). After 'the Emperours were become Christians', pre-publication censorship was unknown, and 'Books were ever as freely admitted into the World as any other birth' (*CPW*, II.505). Biblical precedents for freedom of inquiry include 'the examples of *Moses, Daniel & Paul*, who were skilfull in all the learning of the AEgyptians, Caldeans, and Greeks . . . reading their Books of all sorts' (*CPW*, II.507–8). In passage after passage, biblical echoes reinforce the appeal to the audience addressed, treating them as members of a common body and not as narrowly partisan: 'Suffer not these licensing prohibitions to stand at every place of opportunity forbidding and disturbing them that continue seeking, that continue to do our obsequies to the torn body of our martyr'd Saint' (*CPW*, II.550).

Though at no point in *Areopagitica* does Milton attack monarchical government directly, his position in this treatise is implicitly republican, in its egalitarianism, its rejection of hierarchy and the illegitimate imposition of authority. The search for truth is presented both as a sacred duty and as a communal task, performed by free individuals (the 'sad friends of Truth' in their 'careful search') working individually in a common enterprise, with the writer himself as one of many 'faithfull labourers', warriors united in a common cause.[21] In *The Readie and Easie Way* (1660), Milton argues that the best form of government is 'a free Commonwealth', in which 'they who are greatest', bearing the responsibilities of public office, 'are not elevate above thir brethren . . . walk the street as other men, may be spoken to freely, familiarly, friendly, without adoration' (*CPW*, VII.425). Precedents he cites are rooted in ancient Jerusalem, in the teachings of Jesus and the polity of the pre-diaspora Jews. A free commonwealth, without a king at its head, he argues, closely accords with the 'precept of Christ', who warned his disciples against 'heathenish government' in which monarchs 'exercise lordship' over their passive and cowed subjects. A king, in contrast, 'must be ador'd like a Demigod' (*CPW*, VII.424–5).

The two Old Testament proof-texts which Milton and other polemicists regularly use to support their widely differing views on the sacredness of kingship and the relationship between ruler and people are Deuteronomy 17:14–17, and 1 Samuel 8:7–18. It is of course the very nature of a biblical proof-text that it can be wheeled into view to support several incompatible positions, each of which is taken by a particular writer as being the true interpretation of God's word. Divine-right theorists tend to interpret both passages as evidence and justification for the unlimited power of divine-right monarchs. In contrast, Milton in the *Defence*, using similar arguments to those in *Vindiciae contra Tyrannos* and in Samuel Rutherford's *Lex, Rex: The Law and the Prince* (1644), interprets Deuteronomy 17 as setting forth 'a law for Kings', indicating the bounds which a just ruler would be careful not to overstep. 'God also established laws for the prospective king . . . and in these laws warned him against "multiplying for himself horses or wives or riches."'[22] The distinction between a just king and a tyrant, implicit here, is commonplace enough during this period to find its way into the marginal glosses of *An Abridgement of the Late Remonstrance of the Army* (1648), where both Deuteronomy 17 and Romans 13:3–4 are cited to this effect. Yet Milton takes the argument a step further, and in the *Defence*, gives a specifically republican slant to Deuteronomy 17, suggesting that 'a republican form of government . . . as better adapted to our human circumstances than monarchy, seemed to God more advantageous for his chosen people' (*CPW*, IV.i.344). In both *Tenure* and *Defence*, he finds in Deuteronomy 17 scriptural support for the doctrines of popular sovereignty and the right of revolution: 'These words confirme us that the right of choosing, yea of changing their own Government is by God himself in the People' (*Tenure*, *CPW*, III.207). John Lilburne in *Regall Tyranny Discovered* (1647) draws similar conclusions from Deuteronomy 17, seeing it not only as providing 'a *Law* for the chusing of a *King* and his behaviour', but as carrying the 'very cleer' implication 'that all Government whatsoever ought to be by mutuall consent and agreement'.[23]

Free will for Milton, as *Paradise Lost* and *Samson Agonistes* clearly indicate, allows for the possibility of choosing wrongly and suffering the consequences. Milton's treatment of 1 Samuel 8, like that of Lilburne in *Regall Tyranny Discovered*, presents the free choice of a king by the Jews as an error that may well be repeated by future generations. The biblical verse to which Milton, Lilburne, and other republicans give particular emphasis is 1 Samuel 8:18: 'And ye shall cry out in that day because of your king which ye shall have chosen you; and the Lord will not hear you in that day.' Lilburne draws a republican moral from the biblical proof-text: when the Jews sought a king to rule over them, they were overtly rejecting the God who had been their deliverer and had 'set them free on every side', and therefore deserved the punishment they would receive.

> Yet all this would content them, but *they would have a King to reigne over them*, when (saith Samuel) *the Lord God was your King* . . . The People acknowledged that they had added to all their sin, this evil, *even to ask a King*. Whereby we may evidently perceive, that this office of a King, is not in the least of Gods institution; neither is it to be given to any man upon earth. Because none must rule by his will but God alone.[24]

In *The Readie and Easie Way* (1660), Milton likens his own role to that of the prophet Samuel or the prophet Jeremiah, issuing a strong rebuke to a 'headstrong people', a 'misguided and abus'd multitude' determined to have its own way.[25] His gift of prophetic vision enables him to foresee the destruction that may ensue as a consequence of choosing wrongly, but all he can do is to provide a warning, which may well fall on deaf ears. The biblical precedent suggests that those who place the yoke around their own necks will live to regret it.

> This is not my conjecture, but drawn from God's known denouncement against the gentilizing *Israelites*, who though they were governd in a Commonwealth of God's own ordaining, he only thir king, they his peculiar people, yet affecting rather to resemble heathen, but pretending the misgovernment of *Samuel's* sons . . . clamourd for a king. They had thir longing, but with this testimonie of God's wrath: *ye shall cry out in that day because of your king whom ye shall have chosen, and the Lord will not hear you in that day.* Us if he shall hear now, how much less will he hear when we cry heerafter, who once deliverd by him from a king, and not without wondrous acts of his providence, insensible and unworthy of those high mercies, are returning precipitantly, if he withold us not, back to the captivitie from whence he freed us.

Tyrants are thus to Milton both the punishment a just God metes out and, like 'any evill', a burden to be thrown off by 'any honourable means'.[26]

The proponents of absolutism and non-resistance, such as Filmer and Salmasius, read 1 Samuel 8 in a very different way, as carte blanche for those exercising power in the state. Hobbes and Filmer considered the traditional distinction between king and tyrant to be entirely nominal. 'Tyrant' is no more than 'a word of disgrace': 'they that are discontented under *monarchy*', says Hobbes, 'call it *tyranny*'. The same 'patient obedience', they argue, is due to all rulers, even to a 'man . . . that is . . . thought to govern ill'.[27] Where Milton and Lilburne saw in 1 Samuel 8:10–18 a catalogue of abuses by proud and rapacious monarchs – 'and he will take your fields, and your vineyards, and your olive-yards, even the best of them, and give them to his servants' – Filmer and Salmasius interpreted this passage as biblical evidence for the 'unlimited jurisdiction' of kings, their unconditional right to alienate the property of subjects, enabling monarchs to be 'glorious, powerful and abounding in riches'.

> The scope of Samuel was to teach the people a dutiful obedience to their king, even in those things which themselves did esteem mischievous and inconvenient. For, telling them what a king would do, he instructs them what a subject must suffer, yet not so that it is right for kings to do injury, but it is right for them to go unpunished by the people if they do it.[28]

Milton, like the author of *Vindiciae*, used 1 Samuel 8 as a means of defining the difference between a just ruler and a tyrant, 'regarding neither Law nor the common good', who allows his 'own unjust desires' to govern him: 'The prophet then was not maintaining that these royal rights were a divine grant but rather a most depraved method of government usurped by the pride of kings and their lust for rule! This is not what kings should do, but what they wish to.'[29]

In these passages, as in most of those I have been discussing, the distinction between just ruler and tyrant allows at least the theoretical possibility that a particular monarch will resist the temptations of power, bridle his own lusts, and govern wisely. Monarchy, as Aristotle and others have argued, is one of several forms of government, each with advantages and disadvantages. Milton makes this concession in the *Defence:*

> Whether the government of one man or several is in fact the better cannot be discussed here. Monarchy has indeed been praised by many famous men, provided that the sole ruler is the best of men and fully deserving of the crown; otherwise monarchy sinks most rapidly into the worst tyranny. (*CPW*, IV.i.427)

In *Tenure* and *Defence*, Milton only rarely goes so far as to claim, as does the author of *The Armies Vindication* (1649), that '*Monarchy is Tyranny*' and that under any monarchy 'there's nothing left the people but meer slavery'.[30] He does, however, in setting forth 'what the people by thir just right may doe in change of government, or of governours', come close to holding that monarchy is in itself incompatible with that 'free goverment' which best fits the human inheritance of inalienable liberty.

> And surely they that shall boast, to be a free Nation, and not have in themselves the power to remove, or to abolish any governour supreme, or subordinat, with the government it self upon urgent causes, may please thir fancy with a ridiculous and painted freedom, fit to coz'n babies; but are indeed under tyranny and servitude; as wanting that power, which is the root and source of all liberty to dispose and *oeconomize* in the Land which God hath giv'n them, as Maisters of Family in their own house and free inheritance. (*Tenure*, *CPW*, III.236–7)

This is essentially the position argued by the Leveller Richard Overton in *An Arrow against All Tyrants* (1646): each individual has a right of proprietorship over what belongs to him, which cannot be alienated without his consent. Overton is writing here from Newgate prison, protesting against unjust imprisonment, and begins the pamphlet by stating a general principle:

> To every Individual in nature, is given an individuall propriety by nature, not to be invaded or usurped by any: for every one as he is himself, so he hath a selfe propriety, else he could not be himself, and on this no second

> may presume to deprive any of, without manifest violation and affront to the very principles of nature . . . No man hath power over my rights and liberties, and I over no mans . . . For by naturall birth, all men are equally and alike born to the like propriety, liberty and freedome . . . even all whereof God hath made him free.[31]

According to Overton, all legitimate government, not only in its institution but in everyday practice, must be 'by deputation, commission, and free consent', otherwise someone exercising power is no better than 'a Theife and Robber to his kind' (p. 4). Overton's *An Appeale from the Degenerate Representative Body the Commons of England . . . to the Body Represented* (1647), another appeal against his imprisonment, takes the principle of devolved power by 'free consent' literally, applied not only to monarchs but to any person or body entrusted with power:

> *All betrusted powers if forfeit, fall into the hands of the betrusters* . . . and where such a forfeit is committed . . . disobligeth from obedience . . . While the *Betrusters* are *dischargers* of their *trust,* it remaineth in their hands, but no sooner the *Betrusted* betray and forfeit their *Trust,* but (as all things else in dissolution) it returneth from whence it came, even to the hands of the *Trusters.*[32]

When Milton, in the passage quoted above, contrasts 'a free Nation' with the state of servitude, he is arguing what Quentin Skinner calls a neo-Roman theory of liberty: if you are under the power of an individual or group that claims the right of depriving you of liberty or seizing your possessions whenever he or they wish to do so, whether or not he chooses at any moment to exercise that right, then you can no longer be considered free, but a slave.

> Without which natural and essential power of a free Nation, though bearing high thir heads, they can in due esteem be thought no better than slaves and vassals born, in the tenure and occupation of another inheriting Lord. Whose goverment, though not illegal or intolerable, hangs over them as a Lordly scourge, not as a free goverment; and therefore to be abrogated.[33]

In *The Readie and Easie Way*, facing the prospect of an 'ingratefull backsliding', a resumption by free if (to Milton) misdirected choice, of the 'once abjur'd and detested thraldom of Kingship', Milton presents monarchy as inevitably entailing abject servitude: 'It may be well wonderd that any Nation styling themselves free, can suffer any man to pretend hereditarie right over them as thir lord; when as by acknowledging that right, they conclude themselves his servants and his vassals, and so renounce thir own freedom' (*CPW*, VII.422, 423, 427–8).

A recurrent motif in *The Readie and Easie Way*, as earlier in the *Defence*, is the danger of a re-enacted Egyptian captivity, by a misguided people who are tempted in their folly to 'run their necks again into the yoke which they have broken' and, at a moment when they have an opportunity to choose a course that will materially alter their future lives, 'seem now chusing them a captain back for *Egypt*'.[34] These passages contrast the journey out of Egypt under Moses, escaping from bondage to a promised freedom, with the ever-present danger that, 'choosing rather / Inglorious life with servitude', the 'inconsiderate multitude' shall, fearing the uncertainties of freedom and blinded with idolatry, return to Egyptian bondage.[35] Here again the history of the Jews provides cautionary parallels to the immediate situation of contemporary England. The parallel, in 1651 and in 1660, is to the Jews in the wilderness (Numbers, 14:1–4), who, defying their leader and promised 'deliverer' Moses, wished to return to Egypt, thinking that even as slaves they would enjoy greater comfort there. An angry God, Milton warns, will, now as then, punish such cowardice severely. As he writes in *Defence:*

> All slavery indeed is a stain upon any freeborn man, but for you to resist your destiny and wish to return to slavery after your freedom had been won by God's assistance and your own valor . . . would be not a simply a shameful act, but an ungodly and criminal act! Your sin would equal the sin of those who were overcome with longing for their former captivity in Egypt and were at length destroyed by God in countless disasters of all sorts, thus paying to their divine deliverer the penalty for their slavish thoughts. (*Defence*, *CPW*, IV.i.532)

As with other biblical parallels discussed in this chapter, warnings against a 'returne . . . back to *Egypt*' are relatively frequent in polemics by republicans and partisans of the Good Old Cause.[36] A letter to Milton from Moses Wall in 1659 uses the same biblical analogy in criticizing political leaders who, seeking power, betray the principles they profess: 'when those being instated in power, shall betray this good Thing committed to them, and lead us back to Egypt, and by that Force which we gave them, to win us Liberty, hold us fast in Chains'. Here the emphasis is less on the weakness of those who in 'feare' revert to an earlier state of enslavement after a brief interval of freedom, but on the culpability of those rulers who misuse the power entrusted to them.[37] For Milton, in *Defence* and *The Readie and Easie Way*, as in *Paradise Lost* and *Samson Agonistes*, the emphasis is on free choice and its consequences. Though the changing circumstances of 1660 had made the resumption of the monarchical yoke and the extinction of republican hopes almost inevitable, the rhetorical pattern in an eloquent passage in *The Readie and Easie Way* again contrasts glory and shame, an opportunity grasped and an opportunity which may be irrevocably lost:

> That a nation should be so valorous and courageous to winn thir liberty in the field, and when they have wonn it, should be so heartless and unwise in thir counsels, as not to know how to use it, value it, what to do with it or with themselves; but after ten or twelve years prosperous war and contestation with tyrannie, basely and besottedly to run their necks again into the yoke which they have broken, and prostrate all the fruits of thir victorie for naught at the feet of the vanquishd, besides our loss of glorie, and such an example as kings or tyrants never yet had the like to boast of, will be an ignominie if it befall us, that never yet befell any nation possessd of thir libertie; worthie indeed themselves, whatsoever they be, to be for ever slaves. (*Readie and Easie Way*, *CPW*, VII.428)

5

Victory's Crest
Milton, the English Nation and Cromwell

> What may not then our isle presume,
> While Victory his crest does plume!?[1]

I

The subject of this chapter is the ambivalence of Milton and several of his fellow republicans towards military conquest and particularly towards the figure of Oliver Cromwell. The war in Iraq might suggest a modern analogy: conquest looks very different to those delivering and those receiving the bombs. Even from the perspective of the victors, praise of the conqueror Cromwell could be double-edged. Cromwell, 'the War's and Fortune's son', with his sword held erect before him ('Horatian Ode', 113–16), could appear to contemporaries as the patron of liberty, servant of the commonwealth, or as its destroyer, bent on reducing the English people to servitude.

Milton does not always treat Cromwell with such ambivalence, bringing out his potential for harm. Milton's sonnet addressed to Cromwell, 'our cheif of men', in May 1652, while arguing that 'peace hath her victories / No less renownd then warr', sees Cromwell primarily as conqueror, triumphant in a series of battles and ready to take on whatever 'new foes' may arise. 'Peace & truth' are projected as the Lord General's ultimate aims, but these seem a long way off, as the 'blood of Scotts' killed on the battlefield serves as 'Gods Trophies', reminding Cromwell that 'much remaines / To conquer still'.[2] A similar view of Cromwell as God's chosen warrior finds expression in Milton's *Second Defence:*

> He soon surpassed well-nigh the greatest generals both in the magnitude of his accomplishments and in the speed with which he achieved them . . . It is impossible . . . to describe with fitting dignity the capture of the many cities, to list the many battles . . . in which he was never conquered nor

> put to flight, but traversed the entire realm of Britain with uninterrupted victory.[3]

In the extended passage praising Cromwell in the *Second Defence*, Milton emphasizes his 'upright life' and steadfast 'faith dependent on God', presenting his military success as a direct consequence of his exemplary strength of character and 'Christian virtue':

> Commander first over himself, victor over himself, he had learned to achieve over himself the most effective triumph [in se prius imperator, sui victor, de se potissimum triumphare didiceret] . . . There flourished in him so great a power, whether of intellect and genius or of discipline . . . that to his camp, as to the foremost school, not just of military science, but of religion and piety, he attracted from every side all men who were already good and brave, or else he made them such, chiefly by his own example.[4]

The terms of praise in Marvell's 'Horatian Ode' are resolutely secular as well as double-edged – Cromwell in this poem is certainly not 'guided by faith' or represented as doing God's work.[5] But here again, 'uninterrupted victory' testifies to Cromwell's heroic stature as one of the 'greater spirits', giving no quarter to less civilized or less resolute adversaries. Slain or humbled Irish serve the same function as 'the blood of Scotts' for Milton:

> And now the Irish are ashamed
> To see themselves in one year tamed.
> So much one man can do,
> That does both act and know.
> They can affirm his praises best,
> And have, though overcome, confessed
> How good he is, how just,
> And fit for highest trust.
> (44, 73–80)

The ideology of 'civilizing Conquest', in the 'Horatian Ode' as in Milton's *Observations upon the Articles of Peace*, attributes moral superiority to the victors (as in the wholly illegitimate inference that Cromwell's success in battle proves him to be 'good', 'just' and 'fit for highest trust'), while, like Prospero confronted by Caliban, treating the 'Barbarisme and obdurate wilfulnesse' of the subjugated Other with a degree of contempt. Thus, in the *Observations*, the 'savage' Irish are dismissed as impervious to 'reason and demonstration', capable of being taught only by the most violent means, because of 'a disposition not only sottish but indocible and averse from all Civility and amendment'.[6] A similar polemical strategy is central to Marvell's *The Character of Holland* (1653), applied in this case to a powerful rival of the English nation, as the poet seeks to disable an adversary by volleys of wit. The facts of geography prove the barbarity of the 'sordid' Dutch, where the 'civility' of the English justifies their imperial dominion.

> Holland, that scarce deserves the name of land,
> As but th'off-scouring of the British sand . . .
> This indigested vomit of the sea
> Fell to the Dutch by just propriety . . .
> Nor can civility there want for tillage,
> Where wisely for their court they chose a village.
> (1–2, 7–8, 17, 77–8)

Edmund Waller's *Panegyrick to My Lord Protector* (1655), in treating Cromwell's victories over the Irish and over the Scots, until then 'a Race unconquer'd, by their Clyme made bold', occludes any bloodshed or resistance by incorporating the vanquished into the British 'seat of Empire', graciously extending to 'the unwilling *Scotch*' the privilege of becoming English:

> Preferr'd by Conquest, happily o'rethrowne,
> Falling they rise, to be with us made one;
> So kinde Dictators made, when they came home,
> Their vanquish'd Foes, free Citizens of *Rome*.
> Like favor find the *Irish*, with like Fate,
> Advanc'd to be a portion of our State.[7]

In Milton's *History of Britain*, the ideology of 'civilizing Conquest' becomes more problematical, in part because here the barbarians are British and the conquerors Roman. David Quint in *Epic and Empire* has suggested that, running in parallel with the glorification of 'imperial conquest' in the *Aeneid*, there is a rival epic tradition, 'epics of the defeated', originating in Lucan's *Pharsalia*. If rebels against imperial sway are characterized as motivated by a love of freedom or a 'courage never to submit or yield', then at least the possibility of sympathy, of 'dissenting perspectives', is opened up.[8] In the *History of Britain*, the reforms of the Roman conqueror Agricola are on the one hand 'worthie actions; teaching and promoting like a public Father the institutes and customes of civil life', while on the other hand the introduction of 'the *Roman* fashions' among the early Britons 'which the foolisher sort call'd civilitie . . . was indeed a secret Art to prepare them for bondage'.[9] In the *Character of the Long Parliament*, intended for the *History of Britain* but not published until 1681, Milton's own English contemporaries are presented as barbarians, like their ancestors among the ancient Britons, deficient in the virtues of 'civilitie, prudence, love of the public', and 'in good or bad success alike unteachable'.

> For the sunn, which wee want ripens witts as well as fruits; and as wine and oyle are imported to us from abroad, so must ripe understanding and many civil vertues bee imported into our minds from forren writings & examples of best ages: wee shall else miscarry still and com short in the attempt of any great enterprise. Hence did thir victories prove as fruitless as thir losses dangerous, and left them still conquering under the same grievances that men suffer conquerd.[10]

The ancient Britons, as Milton characterizes them in the *History of Britain*, were 'right *Barbarians*': courageous in battle and 'adoring the name of liberty', they nevertheless were ignorant of 'what it was to govern well themselves', showing in their actions 'no rule, no foresight, no forecast, experience or estimation, either of themselves or of thir Enemies'.[11] Under Roman rule, they were 'bred up in liberal Arts' and taught to 'affect the Latine Eloquence': 'Of the *Romans* we have cause not to say much worse, then that they beate us into some civilitie; likely else to have continu'd longer in a barbarous and savage manner of life.'[12] In the unsettled conditions of 1648–9, Milton argues in the 'Digression', the English people faced an opportunity similar to that of their British ancestors at the end of the period of Roman rule. 'The gaining or loosing of libertie is the greatest change to better or to worse that may befall a nation under civil goverment, and so discovers, as nothing more, what degree of understanding, or capacitie, what disposition to justice and civilitie there is among them' (*CPW*, v.441). Milton consistently argues that 'libertie hath a sharp and double edge fitt onelie to be handl'd by just and vertuous men'; according to 'the known rules of antient libertie' as handed down by Aristotle, Cicero, and the republican tradition, 'who loves that, must first be wise and good'.[13] Like the ancient Britons who, 'having such a smooth occasion giv'n them to free themselves as ages have not afforded, such a manumission as never subjects had a fairer', failed to take advantage of the opportunity, Milton's contemporaries faced a moment in history which could lead either to the establishment of 'a just and well amended common-wealth' or to further thraldom, 'miserie and ruin', 'ev'ry where wrong & oppression'.[14]

Towards the beginning of Book III of the *History of Britain*, Milton argues for the value of self-knowledge, facing uncomfortable truths, in nations as in individuals: 'For if it be a high point of wisdom in every private man, much more is it in a Nation to know it self; rather than puft up with vulgar flatteries, and encomiums, for want of self knowledge, to enterprise rashly and come off miserably in great undertakings.'[15] He makes a similar point in the peroration addressed to his 'fellow countrymen' at the end of the *Second Defence*, in juxtaposing great hopes and human weaknesses. The greatest conquest is the conquest over self, the 'perseverance' necessary to bring 'great undertakings' to successful completion.

> If after such brave deeds you ignobly fail, if you do aught unworthy of yourselves, be sure that posterity will speak out and pass judgment . . . It will seem to posterity that a mighty harvest of glory was at hand, together with the opportunity for doing the greatest deeds, but that to this opportunity men were wanting.[16]

Here, as elsewhere, Milton singles out self-mastery as the defining quality distinguishing free men from slaves. Men who are 'slaves within doors', he says in *Tenure*, are for this reason content 'to have the public State conformably govern'd to the inward vitious rule, by which they govern themselves', finding rationalizations to 'colour over thir base compliances' to tyrants. Freedom entails responsibilities: it is easier to be servile than to be free, and freedom gained with painstaking effort can be quickly lost.[17] 'A nation which cannot rule and govern itself', Milton warns his countrymen in the *Second Defence*, may deliver itself into slavery to 'masters whom it does not choose'.

> Such is the decree of law and of nature herself, that he who cannot control himself, who through poverty of intellect or madness cannot properly administer his own affairs, should not be his own master, but like a ward be given over to the power of another . . . If to be a slave is hard, and you do not wish it, learn to obey right reason, to master yourselves.[18]

Milton's arguments for republicanism and against monarchical government in *The Readie and Easie Way* seek to awaken national pride together with a sense of shame in his audience. He praises the 'many thousand faithfull and valiant *English* men', who, in 'all the battels we have wonn', have succeeded in securing 'all *Scotland* as to our conquest . . . which never any of our kings could conquer'. Similar claims of unprecedented victories over the previously 'unconquer'd' Scots can be found in panegyrics of Cromwell by Waller and Payne Fisher.[19] Yet, Milton argues, the victors have by their own folly become the vanquished. In contrasting 'the majesty of a free people' with 'the base necessitie of court flatteries and prostrations', Milton is appealing to patriotism and the instinct of solidarity among those who fought against Charles I. As in *Areopagitica*, he argues that 'brotherly dissimilitudes' are to be welcomed among those united in a common cause.[20] His sonnets to Fairfax, Cromwell, and Sir Henry Vane all present wisdom as a necessary complement to the 'matchless Fortitude' of successful warriors, coupling 'Victory' in battle with the 'sage counsell' which can 'advise how warr may best [be] upheld', the 'nobler task' and 'no less renownd' victories of peace.[21] Marvell, in the 'Horatian Ode', relies on the same traditional coupling of the virtues of Achilles and Ulysses in describing Cromwell as someone who can 'both act and know'.[22]

In *The Readie and Easie Way*, adopting the prophetic stance, Milton strives against the odds 'to forewarne my countrey in time', regretting that 'the effects of wisdom are so little seen among us': 'Shall we never grow old anough to be wise[,] to make seasonable use of gravest autorities, experiences, examples?'[23] Milton's Samson similarly recognizes that the 'high gift of strength', which had previously made him 'the dread of *Israel*'s foes . . . himself an Army', was insufficient without wisdom, self-knowledge, self-mastery.

> O impotence of mind, in body strong!
> But what is strength without a double share
> Of wisdom, vast, unwieldy, burdensom,
> Proudly secure, yet liable to fall
> By wicked subtleties, not made to rule,
> But to subserve where wisdom bears command.[24]

If the English nation at this critical juncture makes the wrong choice – like Samson, 'sole Author' of whatever 'evils hath befall'n' as a result (*Samson Agonistes*, 374–6) – the blame, Milton contends, lies with deficiencies in wisdom, an inability or refusal to heed the lessons of history, 'gravest autorities, experiences, examples' and even to recognize where their true interest lies.

II

In the *Second Defence*, the *History of Britain*, and *The Readie and Easie Way*, Milton cites the lessons of history to help explain how and why 'violent Lords' from time to time 'undeservedly enthrall' man's 'outward freedom', taking advantage of the propensity of fallible men and women to 'give up thir understanding to a double tyrannie, of Custom from without, and blind affections within'.[25] Marchamont Nedham's republican manifesto, *The Excellencie of a Free-State* (1656), gives a number of instances from Roman history to illustrate the maxim that 'Freedom is a Virgin that every one seeks to deflower . . . so great is the Lust of mankinde after dominion'. Like Milton, Nedham sees a degree of complicity between tyrants and their willing slaves, who see their 'interest in base fawning, and the favour of present Great Ones': 'the greatest part' of mankind, he argues, 'was ever inclined to adore the Golden Idol of Tyranny in every Form'.[26] 'Immoderate Power', Nedham suggests, 'soon lets in high and ambitious thoughts', and few men faced with the delicious prospect of 'unbounded Power' are able to resist temptation: 'How many Free-States & Common-wealths have paid dear for their Experience in this particular? who by trusting their own servants too far, have been forced, in the end to receive them for their Masters.'[27] The remedy Nedham suggests, as a 'prime Principle of State', is 'To keep any man, though he have deserved never so well by good success or service, from being too great or popular: it is a notable means (and so esteemeth by all Free-States) to keep and preserve a Commonwealth from the Rapes of Usurpation.'[28] Yet neither Nedham nor his fellow republican James Harrington explicitly states that Cromwell is such a man, greedy for power. Like the Cromwell of the 'Horatian Ode', who 'has his sword and spoils ungirt, / To lay them at the public's skirt', the Lord General is presented by Nedham and Harrington as, for the moment at least, content to act as servant of the people, yet also capable of savagery and destruction.[29]

Nedham's *True State of the Case of the Commonwealth* (1654), though written in support of the Protectorate settlement, nevertheless emphasizes the potential for tyranny in a situation where 'all Power of Government [is] devolved upon the General, as Head of the Army', leaving 'both the instituting and executing of Law to the arbitrary discretion of the Souldier', who is able 'to execute his own will in place of Law, without check or controll'.[30] Harrington in *The Commonwealth of Oceana* (1656), while praising Cromwell as a 'most victorious captain and incomparable patriot', sees the nation as 'ruined by his victory'. Having 'cast herself at his feet' as supplicant, the English nation could develop in either of two directions: 'what is there in nature that can arise out of these ashes, but a popular government, or a new monarchy to be erected by the victorious army?'[31] Harrington's proposal for dealing with the political crisis of 1653–5 differed considerably from that of Milton in the *Second Defence*, Marvell in *The First Anniversary*, and Nedham in *A True State of the Case of the Commonwealth*, all of which urged support for the Protectorate government under Cromwell. In *The First Anniversary*, Marvell presents Cromwell's assumption of power as an unselfish acceptance of burdensome responsibility by a nurturing, benevolent 'Father' and guide, carefully avoiding the extremes of tyranny and anarchic licence.

> For all delight of life thou then didst lose,
> When to command, thou didst thy self depose;
> Resigning up thy privacy so dear,
> To turn the headstrong people's charioteer.
> (*The First Anniversary*, 221–4)

Where the analogies Marvell cites in the 'Horatian Ode' are largely, like those of Harrington and Nedham, from Roman history ('A Caesar he ere long to Gaul, / To Italy an Hannibal'), in *The First Anniversary* he uses a series of biblical parallels to present Cromwell as one who, in spite of having 'grown great' by 'conquest', 'would not . . . be Lord' over his fellow man.[32] Cromwell, Marvell argues, consciously resists the temptation of absolute power and has the self-discipline to 'still refuse to reign'. Here again he is presented as serving others, as wise, provident, and attentive to the public interest, yet the imagery also suggests the twin dangers of anarchic desire and arbitrary power, two kinds of 'will':

> Thou, and thine house, like Noah's eight did rest,
> Left by the war's flood on the mountain's crest:
> And the large vale lay subject to thy will,
> Which thou but as a husbandsman wouldst till:
> And only didst for others plant the vine
> Of liberty, not drunken with its wine.[33]

Harrington uses classical and biblical analogies to provide 'the greatest examples' to buttress his arguments, but to an entirely different effect. To him, a great conqueror, a Caesar or Alexander, is no better than a butcher; indeed, Julius Caesar, as one who has succeeded in having 'perpetrated some heinous crime' in invading the liberty of the Roman people, is 'more execrable than Catiline':

> To begin with Alexander, erecting trophies common with his sword and the pestilence, to what good of mankind did he infect the air with his heaps of carcasses? The sword of war, if it be any otherwise used than as the sword of magistracy for the fear and punishment of those that do evil, is as guilty in the sight of God as the sword of a murderer; nay more, for if the blood of Abel, of one innocent man, cried in the ears of the Lord for vengeance, what shall the blood of an innocent nation?[34]

True heroism, Harrington suggests in this passage, is incompatible with the pursuit of military glory. Like Milton in the later books of *Paradise Lost* and in *Paradise Regained*, Harrington sees the desire for 'the throne of ambition' – 'to gain dominion and to keep it gain'd' – and the worship of military prowess as indicative of false values.

> Of this kind of empire, the throne of ambition, the quarry of a mighty hunter, it hath been truly said that it is but a great robbery. But if Alexander had restored the liberty of Greece, and propagated it unto mankind, he . . . might have been truly called the Great.[35]

In the exchange between Michael and Adam in the last two books of *Paradise Lost*, Milton similarly attacks the adulation commonly accorded to 'great Conquerours', mistakenly gaining 'renown on Earth' for success on the battlefield, allowing them to 'bring home spoils with infinite / Man-slaughter', as contrasted with 'what most merits fame' (*PL*, XI.688–99).

In the writings of Milton's fellow republicans Nedham and Harrington in this period, republican Rome serves as a model for the infant English commonwealth. In *The Excellencie of a Free-State*, Nedham, following Machiavelli, argues that 'the Sword, and Soveraignty, ever walk hand in hand together', praising a citizen army as guardians of the public liberty, where an army of mercenaries, 'a *Praetorian Band*', could easily become the instruments of oppression:

> *Rome* it self, and the Territories about it, was trained up perpetually in Arms . . . so long as *Rome* acted by the pure Principles of a *Free-State* . . . In those days there was no difference, in order, between the Citizen, the Husbandman, and the Souldier: for, he that was a Citizen, or Villager yesterday became a Souldier the next, if the *Publick Liberty* required it.[36]

Like Machiavelli in the *Discourses*, Nedham contrasts the vitality of the Roman republic with the decadence of the later empire, arguing that 'the Romans flourished most when they were a Free-State'. Under kings, the Romans were 'a very inconsiderable People', but as a republic Rome 'laid the Foundation and built the Structure of that wondrous Empire that overshadowed the whole World'. 'Courage and Magnanimity', Nedham argues, are virtues that flourish in a republic and are lost with 'the loss of Freedom' under 'usurping Dictators' and emperors.[37] Characteristically, he cites modern instances – 'the valiant *Swisses*, the *Hollanders*' – along with the history of Rome, with particular application to the immediate situation of England in the mid-1650s, 'our own Nation, when declared a Free-State'.[38]

Though Cromwell's name is not mentioned, *The Excellencie of a Free-State* can be seen as a covert attack on Cromwell as a threat to 'a Re-establishment of our Freedom in the hands of the People' (p. 36). Much more direct attacks on Cromwell as tyrant and usurper can be found in

Leveller, republican, and Fifth Monarchist pamphlets, both in 1647–9 and in the mid-1650s. John Wildman's *A Call to All the Souldiers of the Armie, by the Free People of England* (1647) imagines two Cromwells, good and bad:

> And if Cromwell instantly repent not and alter his course, let him know also that ye loved and honoured just, honest, sincere, and valiant Cromwell that loved his country and the liberties of his people above his life, yea, and hated the King as a man of blood, but that Cromwell ceasing to be such, he ceaseth to be the object of your love.[39]

William Walwyn's *The Bloody Project* (1648) and Richard Overton's *The Hunting of the Foxes* (1649) see a plot by '*Cromwell* and *Ireton*, and their faction of self interessed Officers . . . to grasp the sole dominion into their own hands' in 'a *New Regality*'.[40] The English nation, according to *The Hunting of the Foxes*, is 'under a more absolute arbitrary Monarchy than before. We have not the change of a Kingdom to a Common wealth; we are only under the old cheat, the transmutation of Names, but with the addition of New Tyrannies to the old.'[41] As Walwyn puts it:

> To be short, all the quarrell we have at this day in the Kingdome, is no other then a quarrel of Interests, and Partyes, a pulling down of one Tyrant, to set up another, and instead of Liberty, heaping upon our selves a greater slavery than that we fought against.[42]

Walwyn, directing his appeal to the consciences of 'soldiers and People', bitterly attacks the 'great men in the City and Army' who 'have made you but the stairs by which they have mounted to Honor, Wealth and Power', while 'you and your poor friends that depend on Farms, Trades, and small pay' suffer. War and conquest, as presented here, are no better than murder.

> But if you have not killed and destroyed men enough for this, go on and destroy, kill and sley, till your consciences are swoln so full with the blood of the People, that they burst agen, and upon your death-beds may you see your selves the most horrid Murtherers that ever lived, since the time that Cain kild his brother without a just Cause.[43]

The Hunting of the Foxes, addressed to 'all that have, and are still engaged in the Military Service of the Common-wealth', similarly distinguishes between 'the Grandie-Deceivers', who 'are become masters and usurpers of the name of the Army', and the common soldiers, citizens in arms.[44] Like Nedham and Harrington, Overton contrasts a '*Mercenary Army*, hired to serve any *Arbitrary power* of a *state*', willing 'to butcher the people for pay', with the ideal of independent, conscientious 'English Souldiers, engaged for the Freedoms of *England*'.[45] *The Hunting of the Foxes* is a defence of five soldiers in the New Model Army punished for disobedience, arguing that 'our being Souldiers hath not deprived us of our Right as Commoners'.

> Further we desire you to consider, That the strength, the honour and being of the Officer . . . doth consist in the Arme of the Souldier. Is it not the Souldier that endureth the heat and burden of the day, and performeth that work whereof the Officers beareth the glory and name?[46]

Edward Sexby, an even more ardent republican opponent of Cromwell, advances similar arguments in the Putney debates, again acting as spokesman for the 'many thousands of us soldiers' in the New Model Army:

> We have engaged in this kingdom and ventured our lives, and it was all for this: to recover our birthrights and privileges as Englishmen . . . If we had not a right to the kingdom, we were mere mercenary soldiers . . . I do think the poor and meaner of this kingdom . . . have been the means of the preservation of this kingdom.[47]

In 1654, Wildman published an anonymous broadsheet, *A Declaration of the Free-Born People of England, Now in Armes Against the Tyrannie and Oppression of Oliver Cromwell*, fiercely attacking Cromwell as tyrant, hypocrite, and usurper, and arguing 'the present necessity to take up *Armes* for the defence of our Native Rights and Freedoms, which are wholly invaded and swallowed up in the Pride and Ambition of *Oliver Cromwell Esq.* who calls himself *Lord Protector* of *England*, and hath rendered all English-men no better than his Vassals'.[48] Wildman was arrested in February 1655, accused of planning an armed uprising, and remained in prison until June 1656. In the *Declaration*, Wildman presents Cromwell as having deceived the English people with 'specious pretences and most alluring promises'.

> We did believe, as they told us, that our present sufferings, were onely like a rough stormy passage, to the Haven of Justice, Right, and Freedome: Wee could not suspect these ambitious designes in *Cromwell*, and his Confederates, that are now proclaimed to the World . . . These things rocked us asleep, with the pleasant Dreames of Liberty and Justice, untill he hath made a Sacrifice of all our *Lawes*, *Liberties* and *Properties*, unto his own Ambition.[49]

Both the *Declaration* and the Fifth Monarchist pamphlet *The Protector, (So called) In Part Unvailed* (1655), purporting to be 'By a late Member of the Army', cite Cromwell's speech to the Protectorate Parliament as proof 'that he hath dissolved all civill Government, and that He had in himselfe alone, an absolute unlimited Arbitrary power, without checke or controle'.[50]

> The plain truth is, we are at his mercy, by reason of the power of the sword, which is over us (which was never taken up on our part to this end) and he may do with us what he pleases . . . if he will be good to us and us use well, so . . . if we will cry Grace, Grace, and fall down and worship his Government . . . he will say we are good Boyes, and will use us well.[51]

Though the apocalyptic terminology prominent in *The Protector Unvailed* ('The Monarchical foundation in which he stands, is that which the Lord by his Spirit in his People, and by their hands . . . hath destroyed') differs from the essentially secular, contractual language of Wildman's *Declaration*, both see the Protectorate government as monarchy under another name and Cromwell as tyrant and deceiver.[52]

Republican attacks on Cromwell are carried one step further in Sexby's *Killing Noe Murder* (1657), a call to tyrannicide. Like Milton in *Tenure* – though of course Milton is attacking Charles I and never characterizes Cromwell in these terms – Sexby argues that a tyrant should be treated as an outlaw, 'a common pest, and destroyer of mankinde', outside the bounds of civil society.

> And therefore a Tyrant that submits to no law; but his will and lust are the law, by which he governs himself and others, is no Magistrate, no Citizen or member of any Society, but an Ulcer and disease that destroyes it . . . He is therefore in all reason to be reckoned in the number of those Savage Beasts, that fall not with others into any heard: that have no other defence but their own strength; making a prey of all thats weaker, and, by the same justice, being a prey to all that's stronger then themselves.[53]

He who lives by the sword, Sexby suggests, must expect to die by the sword. Milton in *Tenure* argues that 'justice don upon a Tyrant is no more but the necessary self-defence of a whole Common wealth', and the author of *The Protector Unvailed* claims that a tyrant and 'all those who have been Aiders and Abettors, to him' become subject to a form of citizen's arrest: it is 'lawfull for any well-affected Person or Officer, to proceed to apprehend him, or them, and bring them before the next Justice of the Peace'.[54] Citing Aristotle, Tacitus, and Machiavelli to identify 'the Markes of a Tyrant', Sexby accuses Cromwell of 'spungy eyes, and a supple conscience', of gaining power by deception and maintaining power by ruthlessly suppressing any potential opposition:

> Almost all Tyrants have been first Captaines & Generalls for the people: under pretence of vindicating, or defending theire Liberties. *Ut*

> *imperium evertant Libertatem praeferunt; cum perverterunt, ipsam aggrediuntur*, sayes *Tacitus*, [. . .] to subvert the present Government, they pretend Liberty for the people, when the Government is downe, they then Invade that libertie them selves.[55]

As with the other attacks on Cromwell's Protectorate by Levellers and republicans discussed above, Sexby's immediate audience is 'Officers and Soldiers of the Army' who once fought side by side with Cromwell, seeking to awaken their consciences.

> For you that were the Champions of our Liberty, and to that purpose were raised, are you not become the instruments of our Slavery? and your hands that the people employ'd to take off the yoake from our necks, are not those the very hands they that now doe put it on? . . . Give not Posterity as well as your own Generation the occasion to mention you with infamie, and to curse that unfortunate valour, and successe of yours, that onely hath gained victories . . . against the common-wealth. (*Killing Noe Murder*, Sig. A1^{v})

Here again the contrast is between 'Janizaries', hired killers who are 'pimpes of Tyranny . . . slaves themselves, and making all others so', and free citizens bearing arms in defence of their native birthright (*Killing Noe Murder*, Sig. B2^{v}). In an eloquent prefatory epistle addressed to fellow soldiers of the New Model Army 'from one that was once one amongst you', Sexby presents them with a stark moral choice: to serve God and the cause of liberty or to serve the base lusts of man, as the willing instruments of tyranny and oppression:

> Could ever England have thought to have seen that Armie that was never mentioned without the titles of Religious, Zealous, Faithfull, Couragious, the fence of her libertie at home, the Terrour of her enemies abroad; Become her Gaolers? not her Guard, but her oppressours? not her Souldiers, but a Tyrants executioners?[56]

Like Milton, Sexby locates 'the root and source of all liberty' in the right of each and every individual 'to dispose and *oeconomize* in the Land which God hath giv'n them, as Maisters of Family in their own house and free inheritance' – what Overton in *An Arrow against All Tyrants* (1646) calls 'a selfe propriety', 'an individuall propriety by nature, not to be invaded or usurped by any': 'But sure no English man can be ignorant, that it is his Birth-right to be master of his own Estate; and that none can command any part of it but by his own grant and consent, either made expressly by himself, or Virtually by a Parliament.'[57] Going well beyond Milton, Sexby extends the principle of consent to justify the assassination of Cromwell, citing as precedent the biblical instances of Samson, Ehud and others. Though Milton cites Ehud as an example of justified tyrannicide, he explicitly states his preference for 'faire and op'n tryal . . . to teach lawless Kings, and all who so much adore them, that not mortal man, or his imperious will, but Justice is the onely true sovran and supreme Majesty upon earth' (*Tenure*, *CPW*, III.237).

To Sexby, violent direct action is the ultimate expression of liberty, the remedy of the oppressed:

> The example of Ehud shews us the naturall and almost the only remedie against a Tyrant, and the way to free an opprest people from the slavery of an insulting Moabite, tis done by prayers and teares, with the help of a Dagger . . . Now that which was lawfull for Samson to doe against many oppressours why is it unlawfull for us to do against one? Are our injuries lesse?[58]

Along with these biblical precedents, Sexby invokes the spirit of liberty in 'old Rome', with the pantheon of republican heroes as models for imitation: 'Our nation is not yet so barren of vertue, that we want noble examples to follow amongst ourselves.' The choice facing his fellow Englishmen, and in particular the soldiers who fought in the New Model Army, Sexby argues, is complicity with tyranny and injustice or active resistance:

> To us particularly it belongs to bring this Monster to justice, whom he hath made the instruments of his Villainy, and sharers in the Curse and Detestation that is due to himself from all good men. Others only have their Liberty to vindicate, we our Liberty and our honour . . . What the people at present endure, and posterity shall suffer, will all be laid at our doores . . . for onely we under God have the power to pull down this Dagon which we have set up.[59]

Rather than being presented as God's champion, like Milton's Samson, triumphing over his oppressors and their false deity, Cromwell is depicted here as the enemy of God, an idol to be shattered.

III

The *Second Defence*, like Marvell's *First Anniversary*, is in part an attempt to defend Cromwell, newly installed as Lord Protector, against charges that he is yet another tyrant. In this Latin tract, Milton's primary object is to refute the 'slanderous accusations' in the royalist *Cry of the Royal Blood to Heaven*, where Cromwell is maligned as boasting of his desire 'to overthrow all monarchies, to destroy all kings', and as relying on 'trickery and deceit'. As Laura Knoppers has observed, the extended passage in praise of Cromwell as leader of the New Model Army 'can be seen as responding to attacks on Cromwell by stressing above all his piety'.[60] In presenting the New Model Army as 'obedient to his command in all things', a body of soldiers motivated not by the licentiousness typical of the military but by 'the code of Christian virtue', inspired by the example of a commander 'well-versed in self-knowledge' and discipline, Milton by implication refutes arguments by Levellers that sought to present the interests of proud and ambitious 'grandees' and common soldiers as irreconcilably opposed. In the *Second Defence*, Milton praises Cromwell in republican terms as 'the liberator of your country, the author of liberty, and likewise its guardian and savior'.[61]

It has often been argued that Milton turned against Cromwell and the Protectorate regime during the 1650s and that the apparent praise of Cromwell in the *Second Defence* is in fact 'coded criticism'. When Milton characterizes the restored Rump Parliament in 1659 as 'the authors and best patrons of religious and civil libertie, that ever these Ilands brought forth' and speaks of 'a short but scandalous night of interruption' to the cause of liberty, according to this view, he is retrospectively repudiating 'the whole of the Protectorate'.[62] 'Troubled by Cromwell's elevation', Blair Worden claims, Milton saw the establishment of the Protectorate as a 'failure . . . calamitous to the cause which both the poet and the hero had served'.[63]

The view that the *Second Defence* represented 'opposition from within' and even gives 'veiled expression to the hatred and mistrust which Cromwell inspired so widely' has been contested by Robert Fallon, Paul Stevens, and others.[64] There is no doubt that Milton's commitment to radical republicanism, the conviction that 'a free Commonwealth without single person or house of lords, is by far the best government, if it can be had', is as clear in the preface to *Hirelings* (1659) as it is in *The Readie and Easie Way*, published a year later. The preface to *Hirelings* presents the restoration of the Rump Parliament in 1659, after the brief reign of Richard Cromwell, as instrumental in the great task of delivering the English people 'from the slavish dejection, wherin from father to son we were bred up and taught'.[65] But, as Fallon and Corns have argued, 'a short but scandalous night of interruption' is an odd phrase to describe the six years of the Protectorate, and could equally well refer to the period of anarchy before the return of the Rump, in the two weeks between the forcible dissolution of Richard Cromwell's Parliament and 'the restoration of regular government'. *Hirelings*, along with Milton's other republican pamphlets of 1659–60, suggests the continuity of the non-monarchical commonwealth, in one form or another, throughout the period of the English Revolution, as 'a stable, abiding entity embodied in a series of manifestations'.[66] When Milton uses the word 'interruption' in *The Readie and Easie Way*, 'those unhappie interruptions, which God hath remov'd' and 'the frequent disturbances, interruptions and dissolutions which the Parliament hath had' refer to the naked rule of the sword in such actions as Lambert's dissolution of the Rump in 1659, in a period when there was no settled government, rather than to the entire period of the Protectorate.[67] If by 'a new dawning of Gods miraculous providence', the 'care and tuition' of liberty are in May 1659 'revolvd' upon the 'shoulders' of the Rump Parliament, this does not mean that during the previous ten years other bodies and other individuals could not have been chosen 'by the power of God' to fulfil that role.[68]

Milton treats the Rump Parliament in a much less positive way in the *Second Defence*. There, as he does in the 'Digression' in the *History of Britain*, he presents it as ineffective, faction-ridden, dominated by the power of the few, inattentive to the public welfare:

> When you saw delays being contrived and every man more attentive to his private interest than to that of the state, when you saw the people complaining that they had been deluded of their hopes and circumvented by the power of the few, you put an end to the domination of these few men, since they, although so often warned, had refused to do so.[69]

This is essentially the way in which the Rump Parliament is characterized in Nedham's *True State of the Case of the Commonwealth:* as interested only in perpetuating its own power, exemplifying a tyranny of the few, 'corrupted' by the exercise of 'an unaccountable condition of Authority'.

> But when after the intercurrence of divers years, all our hopes were blasted, in regard particular Members became studious of Parties and private Interests, neglecting the publick . . . a visible designe carried on by some among them, to have perpetuated the Power in their own Hands . . . and were like in a short time to overwhelm the ancient Liberties and Properties of the People.[70]

Cromwell was thus, according to Milton and Nedham, entirely justified in dissolving the Rump, and the dissolution of the Nominated Parliament which followed shortly afterwards was no less inevitable, after that body had disappointed 'the hopes conceived, and expectations raised' when it met. Milton's account of the Nominated Parliament is brief, where Nedham treats its failings more extensively, criticizing those members of parliament whose 'principles led them to a pulling down all, and establishing nothing', led by 'a new Fury of Persecution' and 'fastening a mark of Antichristianism upon every thing they liked not'.[71] According to Milton:

> Another Parliament was convened anew . . . The elected members came together. They did nothing. When they in turn had at length exhausted themselves with disputes and quarrels, most of them considering themselves inadequate and unfit for executing such great tasks, they of their own accord dissolved the Parliament.[72]

In the *Second Defence*, Milton argues that the establishment of the Protectorate under Cromwell had not betrayed the principles of the revolution, that the exercise of power by those most worthy to rule is compatible with, even necessary for, the preservation of liberty. Cromwell is presented as 'defender of liberty' and 'pillar and support of English interests', using his power to 'restore to us our liberty, unharmed and even enhanced'.

> Cromwell, we are deserted! You alone remain. On you has fallen the whole burden of our affairs. On you alone they depend. In unison we acknowledge your unexcelled virtue. No one protests save such as seek equal honours, though inferior themselves, or begrudge the honors assigned to one more worthy, or do not understand that there is nothing in human society more pleasing to God, or more agreeable to reason, nothing in the state more just, nothing more expedient, than the rule of the man most fit to rule. All know you to be that man, Cromwell![73]

Milton's polemical strategy here is similar to that in the opening lines of Waller's *Panegyrick to My Lord Protector* (1655), though Waller's primary audience is former royalists rather than those who fought against the king. Any opposition to the Cromwellian Protectorate is occluded, dismissed as selfish factionalism, jealousy, the narrow perspective of unreasoning 'partial Spirits':

> While with a strong, and yet a gentle Hand
> You bridle Faction, and our Hearts command;
> Protect us from our Selves, and from the Foe,
> Make us Unite, and make us Conquer too;
> Let partial Spirits still aloud complain,
> Think themselves injur'd that they cannot Raign,
> And own no Liberty, but where they may
> Without controule upon their Fellows prey.[74]

Milton not only denigrates anti-Cromwellian sentiment as unworthy and disorderly 'faction', he pretends it does not exist, as 'all' acknowledge 'in unison' Cromwell's fitness to rule, as Cromwell is 'greeted by the spontaneous and heartfelt cries of all upright men' (*CPW*, IV.i.671–2).

In a passage directed at his fellow republicans, Milton goes on to defend Cromwell against the charge that the Protectorate is monarchy under another name. Like Marvell in *The First Anniversary*, Milton presents Cromwell as scorning 'the haughty titles which seem so great in the opinion of the mob'. Both authors are dismissive of the 'false renown' of 'useless', inactive kings, who 'only are against their subjects strong'.[75] Cromwell is described in both works as one who by his accomplishments has 'outstripped . . . the achievements of our kings': since titles are essentially meaningless, 'your deeds recognize no other name as worthy of you'.

> For to be Cromwell was a greater thing,
> Than ought below, or yet above a king:
> Therefore thou rather didst thyself depress,
> Yielding to rule, because it made thee less . . .
> Abroad a king, he seems, and something more,
> At home a subject on the equal floor.[76]

Like Marvell in *The First Anniversary*, Milton sees the conferment of titles and public honours as limiting or bounding public figures, allowing the victorious Cromwell, 'the greatest and most illustrious citizen, the director of public counsels, the commander of the bravest armies', to descend from the heights of heroism to the workaday concerns of ordinary political life, in the interest of 'the public good' (*CPW*, IV.i.672).

In the *Second Defence*, Milton defends the Protectorate government by arguing, as Nedham does in *The True State of the Case of the Commonwealth*, that 'though the Commonwealth may appear with a new face in the outward Form, yet it remains still the same in Substance'.[77] Cromwell's refusal to assume the title of king is presented in the *Second Defence* as a commitment on his part to republican principles.

> The name of king you spurned from your far greater eminence, and rightly so. For if, when you became so great a figure, you were captivated by the title which as a private citizen you were able to send under the yoke and reduce to nothing, you would be doing almost the same thing as if, when you had subjugated some tribe of idolaters with the help of the true God, you were to worship the gods that you had conquered. (*CPW*, IV.i.672)

The equation of monarchy with idolatry in the passage resembles a number of passages in *The Readie and Easie Way*, *Paradise Lost*, and elsewhere, in which the 'yoke' of bondage is contrasted with the strenuous pursuit of freedom. In most of these passages, the resumption of the idol of monarchy is associated with a 'multitude' characterized as 'abject and ignoble . . . spiritless and weak', rather than with ambitious men seeking power.[78] It is wrong to see the passage on Cromwell's spurning the title of king as a coded attack on him, accusing him of harbouring monarchical ambitions. As panegyric traditionally does, it offers counsel, praising the person addressed for doing what the panegyrist would like him to do, reminding him of the responsibilities with which he is entrusted. Cromwell's situation, as Milton presents him here, is closely akin to that delineated in Marvell's 'Horatian Ode' four years earlier: 'Nor yet grown stiffer with command, / But still in the Republic's hand' (81–2).

The paragraph that follows emphasizes the 'high hopes' and 'great confidence' placed in Cromwell as guardian of the liberties of the English nation. When Milton says that these hopes rest in Cromwell 'alone' – 'that which she once sought from the most distinguished men of the entire nation, she now seeks from you alone and through you alone hopes to achieve' (*CPW*, IV.i.673) – he is not in any way endorsing rule by a 'single person', but emphasizing the heavy weight of responsibility on Cromwell, after the failure of the Rump and the Nominated Parliament. Any power invested in Cromwell under the Protectorate government, Milton clearly indicates, is a trust, 'entrusted' to his 'care' (*CPW*, IV.i.673). A series of imperative verbs brings out the choice facing Cromwell and the English nation, appealing to honour as against shame, patriotic feelings and solidarity among those who fought side by side in the New Model Army as contrasted with divisiveness, self-seeking, and the extinction of 'our liberty, so bravely won'. By presenting alternative scenarios, Milton seeks to encourage one possible course of action, while warning against the other.

> Honor the great confidence reposed in you, honor your country's singular hope in you. Honor the faces and wounds of the many brave men, all those who under your leadership have striven so vigorously for liberty. Honor the shades of those who have fallen in that very struggle. Honor too what foreign nations think and say of us, the high hopes which they have for themselves as a result of our liberty, so bravely won, and our republic, so gloriously born. If the republic should miscarry, so to speak, and as quickly vanish, surely no greater shame and disgrace could befall this country. (*CPW*, IV.i.673)

In addressing Cromwell, and later in addressing his 'fellow countrymen' (*CPW*, IV.i.680), Milton presents the defence of liberty as beset with uncertainties. The spectre of Cromwell the tyrant looms over the powerful admonitory address to the Lord Protector. Cromwell, as presented, has the potential for becoming the patron of liberty or its destroyer. As David Loewenstein has pointed out, this passage 'directly confronts the . . . precarious political realities threatening the new state': 'even as he passionately celebrates the new regime, he anxiously envisions its potential demise'.[79] Milton appeals here to republican principles, warning Cromwell that a ruler who violates the liberties of his subjects becomes a slave to an 'inward vitious rule' within himself (*CPW*, III.190). Towards the end of the passage he associates the cause of liberty not only with 'virtue' but with 'religious faith', equating the loss of liberty with the 'first wound', the Fall of Man.

> For if the very patron and tutelary god of liberty, as it were, if that man than whom no one has been considered more just, more holy, more excellent, shall afterwards attack that liberty which he himself has defended, such an act must necessarily be dangerous and well-nigh fatal not only to liberty itself but also to the cause of all virtue and piety. Honor itself, virtue itself will seem to have melted away, religious faith will be circumscribed, reputation will hereafter be a meagre thing. A deeper wound than this, after that first wound, can never be inflicted on the human race. (*CPW*, IV.i.673)

Milton presents the burden of responsibility on Cromwell as a severe 'test'. After projecting two rival scenarios for the future of the English nation, under freedom or under tyranny, Milton indicates the possible scope of the victories of peace, which, according to the sonnet addressed to Cromwell two years earlier, are 'no less renownd than warr'.[80] Cromwell is being challenged 'to live up to his professed ideals', depicted as facing 'arduous tasks' which can confirm or disprove his heroic status, fulfil or disappoint the hope that he has 'been raised by the power of God beyond all other men to this most exalted rank' and that he can remain immune to the temptations of power.[81]

In a powerful peroration, similar in many ways to the closing pages of *The Readie and Easie Way*, Milton warns his 'fellow countrymen' of the possibility that they may be 'unworthy of liberty':

> Many men has war made great whom peace makes small. If, having done with war, you neglect the arts of peace, if warfare is your peace and liberty, war your only virtue, your supreme glory, you will find, believe me, that peace itself is your greatest enemy. Peace itself will be by far your hardest war, and what you thought liberty will prove to be your servitude. (*CPW*, IV.i.680, 683)

Freedom and slavery are redefined in moral terms, with a battlefield within the individual. Once again the emphasis is on self-knowledge and the love of virtue. Surrender to the tyrant within, 'inordinate desires / And upstart Passions', which usurp 'the Government' from 'free Reason', will ultimately lead to the surrender of 'outward freedom' (*PL*, XII.86–96). 'Unless you expel avarice, ambition, and luxury from your minds, yes, and extravagance from your families as well, you will find at home and within that tyrant who, you believed, was to be sought abroad and in the field – now even more stubborn.'[82] As he does consistently, Milton contrasts licence, 'which never hath more scope or more indulgence then under Tyrants', with the self-regulating liberty of those recognizing the need to be 'govern'd by reason': 'For indeed none can love freedom heartilie, but good men' (*Tenure*, *CPW*, III.190). Licence, Milton consistently argues, is the province of beasts 'that bawl for freedom in their senseless mood', unaware that 'truth would set them free'.

> However loudly they shout and boast about liberty, slaves they are at home and abroad, although they know it not. When at last they do perceive it and like wild horses fretting at the bit try to shake off the yoke, driven not by the love of true liberty (to which the good man alone can rightly aspire), but by pride and base desires, even though they take arms in repeated attempts, they will accomplish naught. They can perhaps change their servitude; they cannot cast it off.[83]

Like Nedham in *The Excellencie of a Free-State*, Milton cites 'the ancient Romans, once they had been corrupted and dissipated by luxury', as an instance of those who had proved themselves 'unworthy of liberty' (*Second Defence*, *CPW*, IV.i.683). The 'Digression' to *The History of Britain* similarly finds a lesson in Roman history: 'that libertie sought out of season in a corrupt and degenerate age brought Rome it self into further slaverie'. In the *Second Defence* as in *Samson Agonistes*, Milton couples ingratitude 'to their very liberators', those 'Whom God hath of his special favour rais'd / As their Deliverer', with 'Nations grown corrupt' and justly punished for 'thir vices' with 'servitude'.[84] Unlike such radicals as Rainborough and Wildman, who argued for an extended franchise in the Putney debates, on the grounds that 'every person in England has as clear a right to elect his representatives as the greatest person in England', thus giving 'his own free consent' to the laws by which he is governed, Milton does not identify liberty with the right to vote.[85] Men who are 'easily corrupted', he says bitterly, will elect representatives who replicate their own moral failings.

For why should anyone then claim for you freedom to vote or the power of sending to Parliament whomever you prefer? So that each of you could elect in the cities men of his own faction, or in the country towns choose that man, however unworthy, who has entertained you more lavishly at banquets and supplied farmers and peasants with more abundant drink? . . . Or how could they suddenly become legislators for the whole nation who themselves have never known what law is, what reason, what right or justice, straight or crooked, licit or illicit; who think that all power resides in violence, all grandeur in pride and arrogance?[86]

In redefining liberty in terms of moral probity, here and in *The Readie and Easie Way*, Milton comes close to denying liberty, or justifying the abrogation of rights, for those who fail to measure up to his high standards. The problem, as stated in *A Needful Corrective or Ballance in Popular Government* (1659), by the republican Sir Henry Vane, is 'To shew how that depraved, corrupted, and self-interested will of man, in the great Body, which we call the People, being once left to its own free motion, shall be prevailed with to espouse their true publick interest.'[87] Several passages in *The Readie and Easie Way* show how reluctant Milton was to allow the body of the populace 'its own free motion': the proposal for a permanent senate, whose members hold office for life, and, notoriously, the argument for the right of a virtuous minority to compel the unregenerate multitude if that 'greater number' chose to revert to kingship: 'More just it is doubtless, if it com to force, that a less number compell a greater to retain, which can be no wrong to them, thir libertie, then that a greater number for the pleasure of thir baseness, compell a less most injuriously to be thir fellow slaves.'[88] Vane, like Milton, writing at this time, favoured a severely limited franchise, with the privileges of freedom extended only to a minority of those who had proved to be worthy: where Levellers like Overton and Lilburne considered all Englishmen to be 'free-born', here the term is applied only to the virtuous few.

That in the time of the Common-wealths constituting, and in a Nation much divided in affection and interest . . . none be admitted to the exercise of the right and privilege of a free Citizen, for a season, but either such as are free born, in respect of their holy and righteous principles, flowing from the birth of the Spirit of God in them . . . or else who, by their tryed good affection and faithfulness to common rights and publick freedome, have deserved to be trusted with the keeping or bearing their owne Armes in the publick defence. (Vane, *A Needful Corrective*, pp.7–8)

In the *Second Defence*, as in Michael's stern admonition to Adam in *Paradise Lost*, Book XII, the loss of 'outward freedom' in 'a nation which cannot rule and govern itself' is seen as the 'Judgement just' of God on those nations which 'decline so low / From vertue, which is reason'. Tyrants will always be found who 'will perch on your back and shoulders as if on beasts of burden, who will sell you at public auction, though you be victors in the war'.

> Just as to be free is precisely the same as to be pious, wise, just, and temperate, careful of one's property, aloof from another's, and thus finally to be magnanimous and brave, so to be the opposite of these qualities is the same as to be a slave. And by the customary judgment and, so to speak, just retaliation of God, it happens that a nation which cannot rule and govern itself, but has delivered itself into slavery to its own lusts, is enslaved also to other masters whom it does not choose, and serves not only voluntarily but also against its will.[89]

Passages of this kind can be read in two ways: as theodicy, explaining and justifying the ways of God in punishing transgressors and leaving sinful men and nations 'to thir own polluted ways', or as an exhortation to a people not yet hardened in sin and blinded by folly 'to obey right reason, to master yourselves', exercising their free will 'to ordain wisely as in this world of evill, in the midd'st whereof God hath plac't us unavoidably'.[90] Milton's aim in the address to his 'fellow countrymen', as in *The Readie and Easie Way*, is 'to forewarne my countrey in time':

> For, my fellow countrymen, your own character is a mighty factor in the acquisition or retention of liberty. Unless your liberty is such as can neither be won nor lost by arms, but is of that kind alone which, sprung from piety, justice, temperance, in short, true virtue, has put down the deepest and most far-reaching roots in your souls, there will not be lacking one who will shortly wrench from you, even without weapons, that liberty which you boast of having sought by force of arms.[91]

'Conquerors' and 'conquered', Marvell suggests in an attack on the institution of monarchy in *The First Anniversary*, are alike victims, seen by actual and potential tyrants as cannon fodder, potential rivals who must be crushed:

> Their other wars seem but a feigned contest,
> This common enemy is still opprest;
> If conquerors, on them they turn their might;
> If conquered, on them they wreak their spite.
> (29–32)

In his writings of this period, Milton shares with Marvell and Harrington the conviction that the 'warfare of peace' is 'far more noble than the gory victories of war': 'Unless you be victors here as well, that enemy and tyrant whom you have just now defeated in the field has either not been conquered at all or has been conquered in vain' (*CPW*, IV.i.81).

6

Monarchy and Servitude
The Politics of Paradise Lost

I

One thing that has puzzled and embarrassed critics of Milton, giving rise to any number of different explanations, is that Satan, the father of lies, God's adversary, is again and again given speeches closely resembling Milton's own earlier attacks on monarchy and defences of liberty. This has been interpreted as a disavowal or abandonment of Milton's earlier activist republicanism. C. S. Lewis sees in Satan only 'lies and propaganda', a 'monomaniac concern with himself and his supposed rights': to Lewis, Satan's 'talk about liberty' is a mere pretence.[1] Stanley Fish finds in the appeal of Satan in Books I and II a reminder of the reader's own fallen nature, educating the reader by tricking him into an erroneous response, in a dialectic 'involving the respondent in his own edification'. Both see Satan's rhetoric as corrupt and seductive, and any resemblance to Milton's own republican views as specious or misleading.[2] In contrast, the Romantic Satanists, their heir William Empson and such late twentieth-century historicist critics as Christopher Hill and David Norbrook argue for a fundamental consistency in Milton's political views before and after 1660. In their different ways, writing under different circumstances, Blake, Empson and Norbrook all interpret resemblances between the Satanic rhetoric of republicanism and Milton's own political principles as revelatory and as problematical, in the way they expose irreconcilable conflicts in the ideology of republicanism or in the theology underpinning *Paradise Lost*.[3]

As critics of all schools concede, the vocabulary and rhetoric of Satan and his followers frequently echo Milton's own in works written before 1660. In speeches by Satan, Beelzebub, and Mammon in Books I, II, V, and VI, the monarch of Heaven is a tyrant, to whom 'submission' is base, 'abject', and shameful, a form of 'servility' or 'bondage'. This is the characteristic language of the Good Old Cause, the defiant republicanism of

The Readie and Easie Way.[4] There is a degree of irony or ambivalence in all these passages, since Satan and the other fallen angels make no distinction between God and any other monarch. Readers of the poem know, even before Satan's stirring words, that God never for a moment doubted his empire, shaking in terror at the power of his adversary.

Mammon's speech in Book II treats the 'servile offerings' of 'Subjection' as painfully humiliating, the forced 'worship paid / To whom we hate' (*PL*, II.239, 247–9). His attack on 'vassalage' is consistently republican in its language and assumptions, including the idea, characteristic of the thought of classical republicanism, that the liberty and property of the individual can never be dependent upon the 'leave' or permission of those in power.[5]

> Let us not then pursue
> By force impossible, by leave obtain'd
> Unacceptable, though in Heav'n, our state
> Of splendid vassalage, but rather seek
> Our own good from our selves, and from our own
> Live to our selves, though in this vast recess,
> Free, and to none accountable, preferring
> Hard liberty before the easie yoke
> Of servile Pomp.
>
> (*PL*, II.249–57)

Passages like this not only echo the attacks on the 'carnal admiring of . . . worldly pomp and greatness' in *Tenure* and *The Readie and Easie Way*, but also contrast the 'ease' of comfortable 'bondage' with 'strenuous liberty' in exactly the way Milton does in both *Samson Agonistes* and *The Readie and Easie Way.*[6]

If, as John Toland argued in 1698, Milton's aim in *Paradise Lost* was 'to display the different Effects of Liberty and Tyranny', then both terms are problematical, with shifting, unstable meanings. Liberty and service mean different things to Satan and to Abdiel in their confrontation in Book v.[7] Satan's call to 'cast off this Yoke', refusing to pay 'knee-tribute . . . prostration vile', not only praises freedom and equality as aims to pursue, but also makes the familiar Miltonic point that liberty is compatible with 'Orders and Degrees' (*PL*, v.782, 786, 792–3).

Abdiel's answer to Satan has sometimes, mistakenly, been described as royalist in its assumptions.[8] Against Satan's claim that no one has the right to 'assume / Monarchie' over 'his equals' (*PL*, v.794–6) – more or less what Milton argued in *The Readie and Easie Way* and elsewhere – Abdiel argues that 'the just Decree of God' awarding 'Regal Scepter' to his Son may not be challenged (*PL*, v.814–16). Implicit in these lines, and fully explicit in the Nimrod passage in Book xii, is a clear distinction between 'the Throne and Monarchy of God' (*PL*, i.42) and earthly monarchy, a product of the fallen world and the 'tyrannous' pretensions of whose who, in 'despite of Heav'n', falsely claim divine right to justify their rule (*PL*, xii.32, 34–5). Milton makes this distinction between the kings of the earth and God again and again in his prose tracts, as does Lilburne in *Regall Tyranny Discovered:* 'This office of a King, is not in the least of Gods institution: Neither is it to be given to any man upon earth. Because none must rule by his will but God alone.'[9] Such a distinction is central to the Nimrod episode in *Paradise Lost*, in which Adam expresses horror at the pretensions of anyone who, like Nimrod, seeks to 'arrogate Dominion undeserv'd / Over his brethren':

> O execrable Son so to aspire
> Above his Brethren, to himself assuming
> Authoritie usurpt, from God not giv'n . . .
> Man over men
> He made not Lord; such title to himself
> Reserving, human left from human free.
> (*PL*, xii.27–8, 64–71)

Milton consistently attacked the doctrine 'that all Kings are the Lords Anointed' and rejected as absurd the pretensions of monarchs that they exercise power as 'immediat Vicegerent' of God.[10]

Abdiel's second answer to Satan in Book vi takes up Satan's claim that 'servilitie' or the desire to 'serve' is incompatible with 'freedom' (*PL*, vi.166, 169), by contrasting it with willing service and the rule of the 'worthiest'.[11] Servitude, Milton suggests here, is enthralling oneself. A consequence of the gift of free will, God announces in Book iii, is the possibility of entering into bondage to an unworthy master, surrendering one's freedom: 'I formd them free, and free they must remain, / Till they enthrall themselves' (*PL*, iii.124–5). As Abdiel tells Satan, defining freedom and servitude in similar terms:

> Unjustly thou deprav'st it with the name
> Of *Servitude*, to serve whom God ordains,
> Or Nature; God and Nature bid the same,
> When he who rules is worthiest, and excells
> Those whom he governs. This is servitude,
> To serve th'unwise, or him who hath rebelld
> Against his worthier, as thine now serve thee,
> Thyself not free, but to thyself enthrall'd.
> (*PL*, vi.174–81)

The authorial comments on Abdiel's 'constant mind' that end Book v – 'Among the faithless, faithful only hee; / Among innumerable false, unmov'd' (*PL*, v.896–907) – indicate that Milton saw Abdiel as the winner of this debate. Here and again at the beginning of Book vi, Abdiel is praised in terms that present him as a model for conduct: this is how one should behave, Milton suggests, in difficult conditions 'on evil dayes, though fall'n', and evil tongues' (*PL*, vii.26), surrounded by enemies. In the Restoration context of the poem, as Achinstein points out, Abdiel's courageous stance, 'unshak'n' in 'his Loyaltie . . . his Zeale' to the God he serves (*PL*, v.899–900), is akin to that of Dissenters, suffering persecution for their religious beliefs.[12]

A number of critics dismiss any similarities between Milton's writings before 1660 and the speeches of Satan and his followers by characterizing Satan as a tyrant. Thus, to C. S. Lewis, 'all Milton's hatred of tyranny is expressed in the poem, but the tyrant held up to our execrations is not God. It is Satan . . . He is the Machiavellian prince who excuses his "political realism" by "necessity, the tyrant's plea".'[13] A similar line is argued by Stevie Davies in *Images of Kingship in Paradise Lost* (1983) and by Joan Bennett in *Reviving Liberty* (1989). Citing such passages as the opening lines of Book ii ('High on a Throne of Royal State . . . '), and other references in *Paradise Lost* to 'Kings barbaric', Turkish despotism, and 'tawdry magnificence', Davies sees Satan as the archetype for all earthly monarchs and usurpers.[14] Like Lewis and Davies, Bennett finds in Milton a clear, unproblematical distinction between just kings and tyrants and between divine and Satanic kingship. To Bennett, Charles I was 'the tyrant with whose ways Milton was most familiar', and she seeks to demonstrate 'the fundamental similarity between Charles and Satan', drawing parallels between such pamphlets as *Eikonoklastes* and the portrayal of the 'false heroism' of Satan.[15] Robert Fallon, relying heavily on passages where Milton praises a 'just King' while attacking a 'Tyrant' as the 'common enemie' of mankind, goes so far as to claim that Milton 'has no quarrel with kings' in general, but only criticizes the house of Stuart.[16]

Historicist critics such as Hill, Norbrook and Worden take a different line. They argue that Milton never abandoned his republican principles, but that, in his presentation of Satan and his followers, Milton is commenting indirectly on the failure of the English Revolution. According to Hill, 'the character of Satan alludes to some of the ways in which the Good Old Cause had gone wrong . . . The Revolution had utterly failed . . . because the men were not great enough for the Cause'.[17] Though Hill does not identify Satan with Cromwell in the way that Bennett and

Davies identified Satan with Charles I, he sees parallels in the 'presumptuous aspiration . . . pride and arrogance . . . against which Milton and other radicals had warned Oliver Cromwell and his generals' (p. 368). Norbrook carries the comparison further, likening Milton's Satan to Cromwell and to the Caesar of Lucan's *Pharsalia*, as a charismatic yet dangerous political leader. To Norbrook, Satan illustrates 'how republican ideals can become corrupted by personal ambition': in Satan's speeches, the 'language of liberty is being exploited' in a bid to 'magnify his personal power; but that does not in itself invalidate the language'.[18] Norbrook characterizes Satan's language as oscillating 'between republican and monarchical discourse' and sees this as illustrative of Milton's ambivalence towards the quasi-monarchical aspects of the Cromwellian Protectorate (p. 454).

To Worden, the identification of Satan with Cromwell is complete. In a series of influential essays and in *Literature and Politics in Cromwellian England*, Worden constructs a narrative of Milton's growing disillusionment with Cromwell, coming to see him as a hypocrite, a would-be tyrant. According to Worden, Milton began to turn against Cromwell as early as 1653, never fully gave allegiance to the Protectorate, and in the course of the 1650s 'the suspicions would turn to anger and revulsion'. Passages in praise of Cromwell in the *Second Defence* are read as coded attacks on 'the violator of liberty'. Cromwell, in this view, 'sacrificed the revolution on the altar of his own ambition', becoming to Milton not simply 'a flawed hero, but a villain'.[19] To Worden, Satan's use of republican discourse is 'a false application of political vocabulary', an intellectually dishonest attempt at 'applying virtuous principles to vicious ends'.[20] There is little room for ambivalence in Worden's treatment of the Satanic Cromwell or the Cromwellian Satan.

In contrast to all these critics, Blake, Shelley and, over a century later, William Empson do not recognize any break separating the earlier from the later Milton. What is most radical in the approach of Blake, Shelley and Empson is their attempt to overturn the widely accepted distinction between the Judaeo-Christian God and any earthly tyrant. Shelley, who lists Satan's 'faults' and the 'wrongs' he has suffered, as on a balance sheet, argues in *A Defence of Poetry* that 'Milton has so far violated the popular creed (if this shall be judged to be a violation) as to have alleged no superiority of moral virtue to his God over his Devil'.[21] What is at issue here is not simply whether certain characteristics of Milton's Satan might attract the reader's (or, as Blake argues, the author's) sympathies: Shelley in this passage is directly challenging the ideology underlying the poem.

Empson makes a similar point in arguing that the God of *Paradise Lost* and Christian tradition is 'a wicked God'. According to Shelley:

> Milton's Devil as a moral being is as far superior to his God as one who perseveres in some purpose which he has conceived to be excellent in spite of adversity and torture, is to one who in the cold security of undoubted triumph inflicts the most horrible revenge upon his enemies . . . with the alleged design of exasperating him to deserve new torments.[22]

To Blake in *The Marriage of Heaven and Hell*, the traditional Christian God, the God who, in *Paradise Lost*, Book III, demands 'rigid satisfaction' to punish the 'Treason' of those who defy him (*PL*, III.207–12), is a deity created by man in his own craven image. Urizen is the name Blake gives to this jealous, constricting deity, the God of 'thou shalt not', in his prophetic books.[23] In conventional thought, according to Blake, 'Good is the passive that obeys Reason' and 'Evil is the active springing from Energy': 'Those who restrain desire, do so because theirs is weak enough to be restrained and the restrainer or reason usurps its place & governs the unwilling . . . The history of this is written in Paradise Lost.'[24] In *Paradise Lost*, Blake claims, Milton struggles to break free of this repressive theology – an alliance of 'God & his Priest & King' which, as Blake says in the bitter irony of 'The Chimney Sweeper', colludes in justifying inequality and 'misery', turning the earth into a prison and clothing its inhabitants with 'the clothes of death'. As a 'true Poet', 'at liberty' when writing 'Of Devils & Hell', Milton was 'of the Devil's party without knowing it'. The questions Satan raises throughout the poem cannot be easily answered: as Neil Forsyth says, 'the unpleasant God of the Old Testament in Milton's reconstruction, makes Satan's rebellion against him thoroughly understandable'.[25]

Empson, writing in 1961, endorses the view of Blake and Shelley that the God of Christian tradition was a tyrant – a 'mean-minded', spiteful autocrat, a deity 'peculiarly unfitted to inspire trust'. Empson is particularly horrified by the idea that God sent Raphael to Adam and Eve to 'render man inexcusable', in full knowledge that they would fail the test he set for them.[26] Though he comments on how Satan's attacks on monarchy express sentiments 'identical with that of such persons as Milton who had dared to deny that Charles I had Divine Right' (p. 46), his emphasis is less on Satan's rebellion than on the fall and punishment of Adam and Eve. In his view, Eve's arguments in the separation scene and in the temptation scene, despite the customary denigration of Eve by 'pious critics', show her to be a rational being, a free agent.[27]

One passage frequently cited by twentieth-century critics as 'packed with Milton's libertarian fervor' is Eve's defence of her ability to resist temptation in the separation scene in Book IX, with its echo of the 'doctrines of freedom reminiscent of *Areopagitica*':

> If this be our condition, thus to dwell
> In narrow circuit strait'nd by a Foe,
> Suttle or violent, we not endu'd
> Single with like defence, wherever met,
> How are we happie, still in fear of harm?
> (*PL*, IX.322–6)[28]

These are precisely the arguments that Milton advanced in *Areopagitica* to justify the providence of a God who 'gives us minds that can wander beyond all limit and satiety', exposing men and women to temptation, rather than locking them up as in a hermitage, in 'the forcible hindrance of evill-doing'.[29] Eve continues:

> And what is Faith, Love, Vertue unassaid
> Alone, without exterior help sustaind?
> Let us then not suspect our happy State
> Left so imperfet by the Maker wise,
> As not secure to single or combin'd.
> (*PL*, IX.335–9)

Not only is the idea that virtue must be tested in the field of the world, without the aid of 'exterior help', central to *Areopagitica*, as well as such poems as the Ludlow Masque and *Paradise Regained*, it is also, in a different context, at the heart of the theodicy in Book III, in God's speech describing Adam and Eve as 'sufficient to have stood, though free to fall':

> Not free, what proof could they have givn sincere
> Of true obedience, constant Faith or Love,
> Where onely what they needs must do, appeard,
> Not what they would? what praise could they receive?
> What pleasure I from such obedience paid?,
> (*PL*, III.103–7)

Milton scholars commenting on the separation scene are often uncomfortable with Eve's arguments, labelling her as 'wrong' and saying that she should have recognized her proper subordinate position. Even Tillyard, generally sympathetic to Eve, speaks of Adam's 'real intellectual superiority', while Dennis Burden, confident that 'the liberty which Eve claims is not that liberty which her female nature was created to have', says 'these arguments do not apply to Eve's case'. Fowler, in his note on 'Eve's dangerous individualism', similarly handles the passage with kid gloves: 'We should not assume that because in *Areopagitica* M. rejects "cloistered virtue" he therefore approves Eve's sentiments here, in the very different context of an unfallen world.'[30] To these critics, Adam, in his speech beginning 'O Woman, best are all things as the will / Of God ordain'd them', is plainly in the right, refuting Eve's arguments and acting, as he should, as her wise instructor.

> Seek not temptation then, which to avoid
> Were better, and most likelie if from mee
> Thou sever not: Trial will come unsought.
> Wouldst thou approve thy constancie, approve
> First thy obedience.
>
> (*PL*, IX.343–4, 364–8)

Yet this is not an episode like the confrontation of Satan and Abdiel, an exchange of arguments with a clear winner. As Diane McColley says, 'they are both right' in a colloquy where both, as rational beings, explore the nature of freedom in a world where, even before the fall, good and evil, 'two twins cleaving together', are 'intermixt', with the differences between them 'hardly to be discern'd' (*Areopagitica*, *CPW*, II.514). Eve's arguments in the separation scene, like those of Adam, can be considered 'Milton's argument for Christian liberty', as advanced in *Areopagitica* and other pamphlets, 'translated into prelapsarian terms'.[31]

Adam's parting words to Eve, consenting to their working separately in spite of any danger they might face, have often been judged severely by critics as 'misguided lenience', weakness, a failure to exercise his proper authority over her.[32] But his words and actions here are entirely in keeping with Milton's Arminian doctrine of free will. The unfettered conscience may fall into error, yet such errors are neither predetermined nor irremediable.

> Go; for thy stay, not free, absents thee more;
> Go in thy native innocence, relie
> On what thou hast of vertue, summon all,
> For God towards thee hath done his part, do thine.
>
> (*PL*, IX.372–5)[33]

What is at stake here is the unstable, problematical relationship between freedom and obedience, not easy to discern in the world 'in the midd'st whereof God hath plac't us unavoidably':

> If every action which is good, or evill in man at ripe years, were to be under pittance, and prescription, and compulsion, what were vertue but a name, what praise could be then due to well-doing, what grammercy to be sober, just or continent? (*Areopagitica*, *CPW*, II.526, 527)

Though Milton speaks here of 'man' and of God's 'suffering *Adam* to transgresse' as compatible with 'divin Providence', it is clear that for Milton the conviction that 'God left him free', allowing the opportunity for 'the triall of virtue, and the exercise of truth', is equally applicable to the postlapsarian and the prelapsarian state, and to Eve as well as Adam, women and men as rational beings (*CPW*, II.527–8). At no point does Milton urge unquestioning, mindless obedience to anyone who may be in a position of authority. 'A man may be a heretick in the truth; and if he beleeve things only because his Pastor sayes so, or the Assembly so determine, without knowing other reason, though his belief be true, yet the very truth he holds, becomes his heresie.'[34]

In politics, both before and after 1660, for Milton and his political allies difficulties may arise from a perceived conflict between the sovereign conscience and the external constraints impinging upon it. Milton's position, like that of John Goodwin, Roger Williams, and Henry Robinson, was a radical one. 'Outward force', Milton maintained in *A Treatise of Civil Power* (1659), should have no power over the individual conscience: 'There can be no place then left for the magistrate or his force in the settlement of religion, by appointing either what we shall beleeve in divine things or practice in religious' (*CPW*, VII.255, 271). According to Roger Williams, writing in 1644, '*God* needeth not the helpe of a materiall *sword* of *steele* to assist the *sword* of the *Spirit* in the affaires of *conscience*.' 'God accepts only of willing service, such as we performe of our owne free election, not by compulsion', argued Robinson in *Liberty of Conscience* (1644).[35] Marvell, making a similar point with characteristic wit in the 1670s, contrasting 'Spiritual Armour' with 'Weapons of another Warfare', asked 'Why may they not, as well as force men to Church, cram the Holy Supper too down their Throats . . . and drive them into the Rivers by thousands to be baptized or drowned?'[36] In each of these passages, the particular issue is one of church discipline and the limits of civil power, the question of whether the civil magistrate can 'use force in matters of religion', but the general position being argued is consistent with Milton's treatment of freedom of conscience in *Areopagitica* and in the separation scene. As so often in Milton, the ethical, political, and religious dimensions are inseparable.

> Christ hath a government of his own, sufficient of it self to all his ends and purposes in governing his church; but much different from that of the civil magistrate; and the difference in this verie thing principally consists, that it governs not by outward force . . . First because it deals only with the inward man and his actions, which are all spiritual and to outward force

> not lyable: secondly to shew us the divine excellence of his spiritual kingdom, able without worldly force to subdue all the powers and kingdoms of this world, which are upheld by outward force only.[37]

After the Restoration, Milton lived under a civil magistrate he considered oppressive and illegitimate, and a central issue in *Paradise Lost* and in *Samson Agonistes* is how to conduct oneself under such conditions. Does God counsel obedience to an unjust authority, when one feels oneself to be surrounded by a 'people victor once, now vile and base, / Deservedly made vassal'?[38]

II

The political context most directly relevant to *Paradise Lost*, published in 1667, and *Samson Agonistes*, published in 1671, is Restoration England. This was a period of the persecution of Dissenters under the Clarendon Code and Five Mile Act of 1664–5, a period of 'the Prosperity of the Wicked, and the Adversity of the Godly', one of the recurrent moments in history when, as the Archangel Michael predicts to Adam, 'heavie persecution shall arise / On all who in the worship persevere / Of Spirit and Truth' (*PL*, xii.532–3).[39] When Milton speaks of himself in the invocation to *Paradise Lost*, Book vii as 'unchang'd . . . though fall'n on evil dayes . . . and evil tongues; / In darkness and with dangers compast round, / And solitude' (*PL*, vii.24–8), these dangers were real, a recent memory. After the Restoration, Milton was arrested and threatened with death, his books 'against the late King' were burnt by the common hangman, and many of his former associates, adherents of the Good Old Cause, were brutally executed.[40] The problem facing the postlapsarian Adam and Eve, as well as Samson, is how, 'under change of times' (*Samson Agonistes*, 695), they can retain and exercise their freedom, and not descend into servitude or sink into despair. Having chosen wrongly and been severely punished, what do they do next? In Book x, Adam and Eve face a choice between vain contention, each bitterly accusing the other ('Out of my sight, thou Serpent'), or seeking to find some 'remedie or cure / To evils which our own misdeeds have wrought'.

> But rise, let us no more contend, nor blame
> Each other, blam'd enough elsewhere, but strive
> In offices of Love, how we may light'n
> Each other's burden in our share of woe.
> (*PL*, x.867, 958–61, 1079–80)[41]

The political question implicit in Books X–XII of *Paradise Lost* is how to endure, how to maintain one's allegiance to 'Truth', exercising free choice in a hostile environment, and 'by things deemed weak / Subverting worldly strong' (*PL*, XII.567–9).

Throughout the poem, free choice is presented as problematical, hedged round by uncertainty. Though Eve could not have recognized the full implications of the parallel, the choice facing her in the temptation scene in Book IX is whether to follow Satan's example, replicating the Fall of the Angels in a second Fall. Milton's theology is explicit here, as God in Book III speaks of angels and men alike as 'sufficient to have stood, though free to fall': 'Such I created all th'Ethereal Powers / And Spirits, both them who stood and them who faild: / Freely they stood who stood, and fell who fell' (*PL*, III.99–102). In tempting Eve, Satan, as Serpent, cites his own apparent example, as 'ventring higher then my Lot', rising above his appointed station and defying 'the Threatner' without being punished (*PL*, IX.686–90). As in the earlier episode of Eve's dream, Satan holds forth to a receptive Eve the hope of transcending the limits surrounding her and, through newly attained Knowledge, unlocking a potential hitherto held in check.

> Happie though thou art,
> Happier thou mayst be, worthier canst not be:
> Taste this, and be thenceforth among the Gods
> Thyself a Goddess, not to Earth confind,
> But somtimes in the Air, as wee, somtimes
> Ascend to Heav'n, by merit thine, and see
> What life the Gods live there, and such live thou.
> (*PL*, V.75–81)

Adam's comment on the significance of the dream is sound enough, in terms of the conventional faculty psychology of Milton's day: 'mimic Fansie' unconstrained by 'watchful . . . Reason' can in dreams, 'misjoyning shapes', create monstrous visions, oddly resembling 'deeds long past or late' in the waking state, and yet these are not in themselves evil. 'Evil into the mind of God or Man / May come and go, so unapprov'd, and leave / No spot or blame behind' (*PL*, V.104–6, 110–34, 117–19). But rather than recognizing the dream as a warning, suggesting the need for increased vigilance, Adam sees it as encouraging, and shows no awareness that Eve might have found the dream of flight, with its 'high exaltation', attractive, as responding to her own potential desires, rather than as something emanating from an outside source, and easily cast off. 'That what in sleep thou didst abhor to dream, / Waking thou never wilt consent to do' (*PL*, V.90, 120–1).[42]

In the most powerful lines in his central speech of temptation in Book IX, Satan not only, as a skilled and wily orator, chooses arguments calculated to convince, breaking down Eve's feeble defences, but re-enacts his own rebellion and his arguments justifying it in Book I. God is a tyrant, one who, jealous of any possible rivals, demands worship from his cowed followers, whom he keeps in subjection, ruling by fear. We have seen similar arguments by Milton and his political allies in and around 1649 and again in 1659–60: tyrants, who seek to keep their subjects in darkness, obscuring the truth that might set them free, should be resisted.

> Why then was this forbid? Why but to awe,
> Why but to keep ye low and ignorant,
> His worshippers; he knows that in the day
> Ye eat thereof, your Eyes that seem so cleere,
> Yet are but dim, shall perfetly be then
> Op'nd and cleerd, and ye shall be as Gods,
> Knowing both Good and Evil as they know.
>
> (*PL*, IX.703–9)

Yet in these particular circumstances, the reader, forewarned, is aware that if Eve accepts these highly plausible arguments, she will become Satan's disciple, a trophy in his battle against God. As readers, we are in the privileged position of knowing Satan's plans for Adam and Eve, as laid out (with Satan's connivance) by Beelzebub in Book II:

> Possess
> All as our own, and drive as we were driven,
> The punie inhabitants, or if not drive,
> Seduce them to our Party, that thir God
> May prove thir foe, and with repenting hand
> Abolish his own works.
>
> (*PL*, II.365–70)

In Satan's soliloquy on Mount Niphates, a second possible scenario is shadowed forth, one in which, instead of Adam and Eve following the path taken before them by Satan, Satan might, exercising his free will, seek repentance, hoping to undo an earlier choice which has, contrary to his expectation, left him 'onely Supream / In miserie'.

> Other Powers as great
> Fell not, but stand unshak'n, from within
> Or from without, to all temptations arm'd.
> Hadst thou the same free Will and Power to stand?
> Thou hadst: whom then hast thou then or what to accuse,
> But Heav'ns free Love dealt equally to all?
>
> (PL, IV.63–8, 91–2)

We know that Satan will not repent, and, indeed, we are made aware from the outset that he is deluded in thinking that at any time or in any place he and the other fallen angels 'shall be free', since 'all-ruling Heaven' directs everything he does (*PL*, I.212, 258–9).[43] Whatever freedom of choice Satan and his followers may have possessed in their initial rebellion has been stripped from them as part of their punishment.

> Nor ever thence
> Had ris'n or heav'd his head, but that the will
> And high permission of all-ruling Heaven
> Left him at large to his own dark designs,
> That with reiterated crimes he might
> Heap on himself damnation, while he sought
> Evil to others.
> (*PL*, I.210–16)

Towards Satan, God is implacable: even hardened sinners are given the opportunity to repent before the gates of mercy are closed.

Milton did not share Origen's heretical view that Satan and other fallen angels, as rational creatures, could 'eventually find salvation and be reunited with God'. Nevertheless, the hope of repenting and thus escaping from endless, unbearable pain, along with the fear that such a possibility is no longer open to him, are central to the tragic effect of this great soliloquy.[44] Satan's recognition that God 'deservd no such return' from him, that his motivation in rebelling 'against Heav'ns matchless King' was 'Pride and worse Ambition', that the 'service' to a God who had 'created what I was / In that bright eminence' was in no way 'hard', intensifies the tragic effect, giving Satan a psychological dimension and complexity entirely absent from the colloquy in Heaven in Book III.[45] Blake's aphorism that Milton was 'at liberty' in writing about devils and Hell, and 'in fetters' in writing about Heaven is surely borne out by the agonized twisting and turnings of this great speech, which, like the soliloquies of Macbeth and Hamlet, shows a character no longer obliged to perform a role in the presence of others.[46] Struggling against despair, Satan thrashes about, hoping to find a way out, aware that what has entrapped him is not only the boundless power of his 'punisher', but his own nature.

> But say I could repent and could obtaine
> By Act of Grace my former state; how soon
> Would higth recal high thoughts, how soon unsay
> What feign'd submission swore: ease would recant
> Vows made in pain, as violent and void.
> For never can true reconcilement grow

Where wounds of deadly hate have peirc'd so deep:
Which would but lead me to a worse relapse
And heavier fall.

(*PL*, IV.93–101, 103)

If Satan's tragic dimensions have led a number of critics to see him as a sympathetic figure, then, in contrast, the most problematical passage in *Paradise Lost*, the one which, again and again, readers have found indigestible, is God's exposition in Book III, couched in the first person, of the poem's basic theology. Part of the problem here is the incessant use of 'I' and 'mee', which makes the deity, whose ineffable essence, according to *De Doctrina*, 'is far beyond man's imagination, let alone his understanding' (*CPW*, VI.133), seem petty, excusing himself, defending his actions as though his 'only begotten Son' might raise objections. Though Milton in *De Doctrina* cautions against anthropomorphism or what he calls 'anthropopathy', 'the ascription of human feelings to God', in this passage Milton's attempt to use God as spokesperson turns the deity into a grumpy old man.[47] Critics have found 'ingrate' particularly hard to swallow.

So will fall
Hee and his faithless Progenie: whose fault?
Whose but his own? ingrate, he had of mee
All he could have; I made him just and right,
Sufficient to have stood, though free to fall.

(*PL*, III.95–9)[48]

When, in *Areopagitica*, Milton, making a similar doctrinal point, says of postlapsarian man, 'God uses not to captivat under a perpetuall childhood of prescription, but trust him with the gift of reason to be his own chooser' (*CPW*, II.513–14), there is neither the assumption that man has already made the wrong choice nor any attempt to shift the blame. As Waldock, Empson and others have argued, to begin the account of the Fall of Adam and Eve with a statement that, as earlier in the Fall of the Angels, the end was already known by an omniscient God is akin to pretending neutrality while loading the dice or putting one's finger on the scales. Morally and aesthetically, this passage raises at least as many questions as it purports to answer. Neither the reader nor Adam nor Eve can share God's 'prospect high', in which he can behold 'past, present, future' at once.

And shall pervert
For man will hark'n to his glozing lyes,
And easily transgress the sole Command,
Sole pledge of his obedience.

(*PL*, III.77–8, 92–5)

Ventriloquized through God's mouth, these words sound brutal, punitive, turning 'free to fall', as 'all-ruling' providence sees it (*PL*, I.212), to 'refusing to be grateful for the freedom I've given you, and therefore certain to fall', getting the punishment you deserve – a freedom to do what I know in advance you will do.

As a Puritan with Arminian tendencies, Milton, like Goodwin and Baxter, seeks to get round the problem of reconciling an omniscient, omnipotent providence with freedom of choice by distinguishing foreknowledge from any form of compulsion. According to *De Doctrina:*

> Divine foreknowledge definitely cannot itself impose any necessity; nor can it be set up as a cause, in any sense, of free actions . . . Liberty will be an empty word, and will have to be banished utterly not only from religion, but also from morality . . . But though future events will certainly happen, because divine foreknowledge cannot be mistaken, they will not happen by necessity, because foreknowledge, since it exists only in the mind of the foreknower, has no effect on its object. (*De Doctrina*, I.iii, *CPW*, VI.164–5)

Goodwin argued a similar position in *Redemption Redeemed* (1651): 'no act of God . . . imposeth any necessity upon any free-working cause . . . to act so, or so, determinately' and 'no knowledge, as such, hath any influence at all upon the object, or thing known, to cause it to be, or not to be'.[49] The standard Calvinist position, as expressed for example by William Perkins, rejected free will in Adam and Eve and in their descendants as incompatible with God's eternal, immutable Decrees: 'From the first moment of time the fall of Adam was necessary . . . by reason of the foreknowledge of God: for that which he foreknew would come to passe, must needs of necessitie come to passe . . . necessarie immutably.'[50] Milton's theodicy, as expressed in this lengthy expository speech by God in Book III, denies that God's 'absolute Decree' regarding Adam and Eve 'over-ruld' their will, claiming instead the status of being 'unchangeable, Eternal' for the 'high Decree' of God 'which ordain'd thir freedom'.

> They themselves decreed
> Their own revolt, not I; if I foreknew,
> Foreknowledge had no influence on their fault,
> Which had no less prov'd certain unforeknown.
> (*PL*, III.114–19, 125–8)

Readers, even those conversant with the terminology of seventeenth-century theological controversies, are likely to find these lines puzzling, even fallacious in their logic. If Adam and Eve are genuinely free, why should their fall be certain?[51]

In Milton's version of Arminian theology, God has absolute power over his creation, but freely chooses not to use it. In political terms, God chooses to behave like a limited monarch, rather than an absolute monarch. Goodwin, Milton's fellow republican in 1649–51, who defended the establishment of the Commonwealth and the deposition of Charles I, explicitly makes this comparison: though '*God* hath an absolute Sovereignty and Lordship over his Creature', as monarch God was 'a Lover of his Subjects' and thus refrained from exercising his power over them 'upon the hardest terms, and most grievous'.[52] Edmund Waller, who had praised the combination in a secular ruler of 'a strong, and yet a gentle Hand' in *A Panegyrick to My Lord Protector* (1655), used a similar antithesis in welcoming the return of Charles II five years later: 'With power unbounded, and a will confin'd.' As a model for earthly rulers, such a political formula can be dangerous, if there are no limits on the monarch's will other than self-restraint on his part – the belief, held by Hobbes and Filmer, for example, that the lives, liberties, and possessions of his subjects are alienable, held by these subjects only at the grace of the sovereign, who can seize them whenever he considers it expedient to do so. One of the defining principles of classical republicanism is that no one is free if his liberties are held at the discretion of the state, reducing him to a condition of servitude, ever if the ruler chooses at any given moment not to exercise his discretionary power.[53]

Pamphlets of the radical Levellers Overton and Lilburne illustrate with vivid particularizing detail abuses that may occur when the state's rulers or their emissaries seek to exert such a discretionary power, overriding protests or the ordinary standards of civility. Overton's stance in *An Appeale from the Degenerate Representative Body the Commons of England . . . to the Body Represented* (1647) is an uncompromisingly radical one. Writing as 'Prisoner in the infamous Goale of Newgate', he describes his own arrest and brutal treatment, in terms that, in effect, make the reader an eyewitness to the day-to-day operations of tyranny. After, 'in a warlike manner', officers of the state burst into his house, 'one with his drawn sword, and another with a Pistoll ready cock'd in his hand, and surprized me in my bed without any appearance or shew of any warrant', Overton tells how he was 'most incivilly and inhumanely dragged to *Newgate* headlong through the streets upon the stones through all the dirt and the mire', to remain in prison without redress for several months.[54] Standards of civility and common humanity are invoked, along with 'the liberty of every subject to enjoy the benefit of the Law' and not have their 'lives, persons, and estates . . . laid waste . . . at pleasure', as Overton describes how the officers 'rifled, plundered, and ransacked mine house, exposing my 3. helpless small children to the streets'. His wife, a woman of 'honest and godly conversation', was subjected to the same violent, arbitrary treatment:

> Most inhumanely and barbarously they dragged her away . . . with her tender infant of halfe a yeares of age in her armes headlong upon the stones . . . reviling and abusing her by the way with the scurrilous names of Whore Strumpet, &c.[55]

Lilburne describes similar acts 'of unmanlike cruelty and barbarism' directed at his wife, who was, together with 'eight Gentlewomen more of her friends', attempting to deliver a petition to Parliament.

> [The officer] without any more adoe, laid violent hands upon her, and endeavoured to throw her down the next staires, which are three or four steps . . . but being not content with this, he followed her into the Court of Requests-chamber, and then again . . . took her by the throat, as if he would have throtled her.[56]

At several points in this pamphlet, *Londons Liberty in Chains Discovered* (1646), Lilburne addresses his audience of London citizens directly, reminding them 'how, and by whom your Rights and Liberties have been invaded: and how you are inslaved': 'This briefe relation, thus made unto you, may bee a sufficient discovery of the intentions and sinister ends of your great *Masters*, to continue you still under an enforced slavery and subjection.' Both Lilburne and Overton begin their pamphlets with an epigraph from the Old Testament and end with an appeal to 'the true, faithful, and just God of Heaven and Earth': 'I have discharged my conscience, and what I have done, I have done.'[57]

Though Milton's stance in both *Areopagitica* and *The Readie and Easie Way* is that of a private citizen offering 'publick advice', endeavouring to 'write that which they forsee may advance the publick good', his version of republicanism was never democratic. Where the Levellers and army radicals in the Putney debates and in pamphlets favoured a widening of the franchise, Milton, in *The Readie and Easie Way*, as we have seen, was deeply suspicious of the populace, finding them incapable of rational choice.[58] In this work, written at a time of uncertainty, under a severe threat of 'returning to bondage' and 'readmitting Kingship in this Nation', Milton argued for a severely limited electorate, in an elaborate scheme of indirect voting – oligarchical republicanism, the rule of 'the worthiest'.

> Not committing all to the noise and shouting of a rude multitude, but permitting only those of them who are rightly qualifi'd, to nominat as many as they will; and out of that number others of a better breeding, to chuse a

> less number more judiciously, till after a third or fourth sifting and refining of exactest choice, they only be left chosen who are the due number, and seem by most voices the worthiest.[59]

To Overton, Lilburne, and other Levellers, in their pamphlets and in the Putney debates, oligarchy was a form of tyranny, simply replacing one tyrant and oppressor with another: the common soldier of the New Model Army, Rainborough complained at Putney, 'hath fought to enslave himself, to give power to men of riches, men of estates, to make him a perpetual slave'.[60]

If Milton's attitude towards the Cromwellian Protectorate differed from that of Overton, Lilburne, Ludlow, and other Leveller and republican stalwarts who saw Cromwell as yet another tyrant, reducing free Englishmen to a condition of slavery, it was partly because he viewed Cromwell as both a force for order and a patron of spiritual and civil liberty. Milton's sonnet 16 addresses Cromwell as one who might use his power to protect conscientious men from those who were 'threatning to bind out soules with secular chains': 'Helpe us to save free Conscience from the paw / Of hireling wolves whose Gospell is their maw.'[61] Though Cromwell consistently supported liberty of conscience, neither at this time nor later did he go as far as Milton, since for Cromwell as for such influential Independent ministers as John Owen, 'free Conscience' had to be compatible with a non-persecuting religious establishment, 'religious union', 'the unity of the godly' within a national church.[62] Milton's support of Cromwell in the Republic and Protectorate can be seen as an attempt to reconcile order and liberty, in keeping with his attempt, throughout his career, to draw a distinction between 'licence', raging beyond control, and self-limiting rational liberty: 'For, indeed, none can love freedom heartilie, but good men; the rest love not freedom but license; which never hath more scope or more indulgence then under Tyrants.'[63]

In Milton's theology and in his politics, authoritarian and liberal tendencies are frequently at war with one another. If, like Shelley, we reject the distinction, so important to Lilburne and Overton as to Milton, between earthly rulers, tempted always to act like tyrants, and a God committed to justice, or, like Blake, imagine a jealous, suspicious deity fearing his own overthrow, then it is possible to view the God of Book III as one who 'in the cold security of undoubted triumph' heaps 'new torments' on those who dare to defy him. The God who, demanding 'rigid satisfaction', insists that, for breaking 'fealtie' against 'the high Supremacie of Heav'n', Adam and Eve and their 'whole posteritie must dye' bears some at least of the marks of a tyrant.[64] Milton's Arianism, making the Father the spokesman for an unyielding justice and the Son, who does not share the Father's omniscience, the spokesman for grace, mercy, human feelings, gives rise to the agonizing paradox of 'Dye hee or justice must' (*PL*, III.210). In Book III and, even more insistently, in Books XI and XII, the looming presence of a punitive, Old Testament deity is a constant reminder of the Calvinist theology from which Milton could never entirely escape.

7

God's Just Yoke

Power and Justice in Paradise Lost

I

From the point of view of theodicy, one of the most problematical passages in *Paradise Lost* is God's 'Decree, which unrevok't shall stand', proclaimed before the assembled angels, the origin of Satan's revolt, occasioning civil war in Heaven:

> This day I have begot whom I declare
> My onely Son, and on this holy Hill
> Him have anointed, whom ye now behold
> At my right hand; your Head I him appoint;
> And by my Self have sworn to him shall bow
> All knees in Heav'n, and shall confess him Lord:
> Under his great Vice-gerent Reign abide
> United as one individual Soule
> For ever happie: him who disobeyes
> Mee disobeyes, breaks union, and that day
> Cast out from God and blessed vision, falls
> Into utter darkness, deep ingulft, his place
> Ordaind without redemption, without end.
> (*PL*, v.602–15)

One of the many problems this passage raises is 'This day I have begot'. Since God exists in a timeless dimension, 'this day' does not refer to any calendar accessible to mortal understanding. As Milton points out in *De Doctrina*, 'begot' has both a literal and a metaphorical meaning, and only the second is applicable here: 'In scripture there are two senses in which the Father is said to have begotten the Son: one literal, with reference to production; the other metaphorical, with reference to exaltation.'[1] In arguing in *De Doctrina* that the Son was begotten 'within the bounds of time', Milton challenges the orthodox Trinitarian position that 'the Son is of the same essence as the Father, and generated from all eternity'.[2] The passage in *Paradise Lost* closely follows Psalm 2:6–7, in the Pauline interpretation accepted in the Reformed tradition. According to *De Doctrina*, 'From the second Psalm it will be seen that God begot the Son in the sense of making him a king' (*CPW*, VI.207). The Psalm, in its original biblical context, is directed at 'the heathen', 'the kings of the earth', who, rebelling 'against the Lord, and against his anointed', have brought upon themselves the wrath of an angry, jealous God who, in Psalm 1, sharply distinguishes 'the righteous' from 'the ungodly'. 'Yet have I set my king upon my holy hill of Zion. / I will declare the decree: the Lord hath said unto me, Thou art my Son; this day I have begotten thee.'[3] When Milton translates Psalm 2 in 1653, he adds the parenthetical phrase 'though ye rebel' after 'I saith hee / Anointed have my King', thus, as in *Paradise Lost*, making rebellion a direct consequence of the 'firm decree' anointing the king.[4]

Empson and Forsyth are among the many critics who have found this passage in Book V unsettling, both in its arbitrary nature and in the severity of the punishments threatened. As Empson says, 'to give no reason at all for the Exaltation makes it appear a challenge', emanating from an 'authoritarian' God. 'The sudden decision to change the power structure in heaven' by fiat, according to Forsyth, is 'quite simply inexplicable', the apparent act of an absolute monarch asserting his will.[5] A command that 'all knees in Heav'n' should bow in humble obeisance to someone newly given the title of monarch is hard to reconcile with the republican sentiments of an author who treated with contempt 'the perpetual bowings and cringings of an abject people' as emblems of 'subjection'.[6] In 'civill society', Milton felt, bare proclamations of 'power, not reason', were unacceptable:

> In the publishing of humane laws, which for the most part aime not beyond the good of civill society, to set them barely forth to the people without reason or Preface, like a physicall prescript, or only with threatnings, as it were a lordly command, in the judgment of Plato was thought to be done neither generously or wisely.[7]

And yet, as Milton argues in *De Doctrina*, the prohibition of the tree of knowledge, with the curse attached that death, 'what e'er death is', would follow if that taboo were to be violated, was not a covenant between God and man, but 'a declaration of power'. The prohibition, rather than being in accordance with human reason or common sense, concerned:

> something that was in itself neither good nor evil, so that man's obedience might in this way be made evident. For man was by his nature good and holy, and was naturally disposed to do right, so it was certainly not necessary to bind him by the requirements of any covenant to do something which he would do of his own accord . . . by his own natural impulses, without being commanded.[8]

The Exaltation of the Son in Book v is also a test of obedience: 'him who disobeyes / Mee disobeyes'. As well as refusing to give any explanation, any information (unlike the later prohibition, where Raphael is sent to Eden to deliver advice and warning), the decree threatens extreme, terrifying punishment, with no possibility of redress: 'without redemption, without end' (*PL*, v.615). An omnipotent God here is not only foreseeing the fall of the angels, he is, in effect, bringing it about. The passage is open to the charge often levelled at Calvinist theology, that it makes God the author of sin. Satan as God's adversary is, as it were, 'begotten' at the same moment as the Son, his rebellion and fall made inevitable by God's decree exalting the Son as newly anointed monarch.

A second passage, occurring after the creation of man and the prediction that man, acting freely, will fall but nevertheless may 'find grace' (*PL*, III.131), is less problematical in nature, since it gives reasons for the Exaltation of the Son, here awarded his title of monarch and Son of God 'by Merit'. There, in a passage in Book III which cannot be collapsed into the announcement of the Decree in Book v, the declaration of the Son's Exaltation couples 'Humiliation' with kingship. The new honours are bestowed on the Son as man, consequent on his free choice to offer himself as man's redeemer. Without any punishment attached for those who might challenge the Son's elevation to a heavenly throne, the speech is greeted with universal acclaim by the assembled angels. The Son, the Father says, deserves his elevation because of the 'Love' he has demonstrated and will go on to demonstrate further.

> Because thou . . .
>   Hast been found
> By Merit more than Birthright Son of God,
> Found worthiest to be so by being Good,
> Farr more than Great or High; because in thee
> Love hath abounded more then Glory abounds,
> Therefore thy Humiliation shall exalt
> With thee thy Manhood also to this Throne;
> Here shalt thou sit Incarnate, here shalt Reign
> Both God and Man, Son both of God and Man,
> Anointed universal King; all Power
> I give thee, reign for ever, and assume
> Thy Merits; under thee as Head Supream
> Thrones, Princedoms, Powers, Dominions I reduce:
> All knees to thee shall bow: of them that bide
> In Heaven, or Earth, or under Earth in Hell.
>   (*PL*, III.305, 308–22)[9]

Milton's Arianism, clear enough in this speech, in which the Son is separate from and inferior to the Father, not equipped with foreknowledge, and awarded powers, including Vice-regency, by the Father's free gift, is central to the entire dialogue between Father and Son in Book III.[10] When the Son responds to the Father's assertion that, because of Adam's sin and 'Treason' against God, Adam 'with his whole posteritie must dye', doomed to 'destruction', his offer is free and genuine, not based on foreknowledge.

> Behold mee then, mee for him, life for life
> I offer, on mee let thine anger fall;
> Account mee man; I for his sake will leave
> Thy bosom, and this glorie next to thee
> Freely put off, and for him lastly dye
> Well pleas'd, on me let Death wreck all his rage.
> (*PL*, III.207–9, 236–41)

If he knew that he wouldn't really die, or that the doom pronounced on Adam and his descendants was no more than a gesture, not intended to be carried out, the entire scene would be fraudulent. In Book X, both Adam and Eve use very similar language in accepting responsibility for their actions, unselfishly expressing a willingness to take on themselves the punishment of God's wrath.

> First and last
> On mee, mee onely, as the sourse and spring
> Of all corruption, all the blame lights due;
> So might the wrauth.
>
> There with my cries importune Heaven, that all
> The sentence from thy head remov'd may light
> On me, sole cause to thee of all this woe,
> Mee mee onely just object of his ire.
> (*PL*, X.831–4, 933–6)

In each of these passages, the limited knowledge of the speaker, unable to foresee the consequences of the action they are willing to undertake, brings out the element of free choice. God's wrath is seen as inevitable, not open to question, but perhaps it can be redirected.

Nevertheless, the apparent dichotomy between an Old Testament God dedicated to the 'rigid satisfaction' of Justice – 'death for death' (*PL*, III.212) in the manner of the formula 'an eye for an eye, a tooth for a tooth' – and a Son motivated by charity, the principles of the Sermon on the Mount, creates certain difficulties for Milton in Book III. In the Old Testament, God is frequently represented as angry, disappointed with his creation, even (as with the story of Noah and the Flood) regretting that he ever created man. The prophets Jeremiah, Ezekiel and Isaiah again and again assume the role of spokesman for a God who issues thunderous denunciations of a 'sinful nation, a people laden with iniquity', because they have 'forsaken the Lord thy God'.

> Now is the end come upon thee, and I will send mine anger upon thee, and will judge thee according to thy ways, and will recompense upon thee all thine abominations.
>
> Why have they provoked me to anger with their graven images, and with strange vanities?[11]

The God of the Hebrew Bible, addressing a society in which there are many rival deities, many warring tribes, demands exclusive worship, hating the impurity of those who fail to meet his rigorous demands. Though one passage in Milton speaks of 'the strife / of Mercy and Justice' observable in the Father's face, through most of the dialogue in Heaven in Book III there is little evidence of any inclination towards 'pitie' in the strict and exacting Father (*PL*, III.402, 406–7). Theologically, the dialogue culminates in the familiar contrast of the first and second Adam, fulfilling the conditions of divine justice:

> So Man, as is most just,
> Shall satisfie for Man, be judg'd and die,
> And dying rise, and rising with him raise
> His Brethren, ransomed with his own dear life.
> (*PL*, III.294–7)

Notice the term 'satisfie' and the metaphor of paying a ransom: the emphasis in this passage is on meeting required contractual terms, paying the price demanded. 'High Justice', Michael tells Adam in Book XII, insists that the Son by his sacrifice will 'fulfill the Law' of God, showing both 'obedience' and 'love' and, overcoming death, 'Proclaiming Life to all who shall believe.'[12] Yet even if justice and mercy can, in *Paradise Lost* as in *De Doctrina*, be seen ultimately to be reconciled, in Book III justice is consistently associated with the Father and mercy with the Son, bringing out the contrasts between a theology based on power, ruling by fear and trembling, and one based on compassion for human fallibility.

In some ways, the Father is setting a test for his Son, as he has done for Satan and will do for Adam and Eve. Critics have commented on the parallel between the baffled muteness of the angelic host and the Satanic hordes, where in both cases no one among them 'durst upon his own head' (*PL*, II.220) risk the dangerous enterprise, and more often than not have seen Hell as parodying Heaven. But the comparison can work both ways, so that the echo in Book III of the earlier passage can suggest 'moral equivalence'.[13] The contrast between a deity who knows what the outcome will be, thus exercising control even when it is not apparent he is doing so, and someone who, not aware of the outcome, freely accepts the burden of mortality and suffering, is likely to make the latter a more attractive figure than the stern, unyielding patriarch.

The word 'power' appears seventy-nine times in *Paradise Lost*, as against twelve times in *Samson Agonistes* and eighteen times in *Paradise Regained*, and cognates such as 'powerful' and 'powers' forty-five times in *Paradise Lost.* 'Strength' occurs thirty-four times in *Paradise Lost*, thirty-seven times in *Samson Agonistes*, and only six times in *Paradise Regained*, while the related terms 'strong'/'stronger'/'strongest' occur forty-four times in *Paradise Lost.* In *Samson Agonistes*, the word 'strength' consistently has a moral dimension, presented as 'Heav'n-gifted', a sign of a covenant with God – not simply a gift, but a responsibility.

> My trust is in the living God who gave me
> At my Nativity this strength.
> (*Samson Agonistes*, 1140-1)

> I was no private, but a person rais'd
> With strength sufficient and command from Heav'n
> To free my Countrey.
> (1211-13)

Neither Samson, his father Manoa, nor the Chorus ever considers this strength to be merely a physical attribute, recognizing that, like any free gift, it may be abused, neglected, or misapplied. Milton is consistent in *Areopagitica*, the divorce tracts, *Paradise Lost*, and *Samson Agonistes* in emphasizing how difficult it is 'to ordain wisely as in this world of evill, in the midd'st whereof God has plac't us unavoidably'.

> But what is strength without a double share
> Of wisdom?

> But thee, whose strength, while vertue was her mate,
> Might have subdu'd the Earth.[14]

In *Paradise Lost*, most of the references to 'strength', especially in Books I, II, and VI, are to physical strength alone, showing a refusal by Satan and his followers to admit any moral dimension. Beelzebub in Book I speaks of God's 'high Supremacy', proved by their defeat, as 'upheld by strength, or Chance, or Fate', and Satan, in language that associates trust in strength with the sinner's hardening of the heart, is described as exulting in his strength and that of his assembled forces: 'And now his heart / Distends with pride, and hardning in his strength / Glories.'[15] 'Strength' and 'power' are to Satan material considerations, things that can be measured or counted: if God won the War in Heaven, it was because 'the Potent Victor' had more troops or better weapons at his disposal.

Into what Pit thou seest
From what highth fall'n, so much the stronger prov'd
He with his Thunder: and till then who knew
The force of those dire Arms?

(*PL*, I.91–5)

At one point in Book I, addressing his 'Powers / Matchless but with th'Almighty', Satan even suggests that God had tempted them to rebel prematurely, by disguising the full extent of his 'might'.

But he who reigns
Monarch in Heav'n, till then as one secure
Sat on his Throne, upheld by old repute,
Consent or custome, and his Regal State
Put forth at full, but still his strength conceal'd,
Which tempted our attempt, and wrought our fall.

(*PL*, I.622–3, 637–43)[16]

When Abdiel confronts Satan in battle, he claims that true 'strength and might' must be more than material: Satan's outward appearance, 'towring, armd in Adamant and Gold', to Abdiel hides an inner reality that is far from heroic.

O Heav'n! that such resemblance of the Highest
Should yet remain, where faith and realtie
Remain not; wherefore should not strength and might
There fail where Vertue fails, or weakest prove
Where boldest; though to sight unconquerable?

(*PL*, VI.110, 114–18)

Abdiel then sends a challenge to single combat, while recognizing that 'when Reason hath to deal with force', any such contest is 'brutish': 'His puissance, trusting in th'Almightie's aide, I mean to try' (*PL*, VI.119–20, 124–5).

The War in Heaven, an episode in the poem that few critics have praised, is full of echoes of the epic tradition, while in certain respects being deeply uncomfortable with its awkward mixture of the spiritual and material. Johnson has clearly indicated what the problem is with Book VI:

> Another inconvenience of Milton's design is, that it requires the description of what cannot be described, the agency of spirits. He saw that

> immateriality supplied no images, and that he could not show angels acting but by instruments of action; he therefore invested them with form and matter . . . The confusion of spirit and matter which pervades the whole narration of the war in heaven fills it with incongruity.[17]

But it is arguable that 'the confusion of spirit and matter' is not Milton's, but Satan's, since a process by which spirit is 'imbruted', transformed into or contaminated by matter, is shown throughout the poem as taking place in the fallen angel Satan and in his followers. The Elder Brother in the Ludlow Masque describes how by the 'defilement' of sin 'the soul grows clotted by contagion', and Satan in Book IX expresses dismay at his own 'foul descent', with his original spiritual essence now 'mixt with bestial slime'.[18] At the outset of the War in Heaven, the two opposing armies are described in heroic terms, as equals:

> To such highth
> Of Godlike Power: for likest Gods they seemd,
> Stood they or mov'd, in stature, motion, arms
> Fit to decide the Empire of great Heav'n.
> (*PL*, VI.300–3)

Yet, as the battle proceeds, the two sides are differentiated more and more: the Satanic host for the first time feel 'fear . . . and sense of paine', while, for their opponents, 'Such high advantages thir innocence / Gave them above thir foes, not to have sinnd' (*PL*, VI.394, 401–2). In the midst of battle, at a time when 'horrid confusion' reigns, the Satanic forces are described as struggling in a 'prison' of their own making: 'though Spirits of purest light, / Purest at first, now gross by sinning grown' (*PL*, VI.660–1, 668). Interrupting the narrative of exploits during the battle, Milton comments on how the names of the fallen angels, for all their 'might' displayed in 'Acts of Warr', have been forgotten, relegated to 'dark oblivion'.

> For strength from Truth divided and from Just,
> Illaudable, naught merits but dispraise
> And ignominie, yet to glorie aspires
> Vain glorious, and through infamie seeks fame:
> Therefore Eternal silence be thir doome
> (*PL*, VI.377, 380–5).

Arnold Stein has pointed out that the War in Heaven, rather than being consistently grand and heroic, has a comic element, resembling 'epic farce'.[19] This discordant element enters Book VI with the invention of gunpowder and the cannon by Satan, hoping, with characteristic materialist assumptions, that 'more valid Armes, / Weapons more violent, when next we meet, / May serve to better us, and worse our foes' (*PL*, VI.438–40). Digging into the floor of Heaven, 'Deep under ground, materials dark and crude', Satan and his followers seek 'with infernal flame' to imitate and, in rivalry, overcome God's thunderbolts.

> Such implements of mischief as shall dash
> To pieces, and orewhelm whatever stands
> Adverse, that they shall fear we have disarmd
> The Thunderer of his only dreaded bolt.
> (*PL*, VI.478, 483, 488–91)

The consequences deprive not only Satan's forces but their opponents of the last shreds of heroic dignity: 'down they fell / By thousands, Angel on Arch-Angel rowl'd; / The sooner for thir Arms'.[20] When the good angels respond by tearing up the earth beneath them, with both sides throwing mountains at one another – 'So Hills amid the Air encounterd Hills' – it appears for a moment that Heaven is turned to Hell, and that Satan, if not victorious, has succeeded in bringing his opponents down to his level. Milton comments on the danger, which prompts God the Father to intervene: unless the war is brought to an end, and order restored, 'all Heav'n / Had gone to wrack, with ruin overspred' (*PL*, VI.664, 669–70).

The grotesque anti-heroic or mock-heroic aspects of the War in Heaven are thematically related to the critique of the heroic tradition made explicit in the invocation to Book IX. In these celebrated lines, Milton redefines 'what justly gives Heroic name / To Person or to Poem': not the 'wrauth' or 'rage' of Achilles or Turnus, and not 'Warrs, hitherto the onely Argument / Heroic deem'd' (*PL*, IX.13–17, 28–9, 40–1). In the final books of *Paradise Lost*, in *Paradise Regained*, and in *Samson Agonistes*, Milton presents a number of different instances of 'the better fortitude / Of Patience and Heroic Martyrdom' (*PL*, IX.31–2). If Satan's 'courage never to submit or yield' is one possible way of dealing with affliction, the paradigm of the 'one just Man', bearing the standard of beleaguered truth in 'a dark Age', and, though outnumbered, 'daring single to be just', provides an alternative model of heroic conduct. This, Milton suggests, is another kind of single combat, another kind of courage, in bearing up under adverse circumstances, risking 'Martyrdom' (*PL*, I.108; XI.703, 809, 818).

And yet, in the exchanges between Father and Son at either end of the narrative of the War in Heaven, there is an undercurrent suggesting that any account of 'Battels feign'd' (*PL*, IX.31) must to some extent accept Satan's dangerous assumption that 'Power' can only be conceived in material terms, separated from any idea of justice or morality. In the Father's speech to his Son in Book v, the overall tone includes elements of ironic 'derision', as he pretends not to be 'sure / Of our Omnipotence', while pointing out the need to take measures 'in our defense, lest unawares we lose / This our high place, our Sanctuarie, our Hill' (*PL*, v.721–2, 731–2, 736). Though he describes Satan as preparing 'to try / In battel, what our Power is, or our right', neither the Son's response nor the account of the battle that follows has much to say about 'right'. The Son speaks here of 'all Regal Power' given him and of the 'Glory' that will follow as he proves himself in battle (*PL*, v.727–8, 738–42). When, later on, the Son is armed for the decisive battle, though the words 'deserved right' and 'Vertue' are mentioned, the discourse is primarily about 'Power', once again the 'Glorie' to be achieved in victory. 'Worth' (as with Prince Hal fighting Hotspur) is to be demonstrated through arms, providing proof 'that all may know / In Heav'n and Hell thy Power above compare'.

> Go then thou Mightiest in thy Fathers might . . .
> Bring forth all my Warr,
> My Bow and Thunder, my Almightie Arms
> Gird on, and Sword upon thy puissant Thigh.
> (*PL*, vi.701–5, 709–14)

In addressing the assembled troops before the combat, changing his countenance 'into terrour', 'full of wrauth', the Son is no longer the model for suffering, patience, 'the soveraign edict of charity'. Rather than 'life for life / I offer, on mee let thine anger fall', the Son is transformed into the vehicle of God's wrath.[21] 'Against mee is all thir rage': my proud enemies have scorned me, and I will repay their arrogance, pouring God's indignation upon them by force of arms. As the Son, 'grasping ten thousand Thunders' in his hand, rides into battle, he boasts like any epic hero of his great strength and prowess, challenging his adversary to single combat. At this key point of the narrative, the Son's language would appear to accept Satan's definition of power and strength as material, capable of measurement or concrete proof.

> That they may have thir wish, to trie with mee
> In Battel which the stronger proves, they all,
> Or I alone against them, since by strength
> They measure all, of other excellence
> Not emulous, nor care who them excells;
> No other strife with them do I voutsafe.
> (*PL*, vi.811–13, 818–23, 836)[22]

II

At one point in the dialogue in Heaven in Book III, the Son, showing 'immortal love / To mortal men' along with 'filial obedience', suggests a remedy to God's 'wrauth'. The Father, seemingly no longer intent on punishing disobedience, now says to his Son, 'well thou know'st how dear / To me are all my works, nor Man the least / Though last created' (*PL*, III.267–9, 275–8). The song of the angels at the end of the dialogue in Heaven sees the Father as well as the Son as inclined to 'pitie': here as elsewhere the Son acts as intercessor, pleading for man, yet recognizes a similar impulse in the Father. Passages like this tend to blur the distinction, evident in much of Book III, between an Old Testament God of wrath and a Son in whom the principle of charity is pre-eminent. These lines of 'solemn adoration' by the assembled host, in keeping with Milton's theology generally, distinguish the 'fierce vengeance' appropriate for Satan and the fallen angels from the fate to be meted out to Adam and Eve:

> Him through their malice fall'n,
> Father of Mercie and Grace, thou didst not doome
> So strictly, but much more to pitie encline:
> No sooner did thy dear and onely Son
> Perceive thee purpos'd not to doom frail Man
> So strictly, but much more to pitie enclin'd,
> He to appease thy wrauth, and end the strife
> Of Mercy and Justice in thy face discern'd . . .
> Offerd himself to die
> For mans offence.
>
> (*PL*, III.351, 399–410)

Milton's Arminian doctrine of free will ('I formd them free, and free they must remain / Till they enthrall themselves') is a way of reconciling justice and mercy. To say that 'Man therefore shall find grace', from which Satan and his followers are excluded, means that the possibility of grace is open to Adam, Eve, and their fallible descendants, if they grasp the opportunities offered them.[23] The elect, according to Milton, are defined not by any arbitrary preselection, but by adherence in faith, even in times of tribulation. Justification, he says in *De Doctrina*, is 'the judgment of God, freely given', by which those who believe are absolved of sin:

> So that it is evident that our justification is freely given as far as we are concerned, but it is not free from Christ's point of view. He paid the price, and imputed our sins to himself, and of his own free will washed them away and expiated them. We receive his righteousness, imputed to us, as

> a gift. We pay nothing for it, we merely have to believe. Thus the Father is appeased, and pronounces all believers righteous. There could not be a simpler or more equitable method of satisfaction.[24]

In the passage in Book III where, notoriously, Milton struggles with how to reconcile the foreknowledge of an omniscient, omnipotent deity ('and shall pervert / For man will heark'n to his glozing lyes') with a commitment to human freedom, Milton ends a long expository speech by having God announce that 'Mercy and Justice . . . through Heav'n and Earth', rather than seeming to clash, are one (*PL*, III.92–3, 132–3). The rigid demands of the law are satisfied, thus allowing scope for the operations of grace, extended to fallen man, not yet wholly captive to sin, but denied to those who, like Satan, refuse to repent and admit God's sovereignty.

In Book XI, the Son acts as intercessor, urging God to 'bend thine eare / To supplication', hear the sighs of the repentant Adam and Eve as the first signs of 'thy implanted Grace in Man' (*PL*, XI.22–3, 30–1). The Son associates his advocacy with the sacrifice he has agreed to undertake, 'life for life', recognizing that the sentence already passed on man cannot be rescinded: 'his doom (which I / To mitigate thus plead, not to reverse)'. Here again, in his Arianism, Milton clearly portrays a Son separate from and subordinate to the Father: 'It is quite inconceivable that anyone could be a mediator to himself or on his own behalf . . . The God to whom we were reconciled . . . cannot, if he is one God, be the same as the God by whom we were reconciled, since that God is another person.'[25] Doctrinally, the passage in Book XI, like *De Doctrina*, emphasizes 'Christ's absolutely full satisfaction' of the demands of the Law, a debt fully repaid, while it suggests that, through Christ the mediator, fallible mortals can be 'accounted righteous in the sight of God, not by the works of the Law, but through Faith':

> Let mee
> Interpret for him, mee his Advocate
> And propitiation, all his works on mee
> Good or not good ingraft, my Merit those
> Shall perfet, and for these my Death shall pay.[26]

The Father's response suggests a more strict and severe version of justice: not forgiveness of sin, but the rigid, unsparing separation of the impure, defiled by pollution, from an endangered, vulnerable purity.

> The Law I gave to Nature him forbids:
> Those pure immortal Elements that know
> No gross, no unharmoneous mixture foule,

Eject him tainted now, and purge him off
As a distemper, gross to aire as gross.
(*PL*, XI.49–53)

The expulsion of Adam and Eve from Paradise is described here as a natural, physiological process, akin to the ejection of faeces during digestion, by a law of nature that protects 'pure . . . Elements' against defilement. As we have seen, the fear of pollution, guarding an imagined purity or holiness against an invasive corrupting force, is a recurrent theme in Milton.[27] Later in Book XI, God the Father instructs Michael to 'drive out the sinful Pair, / From hallowd ground', since as 'unholie' they would defile the Paradise in which they had once dwelt, and to expel them 'without remorse' (*PL*, XI.104–6). Though he urges Michael not to dismiss them 'disconsolate', consumed with 'terror', 'least they faint / At the sad Sentence rigorously urg'd' (*PL*, XI.108–9, 111, 113), the deity who emerges from Michael's account of postlapsarian history in Books XI and XII is strict and unforgiving.

If after the Fall 'God . . . oft descends to visit men / Unseen, and through thir habitations walks / To mark thir doings', it is not a friendly visit, but surveillance, observing their folly, at which 'great laughter was in Heav'n', and punishing the blindness and presumption of sinners (*PL*, XII.48–50, 59). The fate of the 'lawless Tyrant' Pharoah and others who remain 'obdurate' is characteristic of the overwhelming destructive force directed at the sinful by a vengeful Old Testament deity.

Thunder mixt with Haile,
Haile mixt with fire must rend th'*Egyptian* Skie
And wheel on th'Earth, devouring where it rouls;
What it devours not, Herb, or Fruit, or Graine,
A darksom Cloud of Locusts swarming down
Must eat, and on the ground leave nothing green.
(*PL*, XII.173, 181–6, 205)

The recurrent pattern in Books XI and XII is for Adam, naively optimistic, to find evidence of hope and to be disabused by Michael, who unrelentingly presents to him evidence to show how 'the world erelong a world of tears must weepe' (*PL*, XI.627).[28] Those few who seek to follow the ways of righteousness are subject to obloquy, persecution, and possible martyrdom. Though Michael presents to Adam the example of the prophet Enoch, saved from 'violent hands' by divine intervention, as illustration of 'what reward / Awaits the good, the rest what punishment', Adam's reaction is to weep, 'all in tears . . . lamenting', at what appears to be injustice, unmerited suffering (*PL*, XI.668–71, 674–5, 709–10).

The deity of the middle books of *Paradise Lost*, in contrast, is a gentler God, a father seemingly fond of his children rather than threatening punishment and ruling by fear. In Books VII and VIII, the deity no longer appears severe and uncompromising in his demands. In the harmonious prelapsarian world, friendly visits by God and by angels dropping in for a meal or a conversation, Milton suggests, were common occurrences.

> For God will deigne
> To visit oft the dwellings of just Men
> Delighted, and with frequent intercourse
> Thither will send his winged Messengers
> On errand of supernal Grace.
> (*PL*, VII.569–73)

Adam reminds Eve in Book IV of how 'Millions of spiritual Creatures walk the Earth / Unseen, both when we wake and when we sleep', and speaks of the pleasure he and Eve have felt in listening to the singing of these 'Celestial voices' (*PL*, IV.677–8, 682). The lines in Book VII suggest that domestic visits by angels continued after the Fall, to those deemed worthy. Henry Vaughan in 'The Retreate' imagines an idealized childhood of man, now lost, as an 'Angell-infancy' in which the presence of God was evident in everyday surroundings, enabling the child, as yet untainted by sin, to 'see a glimpse' of the deity's 'bright-face' in the book of nature.[29] Raphael, a 'sociable Spirit' sent 'as friend to friend' to 'converse with *Adam*', is willing to share a meal with Adam and Eve as a token of friendship and equality before God, partaking of 'Those bounties which our Nourisher, from whom / All perfet good unmeasur'd out, descends'. As he tells Adam, in response to an invitation to 'sit and taste' a meal with them, sheltering from the hot sun:

> *Adam*, I therefore came, nor art thou such
> Created, or such place hast here to dwell,
> As may not oft invite, though Spirits of Heav'n
> To visit thee.[30]

In Book XI, after the Fall, Adam expresses his sorrow at no longer being able to frequent the places where, again and again, he experienced God's visits, recalling them to memory, so that, after expulsion from Eden, 'as from his face I shall be hid'. Milton's language here gives ordinary locations a numinous, magical aura.

> Here I could frequent,
> With worship, place by place where he voutsaf'd
> Presence Divine, and to my Sons relate;

On this Mount he appeerd, under this Tree
Stood visible, among these Pines his voice
I heard, here with him at this Fountain talk'd.
(*PL*, XI.315–22)

Adam's anguished lament is that expulsion from the familiar surroundings of Eden will entail a permanent, irreparable alienation from God, a loss too great to bear. No longer will it even be possible to raise offerings in praise of an 'angrie' God who has cast him off as unworthy and from whom he has fled. 'Nether World' suggests a fear that what remains for him is another Hell, replicating the fate of Satan and his fallen angels: 'In yonder nether World where shall I seek / His bright appearances, or footsteps trace?' (*PL*, XI.328–30). Michael's response is that God is present not only in the Garden of Eden, but throughout the earth, wherever Adam, Eve, and their descendants choose to dwell.

Adam, thou know'st Heav'n his, and all the Earth,
Not this Rock onely; his Omnipresence fills
Land, Sea, and Aire, and every kinde that lives,
Fomented by his virtual power and warmd . . .
Surmise not then
His presence to these narrow bounds confin'd
Of Paradise or *Eden*.
(*PL*, XI.335–42)

In some ways, this speech by Michael anticipates the poem's closing lines, suggesting that, in spite of the 'natural tears' of Adam and Eve occasioned by their forced departure from Eden, 'the World was all before them'. Though with several lines describing the 'flaming Brand' and 'dreadful Faces' surrounding Paradise, the emphasis is on loss, separation from everything they had known, the overall tone is ambivalent: an episode has ended, but 'hand in hand', they can go forward (*PL*, XII.643–8). Michael, who has urged the sorrowing Eve – 'how shall we breathe in other Aire / Less pure?' – that she must 'patiently resigne / What justly thou has lost' (*PL*, XI.284–5, 287–8), reassures Adam that God's 'paternal Love' will accompany him in new, unfamiliar surroundings.

Yet doubt not but in Vallie and in plaine
God is as here, and will be found alike
Present, and of his presence many a signe
Still following thee, still compassing thee round
With goodness and paternal Love.
(*PL*, XI.349–53)

In God's dialogue with Adam in Book VIII, in which Adam acknowledges this 'Heav'nly Power' as his 'Maker' and 'Guide', 'paternal Love' is demonstrated by a friendly, avuncular teasing. Adam, after seeing and naming 'each Bird and Beast . . . After thir kindes', comments on the possible inconvenience of 'solitude', while careful not to offend the God who has 'provided all things' for him: who, he asks, can find happiness or contentment 'alone'?[31] God's response, 'with a smile', is that Adam has plenty of company in the birds and beasts, whose language he knows, and who 'come and play' before him. Adam then says, deploying arguments very similar to passages in Milton's divorce tracts, that rational intercourse, of a kind that raises human beings above 'the brute', necessarily involves equality, a companionship of minds.

> Among unequals what societie
> Can sort, what harmonie or true delight?
> Which must be mutual, in proportion due
> Giv'n and receiv'd . . .
> Of fellowship I speak
> Such as I seek, fit to participate
> All rational delight, wherein the brute
> Cannot be human consort.[32]

God's rejoinder, in a kind of Socratic dialogue – later he says his assertions were intended as test or 'trial', 'to see how thou couldst judge of fit and meet' – is that as a monotheistic deity he is 'alone / From all Eternitie', with no second or equal (*PL*, VIII.405–7, 447–8). Adam, showing both quickness of wit and a due respect, demonstrating the 'freedom' with which he was endowed, responds that where God is by nature unique and perfect, man is incomplete, deficient, and in his 'single imperfection' requires a fit companion. Again the argument resembles that put forth in *Doctrine and Discipline.*

> Thou in thy self art perfet, and in thee
> Is no deficience found; not so is Man,
> But in degree, the cause of his desire
> By conversation with his like to help,
> Or solace his defects . . .
> In unitie defective, which requires
> Collateral love, and deerest amitie.
> (*PL*, VIII.415–19, 423, 425–6, 434)

What follows – presumably intended by the omniscient deity all along, though he pretends not to know what Adam is asking for – is the creation of Eve. This fulfillment of Adam's desire provides not only what he can praise as 'the sum of earthly bliss' and the 'fairest . . . of all thy gifts' (*PL*, VIII.493–4, 522), but a new test for Adam: simultaneously an extraordinary boon, a newly discovered weakness, and a warning. With both Adam and Eve, signs of vulnerability, hints of dangers they may face, are evident from the beginning. Eve, at the moment of her creation, 'with unexperienc't thought', is tempted by the sight of her own reflection in the water, as in the myth of Narcissus: 'there I had fixt / Mine eyes till now, and pin'd with vain desire, / Had not a voice . . . warnd me' (*PL*, IV.457, 465–7). Adam, 'transported' by passion, similarly shows a weakness that could be exploited:

> Here passion first I felt,
> Commotion strange, in all enjoyments else
> Superiour and unmov'd, here onely weake
> Against the charm of Beauties powerful glance.
> (*PL*, VIII.529–33)

Both are warned of a possible danger, yet both are left free to choose, rather than, 'under a perpetuall childhood of prescription', being constrained by what Milton in *Areopagitica* calls 'a rigour contrary to the manner of God and of nature', thus allowing the uncertainties consequent to the trial of virtue exposed to temptation.[33]

III

The word 'just' occurs fifty-two times in *Paradise Lost* (ten times in Book XI), as against nine times in *Paradise Regained*, nine times in *Samson Agonistes*, and eleven times in Milton's translation of the Psalms. 'Justice' occurs seventeen times in *Paradise Lost*, 'justly' ten times in *Paradise Lost*, 'Judge' appears twenty-two times in *Paradise Lost*, 'judged' seventeen times, and 'judgment' ten times. Justice in *Paradise Lost* is always divine justice. 'Civil Justice', a central concern in *King Lear* and *Measure for Measure*, as well as in *Tenure*, is mentioned only once, and then in connection with the 'religious Rites' under the Old Testament, the 'rule by Laws' proclaimed by the 'voice of God' to Moses (*PL*, XII.226–31, 235). Justice in Milton's poem is punitive, retributive, characterized by 'anger and just rebuke, and judgement giv'n' by a deity 'alienated' from man, whose actions have caused the deity to view his creature with 'distance and distaste' (*PL*, IX.8–10). In Book VII, the angels praise a God 'whose just avenging ire / Had driven out th'ungodly from his sight / And th'habitations of the just'. Here a concern for purity, the separation of the godly from the ungodly, is balanced against God's creative powers, shown as he replaces 'Spirits maligne' with a potentially 'better Race' of men in 'thir vacant room' (*PL*, VIII.184–90). 'Dye hee or Justice must' in Book III is a particularly uncompromising formulation of a principle of justice which, allowing no exceptions and accepting no excuses, demands 'rigid satisfaction' (*PL*, III.210–12). 'Strict Laws', Michael tells Adam in Book XII, were given to postlapsarian humans because of 'thir natural pravitie' (*PL*, XII.287–8, 304). Milton speaks of justice after the Fall in similar terms in *Tetrachordon*, referring both to civil laws ('so many and so various Laws', as Adam puts it) and to the commandments of the Mosaic Law:

> In the beginning, had men continu'd perfet, it had bin just that all things should have remain'd, as they began to *Adam & Eve*. But after that the sons of men grew violent & injurious, it alter'd the lore of justice, and put the government of things into a new frame.

'Law', Michael says, is necessarily 'imperfet', appealing to 'servil fear' in an attempt to control man's sinful propensities.[34]

In the Pauline theology of *De Doctrina*, I.xxvi, and a number of passages in Book XII, the Mosaic Law, superseded by the 'better Cov'nant' (*PL*, XII.302) of the Gospel, is no better than an 'elementary, childish and servile discipline'. Milton quotes St Paul's 'contemtuous' characterization of the Law, as laid down in the Hebrew Bible, as 'weak and beggarly rudiments', and other 'ignominious' terms used by St Paul for the Law of the Old Testament are 'a prison that shutteth up, the yoke of bondage, the operation of wrath and of death, the killing letter, the ministerie of death and condemnation'.[35] Yet Milton in *De Doctrina* and in the divorce tracts cites Jesus' statement in the Sermon on the Mount: 'Think not that I am come to destroy the law or the prophets: I am not come to destroy but to fulfil' (Matthew 5:17). There is considerable ambivalence towards the Mosaic Law in Milton's definition of 'satisfaction', the means by which Christ 'fully satisfied divine justice by fulfilling the law and paying the just price'. Here as elsewhere, Milton insists, contesting Calvinist orthodoxy, that Christ's sacrifice was 'on behalf of all men', including sinners, and not just the elect.[36] A strict, unyielding view of God's justice and a more compassionate view of human 'imperfection' often seem at loggerheads in Milton's writings. In the same chapter of *De Doctrina*, where he argues that 'the law causes anger but the gospel produces grace, and as anger and grace are incompatible, it follows that the law and the gospel are incompatible too', he goes on to say, citing Matthew 5:17:

> But in reality the law, that is the substance of the law, is not broken by this abolition. On the contrary its purpose is attained in that love of God and of our neighbor which is born of faith, through the spirit . . . The law is now inscribed on believers' hearts by the spirit.[37]

At times, especially in the divorce tracts, Milton argues for a harmony or continuity of the Law and Gospel, seeing the Mosaic Law not as restricting but as allowing scope for human freedom. A 'monolithic' Pauline interpretation of the Law, expressed in passages in *De Doctrina* and in Books III, XI, and XII of *Paradise Lost*, can be contrasted with a less rigorous view in which Law and Gospel, rather than being presented as incompatible, are united by the overriding principle of charity.[38]

What is surprisingly rare in *Paradise Lost* is any sense that God's justice is ruled by principles of reason, fairness, or equity. There is no passage in *Paradise Lost* equivalent to the following statement in Ralph Cudworth's *True Intellectual System of the Universe* (1678):

> The right and authority of God himself, who is the supreme sovereign of the universe, is also in like manner bounded and circumscribed by Justice. God's will is ruled by his justice, and not his justice ruled by his will; and therefore, God himself cannot command what is in its own nature unjust.[39]

Abdiel in his confrontation with Satan is praised for his victory over those who 'reason for thir Law refuse', but though his arguments defend 'the just Decree of God' and deny Satan's allegation that the elevation of the Son was 'unjust, flatly unjust', Abdiel's answer to Satan equates justice with sovereign power. Since God created all things 'such as he pleasd' and since it is impossible for anyone to 'give Law to God', an all-powerful deity who (Abdiel tells Satan) 'made / Thee what thou art', then anything God pleases to do must by definition be just.[40] Milton's account of the deity in *Doctrine and Discipline* as one who 'binds himself like a just lawgiver to his own prescriptions' is very different, and much closer to the passage just quoted from Cudworth.

> If it be affirm'd that God as being Lord may doe what he will; yet we must know that God hath not two wills, but one will, much less two contrary . . . The hidden wayes of his providence we adore & search not; but the law is his reveled will, his complete, his evident, and certain will; herein he appears to us in human shape, enters into cov'nant with us, swears to keep it, binds himself like a just lawgiver to his own prescriptions, gives himself to be understood by men, judges and is judg'd, measures and is commensurat to right reason; cannot require lesse of us in one cantle of his Law then in another, his legall justice cannot be so fickle and so variable.[41]

Here 'the law' clearly means Scripture as a whole, with no suggestion that the Hebrew Bible has been supplanted or rendered invalid by the New Testament. God no less than man is bound by the laws he has made available to man in the Bible, and God's justice must be bounded by 'right reason'. There is a hint in this passage from *Doctrine and Discipline*, brought out more clearly in the next chapter of the tract, that the precepts of the Mosaic Law, as well as the teachings of Jesus in the Gospel, rest on a pre-existing law of nature, and are in accordance with principles of equity. Again the hidden ways of providence are contrasted with the Law, as openly stated in language ordinary mortals can understand:

> In the delivery and execution of his Law, especially in the managing of a duty so daily and so familiar as this whereof we reason, hath plain anough reveal'd himself, and requires the observance therof not otherwise then to the law of nature and of equity imprinted in us seems correspondent. And hee hath taught us to love and to extoll his Lawes, not onely as they are his, but as they are just and good to every wise and sober understanding.[42]

In *Paradise Lost*, the justice of God is regularly associated with obedience. In Book VI, when the Son prepares for battle, he pledges 'to rid heav'n' of those 'that from thy just obedience could revolt, / Whom to obey is happiness entire' (*PL*, VI.737, 740–1). Michael tells Eve that she should 'patiently resigne / What justly thou hast lost', and Adam, after some tearful questioning, tells Michael 'I yield it just . . . and submit' (*PL*, XI.287–8, 526). In Book X, Adam warns Eve against 'Rancor and pride . . . / Reluctance against God and his just yoke / Laid on our Necks' (*PL*, X.1044–6). After Raphael warns him that their continued happiness depends upon obedience, Adam responds that 'we never shall forget to love / Our maker, and obey him whose command / Single, is yet so just' (*PL*, V.550–2). In this passage, 'just' suggests fairness and rationality, rather than submission to a power who 'may doe what he will'. God's justice is also linked with divine righteousness in the song of the angels in Book X: 'Just are thy ways, / Righteous are thy Decrees on all thy Works' (*PL*, X.643–4). In contrast, submission not only to God's will but to earthly tyrants is presented as a just punishment for human failings in Michael's chilling assertion that 'Tyrannie must be' in the fallen world: 'God in Judgement just' subjects men to 'violent Lords', as 'Justice . . . deprives them of thir outward libertie'[43]

'Just' is used in a very different sense in the central statement of theodicy in Book III, as God says of Adam, 'I made him just and right' and therefore 'Sufficient to have stood, though free to fall' (*PL*, III.98–9). The use of the paired terms 'just and right' suggests the existence of principles imprinted in Adam and Eve before the Fall in accordance with natural law.

> Man was made in the image of God, and the whole law of nature was so implanted and innate in him that he was in need of no command . . . The law of nature . . . is itself sufficient to teach whatever is in accord with right reason (i.e., whatever is intrinsically good).[44]

Though later in Book III, God says that after the Fall, 'once more I will renew / His lapsed powers', Milton does not explicitly state in Book III that the law of nature remains applicable in the postlapsarian world, but this idea lies at the heart of *Areopagitica* and the divorce tracts. In *Tetrachordon* he speaks of 'the rules of nature and eternal righteousness, which no writt'n law extinguishes, and the Gospel least of all'.[45] 'Just and right' are again twinned when Michael, warning Adam against the dangers of passion overcoming reason, tells him 'Oft times nothing profits more / Then self esteem, founded on just and right / Well manag'd' (*PL*, VIII.571–3). Here 'just' is a moral term, applicable to man, who is afforded freedom of choice.

The many references in the later books to 'one just Man' singled out by God from among an unregenerate multitude combine a sense of God's inescapable retributive justice with the hope that courageous individuals will always arise who freely seek to tread 'the paths of righteousness' (*PL*, XI.814). The just man, Milton suggests, is likely to be treated with 'reproach and scorn', even with 'violence', his prophetic warnings ignored, but like Noah or Enoch, though 'derided' by men will be 'of God observd'. Adam says of Noah, saved with his family amid universal ruin:

> Far less I now lament for one whole World
> Of wicked Sons destroyd, then I rejoyce
> For one Man found so perfet and so just,
> That God voutsafes to raise another World
> From him, and all his anger to forget.
> (*PL*, XI.808–18, 874–8)

There are at least six references in Book XI to the beleaguered 'just Man', 'the onely righteous in a World perverse' (*PL*, XI.701), like Abdiel confronting Satan and his army. Such heroes of faith may typologically be seen as forerunners of the incarnate Jesus Christ and the operations of grace, but in the context of Michael's narration in Books XI and XII they all suggest the anger of a God who rains punishment on mankind for sins.[46]

Milton's ultimate source in the Old Testament is Genesis 18:23–6, supplemented by Jeremiah 5:1. In both these biblical passages, God is dissuaded from destroying a city of sinners.

> And Abraham drew near. And said, Wilt thou also destroy the righteous with the wicked? Peradventure there be fifty righteous within the city: wilt thou also destroy and not spare the place for the fifty righteous that are therein? That be far from thee to do after this manner, to slay the righteous with the wicked . . . Shall not the judge of all do right? And the Lord said, If I find in Sodom fifty righteous within the city, then I will spare all the place for their sakes.
>
> Run ye to and fro through the streets of Jerusalem, and see now, and know, and seek in the broad places thereof, if ye can find a man, if there be any that executeth judgment, that seeketh the truth, and I will pardon it.[47]

According to the *Oxford Bible Commentary*, Genesis 18, unusual in 'Abraham's boldness' in speaking up to the deity and the deity's 'readiness to listen to the rebuke', is illustrative of God's justice, initially questioned when Abraham urges him to 'do right'. The emphasis in *PL*, Book XI, as in these two biblical passages, is on righteousness in man, seen as rare: in Jeremiah, the *Oxford Bible Commentary* points out, the prophet is unable to find even one just man in the city. For Milton, the just man is one who 'seeketh the truth', conscious of the difficulties involved in 'daring single to be just'.[48] In the *Oxford English Dictionary*, the first definition listed for 'just' (characterized as 'now chiefly as a biblical archaism') is 'righteous in the sight of God'. Milton, who could read Hebrew, may well have known a Jewish tradition, present in the Talmud and in Hebrew commentaries on Genesis, that at any time there will be a handful of righteous men (no more than thirty-six in number, according to the tradition) for the sake of whom God spares humanity from destruction. These *tzadikim nistarim* (hidden righteous ones) differ from figures such as Noah, Abraham, and Enoch, in that they tend to live in humble obscurity, their identity unknown except to God.[49]

In a number of passages in Books XI and XII, 'the just' are contrasted with the unjust. In such passages, the righteous are frequently described as 'tri'd in sharp tribulations' (*PL*, XI.63). With Cain and Abel, 'th'unjust the just hath slain', and yet Abel is presented, typologically, as one whose 'Faith', unrecognized on earth, is 'approv'd' in Heaven, where he meets his ultimate 'reward' (*PL*, XI.455–9). There are several references in the later books to 'the renovation of the just' at Judgment Day, the longed-for apocalypse when a cleansing fire will create a new world 'wherein the just shall dwell' (*PL*, XI.65, 900–1), as contrasted with a quotidian world stained with sin, described in one passage, pessimistically, as 'To good malignant, to bad men benign / Under her own waight groaning' (*PL*, XII.538–9).

The use of 'just' as a term of measurement (exact, accurate, conformable to a standard) is relatively uncommon in *Paradise Lost*. There is no exact equivalent to 'just note and accent' in the sonnet to Henry Lawes or 'It shall be still in strictest measure eev'n' in sonnet 7.[50] Michael, challenging Satan in Book VII, says that the consequences of his wicked actions will prove 'heaviest by just measure on thy self / And thy adherents' (*PL*, VI.265–6). In the account of the sixth day of the Creation in Book VII, the industrious ant or emmet, member of a commonwealth of fellow workers, is described as 'a pattern of just equalitie', a model for humans to imitate (*PL*, VII.485–9). Here, 'just' means fair or in accordance with reason. The clearest instance in *Paradise Lost* of 'just' as a term of measurement, fixing limits, is the account of God with his compasses creating the world, separating light from darkness, bringing about order from 'Matter unform'd and void', an act intended 'to circumscribe / This Universe, and all created things': 'Thus far thy bounds, / This be thy just Circumference, O World' (*PL*, VII.225–31).

When Satan and his followers describe their own cause as just, Milton's heavy irony convicts the speaker of hypocrisy and self-delusion. The clearest instance of the use of the term 'just' to describe something palpably unjust is 'public reason just' in *PL*, IV.389, but three passages in Book II have a similar effect. Satan, opening the debate in Hell, tells the assembled fallen angels that 'just right, and the fixt Laws of Heav'n' have made him their leader (*PL*, II.18–19), and later in the same speech he says that in renewing the war with God they can claim their 'just inheritance of old' (*PL*, II.38). Near the end of Book II, Satan uses similar self-serving rhetoric in enlisting Sin and Death as his allies, promising them future prey, as he refers to 'all the heav'nly Host / Of Spirits that in our just pretenses arm'd / Fell with us from on high' (*PL*, II.824–6).

God's justice is questioned in two passages in *Paradise Lost*, first by Satan and then by Adam. In tempting Eve, Satan mounts a serious attack on the idea that God is just. Though the biblical account says that 'Eve saw that the tree was good for food, and that it was pleasant to the eyes, and a tree to be desired to make one wise' (Genesis 3:6), Milton's emphasis is primarily on the last of these. Satan's account of the effects of the tree on him, a serpent miraculously endowed with speech and reasoning powers, and his reasoned arguments to show that eating the apple will have an equivalent effect on her, awaken desire in Eve. The power of the magical tree, Satan tells her, is the power of reason, by which beasts and humans can rise above their unjustly restricting limits.

> Now I feel thy Power
> Within me cleere, not onely to discerne
> Things in thir Causes, but to trace the wayes
> Of highest Agents, deemd however wise.
> (*PL*, IX.680–3)

I, a mere serpent, have tasted the tree, and I not only am still alive, defying the taboo, but have attained 'a life more perfet . . . by ventring higher then my Lot': 'Shall that be shut to Man, which to the Beast / Is open? Or will God incense his ire / For such a petty Trespass?' (*PL*, IX.689–93).[51] He then directly challenges the idea that God, in prohibiting knowledge of good and evil, can be just. In terms of deductive logic, as a series of interconnected syllogisms, Satan's argument appears to be impeccable, once you accept his untrue premises.

> Of good, how just? Of evil, if what is evil
> Be real, why not known, since easier shunnd?
> God therefore cannot hurt ye, and be just;
> Not just, not God; not feard then, nor obeyd.
> (*PL*, IX.698–701)

The strongest part of the argument comes in the first two lines, which accord with Eve's own arguments in the separation scene and Milton's claim in *Areopagitica* that, at least in the postlapsarian world, 'knowing good by evill' is both inevitable and necessary: 'what wisdome can there be to choose, what continence to forbeare without the knowledge of evill?' (*CPW*, II.514). How can depriving men and women of the knowledge of good possibly be compatible with justice? And knowledge of evil will aid one to recognize it and avoid it. The next statement, though it observes the forms of a logical argument, is fallacious, invalid in the way it redefines 'just': justice cannot simply mean not hurting someone, and the poem has demonstrated the falsity of that definition thoroughly. But if God is necessarily just, then it is fair to say that if he is not just, he is not God, though it does not follow that a deity who is powerful without being just does not need to be obeyed or feared. An unjust God with overwhelming power at his disposal is even more to be feared than one who limits the exercise of his power in accordance with principles of justice.

Eve's response accepts Satan's central assertion, a claim which Satan has made in Books I and II as well as here: that God is not ruled by any principle of justice, but by envy, fear of overthrow by rivals, whom he therefore keeps in subjection, 'low and ignorant' (*PL*, IX.704). Eve, swallowing the bait, convinces herself that the prohibition is invalid or emanating from hidden motives. A knowledge of good and evil, denied her, she argues, has kept her unjustly in an inferior state. How can such a prohibition be just, and why should she fear it?

> In plain then, what forbids he but to know,
> Forbids us good, forbids us to be wise?
> Such prohibitions binde not . . .
> What fear I then, rather what know to feare
> Under this ignorance of good and Evil,
> Of God or Death, of Law or Penaltie?
> (*PL*, IX.758–60, 773–5)

The magic fruit, as she sees it, schooled by Satan, is 'the Cure of all', in banishing ignorance, allowing access to the privileged realm of knowledge, enabling her to 'be as Gods' (*PL*, IX.776, 710). Eve's claim that her ignorance, in a kind of prolonged infancy, has kept her from understanding what death is, what the penalty will be for disobedience, or what is meant by good and evil has been echoed by Empson and other critics who challenge the poem's basic ideology. By this argument, ignorance or inexperience is deprivation.[52]

The extent to which the fallen Eve has, for the moment at least, become a disciple of Satan is indicated by her expressed hope that God might not notice her, since 'Heav'n is high' and far away. When she raises the possibility that 'our great Forbidder', surrounded by 'all his Spies', might be distracted from his 'continual watch' over his distant subjects, her self-serving arguments resemble those put forth by Belial and Mammon in the debate in Hell (*PL*, IX.811–16). The temptation to keep Adam in ignorance of what she has done, not allowing him 'to partake / Full happiness' with her and by this means gaining advantage over him, shows Eve even more clearly to have accepted the basic premises underlying Satan's revolt. In weighing up the advantages to her if she decides to 'keep the odds of Knowledge in my power / Without Copartner', Eve uses language that echoes Satan's in the earlier books of the poem. To keep Adam from tasting the miraculous fruit, she argues, would: 'render me more equal, and perhaps, / A thing not undesireable, somtime / Superior, for inferior who is free?' (*PL*, IX.817–25). To an appreciable degree, Eve's adoption of such arguments calls into question Satan's earlier claim to be defending principles of freedom and equality in his rebellion. Though Eve's ostensible reason for choosing that '*Adam* shall share with me in bliss or woe' (*PL*, IX.831) by following her example in defying the prohibition is love of Adam, there is an element of selfish calculation even here. Though she claims to value mutual love and companionship over considerations of 'power' and dominance, her expressed motivation includes strong elements of jealousy or envy, in the fear of losing Adam if she dies and he lives on to choose another wife as replacement.

> Then I shall be no more,
> And *Adam* wedded to another *Eve*,
> Shall live with her enjoying, I extinct;
> A death to think.
>
> (*PL*, IX.820, 827–33)

Adam, in contrast, is not deceived, recognizing Eve's 'fatal Trespass' for what it is, but, without hesitation, chooses to follow Eve, moved by 'the Link of Nature', his overwhelming love for Eve.

> For with thee
> Certain my resolution is to Die;
> How could I live without thee, how forgoe
> Thy sweet Converse and Love so dearly joyn'd?
>
> (*PL*, IX.889, 906–9, 913–14)

Though the decision is an instantaneous one, not preceded by detailed deliberation, Milton makes it clear that Adam chooses to fall, giving priority to the motions of the heart over any sense of obligation to God, ignoring the warnings he has received and he has given to Eve, the need to 'beware' of any 'faire appeering good' that would lead one 'to do what God expresly hath forbid' (*PL*, IX.353–6).

Adam's long, anguished speech in Book X as he comes to recognize the consequences of the Fall, a counterpart to Satan's soliloquy on Mount Niphates, from the outset accepts his responsibility for the 'doom' that has befallen him. Mired in despair, Adam feels himself unworthy of God's 'final pardon', while questioning whether the God who has punished him so severely can be just. Addressing his creator, he asks, 'Why hast thou added / The sense of endless woes? inexplicable / Thy Justice seems.'[53] The 'terms' under which God granted Adam and Eve their tenancy in Paradise were 'too hard', making him 'unable to performe' the stipulated conditions. In lines echoed in different circumstances by the Creature in Mary Shelley's *Frankenstein*, Adam, accusing his creator, portrays himself as the unwilling object of an experiment. A key term here is 'will': 'My Will / Concurd not to my being', Adam argues, and yet the will of God is absolute, with no appeal against it.

> Did I request thee, Maker, from my Clay
> To mould me Man, did I sollicite thee
> From darkness to promote me, or here place
> In this delicious Garden?
>
> (*PL*, x.743–7, 750–1)

As with Satan on Mount Niphates, the contortions of Adam's argument reflect the pain he feels, desiring to shift the blame yet unable to escape the conclusions to which, increasingly, he is drawn. Even when he accepts the justice of the punishment handed out, seeing it as 'fair', Adam sees his relationship with his Maker as fundamentally one of power: if there is an element of free choice, it lies with God, who freely, at 'his Will', deals out reward or punishment.

> God made thee of choice his own, and of his own
> To serve him, thy reward was of his grace,
> Thy punishment then justly is at his Will.
> Be it so, for I submit, his doom is fair,
> That dust I am, and shall to dust returne.[54]

Racked with guilt and longing for death and an end to tormented consciousness, Adam now fears the 'dreadful voice' of God, hearing it 'Thunder in my ears' at all times in his imagination: 'For though the Lord of all be infinite, / Is his wrauth also?' God's 'rigour', like his 'anger', is infinite and, Adam fears, can never be 'satisfi'd' (*PL*, x.779–80, 794–5, 801–4). In his challenge to the God who has exacted such dreadful punishment for his transgression, Adam asks the question that subsequent critics, unable to accept Milton's theology, have asked: the case against the idea of original sin has rarely been put more effectively. 'Ah, why should all mankind / For one mans fault thus guiltless be condemn'd, / If guiltless?' (*PL*, x.822–4). Adam, still despairing, and, like Satan in Book iv, able to 'find no way, from deep to deeper plung'd', nevertheless, while condemning himself as 'all corrupt, both Mind and Will deprav'd', is driven to the conclusion that God is in no way to blame, and that his punishment must be endured as just (*PL*, x.825, 844). If Satan is unable to repent, disdaining even 'feign'd submission' and seeing his 'wounds of deadly hate' as incapable of cure or remission, and thus defiantly chooses eternal warfare with God, Adam freely accepts submission to God's power, aware that his attempted 'evasions' are fruitless.

Him after all Disputes
Forc't I absolve: all my evasions vain
And reasonings, though through Mazes, lead me still
But to my own conviction: first and last
On mee, mee onely, as the sourse and spring
Of all corruption, all the blame lights due.
(*PL*, IV.96, 99; X.828–33)

Yet even when he identifies God's justice with Truth, justice to Adam means fulfilling the terms of a terrible bargain, bringing on a deserved death at whatever time God pleases, with any 'prayers or cries' entirely ineffective in moving the stern deity.

Shall Truth fail to keep her word,
Justice Divine not hast'n to be just?
But Death comes not at call, Justice Divine
Mends not her slowest pace for prayers or cries.
(*PL*, X.856–9)

Though he absolves God of any responsibility for the 'endless miserie' he expects, Adam cannot at this point forgive Eve, excoriating her savagely as a 'Serpent . . . false / And hateful': 'But for thee, / I had persisted happie' (*PL*, X.810, 867–9, 873–4). It would have been better if God had left him alone in Paradise, in a universe consisting exclusively of 'Spirits Masculine': woman, 'crooked by nature', is an unnecessary addition to his own 'just number' (*PL*, X.885–90). Only when the contrite Eve, reacting to his misogynist diatribe by begging him, as 'suppliant', not to forsake her, can Adam relent and the two be reconciled. In Eve's appeal to Adam and Adam's response, the emphasis is no longer on the inexorable 'high Decrees' of divine justice, but on the flow of human sympathy,

Bereave me not,
Whereon I live, thy gentle looks, thy aid,
Thy counsel in this uttermost distress,
My onely strength and stay: forlorn of thee,
Whither shall I betake me, where subsist?
(*PL*, X.917–22, 953)

Adam's response, instinctive and immediate, is to seek to comfort the distressed Eve, supplying healing 'counsel' with 'peaceful words': 'As one disarm'd, his anger all he lost' (*PL*, X.944–6). With each providing a 'help meet' for the other, remedying deficiencies, the two can now be seen 'both joyning, / As joyn'd in injuries', in what Milton characterizes in

Tetrachordon as a 'civill fellowship of love and amity'. At the end of Book x, as Adam and Eve recognize the need for mutual 'offices of Love' to face whatever may ensue, a way is opened to possible regeneration and an end to despair. The principle of love, enabling Adam and Eve to go 'hand in hand' into the world that lay 'all before them' after their expulsion from Eden, is seen not as supplanting divine justice, but as modifying its rigour, by providing an element of hope and in this way making life in the fallen world bearable.[55]

8

'Tyrannie Must Be'
Milton and the Restoration

I

The Archangel Michael's grim narrative in *Paradise Lost*, Books XI and XII, presenting postlapsarian history to the stunned Adam as a series of disasters, describes 'true Libertie' as 'lost' after the fall, in a world inexorably declining 'from bad to worse'. Tyranny now becomes the default mode of man as a political animal. Rather than sanctioning or permitting the overthrow of tyrants, God 'in Judgement just' punishes his 'unworthie' creatures by subjecting them to 'violent Lords', as he leaves them 'to thir own polluted wayes': 'Tyrannie must be, / Though to the Tyrant thereby no excuse' (*PL*, XII.83–4, 90–6, 106, 110).

In *Samson Agonistes*, Milton's protagonist struggles against despair, the feeling that he has been abandoned by God. As Blair Worden, Sharon Achinstein, and others have shown, the poem has a specific Restoration historical context, in the situation of former commonwealthsmen and Dissenters, at a time of religious persecution and political unrest.[1] After the Restoration, when England, ignoring his warnings, had chosen a captain back for Egypt, Milton was one of many adherents to the Good Old Cause who had to go into hiding for a time, fearing for his life, and he was imprisoned in the Tower for several months. Others suffered humiliation and martyrdom, and the corpses of Cromwell, Ireton, and Bradshaw were dug up and desecrated. The horrific public spectacle of hanging and disembowelling, with the bodily parts of regicides 'thrown together like butchers meat brought from the shambles', was intended as public warning.[2] Powerful lines in *Samson Agonistes*, describing how even those devoted to the service of God could be plunged in an instant from prosperity to degradation and disgrace, evoke the fate of the regicides and the grim prospects for former commonwealthsmen in Restoration England. What makes the pain especially hard to bear is the sense of being cast off by a God who 'throw'st them lower then thou didst exalt them high', in a darkness from which there seems no escape.

> Oft leav'st them to the hostile sword
> Of Heathen and prophane, thir carkasses
> To dogs and fowls a prey, or else captiv'd:
> Or to th'unjust tribunals, under change of times,
> And condemnation of the ingrateful multitude . . .
> Just or unjust, alike seem miserable,
> For oft alike, both come to evil end.[3]

Under such conditions, the problem for Milton, as for such former republican stalwarts as Edmund Ludlow, was how to overcome the temptation of succumbing to despair: in defeat, had God punished them by leaving them 'a prey' to their enemies? According to Ludlow, on the run after the failure of his hopes after the Restoration, 'all things' in 1660 were 'counter to what the providencyes of the Lord had led to for twenty yeares past': it was God's sovereign pleasure 'to make them the tayle, who before were the head', with their enemies forcing them to 'bow downe'.[4] His fellow republican Robert Overton, a Major General in the New Model Army and Milton's friend, writing from prison, similarly saw God as 'pullinge all downe againe, leading our Strength into captivity, and giveing our Glory into his Enemies hands'. Like Ludlow he sought to reconcile the bitterness of defeat with a unyielding faith in God's providence. The blame, they argued, lay not with a capricious God but with the weaknesses of his sinful creatures.

> The Lorde takes speciall notice on w[ch] side we stand, when he is dealieinge with his owne children for their folly. But his rebuke is not upon his People for their Principle, but for their impious practices, repugnante to [that] principle they held forth, & professed.[5]

In Milton's poem, Samson's anguish comes in part from an overwhelming sense of disappointment, of great hopes crushed:

> Why was my breeding order'd and prescrib'd
> As of a person separate to God,
> Design'd for great exploits; if I must dye
> Betray'd, Captiv'd, and both my Eyes put out,
> Made of my Enemies the scorn and gaze?,
> (*Samson Agonistes*, 30–4)

In dramatizing Samson's journey out of despair, with its violent tragic conclusion, Milton raises a number of ethical and political questions. To what extent does one owe allegiance to an unjust regime? How binding are the commands of conscience? What are the limits and consequences of resistance? Here as elsewhere, Milton, through Samson, suggests a fear of freedom, an unwillingness to accept the responsibilities of 'strenuous liberty', as an explanation for why tyrants thrive:

> But what more oft in Nations grown corrupt,
> And by thir vices brought to servitude,
> Then to love Bondage more then Liberty,
> Bondage with ease then strenuous liberty.
> (268–71)

The underlying theological and ethical position of *Samson Agonistes* is essentially that of *Paradise Lost*: a radical Arminianism dissenting in some ways from more orthodox Reformed theology; in a providentially ordered universe ruled by an demanding (and omniscient) God, each individual is 'sufficient to have stood, though free to fall' (*PL*, III.99). But if *Samson Agonistes* like *Paradise Lost* seeks to 'assert Eternal Providence, / And justifie the wayes of God to men' (*PL*, I.25–6), the ways of God depicted in Milton's tragedy are deeply problematical. In the poem's most powerful passages, the dominant emotion is the sense of loss, a despair that Samson, for much of the poem, finds 'hopeless . . . all remediless' (*Samson Agonistes*, 648). The successive confrontations with Dalila, Harapha, and the Philistine Officer show Samson as combating this overwhelming feeling of inadequacy and failure. But the poem's violent, blood-soaked conclusion, with Samson dying amid the mass slaughter of his enemies, wiping out the 'choice nobility and flower' (1654) of the Philistine nation (except for those fortunate enough not to be able to buy tickets into the arena), is unsettling. In some ways, it can be seen as a fantasy of revenge by those excluded from power, turning the tables on their oppressors.

Michael's admonition to Adam, pointing out the loss of 'true Libertie' as a result of his transgression, can be interpreted in a number of ways. Theologians differed over whether original sin, a 'depravity which all human minds have in common', 'transmitted to posterity by our first parents', brought about the extinction of prelapsarian liberty. In *De Doctrina*, Milton hedges his bets, speaking of 'the loss or at least the extensive darkening of that right reason, whose function it was to discern the chief good . . . We have all committed sin in Adam, therefore we are born slaves.'[6] After Adam inveighs against Nimrod as an 'execrable Son so to aspire / Above his Brethren', Michael explains to him that 'Tyrannie must be' in the fallen world.

> Yet know withall,
> Since thy original lapse, true Libertie
> Is lost, which alwayes with right Reason dwells
> Twinn'd, and from her hath no dividual being:
> Reason in man obscur'd, or not obeyd,
> Immediately inordinate desires
> And upstart Passions catch the Government
> From Reason, and to servitude reduce
> Man till then free.
>
> (*PL*, XII.64–5, 82–90)

Both Luther and Calvin held uncompromisingly that 'man has no free will, but is a captive, servant and bondslave, either to the will of God, or to the will of Satan', and that, as a consequence of the Fall, 'the mind of man has been so completely estranged from God's righteousness' that 'man has now been deprived of freedom of choice and bound over to miserable servitude'.[7] The influential readings of C. S. Lewis and Stanley Fish both assume that 'fallen man is hopelessly corrupt', in effect turning Milton into a strict Calvinist: Adam and his descendants must be taught the bitter lesson of unswerving obedience.[8] William Walker, writing in 2009, argues a similar line: servitude is a 'permanent condition' for postlapsarian man, who lives in 'a state of bondage', incapable any longer of acting 'in accordance with reason'.[9] Mary Ann Radzinowicz interprets this passage in more optimistic terms, arguing 'that Adam's freedom as well as his punishment are inherited by all his sons' and that the fall of Adam and Eve is extended into 'a sequence of falls that, far from necessitating man's fate, reaffirms religious and political liberty'.[10]

The lines that follow, suggesting some political consequences of the fall, tend to bear out Radzinowicz's reading, and are in keeping with Milton's assertion in *De Doctrina* that 'some traces of the divine image still remain within us, which are not wholly extinguished' (*CPW*, VI.396). Those who choose a captain back for Egypt, exercising their free choice to an 'unworthie' end, get the tyrant they deserve.

> Therefore since hee permits
> Within himself unworthie Powers to reign
> Over free Reason, God in Judgement just
> Subjects him from without to violent Lords;
> Who oft as undeservedly enthrall
> His outward freedom: Tyrannie must be,
> Though to the Tyrant thereby no excuse.
>
> (*PL*, XII.90–6)[11]

Michael, who shares Adam's disapproval of the 'proud ambitious' Nimrod and his attempts at 'Empire tyrannous', presents the 'Dominion' of tyrants, falsely claiming 'a second Sovrantie' as God's deputy on earth, as 'undeserv'd' (*PL*, XII.25, 27, 32, 35). The lines, which are consistent with Milton's republican principles though different in their emphasis from *Tenure* or the *Defence*, suggest a repeated pattern: 'oft' (or in the next lines, 'somtimes', when entire 'Nations will decline so low / From vertue') the descendants of Adam and Eve will be faced with a choice and may, 'Authors to themselves', choose wrongly and suffer the consequences (*PL*, III.122; XII.97–101). The loss of inward liberty, presented here as voluntary ('since hee permits / Within himself'), precedes the loss of 'outward freedom' as the just punishment of a stern God. What can happen within the 'Government' of man, when 'sensual Appetite', a usurper, is allowed to rule over 'sovran Reason', can have its parallel in 'Nations'.[12]

There are very few crumbs of comfort for Adam in Michael's dispiriting account of postlapsarian history in *PL*, XI and XII: 'the whole Earth fill'd with violence, and all flesh / Corrupting each thir way', a world in which 'Oppression, and Sword-Law' alternate with 'luxurie and riot' holding unchecked sway (*PL*, XI.672, 715, 888–9). These evils, as Michael presents them, are the result of erroneous choice: even a 'sober Race of Men' who sought 'to worship God aright' – as Samson the Nazarite once did – can fall into the snare and 'yield up all thir vertue, all thir fame / Ignobly, to the traines and to the smiles' of temptresses (*PL*, XI.578, 621–4). The lessons Adam learns in Books XI and XII are humbling and painful. Longing for comfort in a fallen world, Adam is repeatedly swatted down by his unrelenting interlocutor, rendered 'comfortless, as when a Father mourns / His Children, all in view destroyd at once' (*PL*, XI.760–1). In a series of powerful, unsettling tableaux, images of destruction and desolation predominate, dwarfing any offered hope of redemption.[13] At one point, God is presented as ready to give up on creatures who seem incapable of learning from their experience.

> Then will this latter, as the former World,
> Still tend from bad to worse, till God at last
> Wearied with their iniquities, withdraw
> His presence from among them, and avert
> His holy Eyes; resolving from thenceforth
> To leave them to thir own polluted wayes.
> (*PL*, XII.105–10)

Books XI and XII are didactic in intent, with Michael instructing the reader as he patiently educates Adam. Adam's response to the scenes shown him in Book XI and the narrative in Book XII, initially heartfelt and naive, is repeatedly corrected by Michael's authoritative voice. When, for example, Adam, viewing 'a Beavie of fair Women, richly gay / In Gems and wanton dress', says to Michael 'Much better seems this Vision', his tutor sternly tells him 'Judg not what is best / By pleasure, though to Nature seeming meet' (*PL*, XI.582–3, 599, 603–4).[14] At times, the new knowledge Adam has acquired is almost too painful to bear, and his remarks about his disappointed hopes and the fate awaiting his descendants echo his anguished soliloquy in Book X, questioning God's justice:

> O miserable Mankind, to what fall
> Degraded, to what wretched state reserv'd!
> Better end heer unborn. Why is life giv'n
> To be thus wrested from us? rather why
> Obtruded on us thus?,
>
> (*PL*, XI.500–4)

Adam's enlightenment culminates in his recognition of Jesus Christ as saviour and redeemer: in effect, his conversion, making him an exemplar of Faith, the first Christian. The last of Adam's speeches in the dialogue with Michael links faith in Christ with what Milton in the invocation to Book IX calls 'the better fortitude / Of Patience and Heroic Martyrdom', and Michael hails this speech as evidence of having 'attain'd the sum / Of wisdom'.

> That suffering for Truths sake
> Is fortitude to highest victorie,
> And to the faithful Death the Gate of Life;
> Taught this by his example whom I now
> Acknowledge my Redeemer ever blest.[15]

Though the contrast of the First and Second Adam is made explicit only once in the poem, Books XI and XII fulfil the promise of the opening lines: 'Till one greater Man / Restore us, and regain the blissful Seat' (*PL*, I.4–5). As Addison said in 1712, commenting on Book XII, 'The principal Design of this *Episode* was to give *Adam* an Idea of the Holy Person, who was to reinstate Humane Nature in that Happiness and Perfection from which it had fallen.'[16]

Michael's illustrated account of selected horrendous scenes from the Old Testament is designed to demonstrate to Adam the consequences of his sin: 'O sight / Of terrour, foul and ugly to behold', says Adam, dissolving in tears at the spectacle (*PL*, XI.463–4). Book XII is full of reminders that the events of the Old Testament are typological foreshadowings of the redemption, freeing Adam's descendants from the bondage of sin.

In accordance with Milton's post-Calvinist theology, 'by types / And shadowes' the Law prefigures the Gospel by which, in processes of time, it will be superseded (*PL*, XII.232–3). When Moses, accompanied by thunder and lightning, brings down from Mount Sinai the Ten Commandments, the Israelites (or pious Christians, reading the account in scripture) are shown hints of a further truth beyond the 'imposition of strict Laws':

> Instructed that to God is no access
> Without Mediator, whose high Office now
> *Moses* in figure beares, to introduce
> One greater, of whose day he shall foretell,
> And all the Prophets in thir Age the times
> Of great *Messiah* shall sing.
> (*PL*, XII.239–44, 304)[17]

The imperfections of the Law, and the inability of men, unaided, to live up to its exacting requirements, Milton suggests, may instruct them in the need to embrace a 'better Cov'nant', as 'shadowie Types' are supplanted by Christian 'Truth' (*PL*, XII.300–3).

Critics have often found Books XI and XII disappointingly anticlimactic, a distinct falling off from the human drama of Books IX and X. Addison says of Book XII, 'If Milton's Poem flags any where, it is in this Narration, where in some places the Author has been so attentive to his Divinity, that he has neglected his Poetry.' [18] C. S. Lewis has described Books XI and XII is 'inartistic', 'an untransmuted lump of futurity', written in a manner that is 'curiously bad . . . dry and cumbrous'. Martz attributes the problems in Books XI and XII to a 'failure of imagination' in the passages of 'simple didacticism': 'Theologically, the design may be said to work; poetically, it is a disaster.'[19] Michael's narration in Book XII is often inert, as with a lecturer droning on endlessly before an audience struggling to keep awake. In lines 1–465, Adam only manages three interjections of sixteen, fifteen and eleven lines, with all the rest given over to Michael, in passages which at times barely keep up the pretence of telling a story:

> The rest
> Were long to tell, how many Battels fought,
> How many Kings destroyd, and Kingdoms won,
> Or how the Sun shall in mid Heav'n stand still
> A day entire, and Nights due course adjourne.
> (*PL*, XII.260–4)

A further problem with the last two books, as Loewenstein and others have noted, is that the scenes of destructive violence, consequences of the Fall, beginning with the slaughter of the innocent Abel by Cain, are more convincing, presented more vividly, than the promised consolation. Two competing views of history, tragic and apocalyptic, are at war in Books XI and XII, and the conflict is never fully reconciled.[20] On the one hand, the history of postlapsarian man is a series of disasters, missed opportunities, backsliding, in which tyrants and warlords flourish; on the other hand, an ultimate triumph awaits, beyond the limits of recordable time, for those who persevere in their faith. Hope is born out of possible despair, in a time felt to be unpropitious to one 'fall'n on evil dayes', and the danger persists that, surrounded by 'savage clamor', any such hope may prove 'an empty dreame' (*PL*, VII.25, 36–9).

The procession of disasters in Books XI and XII is punctuated by the recurrent presence of a 'just man', the rare individual, who even 'in a dark Age' will seek to serve his divine master, ignoring 'allurement, custom, and a World / Offended' by his conduct (*PL*, XI.808–11). Though in Michael's narrative the series begins with Enoch and Noah and culminates with a saviour who will 'endure . . . a reproachful life and cursed death' to redeem man from the bondage of sin, the example of the 'just man' in a hostile age, Milton suggests here and elsewhere, is applicable to 'the sad friends of Truth', wherever they appear. In any given age, the just man, a tiny, embattled remnant, 'in mind prepar'd, if so befall, / For death, like that which the redeemer did', may have the courage to stand out, in 'a pattern of individual resistance to corrupt, sinful and violent societies'.[21]

Yet even after Adam, 'replete with joy', welcomes the 'deliverer' who can bring redemption to fallen man, Michael sounds a note of caution, warning of an extended reign of darkness, in which the teachings of Jesus will be perverted by those who seek 'secular power, though feigning still to act / By spiritual.' Rather than a gradual process towards enlightenment and renovation, history is presented in 'a grim narrative' of 'degeneration and frustrated historical reform' as an irreversible downward spiral.[22]

> Wolves shall succeed for teachers, grievous Wolves,
> Who all the sacred mysteries of Heav'n
> To thir own vile advantages shall turne
> Of lucre and ambition, and the truth
> With superstitions and traditions taint . . .
> To themselves appropriating
> The Spirit of God, promisd alike and giv'n
> To all Beleevers; and from that pretense,
> Spiritual Lawes by carnal power shall force
> On every conscience.
>
> (*PL*, XII.508–12, 517–22)

In this eruption of rage at corrupt worldly usurpers, those who 'for their bellies sake' seek power and preferment, confounding the carnal and spiritual realms, Milton, using Michael as a spokesman for his own radical Protestant views, returns to the arguments he had put forth in such pamphlets as *Of Reformation in England* and *A Treatise of Civil Power*, as well as in the lines in *Lycidas* on 'our corrupted Clergy then in their height' and in 'On the new forcers of Conscience under the Long Parliament'. Though these works were written under different circumstances, Milton's position in them remains constant. But one difference is that in 1637, 1641, 1647, and 1659, Milton writes in hope of bringing about change, calling the attention of readers to the harm that is being done by those who spread 'foul contagion', predicting their eventual 'ruine'.[23] Milton's prose tracts during the period of the English Revolution are all based on the assumption that those addressed are capable of listening to reason and will give consideration to arguments that, even emanating from those 'in a private condition', seek to 'advance the publick good'. [24] In *Of Reformation*, Milton argues, offering counsel, that 'we must first of all begin roundly to . . . cut away from the publick body the noysom and diseased tumor of Prelacie', and in *A Treatise of Civil Power*, he urges 'the governors of this commonwealth', mixing admonition and discreet flattery, that 'they may, I doubt not, in this treatise, finde that which not only will confirm them to defend still the Christian liberty which we enjoy, but will incite them also to enlarge it'.[25] In Michael's attack on the 'grievous Wolves', in contrast, there is no hope advanced of reform. Milton's rhetoric in this passage, in the verbs 'force', 'binde', and 'unbuild' assumes not only that a reader will agree with the proposition that force is inappropriate in matters of conscience, but also that those in power will pay no attention to these arguments. 'Many will presume' to rule tyrannously by force, and 'heavie persecution shall arise', to punish 'all' who dare to dissent.

> What will they then
> But force the Spirit of Grace it self, and binde
> His consort Libertie; what, but unbuild
> His living Temples, built by Faith to stand[?]
> (*PL*, XII.524–7, 530–2)

Michael, after lamenting the way in which 'the rest, farr greater part, / Will deem in outward Rites and specious formes / Religion satisfi'd', goes on to utter the poem's most bleak and pessimistic lines, foreseeing a world in which the bad prosper and the good suffer, a world 'under her own waight groaning', with no apparent remedy available to the beleaguered, outnumbered virtuous until the long-deferred Day of Judgment (*PL*, XII.533–9). In Books XI and XII as in *The Readie and Easie Way*, with its desperate attempt to 'stay these ruinous proceedings', before the English people 'take our leaves of Libertie' unalterably, Milton regularly presents the warnings of prophets and heroes of faith as unheeded.[26] If the only hope remaining in 'a World devote to universal rack' is for the rare survivor 'to save himself and houshold' (*PL*, XI.820–1), this would leave little or no scope for the amelioration of present ills.

II

Paradise Regained and *Samson Agonistes*, in their different ways, both concern themselves with the problems and temptations facing those who seek to serve God in a hostile, unjust society. The two poems were published together in 1671: the title page reads '*Paradise Regain'd . . . to which is added Samson Agonistes*'.[27] There are a number of verbal parallels linking the two works. Both Samson and Jesus brood on their appointed role as potential 'deliverer', both are beset by 'restless thoughts' at the outset, aware that they have been singled out for some great task, with an angelic messenger bearing witness to their extraordinary status. Both at key points in the action are described as being impelled by 'some strong motion' or 'some rouzing motions'. Where Jesus is presented as a model of conduct in the way he resists temptation and overcomes his assailant, Samson, gifted but imperfect, has succumbed to temptation and must face the consequences.[28]

As a number of critics have pointed out, the juxtaposition of the two poems in a single volume, with striking differences as well as similarities, can be read in very different ways, seeing them either as complementary or as sharply contrasted. Achinstein and Loewenstein, emphasizing the historical context of the 1671 volume in addressing the problematic situation facing dissenters, religious and political, after the Restoration, see the two poems as 'two representations of radical sainthood and two different kinds of literary responses to the political and spiritual crises of the Revolution and Restoration'. To these critics, the central figures of these two poems, each in his own way, exemplify the difficulties facing conscientious individuals in hard times, as moral agents and servants of a demanding deity.[29] An entirely different view of the relationship between the two poems is argued by Joseph Wittreich and other revisionist critics, who, disturbed by the violence of the ending of *Samson Agonistes*, present the figure of Samson as 'a negative example, a warning; a life not to be imitated', as against 'the example set by Jesus' in the companion poem. Wittreich views the two poems as closely interconnected, 'not autonomous but dependent on one another for their meaning', to the extent that *Paradise Regained* can serve as a 'gloss' on the poem published with it.[30] John Carey, arguing a similar line in 1969, says of *Samson Agonistes* that 'its hero serves as a barbaric foil to the new Christian hero' of *Paradise Regained*. According to Wittreich, 'In his own juxtaposition of Samson's story with that of the Son, Milton forces a distinction between those who slay and those who save, between the destroyers and preservers.'[31] A variant of this position is set forth in Derek Wood's *Exiled from Light* (2001), with particular attention to the underlying theology of the two poems, the contrast between the Old Law of the Hebrew Bible and the Gospel that had superseded it. Wood does not denigrate Samson, but sees him as limited in his vision by the Old Testament morality he embodies. As we have seen, Milton in *De Doctrina* and *A Treatise of Cvil Power* argues that under 'the new dispensation of the covenant of grace', believing Christians are entirely exempt from the stipulations of the Mosaic Law of the Old Testament, which he criticizes as a 'childish and servile discipline'. To Wood, this contrast of Law and Gospel is central to *Samson Agonistes*, with its 'savage, pre-Christian morality': 'The fictional protagonist Milton fashioned out of the story in Judges is, I suggest, an emblematic or iconic embodiment of Old Testament consciousness: the state of religion under the Law, rigorous, incomplete, enslaved, literalistic, and uncomprehending.'[32]

Though the two schools of critics disagree strongly about *Samson Agonistes*, they are entirely in agreement in seeing *Paradise Regained* as exemplary, educative, in providing in its hero, undergoing trials and emerging triumphant, a model of conduct available for conscientious Christians faced with situations involving moral choice in their daily lives. According to Loewenstein, 'the inner faith and quiet expectation exemplified by the patient messianic hero who endures constant trials and temptations – and who perseveres' can provide guidance for those in Milton's own day and at other times who find themselves 'tested and proven by trials and tribulations in the hostile wilderness of this world'.[33] As Margaret Kean puts it, concisely, 'his example stands in the text for all willing to follow in his footsteps'. The poem's opening lines suggest a homiletic element in announcing as its subject 'recover'd Paradise to all mankind, / By one mans firm obedience fully tri'd / Through all temptation'.[34] The term 'one man', applying both to Adam and to Jesus, the second Adam, is significant: through the sacrifice of Jesus, voluntarily assuming 'on mans behalf' the burden of mortality, freely choosing 'to die / For mans offence', 'all mankind' are offered the opportunity to gain salvation, overcoming the malign effects of the Fall. *Paradise Regained* thus is a poem that asks, 'How is man to live?' and, as Irene Samuel argues, announces from the outset 'its availability as the mimesis of a universal action, a program for every man'.[35]

The situation of Jesus in *Paradise Regained*, faced by a subtle tempter, who is initially disguised as 'an aged man in Rural weeds', is similar to that of the Lady in the Ludlow Masque, or, indeed, of any 'true warfaring Christian', who can 'apprehend and consider vice with all her baits and seeming pleasures, and yet abstain, and yet distinguish, and yet prefer that which is truly better'.[36] The poem's opening lines, with their contrast of the two Adams, suggest that the contest between the Son of God and Satan is one that will be re-enacted frequently in later times, on occasions when 'the Tempter' can once again be 'defeated and repuls't' (*PR*, I.5–6). When God the Father in Book I, speaking of the Son's forthcoming contest with Satan, tells Gabriel of how 'By Humiliation and strong Sufferance: / His Weakness shall o'recome Satanic strength', the language is that of Adam's final speech to Michael:

With good
Still overcoming evil, and by small
Accomplishing great things, by things deemd weak
Subverting worldly strong, and worldly wise
By simply meek.

In some respects, as Achinstein says, *Paradise Regained* can serve as 'a handbook for talking back to the ungodly', particularly appropriate to 'the Restoration context of religious persecution'.[37]

The emphasis throughout *Paradise Regained* is on the humanity of Jesus, as he stands firm against the tempter. Though he is never misled about Satan's identity and nature ('Knowing who I am, as I know who thou art'), he is not presented as gifted with extraordinary knowledge.

And now by some strong motion I am led
Into this Wilderness, to what intent
I know not yet, perhaps I need not know.
(*PR*, I.290–2, 356)

Jesus is aware that he is 'no Son of mortal man', but he cannot predict what 'the mighty work' to which he is called might entail, 'How to begin, how to accomplish best / His end of being on Earth, and mission high' (*PR*, I.186, 234; II.113–14). In keeping with Milton's Arian theology, the Son in *Paradise Regained* does not share the Father's omniscience: in refuting Satan's arguments, he relies on the same capacities of reason as anyone who, armed with faith, seeks to serve Truth. 'Let her and Falshood grapple; who ever knew Truth put to the wors, in a free and open encounter.'[38]

The sense of uncertainty about the future, 'high hope' mingled with fear and rising 'doubt', is conveyed movingly in the 'troubl'd thoughts' of Mary, who has experienced only 'Afflictions' and is puzzled by what is 'meant' by her son's actions:

> O what avails me now that honour high
> To have conceiv'd of God, or that salute,
> Hale highly favour'd, among women blest;
> While I to sorrows am no less advanc't,
> And fears as eminent, above the lot
> Of other women, by the birth I bore.
> (*PR*, II.II, 65–71, 92, 99)

The disciples, at the beginning of Book II, are equally troubled, thrown into 'perplexity' and doubt:

> Alas, from what high hope to what relapse
> Unlook'd for are we fall'n …
> Now, now, for sure, deliverance is at hand;
> The Kingdom shall to *Israel* be restor'd:
> Thus we rejoyc'd, but soon our joy is turn'd
> Into perplexity and new amaze:
> For whither is he gone, what accident
> Hath rapt him from us?
> (*PR*, II.II–12, 30–1, 35–40)[39]

In the wilderness, Jesus, like his disciples, initially felt that his appointed task might be to become a heroic liberator, a second Judas Maccabeus, the 'great deliverer' that Samson had once promised to be, freeing his oppressed people from the tyrant's yoke. The prospect, for Jesus as for his disciples, is an attractive one, couched in language that combines republican fervour and apocalyptic hope.

> Yet this not all
> To which my Spirit aspir'd; victorious deeds
> Flam'd in my heart, heroic acts, one while
> To rescue *Israel* from the *Roman* yoke,
> Then to subdue and quell o're all the earth,
> Brute violence and proud Tyrannick power,
> Till truth were freed, and equity restor'd.
> (*PR*, I.214–20)

Reza Aslan's recent book *Zealot* (2013) presents Jesus in exactly this way, as a threat to Roman power whose 'messianic aspirations threatened the occupation of Palestine' by Rome. The establishment of the Kingdom of God on earth, in which 'the powerful would be displaced by the powerless', would mean 'the destruction of the present order', an imminent danger both to the Roman authorities and the priestly hierarchy.[40]

To the disciples, it is the apparent dashing of such hopes of liberation from a hated slavery, subjected to the 'pow'r unjust' of their Roman conquerors, that is most troubling. Their plea echoes the lament of the Psalms, coupled with the hope that God will wreak vengeance upon the heathen and 'break them with a rod of iron': 'The kings of the earth set themselves, and the rulers take counsel together, against the Lord, and against his anointed.'[41] 'Now, now', the disciples cry out, hoping that the prophesied 'time is come':

> God of *Israel*,
> Send thy Messiah forth, the time is come,
> Behold the Kings of the Earth how they oppress
> Thy chosen, to what highth thir pow'r unjust
> They have exalted, and behind them cast
> All fear of thee; arise and vindicate
> Thy Glory, free thy people from thir yoke.
> (*PR*, II.35, 42–8)

What is at issue, as John Coffey has argued, is whether such a long-awaited moment is at hand, whether the promise of deliverance would be fulfilled.[42]

In *Samson Agonistes*, after Samson's battle of wits with the Philistine giant Harapha, the Chorus sets forth alternative paths for 'the Spirits of just men long opprest'. It is possible that they will find a 'deliverer', armed by God with 'Heroic magnitude of mind' to overthrow 'Tyrannic power' in 'the mighty of the Earth'. 'More oft', however, in accordance with the will of God, they are assigned the lot of suffering, patience, endurance under hardship as 'the trial of thir fortitude' (*Samson Agonistes*, 1269–75, 1279, 1287–8). As Milton puts it, in the voice of 'patience', in the sonnet on his blindness, 'who best / Bear his milde yoak, they serve him best . . . / They also serve who only stand and waite' (sonnet 19, 8, 10–11, 14). Though in the invocation to *PL*, Book IX, Milton speaks of 'Patience and heroic Martyrdom' as 'better' as a subject for poetry than 'Warrs, hitherto the onely Argument / Heroic deem'd' (*PL*, IX.28–32), there is no denigration of 'heroic acts' in defiance of tyrants and oppressors in *Samson Agonistes* or in Books I and II of *Paradise Regained.* When in Book III Satan reminds

Jesus of the prophecy that 'to a Kingdom thou art born, ordain'd / To sit upon thy Father *David's* Throne', Jesus answers that 'all things are best fulfill'd in their due time' and that he must accept whatever lot has been assigned him.

> What if he hath decreed that I shall first
> Be try'd in humble state, and things adverse,
> By tribulations, injuries, insults,
> Contempts, and scorns, and snares, and violence.
> (*PR*, III.152–3, 182, 188–91)

An implication in such a passage, in the context of Restoration England as 'an age of acute trials and uncertainty', is that the just man will continue to suffer 'contempts, and scorns', and that any deliverance from oppression may be long delayed.[43]

As Lewalski has observed, the action of *Paradise Regained* may be seen as Jesus' attempts, under challenge from Satan, to define what it is to be 'the Son of God', to ascertain his nature and, even more, to work out his mission, his ordained role.[44] When Satan in Book IV, casting aside all pretences, admits that he recognizes Jesus as his 'fatal enemy' and thus has sought 'to understand my adversary, who / And what he is', he claims that the term 'Sons of God' has no one single meaning.

> Thenceforth I thought thee worth my nearer view
> And narrower Scrutiny, that I might learn
> In what degree or meaning thou art call'd
> The Son of God, which bears no single sence;
> The Son of God I also am, or was,
> And, if I was, I am; relation stands;
> All men are Sons of God; yet thee I thought
> In some respects far higher so declar'd.
> (*PR*, IV.514–21, 525–8)

Satan, of course, is not led by mere curiosity, in seeking, as previously with Adam and Eve, 'to win him, or win from him what I can', but the questions he raises here are legitimate ones. In seeking to 'try' or 'sift' his adversary, Satan sets a series of tests by which Jesus can demonstrate his nature as Son of God, in accordance with God's plan to 'expose' his Son to the temptations of Satan and, in triumphing, 'shew him worthy of his birth divine'. As in the earlier trial by temptation of Adam and Eve in *Paradise Lost*, both the test and its outcome are presented by Milton as part of a providential pattern, consistent with a deity who foresees but does not compel.[45]

In their contest, Satan and Jesus begin on more or less equal terms. The young Jesus, with no memory of a previous existence in Heaven, can rely on his careful reading of scripture ('strait I again revolv'd / The Law and Prophets, searching what was writ / Concerning the Messiah') and on the cloudy prophecies coming from an angelic 'messenger' of God, as narrated to him by his mother: 'He fore-told / Thou shouldst be great, and sit on *David's* Throne, / And of thy Kingdom there should be no end.' The Son's principal weapon in answering Satan, along with his steadfast resolution, is the gift of reason he shares with other men, rather than any special gifts consequent on his divine status.[46]

The battle of wits between Jesus and Satan is in part a hermeneutic combat, as the two antagonists brandish rival scriptural passages or interpretations of the same biblical texts. The prophecy that Jesus should one day 'sit on *David's* Throne', a phrase susceptible of any number of meanings, is interpreted by Satan as the exercise of earthly power, to be gained 'by conquest or by league' (*PR*, III.370), overcoming potential military or political rivals. In the last of the temptations, Satan's quotation from scripture is central to the challenge, and Jesus responds with another biblical passage, as he proves himself worthy of the name Son of God, triumphing over the tempter.[47] Satan, bearing Jesus through the air, places his enemy, perilously, on the pinnacle of the Temple of Jerusalem (suggesting, among other things, the dangers consequent on occupying a high position):

> There stand, if thou wilt stand; to stand upright
> Will ask thee skill; I to thy Fathers house
> Have brought thee, and highest plac't, highest is best,
> Now show thy Progeny; if not to stand,
> Cast thy self down; safely if Son of God:
> For it is written, He will give command
> Concerning thee to his Angels, in thir hands
> They shall up lift thee, lest at any time
> Thou chance to dash thy foot against a stone.
> (*PR*, IV.551–9)

In this passage, closely based on Luke 4:9–12, the quotation from Psalm 91:11–12, on how 'no evil' will befall the righteous who trust in God, is accurate, though the interpretation by Satan is self-serving: 'For he shall give his angels charge over thee, to keep thee in all thy ways. They shall bear thee up in their hands, lest thou dash thy foot upon a stone.'[48] The temptation is presumption or arrogance, assuming a special privileged status in being 'Son of God', and demonstrating these extraordinary powers by performing a gratuitous miracle. God will maintain him in the perilous stance on top of the pinnacle, defying the laws of gravity, or, even more spectacularly, will send angels to catch him as he leaps off the pinnacle. Jesus' response uses a second scriptural citation, from Deuteronomy 6:16, to win the exchange, and the victory in words is immediately, conclusively echoed by a physical response, as Satan falls while Jesus stands, unmoved: 'To whom thus Jesus: also it is written, / Tempt not the Lord thy God, he said and stood. / But Satan smitten with amazement fell' (*PR*, IV.560–2). The terms 'stand'/'stood' and 'fall'/'fell' are, of course, both literal and metaphorical: the fall of Satan explicitly re-enacts his earlier Fall, 'Hurld headlong flaming from th'Ethereal Skie', as presented in *Paradise Lost*, and the terms recall the principles of Milton's theodicy, repeated several times in the earlier poem: 'Sufficient to have stood, though free to fall . . . Freely they stood who stood, and fell who fell.'[49]

The words 'Tempt not the Lord thy God' are ambiguous, in the manner of an oracular pronouncement, though their effects on Satan are immediate and direct. Critics have disagreed as to whether Jesus's words tell Satan 'Don't tempt me, because I am God', thus constituting the Son's proclamation or recognition of his own divinity, or, in their primary meaning, are saying that it is wrong to tempt God the Father by asking him to perform a miracle on your behalf. In Deuteronomy, Moses is warning the Israelites not to make God angry with them: 'Ye shall not tempt the Lord your God, as ye tempted him in Massah.'[50] The biblical parallel makes the second reading more likely, and Irene Samuel has argued, citing Calvin's interpretation of the episode in Luke 4, that Jesus's answer to Satan is exemplary in 'defining the right way for every man': 'For they which neglect the means which God appointeth do as if they tried his power and his strength . . . In sum, whoever desireth to take a trial of the divine power, where it is not necessary, he tempteth God, by bringing his power to an unjust examination.'[51] Though Jesus's response is instantaneous, with no element of deliberation or weighing of alternatives, it is presented in the poem as an act of rational choice, a model of how to resist the blandishments of false worldly values.

When in Books III and IV, Satan dangles before Jesus the prospect of regaining 'the Throne of *David*' and bringing about 'deliverance of thy brethren' from 'servitude' (*PR*, III.374, 381–3), it is one of a series of temptations, presented by Milton as glittering but shoddy. The implicit condition, revealed by an angry, defeated Satan at the end of the display, is that Jesus fall down and worship him. Jesus realizes that 'the Kingdoms of the world' (*PR*, IV.182) are Satan's domain, and rejects the gift as tainted. Satan's offer of '*David's* royal seat' (*PR*, III.373) is a central part of the temptation of the kingdoms, which takes up nearly half of the poem, beginning with Satan's taunt:

> Great acts require great means of enterprise;
> Thou art unknown, unfriended, low of birth . . .
> Which way or from what hope dost thou aspire
> To greatness? Whence Authority deriv'st?
> What Followers, what Retinue canst thou gain?
> (*PR*, II.412–13, 417–19)

These trappings of monarchy – 'sumptuous courts . . . the multiplying of a servile crew . . . bred up then to the hopes not of public, but of court office' – are what Milton portrays as most objectionable about a threatened 'returne to Kingship' in *The Readie and Easie Way* (*CPW*, VII.423, 425). Jesus's reply redefines monarchy, presented by Satan in wholly material terms, as a kingdom within. These egalitarian lines allow for the possibility that there can be good kings, servants of the public, conscious of their responsibilities, but dismiss the visual emblems of royal power as 'golden in show' (*PR*, II.458). The only true kingship is rule over oneself. Milton had praised Cromwell in the *Second Defence* as one who, by demonstrating his government over himself, had proved his fitness to rule, and such qualities of self-discipline were common to 'every wise and vertuous man'.

> For therein stands the office of a King,
> His Honour, Vertue, Merit and chief Praise,
> That for the Publick all this weight he bears.
> Yet he who reigns within himself, and rules
> Passions, Desires, and Fears, is more a King;
> Which every wise and vertuous man attains:
> And who attains not, ill aspires to rule
> Cities of men, or head-strong Multitudes,
> Subject himself to Anarchy within,
> Or lawless passions in him which he serves.[52]

Satan then turns to glory, prowess in arms, holding up for emulation such great classical figures as Alexander, Scipio, Pompey and Julius Caesar, 'whom now all the world admires' (*PR*, III.39). Jesus's reply is one of Milton's strongest attacks on false notions of military glory, contrasting 'the flourishing works of peace' (*PR*, III.80) with the slaughterhouse of war. Milton is not simply saying, as in his sonnet to Cromwell, that 'peace has her victories / No less renownd than warr' (sonnet 16, 10–11). Here, as in Michael's remarks to Adam in *PL*, Book XI, Milton describes 'great Conquerours', praised by those who foolishly admire 'Might onely', as 'destroyers rightlier call'd, and Plagues of men' (*PL*, XI.689–97). Milton's sympathies in both passages plainly lie with the victims of conquest rather than the arrogant conquerors. The 'just man' living in humble circumstances is praiseworthy, where those who 'swell with pride', demanding to be worshipped as gods, are 'men not worthy of fame' (*PR*, III.62, 70, 81).

> They err who count it glorious to subdue
> By Conquest far and wide, to over-run
> Large Countries, and in field great Battels win,
> Great Cities by assault; what do these Worthies,
> But rob and spoil, burn, slaughter, and enslave
> Peaceable Nations, neighbouring, or remote,
> Made Captive, yet deserving freedom more
> Than those thir Conquerours, who leave behind
> Nothing but ruin whereso'ere they rove,
> And all the flourishing works of peace destroy.
> (*PR*, III.71–80)[53]

All the 'cumbersome / Luggage of war', Jesus says in a later passage, is a sign of vain ostentation, 'of human weakness rather than of strength' (*PR*, III.387, 400–2).

The temptation of direct political action, fulfilling prophecies that Jesus as Messiah would be the deliverer of his captive, suffering nation, now 'reduc't a Province under Roman yoke', is harder to resist. As we have seen, the idea of a sacred 'Duty to free / Thy country from her Heathen servitude' was one shared by Jesus and his disciples, and exiled or outlawed republicans such as Algernon Sidney, Edmund Ludlow and Sir Henry Vane looked forward to the imminent overthrow of the Stuart monarchy.[54] In his answer to Satan, Jesus does not reject the ideal as false or chimerical, but makes two points. His initial response is that the overthrow of earthly tyrants at this time was not in accordance with the will of God. God has decreed for him and for others who dedicate themselves to the service of their divine master a period of suffering and trial. Later, when Satan takes him up to a mountain top and shows him a vision of how, faced with the power of the contending Roman and Parthian empires, he might come into his inheritance and gain 'that which alone can truly reinstall thee / In *David's* royal seat, his true Successour' (*PR*, III.372–3), Jesus's response is that those he might save are unworthy. It is another version of 'Tyrannie must be', another example of choosing a captain back for Egypt.

> As for those captive Tribes, themselves were they
> Who wrought their own captivity, fell off
> From God to worship Calves, the Deities

> Of *Egypt*, *Baal* next and *Ashtaroth*.
> And all the Idolatries of Heathen round . . .
> Should I of these the liberty regard,
> Who freed, as to their ancient Patrimony,
> Unhumbl'd, unrepentant, unreform'd,
> Headlong would follow; and to thir Gods perhaps
> Of *Bethel* or of *Dan*? no, let them serve
> Thir enemies, who serve Idols with God.
> (*PR*, III.414–17, 427–32)

The history of the Jews in the Old Testament is one of recurrent backsliding, falling off from their professed principles to follow false gods and tawdry earthly values, abusing their gift of freedom. Serving the tyrant within, they succumb to earthly tyrants: 'let them serve'.[55]

After Jesus firmly rejects Satan's offer of the kingdoms, Satan adds a further test, the temptation of '*Athens* . . . Mother of Arts / And Eloquence'. Ancient Greece is presented, attractively, as a repository of wisdom, 'sage Philosophy', as well as 'the secret power / Of harmony', in the works of Homer and 'the lofty grave Tragoedians', teachers of 'moral prudence' (*PR*, IV.240–1, 254–5, 261–3, 272). Jesus, unmoved by Satan's rhetoric, dismisses secular arts and learning as unworthy: there is only one truth, and 'other doctrine' must be cast aside, without hesitation.

> To whom our Saviour sagely thus repli'd.
> Think not but that I know these things, or think
> I know them not; not therefore am I short
> Of knowing what I ought: he who receives
> Light from above, from the fountain of light,
> No other doctrine needs, though granted true;
> But these are false, or little else but dreams ,
> Conjectures, fancies, built on nothing firm.
> (*PR*, IV.285–92)

In the lengthy speech that follows, Jesus condemns all secular learning as no better than 'tedious talk . . . vain boast' by men 'ignorant of themselves, of God much more' and classical literature as 'toys / and trifles', packed with lies, 'swelling Epithetes thick laid / As varnish on a Harlots cheek' (*PR*, IV.307, 310, 328–9, 343–4). Readers of Milton have been troubled by this passage as seemingly inconsistent with Milton's praise of 'the benefit which may be had of books promiscuously read' in *Areopagitica* and the indebtedness to the classical tradition evident throughout his writing. Douglas Bush is representative in characterizing this uncompromising denunciation as 'a painful shock', given the author's 'lifelong devotion to the classical authors' he takes as model in *Paradise Regained* as well as

Paradise Lost.[56] The pitched battle between Athens and Jerusalem, in which one must overcome the other, is often seen as a contest within Milton between Hebraism and Hellenism, Puritanism and humanism, with a 'readiness to make the ultimate sacrifice, if one should be demanded'. Some critics associate this renunciation of the classical world, and *Paradise Regained* generally, with a growing disillusionment and pessimism in the later Milton, after the failure of the English revolution.[57]

Lewalski and others have argued that this episode is compatible with Milton's views expressed elsewhere. The claim that '*Sion's* songs', the Psalms and Hymns of the Hebrew Bible, works that are 'from God inspir'd', excel all classical poetry, can, for example, be found in *The Reason of Church Government*, in a passage that considers possible models for a poet. A Christian writer, whether poet or philosopher, Milton maintains, must necessarily have an advantage over one unaware of the truths of scripture.[58] Even the dubious assertion that 'our Hebrew Songs' preceded the writings of ancient Greece chronologically, and that '*Greece* from us these Arts deriv'd, / Ill imitated' (*PR*, IV.334–9) has precedents in Milton's other writings and that of his contemporaries. What Jesus is saying here is closely akin to passages in Milton's prose writings and in the dialogue between Adam and Raphael in *Paradise Lost*, Book VII: that learning is valuable only when it is applied, pragmatically, to what can be of use in our daily lives. As Adam says, instructed by Raphael:

> That not to know at large of things remote
> From use, obscure and suttle, but to know
> That which before us lies in daily life,
> Is the prime Wisdom, what is more, is fume,
> Or emptiness, or fond impertinence.[59]

Milton's attacks on Salmasius and other opponents in polemical tracts similarly attack 'learned ignorance', a 'swoln visage of counterfeit knowledge' as fraudulent attempts to deceive the credulous: 'In matters of Religion, there is not any thing more intolerable, then a learned foole, or a learned Hypocrite . . . coopt up at his empty speculations, a sot, an ideot for any use that mankind can make of him.' The contrast, in Milton as in the humanist tradition, is between knowledge and wisdom, *scientia* and *sapientia*.[60] In *Hirelings* and in *De Doctrina*, Milton argues against any separate status for the clergy as 'a distinct order in the commonwealth', elevated above the laity, 'bred up for divines in babbling schools and fed at the publick cost'. A 'plaine unlearned man', like the disciples of a 'Saviour . . . anointed to preach the gospel to the poore', may have spiritual gifts lacking in worldly holders of benefices: 'He who disdaind not to be laid in a manger, disdains not to be preachd in a barn.'[61]

> It is a fond error, though too much beleevd among us, to think that the universitie makes a minister of the gospel . . . That which makes fit a minister, the scripture can best informe us to be only from above . . . The Gospel makes no difference from the magistrate himself to the meanest artificer, if God evidently favour him with spiritual gifts, as he can easily and oft have don.[62]

In *De Doctrina*, Milton argues the radical position that 'any believer can preach the gospel, so long as he is endowed with certain gifts' and that, in similar fashion, 'any believer can administer baptism' and 'the communion of the Lord's Supper'. As Christopher Hill points out, the educational reformer William Dell, Independent minister and chaplain to the New Model Army, held similar views, arguing against any distinctions between privileged clergy and subservient laity: 'Must it sadly follow, that all who want human learning must needs also want divinity; and then how shall poor plain people, who live in lawful callings, and have not the leisure to attain human learning, how shall they do to be saved?'[63]

Jesus's reply to Satan in *Paradise Regained*, rejecting the entire classical tradition as tainted, shows Milton's characteristic mixture of egalitarianism and exclusiveness. In Book III, Jesus expresses views about 'the people' similar to what we find in *The Readie and Easie Way* and elsewhere in Milton, saying that 'the peoples praise' is not worth pursuing, since it regularly goes to the unworthy:

> And what the people but a herd confus'd,
> A miscellaneous rabble, who extol
> Things vulgar, & well weigh'd, scarce worth the praise,
> They praise and they admire they know not what;
> And know not whom, but as one leads the other . . .
> His lot who dares be singularly good.
> Th'intelligent among them and the wise
> Are few.
>
> (*PR*, III.48–53, 57–9)

God recognizes 'the just man', looking down on him from on high (60–2), but such men are rare, unrecognized by the undiscerning: goodness here is coupled with wisdom, discernment, rather than with spiritual gifts. At times, Milton, the heir of the Reformed tradition, sees 'the people' as, in their humility and honest labour, free from the pollution of worldly values, while at other times 'the people' are an incorrigible, unregenerate mob, rushing blindly towards their own destruction.[64] For all Milton's emphasis on human freedom and on 'the sovereign edict of charity' – 'no place in Heav'n or Earth, except Hell, where charity may not enter' – the spirit of charity is absent from Jesus's insistence on the single source of truth in *Paradise Regained.* In Milton's theology, the ultimate distinction is between the few who merit salvation and those who refuse to accept the burden of serving an exacting divine master. The God of Milton, like the God of Calvin, is the deity of Exodus, Leviticus, and Deuteronomy, who says, throwing out a challenge, obey me or die.

> I am the Lord thy God . . . Thou shalt have no other gods before me . . . for I the Lord thy God am a jealous God, visiting the iniquity of the fathers upon the children unto the third and fourth generation of them that hate me; And shewing mercy unto . . . them that love me, and keep my commandments.[65]

III

Where the Jesus of *Paradise Regained* is a model of conduct, standing firm against temptation, Milton's Samson is a deeply flawed figure, who is conscious of having abused his calling and, after succumbing to temptation, suffers severe punishment, for which he blames his own weakness. Throughout the poem, both he and his fellow Jews see him as a potential 'deliverer' from the yoke of an unjust conqueror, who has been reduced to the ignominy of slavery, fallen to a state worse than that of a 'beast':

> O glorious strength,
> Put to the labour of a Beast, debas't
> Lower then bondslave! Promise was that I
> Should *Israel* from *Philistian* yoke deliver;
> Ask for this great Deliverer now, and find him
> Eyeless in *Gaza* at the Mill with slaves,
> Himself in bonds under *Philistian* yoke.
> (*Samson Agonistes*, 36–42)

As Guibbory says, he is both like and unlike his fellow Jews, a Hebrew prophet not fully accepted by the people he has tried to serve as divine warrior: 'a Nazarite who has betrayed his vows, he is like biblical Israel – apostate, fallen, but also set apart' in the sense of being chosen.[66] From the outset, Samson recognizes that he is entirely responsible for the terrible situation he finds himself in, blinded and in chains. Free to choose and conscious of having been 'design'd for great exploits' in his earlier state, he has, in effect, enslaved himself.

Nothing of all these evils hath befall'n me
But justly; I my self have brought them on,
Sole Author I, sole cause: if aught seem vile,
As vile hath been my folly, who have profan'd
The mystery of God giv'n me under pledge
Of vow.

(32, 374–9)

'Sole Author' echoes the repentant Adam and Eve in *PL*, Book x: 'On mee, mee onely, as the sourse and spring / Of all corruption'; and 'On me, sole cause to thee of all this woe, / Mee mee onely, just object of his ire' (*PL*, x.832–3, 935–6). For much of the poem, Samson's awareness of his own responsibility simply serves to increase his suffering and sense of failure: 'Now blind, disheartn'd, sham'd, dishonour'd, quell'd, / To what can I be useful, wherein serve / My Nation, and the work from Heav'n impos'd?' (*Samson Agonistes*, 563–5).

Once again, Milton presents the citizens of a country as proving themselves unworthy of freedom, having an opportunity for great accomplishments but throwing it away. In responding to the Philistine giant Harapha, one of three enemies whose taunts serve to lift Samson out of his sense of helplessness and despair, Samson tells him that though 'my Nation was subjected to your Lords', the force of conquest can legitimately be met with equivalent force (1205–7). In effect, Milton is denying the position of Hobbes and others that conquest implies the tacit consent of the conquered and that rebellion against those holding power is unjustified.

I was no private but a person rais'd
With strength sufficient and command from Heav'n
To free my Countrey; if their servile minds
Me their Deliverer sent would not receive,
But to thir Masters gave me up for nought,
Th'unworthier they; whence to this day they serve.
I was to do my part from Heav'n assign'd.

(1211–17)

The republican principles expressed here are identical with those in the two *Defences*, *Tenure* and *Eikonoklastes:* resistance against an unjust ruler or conqueror is a sacred duty, and fidelity to God outweighs any earthly ties. In describing himself as not acting merely as a 'private person', but as motivated to resistance by an 'extraordinary vocation', being 'raysed by God to be a Deliverer', Samson echoes arguments justifying resistance to tyranny in *Tenure* and the *Defence*.[67] According to the *Defence*, 'the heroic Samson', when 'his countrymen reproached him for rising against his Philistine masters', nevertheless, like the righteous tyrannicide Ehud, 'thought it not impious but pious to kill those masters who were tyrants over his country, even though most of her citizens did not balk at slavery' (*CPW*, IV.i.401–2).[68] Earlier in the poem, after the Chorus says that '*Israel* still serves with all his Sons', Samson answers that in spite of 'those great acts which God had done / Singly by me against their Conquerours', the political leaders of Israel refused to assist him or even acknowledge the 'deliverance offer'd', but instead surrendered him to the Philistine authorities (240–6, 259–61).

The situation of Samson, his father Manoa, and the Chorus of Danites, representatives of Samson's 'own Nation' (218) who seek to comfort him in his affliction, is that they live under the 'civil power' of the Philistine conquerors. Samson, in deciding whether or not he should attend the feast celebrating Dagon, as demanded by the Philistine Officer, makes a distinction between religious duties, as commanded by conscience, and 'corporal servitude': 'Not in thir Idol-worship, but by labour / Honest and lawful to deserve my food / Of those who have me in thir civil power' (1336, 1365–7). In *A Treatise of Civil Power*, Milton argues that 'the civil power hath neither right nor can do right by forcing religious things', thus violating the 'birthright of everie true believer, Christian libertie'. 'God by his Secretary conscience', he says elsewhere, presents commands that must be obeyed, even if they constitute 'the meanest under-service'.[69] As Achinstein and others have said, issues addressed in *Samson Agonistes*, immediately relevant to those suffering persecution under the Restoration regime, were 'how to live under oppressive conditions' and, under such conditions, 'how to maintain readiness to serve God's command'.[70]

By compressing the action of the play into a single decisive day yet by narration presenting antecedent action that encompasses Samson's entire career, Milton makes the focus of emotion in *Samson Agonistes* the painful contrast between an abject present and a glorious past. The tragic emotions of pity and fear, in some of the play's most powerful passages, are, again and again, the evocation of the sense of loss, the fear of being abandoned, cut adrift:

> Restless thoughts, that like a deadly swarm
> Of Hornets arm'd, no sooner found alone,
> But rush upon me thronging, and present
> Times past, what once I was, and what am now.
> (19–22)

Samson Agonistes is unusual among tragedies in that its hero is already fallen at the beginning of the play, rather than, like Oedipus in *Oedipus Tyrannus* (or Othello, Lear, and Coriolanus), beginning in prosperity and, with a change of fortune, plunged into adversity. In this respect, Milton's drama resembles *Oedipus at Colonus* and *Philoctetes*, the last two plays of Sophocles. In these two plays, the protagonist is presented as suffering extreme pain as the result of actions performed sometime in the past, and, to those encountering them, attracting a mixture of pity and revulsion. Both the aged, blind Oedipus and the maimed Philoctetes, left alone on a desert island with a foul-smelling, unhealable wound, are, like Samson, cut off from everyday life, isolated by their special gifts and their extraordinary suffering. A major difference between Milton's poem and these two plays by Sophocles is that the Greek gods as depicted there, though powerful, demanding obedience, are in no sense just. The great choral ode in *Oedipus at Colonus* paints an unremittingly bleak picture of life as an intolerable burden, ending in 'strengthless age . . . / Unfriended in that utmost twilight / Where he must live with every bitter thing'. In neither of these plays is there any sense of regeneration or purification by suffering in their tortured protagonists, and in both, as in *Oedipus Tyrannus*, man is seen as the plaything of the gods, rather than as a conscious moral agent, exercising free will.[71]

In the biblical Book of Judges, Samson's betrayal by Dalila and his captivity, with his spectacular revenge on his enemies, comprise the final episode among several, all of which involve violence, where Samson's 'anger was kindled', enabling him to perform 'great slaughter'. In Judges, Samson does not, as in Milton's poem, suffer agonies over his blindness, folly, and humiliation, but immediately after his imprisonment we are told that 'the hair of his head began to grow again', as the Philistines 'rejoice' that their god 'hath delivered Samson our enemy into our hand'.[72] As several critics have pointed out, one notable omission from Milton's poem is Samson's prayer to God before he pulls the Philistines' temple down. In Judges, it is clear that Samson's motive is revenge for the loss of his eyes, and that his action here is in accordance with his earlier actions, as God's scourge:

> And Samson called unto the Lord, and said, O Lord God, remember me, I pray thee, and strengthen me, I pray thee, only this once, O God, that I may be at once avenged of the Philistines for my two eyes . . .
>
> So the dead which he slew at his death were more than they which he slew in his life.[73]

The Samson of Judges, 'who leaves a trail of blood wherever he goes', according to David Grossman in *Lion's Honey: The Myth of Samson*, far from being an independent agent, is used by the deity as an instrument of destruction, 'planted in the world and operated as a lethal weapon of divine will'. 'Samson the hero', Grossman argues, can be seen from two complementary perspectives. On the one hand, the biblical figure serves as a model for those willing 'to apply force without any restraint or moral inhibitions'. But the biblical Samson can also be seen as a tragic figure, doomed by his special gifts – 'a lonely man, forever tortured, enslaved by a God who has chosen him for a demanding mission', with no allowance for human frailties.[74]

Milton's Samson, in contrast, is presented throughout the poem as a free moral agent. To Manoa and the Chorus, he accepts his responsibility for his downfall and his present wretched state, as one who 'like a foolish Pilot have shipwrack't, / My Vessel trusted to me from above' (198–9). At a key moment in the drama, Samson asserts that, in going along with the Philistine messenger to the 'Idolatrous Rites' of the Philistines, he is acting freely, and not under compulsion. Like the Lady in the Ludlow Masque, Samson announces his adherence to 'the freedom' of the 'minde', the sanctity of conscience, unmoved by the mere 'corporal' power of outward force.[75]

> Commands are no constraints. If I obey them,
> I do it freely; venturing to displease
> God for the fear of Man, and Man prefer,
> Set God behind: which in his jealousie
> Shall never, unrepented, find forgiveness.
> (1372–6, 1378)

The situation here is complex. As a Jew and a Nazarite, bound to the service of God by strict vows, Samson is forbidden from the pollution of participating in the 'unclean, prophane' ceremonies of the Philistines – like Shylock, who says, when invited to dinner by a Christian Venetian, 'I will not eat with you, drink with you, nor pray with you.'[76] To do so, Samson says, would be 'prostituting holy things to Idols', doing 'honour to thir *Dagon*' rather than to God, and therefore he initially refuses to go. But 'something extraordinary' in his thoughts, some unspecified 'rouzing motions' within him, dispose him to believe that God will allow him, on this special occasion, to 'dispense with' the normal rules forbidding such behaviour, and not in doing so 'dishonour / Our Law, or stain my vow of *Nazarite*' (1358–62, 1377, 1381–6).[77]

On at least one earlier occasion, Samson cites an 'intimate impulse' (224) that led him to ignore the prudent advice of his parents and customary practice under the Law of the Old Testament, in deciding, of his own free will, to marry outside of his tribe.[78] In Grossman's commentary on this biblical episode, much is made of Samson's 'strangeness and otherness', as one seemingly inhabiting a different world from his uncomprehending parents. In the Book of Judges, according to the *Oxford Bible Commentary*, Samson is 'a wild man caught between the realms of nature and culture and regarded as somewhat dangerous by his own people even while they admire him'.[79] When in *Samson Agonistes*, the Chorus expresses 'wonder / Why thou shouldst wed *Philistian* women', defying parental disapproval for marrying 'the daughter of an Infidel' not once but twice (215–17), Samson gives the same reason for each of the two marriages: an 'intimate impulse', which he interprets as coming from God.

> They knew not
> That what I motion'd was of God; I knew
> From intimate impulse, and therefore urg'd
> The Marriage on; that by occasion hence
> I might begin *Israel's* Deliverance,
> The work to which I was divinely call'd.
> (221–6)

Though the disastrous results of the decision to marry Dalila leaves open the possibility that what Samson took for a divine impulse was self-will, justifying his own morally questionable behaviour by claiming divine sanction, a choral ode basically endorses Samson's position. God is not confined by his own laws, and his 'Heroic' champions have licence to override the strict prohibitions laid down in the Torah, even a Nazarite's vows of purity.

> [God] made our Laws to bind us, not himself,
> And hath full right to exempt
> Whom so it pleases him by choice
> From National obstriction without taint
> Of sin, or legal debt;
> For with his own Laws he can best dispence.
> (309–14, 318)[80]

One reason that *Samson Agonistes* has given rise to endless debate among critics is that at the central crisis of the poem we are not given access to Samson's thoughts. The 'rouzing motions' Samson tells the Chorus he feels can be interpreted in different ways, as can the poem's final moments, with the death of Samson among the slaughtered Philistines. Halfway through the poem, Samson has sunk to the depths of despair, feeling himself 'cast . . . off as never known' by the God he was singled out to serve, as 'his nursling once and choice delight' (*Samson Agonistes*, 633, 641, 1382). Successive encounters with Dalila, Harapha and the Philistine Officer, enemies who seek in one way or another to exploit or gain an advantage over him, each mark a stage towards recovery, a return of inner strength to match the growth of his 'redundant locks . . . clustring down', which the mourning Samson sees as a 'vain monument of strength', lost from being misused (568–70). Several critics have interpreted Samson's gradual recovery from despair in the course of the action in theological terms, as evidence of regeneration, with Samson as a 'hero of faith', whose actions are directed by the hand of Providence. Mary Ann Radzinowicz sees the tragic action as 'exemplary of the acquisition of true knowledge', in which Samson overcomes his human weaknesses. In this view, the encounters with Dalila, Harapha and the Philistine Officer are what Milton describes in *De Doctrina* as 'good temptations', sent by God with the end that men 'may become wiser, and others may be instructed'.

> Good temptations are those which God uses to tempt even righteous men, in order to prove them. He does this . . . either to exercise or demonstrate their faith or patience, as in the case of Abraham or Job, or to lessen their self-confidence and prove them guilty of weakness.[81]

Yet the pattern of the successive confrontations does not, in homiletic fashion, present 'the progressive steps in repentance', leading to 'the spiritual rebirth' of the exemplary hero.[82] If there is a change in Samson in the course of the poem it is not from a state of sin to sainthood, or from blindness to insight, but a gradual recovery from despair, the sense of being abandoned by God. Samson's response to the taunts of Harapha not only acknowledges the justice of his punishment, but, for virtually the first time in the poem, envisages a God who may at last be merciful to his fallible creatures.

> These evils I deserve and more,
> Acknowledge them from God inflicted on me
> Justly, yet despair not of his final pardon
> Whose ear is ever open; and his eye
> Gracious to re-admit the suppliant.
>
> (1169–73)

This passage, as Radzinowicz has noted, reflects Milton's Arminianism in its treatment of free will, conditional election, and the 'final pardon' available through God's grace.[83] It is one of the few moments in which the deity of *Samson Agonistes* appears to be a God of love, rather than relentlessly punishing disobedient sinners with 'wrath divine' (1683).

The final choral ode, beginning with the words 'All is best', is an attempt at closure, drawing a providential lesson from the events portrayed in the play's action: the storms of passion give way to a healthy, serene calmness, in recognition of the power and justice of God.

> His servants he with new acquist
> Of true experience from this great event
> With peace and consolation hath dismist,
> And calm of mind all passion spent.
> (1745, 1755–8)

These lines suggest a cleansing purgation as response to the tragic action, in keeping with the version of Aristotelian theory set forth in Milton's Preface: tragedy has the power 'to purge the mind of those and such-like passions, that is to temper or reduce them to just measure'. The tragic emotions of 'pity and fear, or terror' are seen as unhealthy, 'perturbations of the mind' that need to be brought under control, in order to 'set the affections in right tune', and the tragic poet acts as a kind of physician or apothecary.[84] Yet this curative, homoeopathic model does not do justice to the complex tragic experience or to the extraordinary violence of the play's denouement.

A number of readers, including Irene Samuel and Joseph Wittreich, have found the closing moments of the play deeply disturbing and problematical, not at all productive of 'calm of mind'.[85] If there is a passage in the play calculated to arouse 'fear, or terror', it is the narration of the Messenger, beginning with words that might direct the response of his attentive audience:

> O whither shall I run, or which way flie
> The sight of this so horrid spectacle
> Which earst my eyes beheld and yet behold;
> For dire imagination still persues me.
> (1541–4)

The sight of mass slaughter is not normally consoling. If, according to Aristotle, the best designed tragic plots are those that evoke pity and fear by incidents that 'occur unexpectedly and at the same time in consequence of one another', embodying both reversal (*peripeteia*) and discovery (*anagnorisis*), then the climax of the action, in which Samson pulls the temple down on himself and the Philistines, is the moment in Milton's play most likely to stir up the tragic emotions.[86] The dramatic form by its very nature elicits a variety of responses – as indeed, in Milton's tragedy, the Messenger and Manoa react very differently to the 'horrour' of the 'sad event' (1550–1) the Messenger so powerfully describes. As with the Messenger scenes in such Greek tragedies as *Hippolytus* and *Heracles*, a central moment in the action, both unexpected and inevitable, is narrated by a horrified observer, tasked with bringing the news back and reluctant to do so. The closest equivalents in Greek tragedy to the tragic denouement of *Samson Agonistes* evoke the tragic emotions in response to something beyond human comprehension, rather than any feelings of exultation or consolation. Manoa's reaction to the tragic events is understandable for a father trying to come to terms with his son's death, but it falls short of the full tragic response.

One reason why the tragic denouement of *Samson Agonistes* has seemed problematical to many readers is that it fails to bring about the promised liberation. After hearing of Samson's death, the Chorus, praising him as 'victorious', claims that in his 'dearly-bought revenge' he has 'fulfill'd / The work for which thou wast foretold / To *Israel*' (1660–3). Manoa in his last speech attempts to present 'a death so noble' in wholly positive terms as a fitting end to 'a life Heroic': 'Nothing is here for tears, nothing to wail / Or knock the breast' (1711, 1721–2, 1724). Irene Samuel is one of several critics who have questioned the 'limited vision' of Manoa and the Chorus at the end of the play.[87] Manoa proposes to build a monument to his dead son, 'with all his Trophies hung', to be frequented by his nation's 'valiant youth' and weeping maidens:

> Thither shall all the valiant youth resort,
> And from his memory inflame thir breasts
> To matchless valour, and adventures high:
> The Virgins also shall on feastful days
> Visit his Tomb with flowers.
>
> (1736, 1738–42)

This passage is oddly similar to Dalila's claim that, after overcoming her nation's enemy, she may, among her own people, be acclaimed as a heroine and role-model, 'nam'd among the famousest / Of Women . . . my tomb / With odours visited, and annual flowers' (980–7). There is an undertone of irony in both passages, suggesting that there are other values besides allegiance to a particular tribe and the praise of heroic deeds. Both imagined monuments can be seen as ways of forgetting, editing out moral complexities, rather than of remembering.

In the Book of Judges and in Milton's poem, Samson is a highly equivocal hero, a warrior whose deeds are counted in the number of 'slaughter'd foes' (1667), both early and late in his bloodstained career. In *Samson Agonistes*, as Michael Lieb has argued, 'deity is portrayed in its most archaic and terrifying form'. In this 'work of harsh and uncompromising violence', Samson acts as embodiment of an implacable 'God of Dread', who demands that he be worshipped 'with trembling', and is merciless towards those who would deny or resist his awesome power.[88] The fierce tribal deity of *Samson Agonistes*, victorious over his rival deity Dagon, can welcome the slaughter of multitudes, leaving a legacy of 'years of mourning, / And lamentation' (1712–13) to the stunned survivors. One problem with the readings of the poem that confer a kind of sainthood on *Samson* as 'faithful Champion' is that the poem is so firmly grounded in its Old Testament setting, with a fierce and jealous God demanding absolute loyalty. The Chorus may invoke 'the unsearchable dispose / Of highest wisdom' to support the conclusion that, in God's providential hand, 'all is best', but the deity of Judges, Deuteronomy, and *Samson Agonistes* rules by fear, in the kind of 'servile discipline' Milton disavows in contrasting the Mosaic Law and Gospel in *De Doctrina*.[89] Wittreich and other revisionist critics argue that Samson, ruled by a 'code of vengeance', represents 'that primitive Hebraic element which persists in Renaissance Christianity'.[90]

The Old Testament deity of *Samson Agonistes*, described by one critic as 'the God of Calvin', whom Milton, as 'rational theologian, had spent so much of his career struggling to reject', is a deity who, through Moses, says of those who fail 'to observe and do all his commandments':

> The Lord shall make the pestilence cleave unto thee, until he have consumed thee from off the land, whither thou goest to possess it . . . The Lord shall make the rain of thy land powder and dust: from heaven shall it come down upon thee, until thou be destroyed . . . And thy carcase shall be meat unto all the fowl of the air, and unto the beasts of the earth.[91]

Obey or die: as the strict Calvinist Jonathan Edwards told a captive New England congregation in his sermon 'Sinners in the Hands of an Angry God', a century later: 'The sword of divine justice is every moment brandished over their heads, and it is nothing but the hand of arbitrary mercy, and God's mere will, that holds it back.'[92]

The problematical aspects of the play's violent conclusion have been brought out in John Carey's polemical essay in the *Times Literary*

Supplement, written after 9/11, comparing Milton's Samson to a suicide bomber, who justifies his actions by the conviction that 'his massacre is an expression of God's will'. None of the many responses to Carey, often indignant, satisfactorily answers Carey's objections to readings of the poem that insist 'that we have no alternative but to consider Samson's massacre "virtuous" and "praiseworthy" provided he believes he has divine sanction'. Simply on the basis of 'rouzing motions' that cannot be authenticated (since, as Carey says, Milton 'hides Samson's thoughts' at this moment in the play), there is, according to Carey, no way of distinguishing between Samson's motivation in slaughtering the Philistines and those of any jihadi intent on martyrdom in pursuit of his cause – or of Dalila, impelled to rid her fellow Philistines of a dangerous enemy.[93] Similar arguments can be found in Walter Lim's *John Milton, Radical Politics, and Biblical Republicanism*, characterizing *Samson Agonistes* as 'a text that strongly supports a vision of divine-sanctioned violence' against a despised Other, in the hope of deliverance from a perceived subjection. The Other, in this view, is seen as impure, potentially contaminating, violating 'a divine mandate prohibiting miscegenation'. A 'fundamentalist' text of this kind, with its 'horror of hybridity', divides the world into God's instruments and the loathed enemy, and the same pattern can be applied, 'regardless of the God we follow or the Satan we invent'.[94]

Samson's God is presented by Milton as the true God, and Samson's victory over the Philistines as a manifestation of God's providence, the sudden overthrow of the mighty of the earth. Regina Schwartz has argued that 'for the Bible, as well as for Milton, the Philistines are not part of a pluralistic society that includes many equally legitimate cultures', but are idolators and oppressors, whose tyranny is shown to be unjust. Prophecies that 'a day of vengeance is coming' when God's 'indignation and fury' will break out upon the ungodly and 'utterly consume' his enemies were, as Loewenstein has shown, common currency among radical dissenters living under a hostile, persecuting Restoration regime.[95] But the ending of *Samson Agonistes* can be unsettling to twenty-first-century readers who have lived through many instances of demonizing the Other to justify violence, either by states or by individuals claiming divine sanction. The unsettling final moments of *Samson Agonistes*, like Michael's dispiriting account of the course of postlapsarian history in Books XI and XII of *Paradise Lost*, with its claim that 'Tyrannie must be', as punishment for human failings, reflect the most problematical elements in Milton's post-Calvinist theology and ethics. At the heart of *Paradise Lost* and *Samson Agonistes* is the paradox of tragic freedom: the hidden presence of a deity who, with divine foreknowledge, allows his creatures freedom on the basis that, if they fail to obey his exacting demands, they must bear the terrible consequences.

Postscript

Throughout this book, I have argued that Milton's political and religious beliefs are closely intertwined, and that the classical humanist and ardent Protestant polemicist in Milton at times battle for supremacy, with varying results. If there are inconsistencies in Milton – as, for example, egalitarianism jostling with a belief in hierarchy and discipline – these are the inconsistencies of his age and its dominant ideology. There is no necessary connection between Milton's unorthodox post-Calvinist theology and his political principles or allegiances. Roger Williams, who argued that 'it is the will and command of *God* that . . . *a permission* of the most *Paganish, Jewish, Turkish* or *Antichristian consciences* and *worships*, be granted to *all* men in all *Nations* and *Countries*', a view of Christian liberty more radical than Milton's, was a strict Calvinist in his theology.[1] Though Williams, like Milton and Goodwin, drew a sharp distinction between 'the Civil *Sword*' and a separate 'Spirituall' domain governing conscience, Williams had no hesitation in extending freedom of worship to Roman Catholics, where Milton, notoriously, insisted in *Areopagitica*, 'I mean not tolerated Popery, and open superstition, which as it extirpats all religions, and civill supremacies, so it self should be extirpat'. In the same passage towards the end of *Areopagitica*, Milton excluded from toleration 'that . . . which is impious or evil absolutely either against faith or maners'.[2] His views on liberty of conscience show the same mixture of liberalism and authoritarianism as his views on the strict limitations on the franchise and on the right of the virtuous to enforce their views on an unregenerate majority, as expressed in *The Readie and Easie Way.* Here again, some Leveller leaders and army radicals, strict Calvinists in their theological convictions, argued a position on political liberty far more radical than anything in Milton's republican writings.[3]

Modern critics tend to emphasize the 'discontinuities' or 'evident inconsistencies' in *Areopagitica*, treating 'the grandness of the rhetoric', the 'soaring generalizations' with a degree of scepticism, devoting much of their attention to the brief passage near the end where Milton lists exceptions to the general thesis that it is better 'that many be tolerated, rather than all compell'd'.[4] Stanley Fish, with a deconstructionist zeal to find passages in *Areopagitica* that undercut or 'flatly contradict' the 'extravagant claims' Milton makes, goes so far as to argue that Milton is 'not against licensing', that he has 'no interest at all in the "freedom of the press" . . . and . . . does not unambiguously value freedom at all'. Fish's account of *Areopagitica* is in keeping with his general assault on liberals who would like to claim Milton as one of them:

> Liberals believe that facts . . . are independent of the knower, and that it is the knower's obligation to approach the task of knowing with as few preconceptions as possible . . . with an open mind . . . Liberals believe in . . . the machinery of rationality, of those laws of logic attached to no agenda or vision, but sufficiently general in their scope as to provide a normative perspective . . . Milton believes in none of these things. He believes that all the evidence is in and that it points to a single conclusion – we must discern the will of God and do it – that should form the basis of our thought and action in any and all situations. He believes that there is a great divide between those who have reached that conclusion and those who have reached some other, and that communication between the two groups is impossible.[5]

Fish's version of Milton has no room for ambivalence, respect for different points of view, or any of the virtues praised by Mill in *Of Liberty* and other works that help define the liberal tradition: there is one truth, and those that depart from it are the unregenerate, doomed from eternity to endless night, beyond redemption.

John Stuart Mill's *On Liberty* (1859), like *Areopagitica* and *A Treatise of Civil Power*, is centrally concerned with defining 'the nature and limits of the power which can be legitimately exercised by society over the individual'. Like Milton, Mill places particular emphasis on 'the Liberty of Thought: from which it is impossible to separate the cognate liberty of speaking and writing'. To the Milton of *Areopagitica* and *Paradise Lost*, as to Mill, 'the appropriate region of human liberty' is 'the inward domain of consciousness'.[6] Though, as we have seen, Milton throughout his writings is intent on distinguishing liberty from licence and would not endorse Mill's sweeping claim for the need to insure 'absolute freedom of opinion and sentiment on all subjects, practical and speculative, scientific, moral, or theological', Milton and Mill agree in seeing 'liberty of conscience in the most comprehensive sense' as fundamentally inalienable.[7] To an appreciable extent, Milton and Mill share a common vocabulary, in their emphasis on moral choice and on the central role of 'reason, which is but choosing'. In criticizing 'the disposition of mankind, whether as ruler or as fellow citizens, to impose their own opinions and inclinations as a rule of conduct on others', Mill echoes Milton's remarks on truth and heresy, the 'muddy pool of conformity and tradition', in *Areopagitica*: 'A man may be a heretick in the truth; and if he believe things only because his Pastor sayes so, or the Assembly so determins, without knowing other reason, though his belief be true, yet the very truth he holds, becomes his heresie.'[8] Mill's version, similar both in its wording and in its governing assumptions, is that 'Truth gains even more by the errors of one who, with true study and preparation, thinks for himself, than by the true opinions of those who only hold them because they do not suffer themselves to think', and that when a 'true opinion . . . abides as a prejudice', unexamined, 'Truth, thus held, is but one superstition the more, accidentally clinging to the words which enunciate a truth.'[9]

But for Mill, unlike Milton or Williams, the grounds on which he argues for freedom of conscience are entirely secular. The 'very simple principle' that he claims should 'govern absolutely the dealings of society with the individual in the way of compulsion and control' is 'that the sole end for which mankind are warranted individually or collectively, in interfering with the liberty of action of any of their number, is self-protection'.[10] This is a good deal closer to Hobbes' principle of self-preservation as the first law of nature, overriding all other considerations, than it is to Milton. If such a statement does not go as far as Hobbes in asserting that liberty can simply be defined in material terms as 'the absence of external impediments' that might 'take away part of a man's power to do what he would', it does suggest a kind of reciprocal bargain: individuals need to protect themselves against the societies in which they live, and the society needs to protect itself against the harm that might be done by individuals protecting their own interests. 'The only part of the conduct of any one, for which he is amenable to society, is that which concerns others. In the part which merely concerns himself, his independence is, of right, absolute. Over himself, over his own body and mind, the individual is sovereign.'[11]

Mill's attitude towards religion is highly sceptical, seeing 'the doctrines of Christianity' as for most professing Christians merely 'an hereditary creed . . . to be received passively, not actively': 'What is boasted of at the present time as the revival of religion, is always, in narrow and uncultivated minds, as least as much the revival of bigotry.'[12] For Milton, in contrast, as for Williams, Goodwin, Overton and Lilburne, liberty of conscience is the liberty to follow the promptings of the inner light, obeying God in preference to what earthly masters might demand. This is evident in the language of *Areopagitica*, which again and again treats the capacity to mount rational arguments and to choose among alternatives (or to listen to such arguments, accepting or rejecting them) as dependent on a gift from God: the individual for Milton can never be wholly autonomous. Thus, in familiar passages linking prelapsarian and postlapsarian freedom and the need 'to ordain wisely as in the world of evill, in the midd'st of which God hath plac't us unavoidably':

> When God gave him reason, he gave him freedom to choose . . . God therefore left him free, set before him a provoking object, ever almost in his eyes . . . This justifies the high providence of God, who . . . gives us minds that can wander beyond all limit and satiety. Why then should we affect a rigor contrary to the manner of God and nature . . . For God sure esteems the growth and compleating of one virtuous person, more then the restraint of ten vicious. (*CPW*, II.526–8)

Though Milton in his polemical writings treats sacred and secular history – 'all Stories, Heathen and Christian' – as equivalent when citing precedents, it is always with the reservation that, as the word of God, the Scripture is 'true' in a different way from the accounts of historians and poets. Classical myth and classical history, though available for comparison, are always 'feign'd', human inventions: thus Eve is both like classical goddesses and nymphs, and transcends any imagined beauties, 'more lovely fair / Then Wood-Nymph, or the fairest Goddess feign'd / Of three that in Mount *Ida* naked strove.'[13] The fall of Mulciber, narrated in a gorgeous set-piece, displaying the poet's full resources, Milton warns us, is only 'fabl'd': he cautions, sternly, 'thus they relate, / Erring' (*PL*, I.740–7). The most severe, uncompromising rejection of classical learning to be found in Milton is Jesus's response to Satan in *Paradise Regained*: 'He who receives / Light from above, from the fountain of light, / No other doctrine needs, though granted true.' Though what Satan has offered Jesus as a temptation does not specifically mention the accounts of historians along with philosophers, orators, and poets, Jesus's condemnation is all-encompassing: the only 'Law and Story' he finds untainted are found in scripture: all else is 'false, or little else but dreams'.[14]

Revisionist historians in the past few decades have argued that a similar insistence on the exclusive truth of scripture and on 'godly discipline', submission to the will of God, was characteristic not only of seventeenth-century Puritans but was held by all contending parties, both Milton and his adversaries, throughout this period. According to J. C. Davis:

> Full humanity in this schema is not expressed in autonomy, in self-realization through the exercise of choice, in moral education through civic participation, through what we might call freedom . . . Freedom to respond to God's providential promptings, to submit to his rule and to labour in his service, these aspirations permeate the language of the puritan revolution.[15]

According to this revisionist view, any attempt to argue for a secular dimension in the views of liberty of Milton or any other writer of the period is anachronistic: to Milton and his contemporaries, there can be no liberty other than the liberty to serve God. The recent book by William Walker, angrily rebuking all those who use words like 'republican', 'radical', or 'liberal', or ethical and political abstractions like 'autonomy' or individual rights, constructs a Milton whose instincts are almost entirely authoritarian: his title, spitting defiance at those who hold differing views, is *Antiformalist, Unrevolutionary, Illiberal Milton.* In his emphasis on what he calls anti-formalism, 'an aversion to affirming or repudiating specific forms of government' in Milton's political writings, a feeling that 'at best forms were childish things', Walker is explicitly following in the path of 'Stanley Fish's writings on Milton over the past thirty years', as well as such revisionist historians as Davis.[16] To Walker, quoting chapter and verse from Milton as proof-texts for his assertions, Milton, rather than championing liberty or equality, is one who insists, dogmatically, that there are some who 'are by nature inferior' and that 'all men do not deserve and ought not to be *treated* as equals'. Civil liberties should be extended only to those of whom Milton approves: 'those who are inferior (in wisdom and in virtue)' should 'obey their superiors': 'By "free state" Milton thus means a nation in which the magistrate denies some civil liberties to some men while granting various civil liberties to others, with the aim of conforming to true religion.'[17] In *Milton among the Puritans* (2010), Catherine Gimelli Martin, equally influenced by revisionist historiography, takes a different stance by constructing a Milton uncontaminated by a Puritanism which she sees as 'a reactionary force', deeply repressive, characterized by 'fanatic zeal' in its 'attempt to apply Old Testament sanctions and laws to a new "holy nation"'. Free of any Calvinist pessimism about fallen man's 'total depravity', Martin's version of Milton is an adherent of an 'optimistic humanism', a 'life-affirming religion', as well as being a moderate in his politics, essentially 'secular and rationalist' in his overall approach.[18]

If there is an authoritarian element in Milton's political theory, as in different ways Hammond and Walker have recently argued, it is accompanied by a consistent concern for the advancement of 'liberty, without which civilized life is scarcely possible', a fervent belief, expressed in the *Second Defence* and elsewhere, that a way was opening for the establishment of real liberty, with 'direct progress toward the liberation of all human life from slavery'. As Woodhouse argues throughout the preface to *Puritanism and Liberty*, a potential conflict between liberation and reform lies at the heart of seventeenth-century Puritanism. In Milton, as in many of his contemporaries, a felt need for godly discipline clashes against a longing for a transcendent, triumphant 'liberty . . . that which hath rarify'd and enlightn'd our spirits like the influence of heav'n . . . that which hath enfranchis'd and lifted up our apprehensions degrees above themselves'.[19] These contrary imperatives both unite and divide the opposing sides in the Putney and Whitehall debates, former allies in the Civil War, and, as with Milton, can be found within individuals, locked in internal combat. Ernest Sirluck in 'Milton's Political Thought: The First Cycle' speaks of 'a naturalistic and secular conception of the state' and a second 'contradictory' political theory, in some ways incompatible, which is 'theocratic', at times developed, under differing circumstances, in separate political tracts, and at times uneasily coexisting within a single work.[20] Rachel Foxley, in slightly different terms, speaks of Milton's simultaneous commitment to 'two intellectual worlds: the exclusive classical republicanism which led Milton toward an aristocracy of virtue, and the contractarian and natural law thinking which underpinned his assertions of the right of the people to determine the form of their own state'.[21] Where Woodhouse and Barker emphasize the religious dimension in the political thought of Milton and his fellow Puritans, more recent historicist critics, in the tradition of Skinner and the Cambridge school, emphasize the secular side of the complex, contested tradition of republicanism and its rival doctrines. But for Milton, in his prose works in English and Latin as in his poems, the classical and the biblical can never be disentangled, as 'competing but equally positive values' to which Milton remains committed, even where they seem to clash.[22]

The anti-Trinitarianism evident in *De Doctrina*, *Paradise Lost* and *Paradise Regained* allows Milton to distinguish an all-knowing deity intent on punishing offenders from a Son, not equipped with the ability to foresee the future, but freely offering to deflect his Father's wrath by taking on human form, motivated by 'Divine compassion . . . Love without end'

(*PL*, III.141–2). As Michael explains to Adam in Book XII, 'high Justice' can then be fulfilled, in exacting 'the penaltie to thy transgression due':

> The Law of God exact he shall fulfill
> Both by obedience and by love, though love
> Alone fulfill the Law; thy punishment
> He shall endure by coming in the Flesh
> To a reproachful life and cursed death,
> Proclaiming Life to all who shall believe
> In his redemption.
>
> (*PL*, XII.399, 401–8)

The Law of the Old Testament God, ruling by fear and insisting that his dictates be followed, without excuse or exceptions, is according to this and other passages in *Paradise Lost* and in *De Doctrina*, both fulfilled and transcended by 'a better Cov'nant', in the movement 'from Flesh to Spirit', from 'works of Law to works of Faith' (*PL*, XII.302–6). In his divorce tracts and in *De Doctrina*, Milton argues that an overriding spirit of charity, which he identifies with 'true libertie', must be 'supreme decider of all controversie, and supreme resolver of all Scripture': 'Our Saviours doctrine is, that the end, and the fulfilling of every command is charity; no faith without it, no worship, no works pleasing to God but as they partake of charity.'[23]

And yet in Books XI and XII of *Paradise Lost* and in *Samson Agonistes*, retributive justice, 'the Law of God exact' and its painful consequences on those forced to endure it, is a more dominant presence than the spirit of love, human or divine. This is the God who demands of Abraham, putting him to a trial ('God did tempt Abraham', in the King James translation) by insisting that he sacrifice his beloved son, slaughtering the boy with his own hand, as he chooses obedience to whatever God may tell him to do over the inner workings of parental love or compassion for the innocent victim.[24] The most significant instance of the charity that 'beareth all things, believeth all things . . . endureth all things' in the later books of *Paradise Lost* occurs at the moment when Adam is able to foresee nothing better in prospect than 'a long day's dying to augment our pain', passed on without remission of this 'slow-pac't evill' to their 'hapless Seed' in generations to come. This key episode, though in no way inconsistent with the poem's theology, is not a demonstration of divine forgiveness or mercy that comes 'unimplor'd unsought', bestowed from above in ways beyond human understanding, so much as it embodies the mutual 'offices of Love', by means of which Adam and Eve are able to 'lighten / Each others burden in our share of woe'.[25] What is largely absent from Milton's later writings, the product of 'evil days . . . with dangers compast round, / And solitude' (*PL*, VII.26–8), is the sense of encompassing divine love, the workings of grace even 'to sinners, to the ungodly, to all the world . . . depending on no condition, no performance at all', that we find, for example, in Walwyn's *The Power of Love* (1643), a pamphlet urging freedom of conscience akin in many respects to *Areopagitica* and to the theology of *De Doctrina*:

> God is love, and love makes men God-like; and henceforth let me pray you to marke the workings of love in your owne soules . . . Doe but thinke of the love wherewith Christ hath loved you, and nothing can be so abominably injurious but you will gladly forgive.[26]

Milton's theology is tougher than this, more judgemental, as Adam and Eve look back longingly on the gates of Paradise, guarded by 'dreadful faces throng'd and fierie Armes', as 'with wandring steps and slow', they face an uncertain future (*PL*, XII.641–9).

Notes

Introduction

1 See, for example, *De Doctrina*, I.iv/*CPW*, VI.188–94; and Calvin, *Institutes*, I.228: 'It will be beyond dispute that free will does not enable any man to perform good works, unless he is assisted by grace; indeed, the special grace which the elect alone receive through regeneration.' For an excellent discussion of ways in which Milton and the Dutch Arminians differed from Calvinist orthodoxy in regard to the operations of grace, see Myers, 'Prevenient Grace and Conversion'.

2 This passage is discussed in Fallon, *Milton's Peculiar Grace*, pp. 182–202. See also Danielson, *Milton's Good God*, pp. 82–3.

3 On Milton's conviction, shared with Goodwin and with Arminius, that 'Salvation or Damnation is destin'd to no Man, but either as he believes, or does not believe in Jesus Christ' and persists in this faith, see *De Doctrina*, I.iv/*CPW*, VI.188–90, and Maurice Kelley's introduction, *CPW*, VI.81–4. Throughout this study, I cite *De Doctrina* in the translation of John Carey in *CPW*, VI, edited by Maurice Kelley, checking the text against the recent edition in *Complete Works of John Milton*, vol. VIII, translated and edited by John K. Hale and J. Donald Cullington (Oxford University Press, 2012). Though the Oxford edition of *De Doctrina* has the advantage of including the Latin text, Kelley's edition is far superior in its introduction and notes, particularly those concerned with theology and Milton's relationship with Calvinist tradition. Passages in which the Oxford edition provides a more accurate translation are noted, as are passages in which the Oxford translation can be considered misleading.

4 Woodhouse, *Puritanism and Liberty*, pp. 51–3. Arthur Barker, in *Milton and the Puritan Dilemma*, sees a similar unresolved conflict in Milton, as does Christopher Hill in *Milton and the English Revolution*, pp. 253–67. John Coffey in 'Puritanism and Liberty Revisited', pp. 962–85, argues that within seventeenth-century Puritanism a 'majority' view intolerant of 'error and heresy' can be contrasted with 'a minority of radical puritans who broke decisively with the mainstream puritan view' (p. 964).

5 Calvin, *Institutes*, III.xix; and Luther, *Commentary on Galatians*, p. 85, quoted in Kelley's note to *De Doctrina*, I.xxvii/*CPW*, VI.538–9.

6 *Second Defence*, *CPW*, IV.i.624.

7 *De Doctrina*, I.xxvii/*CPW*, VI.537. In this passage, the translation in the Oxford edition is misleading, translating 'Deo per spiritum veritatis ducem in charitate serviamus' as 'we may be slaves of God in charity through the spirit of truth', rather than 'we may serve God in charity through the guidance of the spirit of truth' (*Complete Works*, VIII.716–17).

8 *De Doctrina*, I.xxvii/*CPW*, VI.521.

9 *De Doctrina*, I.xxvi and xxvii/*CPW*, VI.517, 521. Luther also held that the Gospel abrogated the Mosaic Law but drew different conclusions from this, and Calvin and his followers held that the moral law of the Old Testament remained in force for Christians. See the discussion in Barker, *Milton and the Puritan Dilemma*, pp. 100–7, 236–40, 244–9; and Rosenblatt, *Torah and Law*, pp. 3–9.

10 See Rosenblatt, *Torah and Law*, pp. 45–53, on ways in which Milton's position in the divorce tracts differs from that argued in *De Doctrina*. Barker finds greater consistency in the divorce tracts and *De Doctrina*: see *Milton and the Puritan Dilemma*, pp. 102–7, 112–18.

11 *Second Defence*, *CPW*, IV.i.624.

12 *Doctrine and Discipline*, *CPW*, II.229. On how in Milton 'domestic themes spill out into the public sphere', cf. Achinstein, 'Contextualizing Milton's Divorce Tracts', pp. 174–85.

13 *Tetrachordon*, *CPW*, II.661, 665. The passage from *Tetrachordon* is discussed in Barker, *Milton and the Puritan Dilemma*, pp. 113–16. Rosenblatt has pointed out that in *Tetrachordon* and *Doctrine and Discipline*, rather than arguing that the Mosaic Law has been rendered invalid by the Gospel, Milton 'argues the emancipation of Christians, not from, but through the Mosaic law' (*Torah and Law*, p. 47).

14 See Parker, *Milton's Contemporary Reputation*, pp. 74, 82–3, quoting Daniel Featley, *The Dippers Dipt* (1645) and Clement Walker, *Anarchia Anglicana* (1649).

15 *Tenure*, *CPW*, III.189, 206.

16 See Milton, *Political Writings*, ed. Dzelzainis, pp. xi–xii, xvi–xvii; and Dzelzainis, 'Milton's Politics', pp. 78–81. On the 'constitutional theory of resistance' as argued by sixteenth-century Lutherans and Calvinists, see Skinner, *Foundations*, II.204–17.

17 *Vindiciae contra Tyrannos: A Defence of Liberty against Tyrants* (London, 1648), pp. 28, 40. Cf. Dzelzainis, 'Milton's Politics', pp. 79–81. Calvin, on the other hand, counselled obedience even to 'a very wicked' prince 'utterly unworthy of all honour': 'We are not only subject to the authority of princes who perform their office towards us uprightly and faithfully as they ought, but also to the authority of all who, by whatever means, have got control of affairs', even if those princes 'rule unjustly and incompetently': *Institutes*, IV.xx, para. 25, quoted in Skinner, *Foundations*, II.193–4.

18 *Tenure*, *CPW*, III.189, 242, 257. See the discussion in Milton, *Political Writings*, pp. xviii–xix; and Fallon, 'Milton's *Tenure*', pp. 241–51.

19 *Tenure*, *CPW*, III.236–7. For the view that these two arguments are fundamentally incompatible, see Fallon, 'Milton's *Tenure*', pp. 246–9. On ways in which Milton in *Tenure* 'moves beyond the Reformation theorists of resistance' he cites, see *Complete Works of John Milton*, vol. VI: *Vernacular Regicide and Republican Writings*, ed. N. H. Keeble and Nicholas McDowell (Oxford University Press, 2013), pp. 26–7, 42–3.
20 *Tenure*, *CPW*, III.197; *Defence*, *CPW*, IV.I.457. 'Sounder' is Filmer's translation of Milton's Latin, closer to the original than 'sound' in *CPW*, IV.I.457.
21 *Tenure*, title page, *CPW*, III.189.
22 *Defence*, *CPW*, IV.I.457.
23 Filmer, *Observations*, p. 199.
24 Filmer, *Observations*, pp. 202–3. The passages quoted by Filmer are in *CPW*, IV.i, 332–3, in a different translation. See the discussion of Filmer's attacks on Milton's 'sleight of hand' in Hammond, *Milton and the People*, pp. 120–1, 161–5.
25 Goodwin, *Right and Might Well Met* (1648), p. 14.
26 Sedgwick, *A Second View of the Army Remonstrance* (1649), p. 11.
27 *Readie and Easie Way*, *CPW*, VII.431, 442, 455.
28 *Areopagitica*, *CPW*, II.554; Barker, *Milton and the Puritan Dilemma*, p. 272. On how in the classical republican tradition 'the people' are often 'defined in qualitative rather than quantitative terms', see *Complete Works*, VI, ed. Keeble and McDowell, p. 44. Rachel Foxley in 'Due Libertie and Proportiond Equalitie', pp. 614–38, finds a hostility to 'democracy' or mob rule characteristic of the Greek tradition within republican discourse.
29 Brown, 'Great Senates and Godly Education', pp. 43–60, especially pp. 49–50. On 'the politics of virtue', see Pocock, *Virtue, Commerce, and History*; and Cable, 'Secularizing Conscience', pp. 268–74.
30 Barker, *Milton and the Puritan Dilemma*, p. 273. For a similar view, see Corns, *Uncloistered Virtue*, pp. 281, 290; and Sirluck, 'Milton's Political Thought', pp. 209–24. On the idea of the 'godly remnant' as a central element in Milton's republicanism, see *Complete Works*, VI, ed. Keeble and McDowell, pp. 102–6.
31 Barker, *Milton and the Puritan Dilemma*, p. xxiii; Woodhouse, *Puritanism and Liberty*, pp. 36–7. For a similar view of Milton as Puritan, see Hill, *Milton and the English Revolution*, pp. 242–78; and N. H. Keeble's essay 'Milton and Puritanism', pp. 124–40.
32 Woodhouse, *Puritanism and Liberty*, pp. 67–8. Cable argues that Milton in *The Readie and Easie Way* 'defines his free republican commonwealth as a contradiction in terms: secular theocracy', liberty that 'you have to be a Christian to deserve' ('Secularizing Conscience', p. 274).
33 *Hirelings*, *CPW*, VII.292. On Milton and Congregationalism, see Escobedo, 'The Invisible Nation', pp. 178–92; Nuttall, 'Milton's Churchmanship in 1659', pp. 227–31; and Keeble, 'Milton's Christian Temper', pp. 114–18.
34 *De Doctrina*, I.xxiv, xxvii/*CPW*, VI.500, 521; Nuttall, *Visible Saints*, pp. 55–7, 107–8. Cf. Lake, 'The Godly and Their Enemies', pp. 152–6.

35 *Areopagitica*, *CPW*, II.555, 564. See Tolmie, *The Triumph of the Saints*, pp. 111–16; and Coffey, *John Goodwin and the Puritan Revolution*, pp. 122–30.
36 Schwartz, *The Curse of Cain*, pp. 19–23, quoting Genesis 15:18–21. The passage from Genesis is also discussed in Stevens, 'Leviticus Thinking', pp. 441–61.
37 Genesis 22:17–18, quoted in Stevens, 'Leviticus Thinking', pp. 448–9. In the King James Bible, the word for 'descendants' is 'seed', and Milton uses this word in Michael's narrative in *PL*, XI.120–51, where typologically Abraham's 'seed' is taken to prefigure Jesus Christ.
38 Stevens, 'Leviticus Thinking', p. 445, quoting Leviticus 20:24–6.The translation in the King James Bible reads 'other people' in verses 24 and 26, 'severed' in verse 26.
39 Stevens, 'Leviticus Thinking', p. 451. Where the translation in *CPW*, VI, contrasts 'the obedient' and 'the disobedient', the translation in *Complete Works* is closer to the Latin in contrasting 'those who had carried them out' and 'those who had not carried them out' (VIII.678–9).
40 Schwartz, *The Curse of Cain*, p. 73, quoting Jeremiah 31:32 and 32:39. The King James Bible in Jeremiah 31:32 reads 'although I was an husband to them', but in Jeremiah 32:37–40 the King James translation again and again depicts a punitive God: 'in mine anger, and in my fury, and in great wrath'; 'that they may fear me for ever', 'I will put my fear into their hearts, that they shall not depart from me'.
41 'The Flower', 15–17, 43; 'Love', 9, in Herbert, *Complete English Poems*.
42 *De Doctrina*, I.ii/*CPW*, VI.133–4; Genesis 6:8 and Deuteronomy 9:13–14. 'The ascription of human feelings to God' is an expansion of the term 'anthropopathy' in Milton's original text, not present in the Oxford edition (*Complete Works*, VIII.28–9). Cf. Lieb, *Theological Milton*, pp. 77–80, 143–50. For the passage quoted above from Genesis, cf. *PL*, XI.885–7: 'So willingly doth God remit his Ire, / Though late repenting him of Man deprav'd, / Griev'd at his Heart.'
43 See Lieb, *Theological Milton*, pp. 163–83.
44 *An Apology*, *CPW*, I.899–900. In this passage, Milton seeks to justify on rhetorical grounds the use of 'a vehement vein throwing out indignation, or scorn upon an object that merits it', 'bitter and ireful rebukes', against the claim that such writing is indecorous (*CPW*, I.899).
45 *Of Reformation in England*, *CPW*, I.616–17.
46 *PL*, XI.885, 891; XII.305, 318–19. Cf. Rogers, *The Matter of Revolution*, pp. 152–3, 159–66.
47 For examples of the view that Milton's later works represent a 'retreat from politics', see Worden, 'Milton's Republicanism', pp. 244–5; Bush, *English Literature in the Earlier Seventeenth Century*, pp. 392–4; and Martz, *The Paradise Within*.
48 *Doctrine and Discipline*, *CPW*, II.264.
49 See Shuger, 'Milton's Religion', pp. 13–53; and McDowell, 'How Laudian Was the Young Milton?', pp. 3–22.
50 *The Reason of Church Government*, *CPW*, I.822–3; *Lycidas*, preface, 127.

51 *Letter to a Friend*, *CPW*, I.319–20; Sonnet 7, 14. The *Letter to a Friend*, in two versions, much corrected, is included in the Trinity Manuscript. See the discussion of the *Letter to a Friend* in Fallon, *Milton's Peculiar Grace*, pp. 14–20; and Haskin, *Milton's Burden of Interpretation*, pp. 30, 36–8. Sonnet 7 is discussed more fully in Chapter 2.
52 *Ad Patrem*, in *Complete Shorter Poems*, pp. 240–7; *Reason of Church-Government*, *CPW*, I.810; *Letter to a Friend*, *CPW*, I.319. *Ad Patrem*, addressed in the mid-1630s to the father who had been supporting him, justifies his choice of a life dedicated to poetry over a more practical career.
53 See Campbell and Corns, *John Milton*, pp. 32–3; and, on the standard formulas of neo-Latin funeral elegies, Revard, *Milton and the Tangles of Neaera's Hair*, pp. 40–50. The elegy to Andrewes is also discussed in Miller, 'Milton and the Conformable Puritanism of Richard Stock and Thomas Young', pp. 92–5.
54 *Elegia quarta, Ad Thomas Junium* (translation by Laurence Revard), in *Complete Shorter Poems*, pp. 84–8, and note on p. 164; Lewalski, *The Life of John Milton*, pp. 25–6.
55 *Of Reformation in England*, *CPW*, I.527, 586, 598.
56 *Areopagitica*, *CPW*, II.550, 555, 564.
57 *Of Reformation in England*, *CPW*, I.599; *Tenure*, *CPW*, III.203. On Milton's changing attitudes toward monarchy, see Corns, 'Milton and the Characteristics of a Free Commonwealth', pp. 25–42.
58 *PR*, III.152–3, 182, 190–1.
59 Marvell, 'A Dialogue, between the Resolved Soul, and Created Pleasure', 47.
60 *Samson Agonistes*, 270–1; *Tenure*, *CPW*, III.190.

Chapter 1: Milton's Post-Calvinist Theology

1 Martin, *Milton among the Puritans*, pp. xi, 62, 80, 85; Achinstein, *Literature and Dissent in Milton's England*.
2 Campbell and Corns, *John Milton: Life, Work, and Thought*, pp. 43, 98–100. The conventional view that Campbell and Corns argue against in presenting the early Milton as 'an ecclesiastical and ideological conservative' is that Milton was the 'puritan son of a puritan father, educated by puritans, writing on puritan themes against puritan enemies' (pp. 1, 43). To Campbell and Corns, 'the process of ideological relocation' in Milton was protracted (p. 100). Comments quoted above include Alistair Fowler, *Milton Quarterly*, 44 (2010), 58; William Poole, *TLS*, 11 March 2009, p. 6 (on Campbell and Corns); and John Coffey, *Journal of Ecclesiastical History*, 63 (2012), 827 (on Martin).
3 Cambell and Corns, *John Milton*, pp. 32, 67–8, 84. For similar arguments, see Corns' essay, 'Milton before "Lycidas"', pp. 23–36. For the view of young Milton as incipient radical, see Lewalski, 'How Radical Was the Young Milton?', pp. 49–72.
4 Lewis, *A Preface to Paradise Lost*, pp. 82, 92.
5 Bush, *English Literature in the Earlier Seventeenth Century*, pp. 395, 398–9, 401–2.

6 Patrides, *Milton and the Christian Tradition*, pp. 5, 102.
7 Patrides, *Milton and the Christian Tradition*, pp. 58, 86, 197–8.
8 Patrides, *Milton and the Christian Tradition*, p. 195.
9 *De Doctrina*, Epistle/*CPW*, VI.121; Patrides, *Milton and the Christian Tradition*, pp. 15–25, 96; Hunter et al., *Bright Essence*.
10 Patrides, 'The Godhead in *Paradise Lost*: Dogma or Drama?, *Bright Essence*, p. 72. For 'subordinationism', see Hunter, 'Milton's Arianism Reconsidered', *Bright Essence*, p. 50; for the terms 'substance' and 'essence', see Hunter, 'Further Definitions: Milton's Theological Vocabulary', *Bright Essence*, pp. 15–25. Kelley makes the case for Milton's Anti-Trinitarianism in *This Great Argument*, pp. 84–106, 118–22; and in *CPW*, VI.47–73.
11 Hunter, *Visitation Unimplor'd*, pp. 8, 14.
12 Hunter, *Visitation Unimplor'd*, pp. 99, 114. Barbara K. Lewalski in 'Milton and *De Doctrina Christiana*: Evidences of Authorship', *Milton Studies*, 36 (1998), 203–28, argues, against Hunter, that the evidence for Milton's authorship of *De Doctrina* is overwhelming', citing detailed examples to show 'how closely, in ideas, language, and characteristic attitudes, *De Doctrina Christiana* conforms to Milton's other writing'.
13 Campbell et al., *Milton and the Manuscript of* De Doctrina *Christiana*, p. 161; Gordon Campbell et al., 'The Provenance of *De Doctrina Christiana*', *Milton Quarterly*, 31 (1997), 61–117.
14 Campbell et al., *Milton and the Manuscript of* De Doctrina *Christiana*, pp. 82, 159–61. The earlier draft report in *Milton Quarterly* is more sympathetic toward a 'disintegrationist hypothesis', arguing that 'some parts of the manuscript show more evidence of Miltonic composition than others': 'The relationship of *De Doctrina Christiana* to the Miltonic oeuvre must remain uncertain' ('Provenance', p. 110). In the *Oxford Handbook*, Campbell and Corns conclude that *De Doctrina* is 'beyond reasonable doubt' by Milton, 'though its derivative nature, a feature of the genre, means that it has close verbal affinities with the work of other systematic theologians of the Reformation period' (p. 427).
15 Myers, *Milton's Theology of Freedom*, pp. ix, 2–5.
16 *De Doctrina*, Epistle and title page/*CPW*, VI.117, 120, 125.
17 *De Doctrina*, Epistle/*CPW*, VI.117, 120, 123; *Areopagitica*, *CPW*, II.554.
18 *Of Reformation*, *CPW*, I.540; *Reason of Church-Government*, *CPW*, I.788; Barker, *Milton and the Puritan Dilemma*, p. 338. On 'Puritan' as an opprobrious term, often loosely defined ('I find many that are called Puritans, but few or none that will own the name'), see Hill, 'The Definition of a Puritan', pp. 13–29; and Keeble, 'Milton and Puritanism', pp. 124–6.
19 *A Treatise of Civil Power*, *CPW*, VII.242–3; cf. Nuttall, *The Holy Spirit in Puritan Faith and Experience*, p. 22. 'Every man shall bear his own burden' (Galatians, 6:6) is cited by Milton in *A Treatise of Civil Power* as 'what God himself . . . commands us' (*CPW*, VII.243).
20 Keeble, 'Milton and Puritanism', pp. 124–38.
21 *Areopagitica*, *CPW*, II.543. On the contrast between 'strenuous liberty' and 'bondage with ease', see *Samson Agonistes*, 271, and discussion in Chapter 8.

22 'Sobriety means forbearance from over-eating and from drinking too much' (*De Doctrina*, II.ix/*CPW*, VI.724). On the relationship of *De Doctrina* to the systematic treatises by Wolleb and Ames, see Kelley's introduction, *CPW*, VI.17–22, 45, and Maurice Kelley, 'Milton's Debt to Wolleb's *Compendium Theologiae Christianae*', *PMLA*, 50 (1935), 156–65. In the index to *De Doctrina* in *CPW*, VI, there are over 240 references to Wollebius and over seventy to Amesius.

23 'In the opinion of the Papists it is as absurd to say that we are made righteous by the righteousness of another, as to say that a man is learned by the learning of another. But this is not really an analogy. For the relationship between one man and another is not at all the same as that between a believer and Christ his head': *De Doctrina*, I.xxii/*CPW*, VI.492, 489. Hunter points out that 'the general organization of this chapter of the treatise . . . depends . . . upon that of Wolleb's *Compendium*' and that roughly a quarter of the eighty biblical proof-texts in this chapter also occur in the equivalent chapter in Wolleb: see *Visitation Unimplor'd*, p. 89. 'Our theologians' in this passage clearly means 'Reformed theologians'.

24 *De Doctrina*, I.v/*CPW*, VI.203. After the words 'offended with me' and, earlier, in 'the received opinion', I have substituted the translation by John K. Hale and J. Donald Cullington in Milton, *Complete Works*, VIII.127, as closer to Milton's Latin.

25 Tyacke, *Anti-Calvinists*, pp. 1–5; 'Puritanism, Arminianism and Counter-Revolution', p. 129; Cummings, *The Literary Culture of the Reformation*, p. 291. According to Collinson, 'the orthodox protestant religion' in England at this time was Calvinist: *The Religion of Protestants*, pp. 81–2.

26 Fincham, 'Introduction', *The Early Stuart Church*, p. 5; Lake, 'The Laudian Style', pp. 161–85. On differences between the Laudians and the Dutch Arminians, see Anthony Milton, *Catholic and Reformed*, pp. 436–9. Marvell in *The Rehearsal Transpros'd* (1672) comments acidulously of the Laudians that they 'provided themselves of a new Religion in Holland. It was Arminianism, which though it were the Republican Opinion there, and so odious to King James . . . yet now they undertook to accommodate it to Monarchy and Episcopacy': Marvell, *Prose Works*, I.189.

27 *Of Reformation*, *CPW*, I.525–7.

28 *Of Reformation*, *CPW*, I.576–7. On the charge of carnality, 'the pollution of what should be purely "spiritual" religious worship through the use of bodily ceremonies', see Guibbory, *Ceremony and Community from Herbert to Milton*, pp. 149–56.

29 According to Janel Mueller, Milton's position here is explicitly Calvinist, that of 'nonseparating radical Puritanism, 'a would-be reformer from within the national church': 'Embodying Glory', p. 18.

30 Brautigan, 'Prelates and Politics', pp. 53–4.

31 Anthony Milton, *Laudian and Royalist Polemic in Seventeenth-Century England*, pp. 211, 229. Heylyn in his biography of Laud saw Laud as heroically

'battling against the forces of doctrinal and ceremonial error that had taken over the church' (ibid., p. 208).

32 I am indebted to John Morrill for the term 'post-Calvinist' and for directing me to Jonathan Moore's book on Preston, *English Hypothetical Universalism*. On Baxter, the General Baptists, Goodwin and Milton as providing 'a rival puritan theology' in which 'the scope of salvation was wider than taught in orthodox Calvinism', see Spurr, *English Puritanism*, pp. 168–9; and Campbell and Corns, *John Milton*, pp. 193–5.

33 Tyacke, 'Puritanism, Arminianism and Counter-Revolution', pp. 129–30. On Amyraut, see Armstrong, *Calvinism and the Amyraut Heresy*, pp. xviii, 99–100. On Arminius as working 'within the ecclesiastical and intellectual structure of the Reformed Church' and treating Calvin as 'incomparable' in his interpretation of the Scriptures, see Bangs, *Arminius*, pp. 287, 333–4.

34 Miller, 'Milton and the Conformable Puritanism of Richard Stock and Thomas Young', pp. 73–4, 84–92; Lewalski, *The Life of John Milton*, pp. 5–6, 25–6.

35 See Moore, *English Hypothetical Universalism*, pp. 78–93.

36 Hughes, *Gangraena and the Struggle for the English Revolution*, p. 172; Coffey, *John Goodwin*, p. 162; Goodwin, *Redemption Redeemed* (London, 1651), sig. A2^v.

37 Goodwin, *Redemption Redeemed*, sig. C4. Cf. Coffey, *John Goodwin*, pp. 202, 211.

38 Coffey, *John Goodwin*, pp. 210, 216, quoting Goodwin, *Redemption Redeemed*, pp. 13, 54. The theological and political views of Milton and Goodwin are compared in Barker, *Milton and the Puritan Dilemma*, pp. 87–91, 171–3, 308–13, 358; and in Loewenstein, 'Toleration and the Spectre of Heresy in Milton's England', pp. 45–71.

39 Spurr, *English Puritanism*, p. 168. On the General Baptists and their belief 'that Christ had died in atonement for the sins of all mankind', rather than 'only for a predestined elect', see Tolmie, *The Triumph of the Saints*, pp. 72–7.

40 Lambe, *The Fountaine of Free Grace*, pp. 5, 10. On Overton's role as underground printer of 'a stream of tracts' notable for 'their radical political contents', including *The Fountaine of Free Grace* and tracts by Walwyn, Lilburne, and Overton himself, see Adams, 'The Secret Printing and Publishing Career of Richard Overton', 3–88; and Tolmie, *The Triumph of the Saints*, pp. 75–6.

41 Overton, *Mans Mortalitie*, p. 35. See the discussion of this passage in Burns, *Christian Mortalism from Tyndale to Milton*, p. 173.

42 Overton, *Mans Mortalitie*, title page.

43 *De Doctrina*, I.xiii/*CPW*, VI.400–14. See Kelley's introduction, *CPW*, VI.91–5. On parallels between Overton and Milton, see Burns, *Christian Mortalism*, pp. 170–81; and McDowell, 'Ideas of Creation in the Writings of Richard Overton the Leveller and Paradise Lost', 59–78.

44 Bauman, *Milton's Arianism*; Rumrich, 'Milton's Arianism: Why It Matters', and Fallon, 'Elect Above the Rest', in *Milton and Heresy*, pp. 75–118; Myers,

Milton's Theology of Freedom. Fallon's essay was reprinted, with revisions, in *Milton's Peculiar Grace*.

45 *De Doctrina*, Epistle, I.x/*CPW*, VI.121, 356. In this chapter of *De Doctrina*, in which he argues that marriage is not a sacrament and that polygamy is allowed by the law of God, Milton first defines marriage in terms similar to those set forth in *Doctrine and Discipline*, goes on to discuss polygamy, and then argues in detail that marriage, intended to provide 'the mutuall good-will, love, help and solace of husband and wife' should not be considered 'indissoluble' (*CPW*, VI.370–8). For further discussion, see Chapter 3.

46 *CPW*, VI.203. He says in a later chapter (I.xiv) that 'there is . . . not a single word in the Bible about the mystery of the Trinity' (*CPW*, VI.420).

47 *De Doctrina*, I.xiv/*CPW*, VI.421, 423. On anti-Trinitarianism in *Paradise Lost*, see the detailed listing of parallels in Kelley, *This Great Argument*, pp. 93–106; and Bauman, *Milton's Arianism*, pp. 205–318.

48 *De Doctrina*, I.v/*CPW*, VI.243, 263. On Milton and Calvin on the Trinity, see MacCallum, *Milton and the Sons of God*, pp. 28–36.

49 In *De Doctrina*, Milton says, 'When we talk of knowing God, it must be understood in terms of man's limited powers of comprehension. God, as he really is, is far beyond man's imagination, let alone his understanding.' Here he is stating a position entirely orthodox in arguing the principle of accommodation: 'we ought to form such a mental image of him as he, in bringing himself within the limits of our understanding, wishes us to form' (*De Doctrina*, I.ii/*CPW*, VI.133).

50 See Calvin, *Institutes*, I.xiii, I.112, 129; and Hughes, *Gangraena and the Stuggle for the English Revolution*, pp. 159–60, 191–2. On the term 'Arianism', see Kelley's introduction, *CPW*, VI.53; Bauman, *Milton's Arianism*, pp. 94–120, 145–63; and Rumrich, 'Milton's Arianism', pp. 79–82.

51 Daniel Defoe, *The History of the Devil*, quoted in Bauman, *Milton's Arianism*, pp. 283–5; Kelley, *This Great Argument*, pp. 105–6. For further commentary on this passage in *PL*, Book V, see Chapter 7.

52 See Kelley's introduction, *CPW*, VI.68.

53 See Danielson, *Milton's Good God*, pp. 77, 80–8; and Kelley, *This Great Argument*, pp. 15–19.

54 *Areopagitica*, *CPW*, II.519–20. In *Of True Religion* (1673), written after *Paradise Lost* and *De Doctrina*, Milton includes a sympathetic account of Arminian doctrines, while not identifying his own position as Calvinist, Armininian, or Lutheran: those holding such beliefs, 'painful and zealous labourers' in the pursuit of truth, are 'Learned, Worthy, Zealous, and Religious Men', who hold differing theological opinions, all sincerely held (*CPW*, VIII.425–6).

55 Editor's note, *Doctrine and Discipline*, *CPW*, II.293.

56 *PL*, III.195, 198–200; *De Doctrina*, I.iv/*CPW*, VI.194–5. On the Calvinist doctrine of double predestination, 'whereby he extendeth or witholdeth mercy as he pleaseth, for the glory of his sovereign power over his creatures', see Kelley, *This Great Argument*, pp. 15–19; and Kelley's introduction, *CPW*, VI.77–81. According to Kelley, Milton goes beyond Arminius in rejecting the

idea of predestined reprobation *(CPW,* VI.84–5). Myers similarly emphasizes the radicalism of Milton's position: 'In resisting the division of predestination into election and reprobation, *Paradise Lost*'s theology is sharply discontinuous with all the post-Reformation theological tradition' (*Milton's Theology of Freedom*, pp. 76–8, 81–6).

57 John Preston, for example, as a 'hypothetical universalist', held, like Arminius, Baxter and Milton, that Christ died for all men, not simply for the predestined elect: see Moore, *English Hypothetical Universalism*, pp. 105–11, 116–24. Goodwin held that even the reprobate may 'possibly be saved, any Decree of God notwithstanding' (Myers, *Milton's Theology of Freedom*, p. 86).

58 On the defeat of the Remonstrants at the Synod of Dort and the 'bitter persecution' of the Remonstrants and their lay supporters that followed, see MacCulloch, *Reformation*, pp. 373–8.

59 *De Doctrina*, I.iv/*CPW*, VI.176; Danielson, *Milton's Good God*, p. 73.

60 Kelley, Introduction, *CPW*, VI.81–4. Goodwin argues a similar position in *Redemption Redeemed*; see Coffey, *John Goodwin*, p. 217. It is also central to the General Baptist *Fountaine of Free Grace*, discussed earlier in this chapter.

61 The translation in *Complete Works*, VIII.71 reads 'by its own agency' and omits 'in the future'.

62 Kelley, introduction, *CPW*, VI.84; *PL*, III.173–7. See the discussion of these issues in Myers, 'Prevenient Grace and Conversion', pp. 23–6. According to Phillip Donnelly in *Milton's Scriptural Reasoning*, 'Arminianism is not the mere assertion of conditional election but a way to unite the Reformed insistence that all power for human deliverance comes from God together with the claim that grace is conditional and resistable . . . The primacy of God in providing the gift of salvation is not the crux of the difference between Calvinists and Arminians. The difference lies in whether grace is offered universally and in whether the individual human experience of that divine gift is conditional or not upon human acceptance' (p. 95).

63 The translation in *Complete Works*, VIII.59 reads 'in order to let free causes operate out of that freedom which he himself put into them'.

64 Myers, 'Prevenient Grace and Conversion', pp. 22–7; Article 5, Five Articles of Remonstrance, available at http://www.theopedia.com/Five_articles_of_Remonstrance.

65 Introduction, *CPW*, VI.77, quoting Calvin, *Institutes*, II.v.19. For Milton's scepticism about the term 'original sin', see *De Doctrina*, I.xi/*CPW*, VI.389.

66 'Total depravity' in Canons of Dort (http://www.theopedia, com/TULIP). Myers argues that 'the portrayal of original sin in *Paradise Lost* brings the poem's theology remarkably close to the Reformed orthodox conception of "total depravity" ' (*Milton's Theology of Freedom*, pp. 134–6).

67 Article 3, Five Articles of Remonstrance (http://www.theopedia.com/Five_articles_of_Remonstrance). Danielson argues that Article 3 'is clearly in the tradition of Reformed theology' and is misrepresented in Calvinist polemic,

which accuses it of claiming that fallen man can reach salvation by his own unaided efforts, by 'the light of nature': see *Milton's Good God*, pp. 73–4.

68 Sonnet 19, 9–10, 12–13. The numbers assigned to Milton's sonnets in different editions are inconsistent. The sonnet on his blindness ('When I consider') is sometimes Sonnet 16, sometimes Sonnet 19, where as the sonnet 'To the Lord General Cromwell' in some editions is not given a number and in some editions is Sonnet 16. For consistency, the sonnet on his blindness ('When I consider') is throughout this book Sonnet 19 and the sonnet to Cromwell Sonnet 16.

69 Holy Sonnet 4, 9–10, in Donne, *Complete Poems*, ed. Smith.

Chapter 2: 'Providence Thir Guide'

1 *Areopagitica*, *CPW*, II.527.

2 Calvin, *Commentaries on Isaiah*, quoted in Waddington, *Looking into Providences*, p. 33.

3 Calvin, *Institutes*, I.xvi, I.177, 179. The deity of Calvin and English Calvinism, according to Alexandra Walsham, was activist and interventionist, demonstrating his power in daily life, punishing sinners at times by direct acts of retribution, often appropriate for their particular sins. Such seemingly miraculous occurrences (reports of sinners being consumed by fire or swallowed up by the earth) 'were not hasty improvisations but events which fitted perfectly into the programme for history framed and fixed before time began': *Providence in Early Modern England*, pp. 13, 65–115.

4 *De Doctrina*, I.viii/*CPW*, VI.340. For parallels with definitions in Ames, see Kelley's notes (*CPW*, VI.340–1).

5 *De Doctrina*, I.viii/*CPW*, VI.340–1. On the watchmaker God, see Calvin, *Institutes*, I.175; and Rogers, *The Matter of Revolution*, pp. 153–9.

6 Calvin, *Institutes*, I.xvi, I.175, 176, 179.

7 *The Rehearsal Transpros'd*, Part II, in Marvell, *Prose Works*, I.321.

8 Marvell, *Prose Works*, I.322; *De Doctrina*, I.iii/*CPW*, VI.160–1.

9 *De Doctrina*, I.iii/*CPW*, VI.164–5. On problematical elements in reconciling divine foreknowledge and free will, see Danielson, 'The Fall and Milton's Theodicy', pp. 148–54.

10 Howe, *The Reasonableness of God's Prescience*, p. 119. On Howe and his dissent from strict Calvinist doctrines of predestination, see the discussion in Marvell, *Prose Works*, II.381–92.

11 The autobiographical aspects of this sonnet are evident in its inclusion in a letter to a friend, possibly Thomas Young, in the Trinity Manuscript, commenting on Milton's own 'belatednesse' and 'expectations'.

12 In an interesting commentary on the poem, Dayton Haskin says that the change of direction in the sestet 'corresponds structurally to the archetypal conversion narrative . . . that is, it envisages a period of affliction as a prelude to assurance': Haskin, *Milton's Burden of Interpretation*, p. 115.

13 *Letter to a Friend*, *CPW*, I.320. See the discussion of the scriptural allusions in the *letter* in Fallon, *Milton's Peculiar Grace*, pp. 14–20.
14 Matthew 25:13. As Fallon points out, the letter begins by calling the friend a 'good watch man to admonish that the howres of the night passe on' (*CPW*, I.319), an allusion to John 1:4 as well as Matthew 25:13: *Milton's Peculiar Grace*, pp. 18–20.
15 Myers, 'Prevenient Grace and Conversion', pp. 22–9; cf. Danielson, *Milton's Good God*, pp. 85–90. John Goodwin held a similar position, arguing that 'divine grace assisted the will and made it possible to repent and believe, but it did not compel the will': see Coffey, *John Goodwin*, p. 204.
16 Letter to Richard Mayor, 2 April 1650, in Oliver Cromwell, *Writings and Speeches*, II.235–6, quoted in Worden, *God's Instruments*, p. 14. For the biblical echoes, see Romans 8:31 and the prophecy of the restoration of Israel in Jeremiah 31:10.
17 Worden, *God's Instruments*, pp. 41, 51.
18 Worden, *God's Instruments*, p. 50. On 'the hand of God', cf. Waddington, *Looking into Providences*, p. 107; and Walsham, *Providence in Early Modern England*, pp. 88–9.
19 *Eikonolastes*, *CPW*, III.428–9. Milton makes a similar point in *Tenure*, satirizing claims of providential intervention by those whose actual motives are their own advancement: 'And Providence onely must be the drumme, Providence the word of command' (*CPW*, III.255).
20 For a number of perspectives on Milton's nationalism, as expressed in passages such as these, see the essays included in *Early Modern Nationalism and Milton's England*, ed. Loewenstein and Stevens.
21 *Second Defence*, *CPW*, IV.i.685.
22 *Readie and Easie Way*, *CPW*, VII.463; *De Doctrina*, II.iii/*CPW*, VI.662. Kelley's note points out that this passage in *De Doctrina* is thoroughly orthodox, closely following the Calvinist Wollebius.
23 *Samson Agonistes*, 650, 655, 669–70, 692–6, 703–4. On the treatment of the regicides and imprisonment of other Commonwealthmen after the Restoration, see Worden, 'Milton, *Samson Agonistes*, and the Restoration', pp. 122–6; and Knoppers, *Historicizing Milton*, pp. 42–60.
24 Cooper, *Certaine Sermons* (1580), pp. 164, 176, quoted in Thomas, *Religion and the Decline of Magic*, p. 91.
25 Cunningham, *Children and Childhood in Western Society Since 1500*, p. 51. On afflictions as a trial by fire for the virtuous, see Walsham, *Providence in Early Modern England*, pp. 15–17.
26 Bodleian MS. Fairfax 40, p. 600, quoted in Patterson, *Marvell and the Civic Crown*, p. 97
27 Quoted in Worden, *God's Instruments*, p. 50.
28 For parallels between Milton's situation in the 1660s and that of Ludlow, see Worden, 'Milton, *Samson Agonistes*, and the Restoration', pp. 112–13, 118–26; and Coffey, 'Pacifist Quietist, or Patient Militant?', pp. 149–74.

29 Ludlow, *A Voyce from the Watch Tower*, Part Five: 1660–1662, ed. A. B. Worden, p. 149. As Worden points out, when an edited version of Ludlow's Memoirs was published in 1698–9, many of the passages with religious content were removed or rewritten.

30 *PR*, II.39–40, 53–7.

31 On 'waiting on God', see Loewenstein, *Representing Revolution*, pp. 260–5; and Worden, *God's Instruments*, pp. 39–40, 54–6. Ludlow, in a passage quoted earlier, speaks of the need to wait in readiness until 'when the Lord's tyme is come'.

32 Letter to Leonard Philaras, 28 September 1654, *CPW*, IV.ii, 870 (translation by W. Arthur Turner and Alberta Turner); *PL*, III.45–7.

33 Letter to Philaras, *CPW*, IV.ii.870. Cf. Sonnet 19, 1–9.

34 *Eikonoklastes*, *CPW*, III.564; *Hirelings*, *CPW*, VII.285.

35 *Doctrine and Discipline*, *CPW*, II.292, 297.

36 On the controversy over the meaning of the words 'a short and scandalous night of interruption' and whether they amount to an attack on the Cromwellian Protectorate, see the discussion in Chapter 5.

37 *Samson Agonistes*, 69–70, 679–80, 689, 701.

38 *Areopagitica*, *CPW*, II.527; *Doctrine and Discipline*, *CPW*, II.254.

39 The word 'bondage' occurs fifty-four times in Milton's prose and 'bondage'/'bondslave'/'bonds' seven times in *Samson Agonistes*. 'Captive'/'captivity' occurs fifty-one times in Milton's prose, seven times in *Samson Agonistes*, eleven times in *PL/PR*, while 'yoke' and its cognates appear seventy-one times in the prose, eighteen times in the poems.

40 *Doctrine and Discipline*, *CPW*, II.253–4.

41 *Samson Agonistes*, 410–19; *Doctrine and Discipline*, *CPW*, II.259–60.

42 Sonnet 19 (When I consider), 8, 11; Sonnet 22 (Cyriack, this three years day), 3, 6–9, 14.

43 Sonnet 19, 9–10, 14.

44 Henry King, 'Obsequies', 1–4, in *Justa Edouardo King* (1638), sig. F2. A second poem by Samson Briggs says ''tis not for thee to question Providence', since 'it ill sutes / Men thus to expostulate with God' (sig. H1).

45 Tillyard, *Milton* (1930), pp. 70–4, quoted in *Milton's Lycidas: The Tradition and the Poem*, ed. Patrides, pp. 63–4; Abrams, 'Five Types of *Lycidas*', p. 228.

46 In a recent essay, Gordon Teskey sees the poem's stance as 'one of continual, uncertain, and perilous questioning', arguing that 'these disturbances and the effort they demand' outweigh 'any resolution beyond them, though the poem pretends to give one at last': 'Dead Shepherd: Milton's *Lycidas*', pp. 31–56.

47 *Reason of Church Government*, *CPW*, I.810.

48 *Lycidas*, 64–76. In his essay on *Lycidas* in the *Cambridge Companion*, J. Martin Evans argues that the 'provisional solutions' in the voice of Apollo and St. Peter are not 'entirely satisfying', not providing any 'genuine solace': 'one is left with a sense of incompleteness, of answers yet to be given' (pp. 44–9).

49 *Lycidas*, 130–1. For some of the speculation about the 'two-handed engine', see the note in *Complete Shorter Poems*, p. 78; and Milton's *Lycidas*, ed. Patrides, pp. 356–7.

50 For a sensitive commentary that finds a unifying factor in the speaker's 'gradual . . . growth of understanding that accompanies and emerges from the tides of conflict which shape the surfaces and structures of the poem', see Donald M. Friedman, '*Lycidas*: The Swain's Paideia', pp. 281–302.
51 See, for example, the Son's 'holy Meditations' in the Wilderness in *PR*, Book I, beginning 'O what a multitude of thought at once / Within me swarm' and ending 'And now by some strong motion I am led / Into this Wilderness, to what intent / I learn not yet, perhaps I need not know; / But what concerns my knowledge God reveals' (*PR*, I.195–7, 290–3).
52 *An Apology*, *CPW*, I.927.
53 *An Apology*, *CPW*, I.927–8; *De Doctrina*, II.iii/*CPW*, VI.662.
54 Letter to Philaras, *CPW*, IV.ii.870; Sonnet 22, 6–7.
55 Sonnet 22, 4–6; *Samson Agonistes*, 81–2.
56 *Doctrine and Discipline*, *CPW*, II.253–4; Sonnet 19, 9; Sonnet 22, 6.
57 Sonnet 22, 9–10, 13–14; *PL*, III.194–5.

Chapter 3: The Unpolluted Temple of the Mind

1 *Areopagitica*, *CPW*, II.514–15.
2 *A Maske Presented at Ludlow Castle* (London, 1637), title page.
3 *Complete Shorter Poems*, pp. 82–4. See Brown, *John Milton's Aristocratic Entertainments*.
4 Jonson, *Pleasure Reconciled to Virtue*, 1–2, 142, 159–60, in Lindley, *Court Masques*.
5 Townshend, *Tempe Restored*, 332–3, in Lindley, *Court Masques*.
6 See Shullenberger, *Lady in the Labyrinth*, p. 19: 'The central character . . . and the incarnate human form that its virtue takes, is female, a surprise that seriously challenges the gender bias built into the masque form . . . Milton's exemplary moral agent . . . is a young woman'.
7 *Areopagitica*, *CPW*, II.514–16. Milton gets the details slightly wrong, since the palmer, a figure similar in some ways to Milton's Attendant Spirit, is present at the Bower of Bliss but not the Cave of Mammon. The best account of Milton's indebtedness to Spenser in the Ludlow Masque is Martin, 'Milton's Spenserian Masque', *Milton Quarterly*, 37 (2003), 215–44; a revised version of this essay is included in Martin's *Milton among the Puritans*, pp. 141–73.
8 Spenser, *The Faerie Queene*, II.xii, stanza 72.
9 Marvell, 'Dialogue', 51–4, in *Poems*, ed. Smith.
10 Marvell, 'Dialogue', 46–7.
11 See Mary Nyquist, 'Gendered Subjectivity', pp. 99–127; Turner, 'The Aesthetics of Divorce', p. 51; and Turner, *One Flesh*, pp. 113–23, 216–18.
12 See Nyquist, 'Gendered Subjectivity', pp. 100–5, 109–12. The Calvinist commentary on Genesis issued by the Westminster Assembly (1645) seeks to resolve the contradiction: 'The word *man*, or the Hebrew, *Adam*, taken not personally or individually for one single person, but collectively in this verse,

comprehendeth both male and female of mankind: and so it may well be said, not *let him*, but *let them* have dominion' (p. 109).

13 Bolton, *Some General Directions for a Comfortable Walking with God* (London, 1626), quoted in Martin's introduction to *Milton and Gender*, p. 6; McGuire, *Milton's Puritan Masque*, p. 149.

14 *Areopagitica*, *CPW*, II.515; *A Mask*, 476. In *Areopagitica*, Milton qualifies the general principle that 'God uses not to captivat under a perpetuall childhood of prescription, but trusts him with the gifts of reason to be his own chooser' by, a few sentences earlier, speaking of 'every grown man' (*CPW*, II.513–14). For Milton as for Locke, a child has not yet entirely come into the legacy of reason.

15 *Areopagitica*, *CPW*, II.514. See Brown, *John Milton's Aristocratic Entertainments*, pp. 92–7, 101–3, 137–41.

16 William Shakespeare, *Much Ado about Nothing*, ed. Humphreys, 4.1.31, 139–43.

17 See Fallon, *Milton among the Philosophers*, pp. 79–110; and Kerrigan, *The Sacred Complex*, pp. 31–5.

18 *An Apology*, *CPW*, I.891–2.

19 *An Apology*, *CPW*, I.892–3. See the discussion in Shullenberger, *Lady in the Labyrinth*, pp. 203–9; and Kerrigan, *The Sacred Complex*, pp. 26–9.

20 'Elegia sexta', 61–4, in *Complete Shorter Poems*; translation by Lawrence Revard.

21 *An Apology*, *CPW*, I.890, 892.

22 *A Mask*, 393–400. See the discussion of 'the purity of virgin lady, chaste reader, and honorable author' in Fallon, *Milton's Peculiar Grace*, pp. 103–9. Achsah Guibbory in *Ceremony and Community from Herbert to Milton* points out that the emphasis on purity and pollution here and elsewhere in Milton has a political and religious dimension, as representing 'the temptation of false worship and idolatry' threatening 'the godly Christian' (pp. 165–71).

23 *A Mask*, 204, 210–12, 337. These lines are not in the Bridgewater manuscript and thus were not spoken in performance in 1634, but they are present in the Trinity manuscript. Lines 780–7, in which the Lady, defying Comus, speaks of the 'Sun-clad power of Chastity' and 'the sage / And serious doctrine of Virginity', are absent from the Bridgewater manuscript and also from the Trinity manuscript.

24 In the Trinity manuscript, 'cherub' is corrected to 'guardian', and the draft lines '& while I see yee /this dusky hollow is a paradise /& heaven gates ore my head', after 'I see yee visibly', are crossed out.

25 *A Mask*, 658; *Areopagitica*, *CPW*, II.561.

26 'You took away all the oceans and all the room' (1935), in Osip Mandelstam, *Selected Poems*, trans. Clarence Brown and W. S. Merwin.

27 *A Mask*, 537–8, 697–8; *Areopagitica*, *CPW*, II.514.

28 According to Stephen Orgel in 'The Case for Comus', *Representations*, 81 (2003), 31–45, though Comus's argument here 'has its specious elements . . . it produces some of the best poetry in the masque . . . rich, sensuous, wonderfully inventive'. See also Tillyard, *Studies in Milton*, pp. 82–96.

29 Marcus, *The Politics of Mirth*, pp. 187–91.
30 See, e.g., Brown, *John Milton's Aristocratic Entertainments*, pp. 72–5, 88–92; and Lewalski, *The Life of John Milton*, pp. 77–80. Martin, who argues against the idea that *A Mask* can be considered a 'Puritan masque', cites similar passages in *The Faerie Queene*, in 'Guyon's rejection of Mammon's ill-gotten goods': see 'Milton's Spenserian Masque', pp. 215, 232–3.
31 These lines are in the Trinity manuscript but not the Bridgewater manuscript. On the process of composition and revision, see Brown, *John Milton's Aristocratic Entertainments*, pp. 132–41, 168–78. The Bridgewater manuscript is included in *Complete Shorter Poems*.
32 Kerrigan, *The Sacred Complex*, pp. 26, 32.
33 Woodhouse, '*Comus* Once More', in Diekhoff, ed., *A Maske at Ludlow*, pp. 74–7; Woodhouse, 'The Argument of Milton's *Comus*', pp. 17–42 (p. 29).
34 Corns, 'Milton before "Lycidas"', pp. 34–5; Campbell and Corns, *John Milton*, pp. 83–4.
35 Sonnet 13, 'To Mr. H. Lawes, on his Aires', 1–3. Of lines 780–908 in the Bridgewater manuscript, all but twenty are set to music, though the stage directions, 'The verse to singe or not' (788) and 'the daunces all ended, the Daemon singes or sayes' (897) present alternative ways of staging. See Chernaik, 'Linked Sweetness: Milton and Music', 23–43.
36 Patterson, 'No Meer Amatorious Novel?', p. 85. In 'Milton, Marriage and Divorce', Patterson argues that in *Doctrine and Discipline* 'a logical case for the reform of the divorce laws' is 'superimposed on a subtext of emotional chaos' (p. 286).
37 *CPW*, II.258–9, 275. See Turner, *One Flesh*, pp. 194–9, 224–9; and Patterson, 'No Meer Amatorious Novel?', pp. 97–101. 'The carnal act', unless it is somehow made 'legitimate', Milton says, 'might seem to have something of pollution in it' (*CPW*, II.326).
38 *CPW*, II.327–8. For Milton's exegesis of this passage in Genesis, see Turner, *One Flesh*, pp. 190–5.
39 *De Doctrina*, I.x/*CPW*, VI.381.
40 Sonnet 12, 3–4; *De Doctrina*, I.x/*CPW*, VI.381.
41 *PL*, IV.750, 758–9; Turner, *One Flesh*, p. 235. On Milton's unconventional treatment of prelapsarian sex, see Turner, *One Flesh*, pp. 232–46; and Haller, 'Hail Wedded Love'.
42 *PL*, VII.389–91, 588, 593, 602–4.
43 *Doctrine and Discipline*, *CPW*, II.345–6. On the desacralization of marriage, see *Doctrine and Discipline*, *CPW*, II.275–8; *De Doctrina*, I.xxviii/*CPW*, VI.554–62; and Achinstein, 'Contextualizing Milton's Divorce Tracts', pp. 176, 181–3.
44 *CPW*, II.589–90. The passage in *Tetrachordon* is discussed in Patterson, 'Milton, Marriage and Divorce', pp. 289–92.
45 *Tetrachordon*, *CPW*, II.626. In *Doctrine and Discipline*, in contrast, Milton attacks arguments that in Deuteronomy divorce was granted for 'afflicted wives' and not for husbands as 'palpably uxorious' (*CPW*, II.324).

46 *Tetrachordon*, *CPW*, II.592, 607. I am grateful to Peter Medine for calling my attention to these and other passages in *Tetrachordon* suggesting that men and women are equally 'the image of God' and deserve to be treated accordingly.

47 *De Doctrina*, I.xxvii/*CPW*, VI.525–7. On Milton's divergence from Calvinist orthodoxy here, see Barker, *Milton and the Puritan Dilemma*, pp. 102–7, 319–24, 363; and Kelley's note, *CPW*, VI.521–2.

48 *Tetrachordon*, *CPW*, II.637; *De Doctrina*, II.xxvii/*CPW*, VI.533. Cf. the appeal to charity in the preface to *Doctrine and Discipline*, addressed to Parliament: 'Yet now a civil, and indifferent, a somtime diswaded Law of mariage must be forc't upon us to fulfill, not only without charity, but against her. No place in Heav'n or Earth, except Hell, where charity may not enter' (*CPW*, II.228–9).

49 *Doctrine and Discipline*, *CPW*, II.330–1; *De Doctrina*, I.x/*CPW*, VI.379. On the contrast between a 'negative Pauline conception' of the Mosaic Law in *De Doctrina* and *PL*, XI–XII and a 'more charitable' view in the divorce tracts, see Rosenblatt, *Torah and Law*, pp. 42–50.

50 *Doctrine and Discipline*, *CPW*, II.253, 349–50. OED defines 'injury' as 'a wrongful action or treatment; violation or infringement of another's rights; suffering or mischief wilfully or unjustly inflicted'.

51 *Doctrine and Discipline*, *CPW*, II.229. For discussion of the political implications of Milton's divorce tracts, see Achinstein, 'Contextualizing Milton's Divorce Tracts', pp. 174–85; and Victoria Kahn, *Wayward Contracts*, pp. 197–203.

52 Henry Ferne, *Conscience Satisfied*, p. 12; cited in Shanley, 'Marriage Contract and Social Contract in Seventeenth Century Political Thought', 79–91.

53 Robert Baillie, *A Dissuasive from the Errours of the Time* (London, 1646), p. 116.

54 Herbert Palmer, *The Glasse of Gods Providence toward His Faithfull Ones* (London, 1644), p. 57, in Parker, *Milton's Contemporary Reputation*, pp. 73–6. On how 'Milton's writings on divorce were implacably hounded by the enemies of toleration' in the 1640s, see Campbell and Corns, *John Milton*, pp. 164–71.

55 Clement Walker, *Anarchia Anglicana: Or the History of Independency. The Second Part* (1649), p. 199, in Parker, *Milton's Contemporary Reputation*, pp. 82–3; Christopher Wase, *Electra of Sophocles . . . With an Epilogue* (The Hague, 1649), sig. E8, in Parker, *Milton's Contemporary Reputation*, pp. 83–4.

56 See the discussion of Milton's invocation of natural law to argue the principle that no ordinance or covenant can bind against 'the good of man' in Barker, *Milton and the Puritan Dilemma*, pp. 110–12. On political applications of the principle that 'the supreme of all humane laws is *salus populi*', see Sommerville, *Politics and Ideology in England*, pp. 69–80.

57 *Tetrachordon*, *CPW*, II.624. On equity and the letter of the law in Milton and in political and theological discourse during this period, see Kahn, *Wayward Contracts*, pp. 43–5, 52–5, 199–203. As Kahn points out, in seventeenth-century

discussions of the political contract, the terms 'contract', 'compact' and 'covenant' are treated as synonyms (p. 292).

58 *The Armies Vindication* (1649), pp. 47–8, cited in Barker, *Milton and the Puritan Dilemma*, pp. 371–2.

59 Samuel Rutherford, *Lex Rex* (1644), in Woodhouse, *Puritanism and Liberty*, p. 208.

60 *First Defence*, in *Works*, ed. Patterson, VII.359–61. In this passage, the translation from the Latin by Samuel Wolff is preferable to the one in *CPW*, IV.i.

Chapter 4: Classical and Biblical Republicanism

1 Hobbes, *Leviathan*, Chapter 29, p. 214.

2 Hobbes, *Behemoth*, pp. 174–81.

3 *An Abridgement* (1649), title page, pp. 6–7. On the scriptural references to the punishment of wicked kings in the *Abridgement*, see *Complete Works*, VI, ed. Keeble and McDowell, pp. 18–19.

4 McLaren, 'Rethinking Republicanism', p. 33.

5 *Scripture and Reason Pleaded for Defensive Armes*, title page, p. 15.

6 *Scripture and Reason Pleaded for Defensive Armes*, pp. 9–13, 15, 53.

7 John Goodwin, *Anti-Cavalierisme; or, Truth Pleading as Well the Necessity, as the Lawfulness of This Present War* (1642), p. 5, in William Haller, ed., *Tracts on Liberty*, vol. II, pp. 217–69.

8 *Defence of the English People*, *CPW*, IV.i, 386. Milton advances a similar argument in *Tenure*: 'Those powers that doe the contrary, are no powers ordain'd of God, and by consequence no obligation laid upon us to obey or not to resist them' (*CPW*, III.210).

9 *CPW*, III.189, 202, 206. Such bold statements in the title page and elsewhere in *Tenure*, according to Keeble and McDowell, are 'a direct retort' to Presbyterian objections to 'wicked and bloody tenets' justifying 'the murthering of Kings' (*Complete Works*, VI, ed. Keeble and McDowell, 36–40).

10 *CPW*, III.206. See Dzelzainis, 'Milton's Classical Republicanism', p. 20. *Vindiciae* presents a tyrant as 'opposite to a King': 'he is a King, which lawfully governes a Kingdome', where a tyrant 'governes it not according to law and equitie': *Vindiciae*, p. 103. On the question of 'whether private men may resist by Armes' a prince who 'doth oppresse or ruine a publike State', *Vindiciae* consistently distinguishes between 'private men' and legally constituted magistrates or 'the representative body of the people': see *Vindiciae*, pp. 39–41, 46, 116–20, 133–4.

11 *CPW*, III.198–9, Hobbes, *Leviathan*, Part III, 'Of a Christian Commonwealth', Chapters 32–43. On a possible conflict between a 'secular and naturalistic' and 'theocratic' view of politics in Milton during this period, see Sirluck, 'Milton's Political Thought', pp. 218–19, 224.

12 Harrington, *The Commonwealth of Oceana*, pp. 25–42. On the commonwealth of Israel in the Old Testament as providing a model for Harrington, see Nelson, *The Hebrew Republic*, pp. 50–2, 78–87.

13 *CPW*, VII.432, 436. In this passage in the second edition of *The Readie and Easie Way*, Milton is explicitly or implicitly in dialogue with Harrington: see the introduction and notes to *CPW*, VII.102–4, 210–11, 433–45.

14 Nedham, *Excellencie of a Free-State*, pp. 31–6.

15 Nedham, *Excellencie of a Free-State*, pp. 107–8. *The Excellencie of a Free-State* is largely based on a series of essays included in Nedham's newsbook *Mercurius Politicus* in 1651–2, updated and revised to fit the different political circumstances of 1656. The 'Reason of State' essay is from *Mercurius Politicus*, 108, 24 June–1 July 1652.

16 Nedham, *The Case of the Commonwealth, Stated*, title page, pp. 6–9, 63–5.

17 Nedham, *Excellencie of a Free-State*, p. 151. In *Literature and Politics in Cromwell's England*, pp. 204–7, Worden argues for 'a close working partnership between Milton and Nedham' during 1651–2 and suggests that the similarity here to arguments in Milton's defences of regicide may be due to Milton's authorship or co-authorship of this essay in *Mercurius Politicus*. But the same words appear in an anonymous pamphlet by Nedham, *Anglia Liberata . . . an Additional Reply to All the Pretended Arguments* (1651), pp. 60–1.

18 Goodwin, *The Obstructors of Justice* (1649), pp. 78–80; Parker, *Milton's Contemporary Reputation*, pp. 80–2. On *The Obstructors of Justice*, see Coffey, *John Goodwin*, pp. 180–2.

19 *Tenure*, *CPW*, III.189 (title page), 212–16. In a series of essays, Kevin Killeen argues that historians of the Early Modern period 'have not sufficiently taken stock of the way in which biblical exegesis was seen as an analytical tool for political affairs' in the seventeenth century. 'Far from conceiving monarchs hedged in untouchability, the era was wholly, obsessively aware of the contingency and, indeed, the "killability" of kings', finding in Scripture 'a history of regicide and usurpation, much of it commissioned and at the bidding of God: regicide with an apparently quotidian ease': '"Hanging up Kings": The Political Bible in Early Modern England', *Journal of the History of Ideas*, 72 (2011), 549–70. See also Killeen, 'Chastising with Scorpions'.

20 Sonnet 12, 'On the detraction which follow'd upon my writing certain treatises', 1–4; *Areopagitica*, *CPW*, II.489. On attacks on Milton's divorce pamphlets, see Lewalski, *The Life of John Milton*, pp. 178–80.

21 *CPW*, II.549, 553–4. On the relationship of *Areopagitica* to the republican tradition, see Smith, '*Areopagitica*: Voicing Contexts, 1643–4', pp. 115–18; and Lewalski, *The Life of John Milton*, pp. 190–1, 196–7.

22 *Vindiciae*, p. 95; *Defence*, *CPW*, IV.i, 344. Milton is paraphrasing Deuteronomy 17:16–17: 'But he shall not multiply horses to himself . . . neither shall he multiply wives to himself . . . silver and gold.' On competing interpretations of Deuteronomy 17 and 1 Samuel 8 by conservatives and republicans, see Nelson, *The Hebrew Republic*, pp. 26–32, 50–3.

23 Lilburne, *Regall Tyranny Discovered*, pp. 8–9.

24 Lilburne, *Regall Tyranny Discovered*, pp. 13–14. Cf. *Defence*, *CPW*, IV.i.353: 'The prophet warned them beforehand that their stubbornness in that request would result in their own punishment . . . through their own deserts.'
25 *Defence*, *CPW*, IV.i.353; *Readie and Easie Way*, *CPW*, VII.463.
26 *Readie and Easie Way*, *CPW*, VII.449–50; *Defence*, *CPW*, IV.i.354.
27 Hobbes, *Leviathan*, Chapter 19, p. 121; Filmer, *Patriarcha and Other Writings*, pp. 36, 207.
28 Filmer, *Patriarcha and Other Writings*, pp. 35–7. Salmasius similarly interprets this passage as setting forth 'the rights of kings': see *CPW*, IV.i.348–53.
29 *Tenure*, *CPW*, III.212; *Vindiciae*, p. 94; *Defence*, *CPW*, IV.i.349. *Vindiciae* makes a similar point: not what 'they may justly do', but what 'they unjustly usurp' (pp. 94–5).
30 *The Armies Vindication* (1649), pp. 63–4. William Walker in his revisionist study *Antiformalist, Unrevolutionary, Illiberal Milton*, argues that Milton, no republican, never repudiates monarchy in principle, but even in *The Readie and Easie Way* is 'not against monarchy per se but against a particular kind of monarchy in a particular place at a particular time: a Stuart monarch in England in 1660' (pp. 35, 47).
31 Overton, *An Arrow Against All Tyrants* (1646), p. 3. On 'self-propriety' and consent in Overton, see Rachel Foxley, *The Levellers*, pp. 23–5, 30, 44–5, 92; and, for a comparison with Milton, see *Complete Works*, VI, ed. Keeble and McDowell, p. 27.
32 Overton, *An Appeale*, p. 162.
33 *Tenure*, *CPW*, III.237. Cf. Skinner, *Liberty before Liberalism*, pp. 66–76.
34 *Readie and Easie Way*, *CPW*, VII.428, 463.
35 *PL*, XII.219–20; *Readie and Easie Way*, *CPW*, VII.446. For further discussion, see Chapter 8.
36 John Coffey in 'Quentin Skinner and the Religious Dimension of Early Modern Political Thought', pp. 60–7, devotes particular attention to the metaphor of Egyptian bondage in arguing that Milton's 'language of slavery, while indebted to the classics, is shot through with echoes of Scripture'.
37 Letter of Moses Wall to Milton, 26 May 1659, *CPW*, VII.511; *PL*, XII.218. Wall goes on to say that 'whilst People are not free but straitened in Accommodations for Life, their Spirits will be dejected and servile'. For other instances of the metaphor of Egyptian bondage by Milton's contemporaries, see Knoppers, 'Milton's *The Readie and Easie Way* and the English Jeremiad', pp. 211–25.

Chapter 5: Victory's Crest

1 'Horatian Ode', 97–8.
2 'To the Lord General Cromwell', 1, 4, 6–7, 9–11.
3 *Second Defence*, *CPW*, IV.i.667–8.

4 *CPW*, IV.i.667–8 (Latin text in *Works*, Columbia edition, VIII.214–16). This passage is discussed in Knoppers, *Constructing Cromwell*, p. 93. As Knoppers points out (pp. 89–95, 207), a similar emphasis on Cromwell's piety and self-denial is evident in Payne Fisher's Latin panegyrics and in the English translation by Thomas Manley, *Veni; Vidi; Vici* (London, 1651): 'Blest Hero, whose uprightness all commands / Whose joy in vertue more than triumph stands / . . . Thus doest thou valiant Leader overthrow / Thine enemies, thy selfe thus conquer too' (p. 11).

5 'To the Lord General Cromwell', 3, 6.

6 *CPW*, III.304. See the discussion of the *Observations* in Corns, 'Milton's *Observations upon the Articles of Peace*,' pp. 123–34; and Stevens, 'Leviticus Thinking', pp. 456–8.

7 Waller, *A Panegyrick to My Lord Protector*, pp. 4–6. All quotations of the *Panegyrick* are from the 1655 folio edition.

8 Quint, *Epic and Empire*, pp. 8–11; *PL*, I.108.

9 Milton, *History of Britain*, *CPW*, V.85.

10 *Character of the Long Parliament* ('The Digression'), *CPW*, V.451. The 'Digression' was originally intended for Book III of the *History of Britain*, with an explicit 'parallel betweene their state and ours in the late commotions': 'the late civil broils had cast us into a condition not much unlike to what the Britans then were in' (*CPW*, V.129, 441).

11 *History of Britain*, *CPW*, V.80, 131. On parallels between such passages in the *History of Britain* and the characterization of the Irish in *Observations*, see *Complete Works*, VI, ed. Keeble and McDowell, pp. 52–5.

12 *CPW*, V.61, 85.

13 'Digression', *CPW*, V.449; sonnet 12 (I did but prompt the age), 2, 12.

14 'Digression', *CPW*, V, 441, 443. Nicholas von Maltzahn in *Milton's History of Britain* has argued that the probable date of the 'Digression' is February 1649, after the execution of Charles I, reflecting 'Milton's corrosive misgivings about the Long Parliament and the Presbyterian Assembly' at a time when 'the form of government was yet to be decided' (pp. 31, 37).

15 *CPW*, V.130.

16 *Second Defence*, *CPW*, IV.i.685. For the metaphor of the 'mighty harvest', cf. *Areopagitica*, *CPW*, II.554.

17 *Tenure*, *CPW*, III.190–1.

18 *Second Defence*, *CPW*, IV.i.684. On the basis of these ideas in Roman law, cf. Dzelzainis, 'Republicanism', pp. 302–3.

19 *CPW*, VII.423–4. Cf. Knoppers, *Constructing Cromwell*, pp. 56–66. Fisher, like Marvell in the 'Horatian Ode', praises the victorious Cromwell as 'a hero who serves the republic rather than fighting to gain glory for himself' (Knoppers, *Constructing Cromwell*, p. 61).

20 *Readie and Easie Way*, *CPW*, VII.428; *Areopagitica*, *CPW*, II.555.

21 'To the Lord General Cromwell', 3, 10–11; 'On the Lord General Fairfax at the Siege of Colchester', 5–6, 9; 'To Sir Henry Vane the Younger', 1, 5–7.

22 'Horatian Ode', 75–6.

23 *CPW*, VII.448, 461.
24 *Samson Agonistes*, 47, 52–7, 342, 346.
25 *Paradise Lost*, XII.92–6; *Tenure*, *CPW*, III.190.
26 Nedham, *Excellencie of a Free-State*, pp. 30, 45. Cf. *Tenure*, *CPW*, III.190–1.
27 Nedham, *Excellencie of a Free-State*, pp. 101–2.
28 Nedham, *Excellencie of a Free State*, p. 44.
29 'Horatian Ode', 89–90. Blair Worden has argued that both *The Excellencie of a Free-State* and *The Commonwealth of Oceana* are 'anti-Cromwellian publications', satirizing the Protectorate regime and showing 'hatred and mistrust' of Cromwell: see 'Milton and Marchamont Nedham', p. 175; and *Literature and Politics in Cromwellian England*, pp. 110–15, 306–13. The publication history of *The Excellencie of a Free-State*, much of which recycles material previously used by Nedham in *The Case of the Commonwealth, Stated* (1650) and *Mercurius Politicus* (1651–2), would argue against a reading of *Excellencie* as a straightforward attack on Cromwell.
30 Nedham, *True State*, p. 22.
31 Harrington, *Oceana*, pp. 56, 66.
32 'Horatian Ode', 101–2; *The First Anniversary*, 250, 256.
33 *The First Anniversary*, 258, 293–8. For a discussion of these biblical analogies, see Patterson, *Marvell and the Civic Crown*, pp. 79–88.
34 Harrington, *Oceana*, pp. 249–50. In treating Julius Caesar as an instance of false renown and as the enemy of Roman liberty, Harrington is echoing Machiavelli: see *Discourses*, I.10, pp. 135–8. Nedham in *The Excellencie of a Free-State* similarly treats Julius Caesar as one who abandoned his former principles and 'turn'd his Armes on the Publick Liberty' (p. 102).
35 Harrington, *Oceana*, pp. 249–50; *PR*, II.434.
36 Nedham, *Excellencie of a Free-State*, pp. 90, 92.
37 Nedham, *Excellencie of a Free-State*, pp. 16, 34–6. On the Roman republic compared with the Roman Empire, see Machiavelli, *Discourses*, I.10.
38 Nedham, *Excellencie of a Free-State*, pp. 35–6.
39 [John Wildman], *A Call to All the Souldiers of the Armie*, p. 6. Cf. Overton, *The Hunting of the Foxes*, in Wolfe, *Leveller Manifestoes*, p. 369: 'O Crumwell, O Ireton, how hath a little time and successe changed the honest shape of so many Officers!' For a discussion of other attacks on Cromwell by Levellers and republicans during 1647–9 and the mid-1650s, see Morrill, 'Cromwell and His Contemporaries', pp. 259–81.
40 Overton, *Hunting of the Foxes*, pp. 362, 364, 366.
41 Overton, *Hunting of the Foxes*, p. 372.
42 Overton, *Hunting of the Foxes*, pp. 362, 364, 366, 372; Walwyn, *The Bloody Project*, p. 301.
43 Walwyn, *The Bloody Project*, pp. 301, 306. Walwyn, unlike his fellow Leveller Overton, does not name Cromwell or Ireton but directs his attack at 'the severall Grandee Factions' (p. 296).
44 Overton, *Hunting of the Foxes*, pp. 358, 366.

45 Overton, *Hunting of the Foxes*, pp. 361, 372, 373. David Loewenstein compares *The Hunting of the Foxes* to a number of pamphlets by John Lilburne attacking Cromwell and the Grandees as dissemblers, contrasting them with 'the honest Soldiers, and the rest of the Free-people of England': see *Representing Revolution*, pp. 37–42.

46 Overton, *Hunting of the Foxes*, pp. 373–4. Though *The Hunting of the Foxes* purports to be by the five soldiers, its probable author is Overton: see Wolfe's introduction, *Leveller Manifestoes*, pp. 356–7.

47 Woodhouse, *Puritanism and Liberty*, pp. 69–70.

48 [John Wildman], *Declaration of the Free-Born People* (1654), broadsheet. As Morrill points out, republican attacks on Cromwell at this time treat him as 'corrupted by power', covering his 'ruthless ambition' with a pretended devotion to liberty ('Cromwell and His Contemporaries', pp. 267–9).

49 Wildman, *Declaration of the Free-Born People.*

50 *The Protector Unvailed*, title page; Wildman, *Declaration of the Free-Born People.*

51 *The Protector Unvailed*, p. 42.

52 *The Protector Unvailed*, p. 18.

53 *CPW*, III.212; [Sexby], *Killing Noe Murder* (1657), sig. A4.

54 *CPW*, III.254; *The Protector Unvailed*, 3. Sexby argues that 'by the law of nature, *ubi cessat judicium*, when no justice can be had, every man must be his own magistrate, and do justice for himself' (*Killing Noe Murder*, sig. A4–A4^{v}).

55 [Sexby], *Killing Noe Murder*, sig. A3. On the classical republicanism of *Killing Noe Murder*, see Smith, *Literature and Revolution in England*, pp. 151–3.

56 [Sexby], *Killing Noe Murder*, sig. A1^{v}.

57 *Tenure*, *CPW*, III.237; [Sexby], *Killing Noe Murder*, sig. A4v; Overton, *An Arrow Against All Tyrants*, p. 3. See the discussion of 'self-propriety' in Chapter 4.

58 [Sexby], *Killing Noe Murder*, sig. B1^{v}. Milton's Samson is not motivated by revenge for injuries done him though his action against 'many oppressours' is no less violent. On the biblical precedents of Ehud, Jehu and other divinely inspired regicides, see Killeen, 'Hanging Up Kings', pp. 554–60.

59 [Sexby], *Killing Noe Murder*, sig. B4, B3^{v}.

60 *CPW*, IV.i.662–3, 666; Knoppers, *Constructing Cromwell*, p. 93.

61 *CPW*, IV.i.667–9, 672.

62 Woolrych, 'Milton and Cromwell', pp. 185–218; *CPW*, VII.274.

63 Worden, 'John Milton and Oliver Cromwell', pp. 244, 255.

64 Worden, 'Milton and Marchamont Nedham', p. 175. See Fallon, 'A Second Defence: Milton's Critique of Cromwell?', and Stevens, 'Milton's "Renunciation" of Cromwell'.

65 *Readie and Easie Way*, *CPW*, VII.429; *Hirelings*, *CPW*, VII.274.

66 Corns, *Uncloistered Virtue*, p. 274; Fallon, 'Milton in the Anarchy', pp. 123–46; Woolrych, 'Milton & Cromwell', p. 201.

67 *Readie and Easie Way*, *CPW*, VII.421, 430. Woolrych gives a full account of rival interpretations of 'a short but scandalous night of interruption', 'Milton and Cromwell', pp. 201–9.

68 *Hirelings*, *CPW*, VII.274.

69 *CPW*, IV.i.671. Cf. 'Digression', *CPW*, V.443: 'But when once the superficial zeale and popular fumes that acted thir new magistracie were cool'd and spent in them, straite every one betooke himself, setting the common-wealth behinde and his private ends before, to doe as his own profit or ambition led him. Then was justice delai'd & soone after deny'd, spite and favour determin'd all: hence faction, then treacherie both at home and in the field, ev'ry where wrong & oppression.'
70 Nedham, *True State*, pp. 9, 11.
71 Nedham, *True State*, pp. 13, 14.
72 *CPW*, IV.i.671.
73 *CPW*, IV.i.670, 671–2, 674.
74 Waller, *Panegyrick*, 1–8. Waller's appeal, like Milton's, is in part patriotic. The subtitle of the 1655 quarto links 'the present greatness and joynt interest of His Highness and this nation'.
75 *Second Defence*, *CPW*, IV.i.672; *The First Anniversary*, 24, 28, 41.
76 *Second Defence*, *CPW*, IV.i.672; *The First Anniversary*, 225–8, 389–90.
77 Nedham, *True State*, p. 28.
78 *Defence*, *CPW*, IV.i.532; *Readie and Easie Way*, *CPW*, VII.462–3.
79 Loewenstein, 'Milton and the Poetics of Defense', pp. 188–9.
80 Sonnet 16, 'To the Lord General Cromwell', 10–11.
81 Knoppers, *Constructing Cromwell*, p. 95; *CPW*, IV.i.673–4.
82 *CPW*, IV.i.680.
83 Sonnet 12, lines 9–10; *Second Defence*, *CPW*, IV.i.683.
84 *History of Britain*, *CPW*, V, 449; *Samson Agonistes*, 268–76.
85 Woodhouse, *Puritanism and Liberty*, p. 66.
86 *CPW*, IV.i.682. The 'Digression' directs similar accusations at the members of the Long Parliament, with particular scorn directed at 'some who had bin call'd from shops & warehouses without other merit to sit in supreme council, ' who 'fell to hucster the commonwealth' (*CPW*, V, 445).
87 Vane, *A Needful Corrective*, p. 6. Vane's tract, a letter to Harrington, is discussed in *CPW*, VII, 105.
88 *CPW*, VII.455. This and other passages urging compulsion of the unregenerate multitude by the virtuous few are discussed above in the Introduction. See also Hammond, *Milton and the People*, pp. 173–85, 197–9, 204–5; Foxley, 'Due Libertie and Proportiond Equalitie', pp. 623–38; and introductory essays by McDowell and Keeble in *Complete Works*, VI.43–4, 101–6, 122–3.
89 *PL*, XII.86–101; *Second Defence*, *CPW*, IV.i.680, 684. For further discussion of *PL*, XII, see Chapter 8.
90 *PL*, XII.106–10; *Second Defence*, *CPW*, IV.i.684; *Areopagitica*, *CPW*, II.526.
91 *Readie and Easie Way*, *CPW*, VII.462; *Second Defence*, *CPW*, IV.i.680.

Chapter 6: Monarchy and Servitude

1 Lewis, *A Preface to Paradise Lost*, pp. 78, 99, 102.
2 Fish, *Surprised by Sin*, pp. 38–40, 48–9.

3 Empson, *Milton's God*; Hill, *Milton and the English Revolution*; Norbrook, *Writing the English Republic*.
4 *PL*, I.322, 658, 661; II.321. On Satan's republican language, see Worden, 'Milton's Republicanism', pp. 235–41; Norbrook, *Writing the English Republic*, pp. 444–6; and Stevens, 'The Pre-secular Politics of *Paradise Lost*', pp. 103–6.
5 See Skinner, 'John Milton and the Politics of Slavery', pp. 1–22; and *Liberty Before Liberalism*, pp. 36–77.
6 *Tenure*, *CPW*, III.193; *Samson Agonistes*, 269–71.
7 Toland, *The Life of John Milton*, p. 42, quoted in Newlyn, *Paradise Lost and the Romantic Reader*, p. 35.
8 See Fallon, *Divided Empire*, pp. 123–5. Fallon claims that Abdiel's arguments resemble those of Salmasius, which Milton sought to refute in the *First Defence*. More plausibly, Sharon Achinstein likens the courageous Abdiel, speaking out 'fearless, though alone' against the overwhelming numbers of the Satanic host to defend 'the Cause / Of Truth' (*PL*, V.875; VI.31–2), to the situation of Dissenters after the Restoration: see *Literature and Dissent in Milton's England*, pp. 119–22.
9 Lilburne, *Regall Tyranny Discovered*, pp. 13–14.
10 *Eikonoklastes*, *CPW*, III.586, 589.
11 On voluntary service to God as compatible with freedom of the will, see the discussion of Abdiel's confrontation with Satan in Radzinowicz, 'The Politics of *Paradise Lost*', pp. 222–5; and in Loewenstein, *Representing Revolution*, pp. 229–30.
12 *PL*, V.896–907. On Abdiel as model of 'the true (inner) heroism of obedience', see Fish, *Surprised by Sin*, pp. 180–206. On Abdiel, Dissent, and persecution, see Achinstein, *Literature and Dissent in Milton's England*, pp. 119–22; and Keeble, 'Restoration Images of Milton and Bunyan', pp. 10–14.
13 Lewis, *A Preface to Paradise Lost*, p. 78.
14 *PL*, II.1–5: Davies, *Images of Kingship in Paradise Lost*, pp. 10–39, 49–93.
15 Bennett, *Reviving Liberty*, pp. 33–58.
16 Fallon, *Divided Empire*, pp. 31–5; *Tenure*, *CPW*, III.212.
17 Hill, *Milton and the English Revolution*, pp. 366–7.
18 Norbrook, *Writing the English Republic*, pp. 442, 446.
19 Worden, *Literature and Politics in Cromwellian England*, pp. 293–6; Worden, 'Milton's Republicanism', p. 246.
20 Worden, *Literature and Politics in Cromwellian England*, pp. 344, 346; 'Milton's Republicanism', pp. 241–3. For a different view of the treatment of Cromwell in the *Second Defence*, see Chapter 5.
21 Percy Bysshe Shelley, *Preface to Prometheus Unbound* (1820) and *A Defence of Poetry* (1821), in *Shelley's Poetry and Prose*, pp. 133, 498.
22 Shelley, *A Defence of Poetry*, p. 498; Empson, *Milton's God*, pp. 10–11. On 'subversive Satan' in Blake, Shelley and Empson, see Forsyth, *The Satanic Epic*, pp. 66–76. According to Forsyth, Shelley 'makes clear that he is opposed to the Christian God in general, not just Milton's' (p. 70).

23 On Blake's 'wholesale rewriting of the Bible's account of Creation' in *The Marriage of Heaven and Hell, The Book of Urizen* and his other prophetic books, see Newlyn, *Paradise Lost and the Romantic Reader*, pp. 13–44; and, on the 'dethroning' of the God of *Paradise Lost* in Blake's poem 'Milton', pp. 157–78.

24 *The Marriage of Heaven and Hell*, Plates 4–6, in Blake, *Complete Writings*, pp. 149–50.

25 *The Marriage of Heaven and Hell, Complete Writings*, p. 50; 'The Chimney Sweeper', 7, 11–12, *Songs of Experience, Complete Writings*, p. 212; Forsyth, *The Satanic Epic*, p. 73.

26 Empson, *Milton's God*, pp. 151–4, 158, 189, 202. Cf. the argument to *PL*, v.4–5: 'God to render man inexcusable sends Raphael to admonish him of his obedience.'

27 Empson, *Milton's God*, pp. 154–63; on Eve as free moral agent in the temptation scene, cf. Forsyth, 'Satan', p. 24. Empson is attacking 'neo-Christian' critics such as C. S. Lewis who consider Satan contemptible, denying him any tragic or heroic stature, and are equally dismissive of Eve. For examples of critical denigration of Eve, see McColley, *Milton's Eve*, pp. 3, 19, 141–3.

28 Tillyard, 'The Crisis of *Paradise Lost*', *Studies in Milton*, p. 19; McColley, *Milton's Eve*, p. 172. See also Myers, *Milton's Theology of Freedom*, pp. 125–8.

29 *Areopagitica, CPW*, ii.528.

30 Tillyard, *Studies in Milton*, p. 19; Burden, *The Logical Epic*, p. 88; *Paradise Lost*, ed. Fowler, note to *PL*, ix.335. On critical claims of 'Eve's insufficiency', see McColley, *Milton's Eve*, pp. 141–5, 182–3.

31 McColley, *Milton's Eve*, pp. 176, 180.

32 Tillyard, *Studies in Milton*, p. 20. According to Tillyard, Adam 'offends against the natural order by failing to maintain the hierarchical principles in his dealings with Eve' (p. 24). Burden accuses Adam of 'uxoriousness' in 'yielding to his wife's arguments that they should garden separately' (*The Logical Epic*, pp. 89–93).

33 Neil Forsyth, in private correspondence, has suggested an alternative interpretation: 'on the human level it is Adam doubting that she loves him enough to tell him to stay'. Stella Revard, commenting on 'the emotional climate of the scene', argues that 'Adam, hurt at Eve's gesture of independence, has interpreted her desire for personal integrity as a want of love', and yet 'Adam, if he would affirm Eden the true mirror-image of heaven, must leave Eve free to choose': 'Eve and the Doctrine of Responsibility in Paradise Lost', *PMLA*, 88 (1973), 69–78.

34 *Areopagitica, CPW*, ii.543. Cf. *Treatise of Civil Power, CPW*, vii.248: 'He who to his best apprehension follows the scripture, though against any point of doctrine by the whole church receivd, is not the heretic; but he who follows the church against his conscience and perswasion grounded on the scripture'.

35 Williams, *The Bloudy Tenent, of Persecution, for Cause of Conscience*, p. 105; Robinson, *Liberty of Conscience*, in Haller, *Tracts of Liberty*, ii.119.

36 Marvell, *Prose Works*, II.49, 105.
37 *A Treatise of Civil Power*, *CPW*, VII.255.
38 *PR*, IV.132–3. In this passage, Jesus is responding to Satan's appeal to him to rescue the Roman people, making them 'free from servile yoke' under a vicious Emperor (*PR*, IV.102).
39 See Keeble, *The Literary Culture of Nonconformity*, pp. 43–7, 118–19. On the persecution of Dissenters and on Milton's later writings as 'a response to the agonies of the present', see Achinstein, *Literature and Dissent in Milton's England*, pp. 1–22, 115–53.
40 See Knoppers, *Historicizing Milton*, pp. 42–57; and Lewalski, *Life of Milton*, pp. 398–404.
41 See the discussion of Book x in Tillyard, *Studies in Milton*, pp. 39–44.
42 It has been argued that Eve's dream shows Adam and Eve to be 'already . . . fallen' in their prelapsarian state. See, for example, Waldock, *Paradise Lost and Its Critics*, p. 61; and Tillyard, *Studies in Milton*, pp. 10–12: 'He anticipates the Fall by attributing to Adam and Eve feelings which though nominally felt in the state of innocence are actually not compatible with it'. For a contrary view, see Fish, *Surprised by Sin*, pp. 216–32.
43 As Neil Forsyth has reminded me (private correspondence), this is precisely what Shelley and Empson disliked about Milton's God. See, for example, Empson, *Milton's God*, pp. 41–4, 118–24. 'God's opening speech mixes present and past tenses, as if there were no distinctions between them – and of course, there are not from an eternal perspective . . . Milton's initial representation of God places us . . . outside the normative ken of the reality we inhabit, which is where God exists, inscrutably': Stuart Curran, 'God', p. 527.
44 See Robins, *If This Be Heresy*, pp. 113–15, 137–8; and Forsyth, *The Satanic Epic*, pp. 148–52, 155–7.
45 *PL*, IV.40–5.
46 Blake, *Complete Writings*, p. 150. On Milton's use of soliloquy in presenting Satan as a tragic figure, see Gardner, 'Milton's Satan and the Theme of Damnation in Elizabethan Tragedy', in *A Reading of Paradise Lost*, pp. 99–120; and Carey, 'Milton's Satan', pp. 162–5.
47 *De Doctrina*, I.ii/*CPW*, VI.134. On the problems inherent in the first-person address, see Danielson, 'The Fall and Milton's Theodicy', p. 149; and Lieb, *Theological Milton*, pp. 138–62.
48 See, for example, Waldock, *Paradise Lost and Its Critics*, pp. 100–4; and Empson, *Milton's God*, pp. 115–20, 145–6. Attempts to explain and justify the 'cold and impersonal . . . voice of the omnipotent moral law' in this passage, while 'admitting that the difficulties Milton's God poses for most readers remain', include Irene Samuel, 'The Dialogue in Heaven', pp. 601–11; and Fish, *Surprised by Sin*, pp. 80–7.
49 Goodwin, *Redemption Redeemed*, pp. 53, 27, quoted in Coffey, *John Goodwin*, pp. 216–17.
50 Perkins, *Treatise on . . . Predestination*, quoted in *CPW*, VI.162. Milton, in contrast, argued that 'it is quite impossible that God should have an inflexible

decree about something which we know man is still at liberty to do or not to do' (*CPW*, vi.162).

51 For a thoughtful discussion, see Danielson, 'The Fall and Milton's Theodicy', pp. 148–52.

52 Goodwin, *Redemption Redeemed*, pp. 68, 408; see Coffey, *John Goodwin*, pp. 210–11; and Bennett, *Reviving Liberty*, pp. 82–3.

53 Waller, *Panegyrick*, 1; *To the King, Upon His Majesties Happy Return*, p. 8. In the *Panegyrick*, the equivalent phrase is 'so much Power and Clemency in one' (p. 6). See Skinner, *Liberty Before Liberalism*, pp. 13–28, 36–51.

54 Overton, *An Appeale*, pp. 156, 163–4.

55 Overton, *An Appeale*, pp. 164–5, 166–8.

56 Lilburne, *Londons Liberty in Chains Discovered*, p. 33.

57 Lilburne, *Londons Liberty in Chains Discovered*, pp. 6, 9, 42; Overton, *An Appeale*, p. 188.

58 *Areopagitica*, *CPW*, ii.486, 488. On Lilburne, Overton and classical republicanism, see Glover, 'The Putney Debates: Popular versus Elitist Republicanism'. See the discussion of Milton's sometimes inconsistent treatment of 'the people' and 'freedom to vote' in the Introduction and in Chapter 5.

59 *Readie and Easie Way*, *CPW*, vii.405, 407, 442–3. On the 'aristocracy of virtue' in *The Readie and Easie Way*, see Austin Woolrych's introduction, *CPW*, vii.215–18; and Hammond, *Milton and the People*, pp. 173–7, 201–5.

60 Woodhouse,*Puritanism and Liberty*, p. 71. Overton makes similar charges in *The Hunting of the Foxes* (1649): 'We are onely under the old cheat, the transmutation of Names, but with the addition of new Tyrannies to the old' (Wolfe, *Leveller Manifestoes*, p. 372).

61 Sonnet 16, 10–12. The title of this sonnet in the Trinity manuscript is 'To the Lord Generall Cromwell May 1652. On the proposalls of certaine ministers at the Committee for Propagation of the Gospell.'

62 See Worden, *God's Instruments*, pp. 71–9; Davis, 'Cromwell's Religion', pp. 190–208. Owen was a leading figure among the 'certaine ministers' whose proposals Milton attacked in Sonnet 16.

63 *Tenure*, *CPW*, iii.190. Cf. Sonnet 12 ('I did but prompt the age'), with its attack on those who, ignoring 'the known rules of antient libertie', 'bawle for freedom in their senceless mood': 'Licence they mean when they cry libertie; / But who loves that, must first be wise and good' (2, 9, 11–12).

64 Shelley, *Defence of Poetry*, in *Shelley's Poetry and Prose*, p. 498; *PL*, iii.203–5, 209, 212.

Chapter 7: God's Just Yoke

1 *De Doctrina*, i.v/*CPW*, vi.205.

2 Cf. *CPW*, vi.209–10: 'So God begot the Son as a result of his own decree. Therefore it took place within the bounds of time, for the decree itself must have preceded its execution (the insertion of the word today makes this quite

clear)'. For examples of the orthodox view Milton is contesting, see Kelley's notes, *CPW*, VI.205, 208–10.

3 Psalm 2:1–2, 5, 6–7 (King James Bible). For discussion of the Old Testament content of Psalm 2 and its interpretation as 'the highest article of faith' in the Reformed tradition, see Forsyth, *The Satanic Epic*, pp. 184–7.

4 Psalm II.11–13, in *Complete Shorter Poems*.

5 Empson, *Milton's God*, pp. 102–3; Forsyth, *The Satanic Epic*, p. 176. For similar comments about the exaltation as 'pure fiat', in which a God 'for whose will no cause may be laid down' demands absolute obedience, see Strier, 'Milton's Fetters', pp. 30–4; and Rogers, 'Political Theology', pp. 70–7.

6 *Readie and Easie Way*, *CPW*, VII.426.

7 *The Reason of Church Government*, *CPW*, I.746, quoted in Forsyth, *The Satanic Epic*, p. 176. On the decree proclaimed in Book V as an assertion of 'power, not of reason', see Poole, *Milton and the Idea of the Fall*, pp. 160–1; and Rogers, 'Political Theology', pp. 75–80.

8 *PL*, IV.425; *De Doctrina*, I.x/*CPW*, VI.352.

9 For discussion of the differences between the two Exaltations of the Son in Books III and V, see Herman, *Destabilizing Milton*, pp. 54–7, 193–4; and Hunter, 'Milton on the Exaltation of the Son'. In standard theology, the Exaltation of the Son is associated with the Incarnation and his role as mediator and redeemer. In some biblical passages it is imagined as taking place at his resurrection from the dead three days after the crucifixion.

10 Paul Stevens points out a possible classical parallel in the *Aeneid*, Book I, where Venus, a subordinate deity, intercedes with Jupiter on behalf of Aeneas: 'The Pre-Secular Politics of *Paradise Lost*', p. 100.

11 Isaiah 1:4, Jeremiah 2:17, Ezekiel 7:3, Jeremiah 8:19 (King James Bible).

12 *PL*, XII.401–4, 407. Cf. the discussion of 'the satisfaction of divine justice' by Christ the redeemer in 'fulfilling the law and paying the just price on behalf of all men' in *De Doctrina*, I.xvi/*CPW*, VI.443.

13 *PL*, III.417–26. See Strier, 'Milton's Fetters', p. 39; and Evans, *Paradise Lost and the Genesis Tradition*, pp. 235–7. For an eloquent defence of the dialogue in Book III, emphasizing the differences between Satan's offer, as that of 'an actor taking his cue in a scene he had written for himself', and the Son's volunteering to sacrifice himself, see Samuel, 'The Dialogue in Heaven', pp. 601–11.

14 *Samson Agonistes*, 53–4, 173–4; *Areopagitica*, *CPW*, II.526.

15 *PL*, I.133–4; I.571–3. On hardening of the heart, see *PL*, III.198–201.

16 See the discussion of Satan's 'denial of values outside the self and . . . assertion of the materialistic value of might' in Stein, 'The War in Heaven', pp. 17–37.

17 Johnson, *The Lives of the Poets*, I.290.

18 *A Mask*, 465–9; *PL*, IX. 163–6. See the discussion of related themes in the Ludlow Masque and the divorce tracts in Chapter 3.

19 Stein, 'The War in Heaven', pp. 22–5. For a discussion of ways in which Milton draws on the heroic tradition in Book VI see Revard, *The War in Heaven*, pp. 198–234.

20 *PL*, VI.593–5. This episode may exemplify 'the confusion of spirit and matter' of which Johnson complained, though it can be explained by the paradox of angels, creatures of pure spirit, encumbered by the heavy armour they wear. The lines that follow make it explicit that 'unarm'd they might / Have easily as Spirits evaded' the missiles thrown at them (*PL*, VI.595–7).
21 *Doctrine and Discipline*, *CPW*, II.229; *PL*, III.236–8; VI.824–6. See the discussion of the Son as warrior prince in this episode in Bryson, *The Tyranny of Heaven*, pp. 134–5.
22 For a different view of the Son in Book VI as 'a new kind of hero', transcending such parallels with 'the old heroic ideal' as the challenge to single combat and redefining 'true glory', see Revard, *The War in Heaven*, pp. 254–6, 262–3.
23 *PL*, III.124–5, 131–2.
24 *De Doctrina*, I.xxii, *CPW*, VI.485–6; *PL*, III.124–5, 131–2. See the discussion of the Arminian doctrine of conditional election in Chapter 1.
25 *PL*, III.236; XI.40-1; *De Doctrina*, I.v, *CPW*, VI.218.
26 *De Doctrina*, I.xxii, *CPW*, VI.485; *PL*, XI.32–6.
27 On imagery of purity and pollution in Milton and in the Old Testament, see Schwartz, *Remembering and Repeating*, pp. 14–19; Rogers, *The Matter of Revolution*, pp. 133–42, 147–52; and my discussion in Chapter 3.
28 See the discussion of postlapsarian history in Books XI–XII as a 'forum for God's retributive justice' in Rogers, *The Matter of Revolution*, pp. 160–1, 166–72.
29 Vaughan, 'The Retreate', 1–2, 10, in *Works*, ed. Martin.
30 *PL*, V.221, 229–30, 369, 372–5, 397–9. On Milton's unconventional view of the materialism of angels, able to feel 'real hunger' (*PL*, V.437) and eat, as well as to enjoy an angelic version of sexual union, see Fallon, *Milton among the Philosophers*, pp. 98–107, 137–67.
31 *PL*, VIII.312, 342–3, 363–6, 379–80.
32 *PL*, VIII.368, 372–3, 383–6, 389–92. For similar arguments in *The Doctrine and Discipline of Divorce*, see *CPW*, II.235–6, 251–3, and my discussion in Chapter 3.
33 *Areopagitica*, *CPW*, II.514, 528.
34 *PL*, XII.282, 300, 304–6; *Tetrachordon*, *CPW*, II.665.
35 *De Doctrina*, I.xxvi, *CPW*, VI.517. On 'weak and beggarly rudiments', see *CPW*, I.765 and *CPW*, VII.262. On the Pauline theology of such passages in Milton, see Rosenblatt, *Torah and Law*, pp. 44–7.
36 *De Doctrina*, I.xvi, *CPW*, VI.443–9.
37 *De Doctrina*, I.xxvii, *CPW*, VI.528, 531–2.
38 For further discussion, see Rosenblatt, *Torah and Law*, pp. 41–53. Woodhouse paraphrases Milton: 'the essence of the Law was not abolished but accepted and obeyed in a new spirit of free and voluntary activity' (*Puritanism and Liberty*, p. 65).
39 Cudworth, *The True Intellectual System of the Universe*, III.512, quoted in Rogers, *The Matter of Revolution*, p. 155. Cudworth is arguing against Hobbes and the claim that 'the arbitrary will of the commander should be the very rule of justice itself' (512).

40 *PL*, VI.41; V.814, 818–19, 822–5.
41 *Doctrine and Discipline*, *CPW*, II.292.
42 *Doctrine and Discipline*, *CPW*, II.297–8. Cf. Rosenblatt, *Torah and Law*, pp. 70, 82.
43 *PL*, XII.92–101. The passage is discussed more fully in Chapter 8.
44 *De Doctrina*, I.x, *CPW*, VI.353.
45 *PL*, III.175–6: *Tetrachordon*, *CPW*, II.636. On the centrality of the law of nature in Milton's prose writings, see Barker, *Milton and the Puritan Dilemma*, pp. 112–17, 168–70.
46 On the 'one just Man' in *PL*, XI–XII, see Corns, *Regaining Paradise Lost*, pp. 86–93; and Loewenstein, *Milton and the Drama of History*, pp. 101–7.
47 Genesis 18:23–6; Jeremiah 5:1 (King James Bible). In Genesis 18:38–31, Abraham asks God to reduce the number of just men that might lead him to spare Sodom and Gomorrah, finally arriving at the figure of ten. Eventually the two cities are destroyed, and only Lot is spared.
48 Barton and Muddimann eds., *The Oxford Bible Commentary*, pp. 52, 494; *PL*, XI.703.
49 On Milton's knowledge of Hebrew and of commentaries in Hebrew on Genesis, see Rosenblatt, *Torah and Law*, pp. 83–8. Rashi's commentary was included in most editions of the Hebrew Bible in Milton's day. A bitterly ironic version of 'the legend of the just man', emphasizing persecution and pogroms through the generations, is André Schwarz-Bart, *The Last of the Just*.
50 Sonnet 13, 3; Sonnet 7, 10.
51 See the discussion of the temptation of Eve in Forsyth, *The Satanic Epic*, pp. 265–8; and Evans, *Paradise Lost and the Genesis Tradition*, pp. 275–81.
52 See Empson, *Milton's God*, pp. 158–63. On versions of the Fall that liken Adam and Eve to children, see Poole, *Milton and the Idea of the Fall*, pp. 16–17, 165–70.
53 *PL*, X.753–5, 769. Cf. *PL*, X.725–7: 'Yet well, if here would end / The miserie, I deserv'd it, and would beare / My own deservings'. For God's 'final pardon', cf. *Samson Agonistes*, 1171.
54 *PL*, X.766–70. In *De Doctrina*, Milton argues that God's begetting of the Son, like his other decrees and actions, was in no sense an act of necessity, but of free choice by the deity: see *De Doctrina*, I.v/*CPW*, VI.208–9; and I.iii/*CPW*, VI.159. Adam's lament in some ways resembles passages in the Bible that counsel against challenging the justice of God: 'Woe unto him that striveth with his Maker . . . Shall the clay say to him that fashioneth it, What makest thou?' (Isaiah 45:9); or 'Wilt thou condemn him that is most just?' (Job 34:12–17).
55 *PL*, X.924–5, 960; XII.646–9; *Tetrachordon*, *CPW*, II.599. Cf. Turner, *One Flesh*, p. 306: 'Eve is the first to break the icy deadlock of hatred, and her emotive plea for forgiveness initiates the process of repentance'. Fish characterizes their reconciliation as 'rooted not in justice or adjudication, but merely in love' (*Surprised by Sin*, p. 274). See also Tillyard, *Studies in Milton*, pp. 39–44.

Chapter 8: 'Tyrannie Must Be'

1 See Achinstein, *Literature and Dissent in Milton's England*, pp. 130–3, 138–44; Worden, 'Milton, *Samson Agonistes*, and the Restoration', pp. 112–28; and Knoppers, 'England's Case: Contexts of the 1671 Poems', pp. 572–6, 586–8.

2 See Knoppers, *Historicizing Milton*, pp. 42–57.

3 *Samson Agonistes*, 689, 692–6, 703–4. The lines are discussed in Worden, 'Milton, *Samson Agonistes*, and the Restoration', pp. 122–4; and Knoppers, *Historicizing Milton*, pp. 56–7.

4 Ludlow, *Voyce from the Watch-Tower*, pp. 123, 159, quoted in Worden, 'Milton, *Samson Agonistes* and the Restoration', p. 113. See earlier discussion in Chapter 2.

5 Robert Overton, *Gospell Observations and Religious Manifestations*, quoted from manuscript in Achinstein, *Literature and Dissent in Milton's England*, p. 73. According to Ludlow, God 'seemes to take the rod into his own hand to correct them for their disobedience' (*Voyce from the Watch-Tower*, p. 149).

6 *De Doctrina*, I.xi/*CPW*, VI.389; I.xii/*CPW*, VI.395.

7 Luther's *Doctrine of Free Will* and Calvin's *Institutes*, quoted in Maurice Kelley's introduction, *De Doctrina*, *CPW*, VI.77; on the doctrine of original sin and total depravity, see also Patrides, *Milton and the Christian Tradition*, pp. 97–102; and Williams, *The Common Expositor*, pp. 247–52.

8 Fish, *Surprised by Sin*, pp. 38–45; Lewis, *A Preface to Paradise Lost*, pp. 66–72. According to Lewis, 'Milton's version of the Fall story is substantially that of St Augustine, which is that of the Church as a whole' (p. 66).

9 Walker, *Paradise Lost and Republican Tradition from Aristotle to Machiavelli*, p. 60.

10 Radzinowicz, 'The Politics of *Paradise Lost*', pp. 217–18. For a similar view of renewal of 'lapsed powers' (*PL*, III.176) through God's grace, allowing 'the possibilities of contingent freedom', see Myers, 'Prevenient Grace and Conversion in *Paradise Lost*', pp. 20–36.

11 Lewalski's note to this passage says that it 'implicitly presents the Restoration of Charles II as a divine judgment on the baseness of the English' (*Paradise Lost*, ed. Lewalski, p. 315).

12 *PL*, IX.1127–31; XII.86–96.

13 On the possible conflict in Books XI and XII between ideas of history as tragic and as redemptive, see Loewenstein, *Milton and the Drama of History*, pp. 92–101, 118–21; and Martz, *The Paradise Within*, pp. 150–3.

14 According to Fish, 'the reader stands in relation to [Adam] as an advanced pupil to a novice. The pedagogical aspect to the situation is formalized and objectified to a degree we have not seen before' (*Surprised by Sin*, p. 288). On the education of Adam and the reader, see also Sasek, 'The Drama of *Paradise Lost*, Books XI and XII', pp. 341–56.

15 *PL*, IX.31–2; XII.569–72, 575–6. On the themes of redemption and conversion in Book XII, see Waddington, *Looking into Providences*, pp. 191–2, 196–7; and MacCallum, *Milton and the Sons of God*, pp. 193–200.

16 Joseph Addison, *Spectator*, No. 369, in *The Spectator*, IV.158, quoted in Waddington, *Looking into Providences*, p. 173. On the two Adams, see Waddington, *Looking into Providences*, p. 177.
17 According to *De Doctrina*, 'there was a kind of manifestation or foreshadowing of the covenant in Moses' time'. The Gospel 'was first announced, obscurely, by Moses and the Prophets, and then with absolute clarity by Christ himself and his apostles and the evangelists' (*De Doctrina*, I.xxvi, xxviii/*CPW*, VI.516, 523).
18 Addison, *Spectator*, No. 369, *The Spectator*, IV.157.
19 Lewis, *A Preface to Paradise Lost*, p. 129; Martz, *The Paradise Within*, pp. 141–2, 150–2, 159.
20 See Loewenstein, *Milton and the Drama of History*, pp. 93–4, 115–24. Loewenstein finds a similar 'uneasy juxtaposition of tragic and apocalyptic versions of history' in Milton's prose writings of the 1640s and 1650s (p. 124).
21 *PL*, XII.405–6, 444–5; *Areopagitica*, *CPW*, II.549. For the 'just man' in Milton's writings, see Corns, *Regaining Paradise Lost*, pp. 86–93; and the discussion in Chapter 7.
22 *PL*, XII.468, 479, 517–18; Loewenstein, *Milton and the Drama of History*, pp. 116–20.
23 *Lycidas*, headnote, 114, 127.
24 *Areopagitica*, *CPW*, II.486.
25 *Of Reformation*, *CPW*, I.598; *Treatise of Civil Power*, *CPW*, VII.241.
26 *Readie and Easie Way*, *CPW*, VII.409, 463. On the prophetic voice in *The Readie and Easie Way*, written 'as much out of duty to God as from hope that the people will listen', see Knoppers, 'Milton's *The Readie and Easie Way* and the English Jeremiad', pp. 213–25.
27 As Achinstein points out, the two poems have separate pagination in the 1671 edition, but the signatures are continuous: see *Literature and Dissent in Milton's England*, pp. 130–1.
28 See *Samson Agonistes*, 19, 38–40, 225–6, 1214; and *PR*, II.35 and I.290. A number of parallels are discussed by Balachandra Rajan in 'To Which is Added *Samson Agonistes*', pp. 103–5. On the theme of deliverance in the two poems, see Guibbory, *Christian Identity*, pp. 279–89.
29 Loewenstein, *Representing Revolution*, p. 191; Achinstein, *Literature and Dissent in Milton's England*, p. 131. On the question of whether the poems can be considered complementary, with 'a striking consistency between the two', or sharply contrasted, even in some respects incompatible, see the essays by Barker and Rajan in Rajan, ed., *The Prison and the Pinnacle*, pp. 13–16, 96–105; and Coffey, 'Pacifist Quietist, or Patient Militant', pp. 168–9.
30 Wittreich, *Interpreting Samson Agonistes*, pp. 330–1, 343. Elsewhere, Wittreich describes Milton's Samson as 'at once a positive and a negative example' and as 'a manifestation of the dark side of a deity' whose 'claims for justice . . . express themselves in vengeance and violence' (pp. 318, 351).
31 Carey, *Milton*, p. 138; Wittreich, *Shifting Contexts*, p. 217. The title of Carey's chapter, consistently hostile toward Milton's Samson, is 'The Outmoded Hero: Samson'.

32 *De Doctrina*, I.xxvi and xxvii/*CPW*, VI.517, 521; Wood, *Exiled from Light*, pp. xvii, xx. Cf. *A Treatise of Civil Power*, *CPW*, VII.259.
33 Loewenstein, *Representing Revolution*, p. 247. Cf. Wittreich, *Interpreting Samson Agonistes*, p. 343, on 'the example set by Jesus, every aspect of whose life, especially the phase of it spent in the wilderness, was subject to imitation'. See also Keeble, 'Wilderness Exercises'.
34 Margaret Kean, '*Paradise Regained*', p. 436; *PR*, I.3–5.
35 *PL*, III.218, 222, 409–10; Samuel, 'The Regaining of Paradise', pp. 111, 126.
36 *PR*, I.314; *Areopagitica*, *CPW*, II.514–15.
37 *PR*, I.160–1: *PL*, XII.565–9; Achinstein, *Literature and Dissent in Milton's England*, pp. 131–3. Cf. Keeble, 'Wilderness Exercises', pp. 91–9. Both passages echo the Sermon on the Mount and 1 Corinthians 1:27: 'But God hath chosen the foolish things of the world to confound the wise; and God hath chosen the weak things of the world to confound the things which are mighty.'
38 *Areopagitica*, *CPW*, II.561. On Arianism and the humanity of Jesus in *Paradise Regained*, see Lewalski, *Milton's Brief Epic*, pp. 134–48; and Kean, '*Paradise Regained*', p. 432: 'The Son must be seen to undergo temptation in all humility as a man, and it does not follow that the Son must be aware at this moment of his own divine nature for his victory over Satan's machinations to be complete.'
39 Achinstein has suggested that such passages, which have no equivalent in Milton's New Testament sources, reflect the situation of Restoration Dissenters at a time of persecution and uncertainty: see *Literature and Dissent in Milton's England*, pp. 135–7. On parallels between 'the experience of the disciples' and that of the post-Restoration 'godly', see Coffey, 'Pacifist Quietist, or Patient Militant', p. 162.
40 Aslan, *Zealot*, pp. 79, 119. Aslan's revisionist study, which compares Jesus and his disciples with other would-be Messiahs and opponents of Roman power at the time, was a best-seller in the USA.
41 Psalms, 2:2, 9 (King James Bible). This psalm is often interpreted as a Messianic prophecy.
42 Coffey, 'Pacifist Quietist, or Patient Militant', pp. 158–63. On the concept of 'waiting for God', not knowing when the 'due time' will arrive, see Loewenstein, *Representing Revolution*, pp. 262–5; and Knoppers, *Historicizing Milton*, pp. 137–40.
43 Loewenstein, *Representing Revolution*, p. 268. On militant action and patient suffering as 'alternative models of radical sainthood', see Loewenstein, *Representing Revolution*, pp. 292–5; and Coffey, 'Pacifist Quietist, or Patient Militant', pp. 169–71.
44 See Lewalski, *Milton's Brief Epic*, pp. 133–6; and MacCallum, *Milton and the Sons of God*, pp. 226–7, 240–3.
45 *PR*, IV.530, 532; I.141–3. As Martz points out, the phrase 'the sons of God' is applied to the Faithful several times in the New Testament (*The Paradise Within*, pp. 180–2).

46 *PR*, I.238–41, 259–61. On Jesus's reliance on the gift of reason rather than any divine revelation, see Samuel, 'The Regaining of Paradise', pp. 111–27; Lewalski, *Milton's Brief Epic*, pp. 159–62; and MacCallum, *Milton and the Sons of God*, pp. 240–5.
47 See Radzinowicz, 'How Milton Read the Bible', pp. 205–8; and Sims, 'Jesus and Satan as Readers of Scripture in *Paradise Regained*'.
48 Psalm 91:11–12 (King James Bible).
49 *PL*, I.45; III, 99–102. See Samuel, 'The Regaining of Paradise', pp. 120–3; and MacCallum, *Milton and the Sons of God*, pp. 258–61.
50 Deuteronomy 6:16 (King James Bible).
51 Deuteronomy 6:16 alludes to Exodus 17:1–7, in which the Israelites, in the wilderness and suffering from thirst, complain against Moses and God. See Samuel, 'The Regaining of Paradise', pp. 116–17, citing John Calvin, *A Harmonie upon the Three Evangelists* (1584), p. 132. On differing interpretations of this crux, see Martz, *The Paradise Within*, p. 182; MacCallum, *Milton and the Sons of God*, pp. 313–15; and the headnote in *The Complete Shorter Poems*, ed. Carey, pp. 417–19.
52 *Second Defence*, *CPW*, IV.i.667–8; *PR*, II.463–72. See the discussion of these lines as a 'critique of the values and practices of secular monarchies' in Lewalski, *Life of Milton*, pp. 516–19. On the *Second Defence* and Cromwell, see Chapter 5.
53 Lewalski sees the influence of stoicism here (*Milton's Brief Epic*, pp. 234–41), and Loewenstein finds parallels in the religious and political beliefs of Quakers such as Milton's friend Thomas Ellwood (*Representing Revolution*, pp. 251–9). On attitudes towards military conquest by Milton and some of his contemporaries, see the discussion in Chapter 5.
54 *PR*, III.158, 175–6. On the unstinting opposition to the post-Restoration regime by the republicans Ludlow, Sidney and Vane, see Worden, 'Milton, *Samson Agonistes*, and the Restoration', pp. 112–26; and Coffey, 'Pacifist Quietist, or Patient Militant', pp. 150–5.
55 On 'the relation between the English and biblical Israel' in *Paradise Regained*, see Guibbory, *Christian Identity*, pp. 276–82.
56 *Areopagitica*, *CPW*, II.517; Bush, *The Renaissance and English Humanism*, pp. 124–6. See also Festa, 'The Temptation of Athens and the Variorum'.
57 Martz, *The Paradise Within*, pp. 197–9; Worden, 'Milton's Republicanism and the Tyranny of Heaven', pp. 244–5. For a similar view from a critic of an earlier generation, see Tillyard, *Milton*, p. 309.
58 *PR*, IV.346–50; *Reason of Church Government*, *CPW*, I.223. See Lewalski, *Milton's Brief Epic*, pp. 281–8, 298–300; and Samuel, 'Milton on Learning and Wisdom'. On the superiority of the poetry of the Hebrew Bible as an 'opinion which Milton had, in some form or other, held all his life', see Lewis, *Preface to Paradise Lost*, pp. 3–5; and *Complete Shorter Poems*, pp. 378, 441.
59 *PL*, VIII.191–5. See Samuel, 'Milton on Learning and Wisdom', pp. 717–22; Lewalski, *Milton's Brief Epic*, pp. 288–301; and Festa, 'The Temptation of Athens', pp. 15–18.

60 *Doctrine and Discipline*, *CPW*, II.223; *Animadversions*, *CPW*, I.720. Milton says of Salmasius that compared to a virtuous, upright plebeian, 'learned without much reading'. 'you have read without profit, and for all your skill in languages . . . are but a brute beast at the end': *Defence*, *CPW*, IV.i.339.

61 *Animadversions*, *CPW*, I.720; *Hirelings*, *CPW*, VII.302, 304, 319.

62 *Hirelings*, *CPW*, VII.315–16, 319. On 'the term clergy, which ecclesiastics have . . . appropriated to themselves', see *De Doctrina*, I.xxix/*CPW*, VI.572.

63 *De Doctrina*, I.xxix/*CPW*, VI.570–3; William Dell, *The Tryal of Spirits* (1653), quoted in Hill, *The World Turned Upside Down*, p. 301; cf. Hill, *The World Turned Upside Down*, pp. 100–1; and Hill, *Milton and the English Revolution*, p. 424. On Milton's belief in the priesthood of all believers, see Simpson, *Spiritual Architecture and Paradise Regained*, pp. 30–1, 84–9.

64 See Hammond, *Milton and the People*, on the contrast between 'his vision of an ideal people summoned by God to fulfil their historic vocation, and his recognition that many, perhaps most, are incapable of responding to that calling' (p. 12).

65 *Doctrine and Discipline of Divorce*, *CPW*, II.229; Exodus 20:2–6 (King James Bible). On the spirit of charity in Milton, see Schwartz, 'Milton on the Bible', pp. 37–54.

66 Guibbory, *Christian Identity*, p. 285. On the Jews as 'one peculiar nation' selected by God 'from all the rest', who nevertheless frequently fell into apostacy, see *PL*, XI.111–13.

67 See Serjeantson, '*Samson Agonistes* and "Single Rebellion"', pp. 613–31. According to Serjeantson, Reformed commentaries on the Book of Judges regularly make a similar distinction between 'a private person' and one acting under a 'command by God': 'by all the accepted canons of good Protestant political theory, his actions are just' (pp. 625–7). See also Killeen, 'Hanging Up Kings', pp. 554–61.

68 This passage in the *Defence* leaves it open whether Samson in his actions was 'prompted by God or by his own valor'. See the discussion in Gregory, 'The Political Messages of *Samson Agonistes*', pp. 186–7, on how this passage uses the figure of Samson 'to evoke heroic precedents for the regicide', countering the arguments of Salmasius.

69 *A Treatise of Civil Power*, *CPW*, VII.262; *Reason of Church Government*, *CPW*, I.822.

70 Achinstein, *Literature and Dissent in Milton's England*, p. 152. See also Loewenstein, *Representing Revolution*, pp. 269–76; and Knoppers, 'England's Case', pp. 586–8.

71 Sophocles, *Oedipus at Colonus*, trans. Fitzgerald, II.1245–8.

72 Judges 14:19, 15:8, 16:22–3 (King James Bible). See the discussion in Grossman, *Lion's Honey*.

73 Judges 16:28, 30. Among the critics who comment on Milton's omission of Samson's prayer to God at this central moment of the story are Wittreich, *Interpreting Samson Agonistes*, pp. 73–6; Fish, *How Milton Works*, pp. 418–21,

447–55; and Carey, 'A Work in Praise of Terrorism?' *TLS*, 6 September 2002, pp. 15–16.

74 Grossman, *Lion's Honey*, pp. 66, 87–8, 124. On the biblical Samson as embodiment of 'a blind, uncontrolled force, leaving a terrible swath of destruction behind, finally consuming itself together with what stands in its way', see Alter, *The Art of Biblical Narrative*, p. 95.

75 *A Mask*, 662–4. See Achinstein, *Literature and Dissent in Milton's England*, pp. 141–3.

76 Shakespeare, *The Merchant of Venice*, I.iii.32–3; *Samson Agonistes*, 1362.

77 Victoria Kahn in *Wayward Contracts* argues that *Samson Agonistes* 'explores the tragic dilemma of the individual compelled to judge and act in the absence of cognitive certainty' (pp. 254, 267–8). Fish, in his commentary on this passage, claims that Samson's final position here is one of 'radical uncertainty', and that his action, rather than assuming 'heavenly authorization', 'has no final warrant except what he himself thinks best to do' (*How Milton Works*, pp. 458–65).

78 On the interdiction of exogamy in the Old Testament, the preservation of the purity of the chosen as against the infidel, see Sauer, *Milton, Toleration, and Nationhood*, pp. 145–9.

79 Grossman, *Lion's Honey*, pp. 40–7, 60–3; Barton and Muddiman, eds., *Oxford Bible Commentary*, pp. 177, 186. Grossman sees the biblical Samson as entirely God's instrument here, lacking in free will in taking a consort from among his people's enemies (pp. 39–42).

80 Norman Burns has argued that Milton's position, here and elsewhere, is antinomian – a radical belief that, to the regenerate, led by the promptings of conscience, the restrictions of civil and religious law no longer apply: see ' "Then stood up Phinehas": Milton's Antinomianism, and Samson's'; and, for a similar view, Barker, *Milton and the Puritan Dilemma*, pp. 320–3.

81 *De Doctrina*, I.viii/*CPW*, VI.338; Radzinowicz, *Toward Samson Agonistes*, pp. 104–8, 230–7, 251. Other critics who see Samson's 'spiritual rebirth' as enacted in the poem include Steadman, 'Faithful Champion'; and Gossman, 'Milton's Samson as the Tragic Hero Purified by Trial'.

82 Steadman, 'Faithful Champion', p. 13.

83 See Radzinowicz, *Toward Samson Agonistes*, pp. 339–47.

84 Preface, 'Of That Sort of Dramatic Poem Which Is Call'd Tragedy', *Complete Shorter Poems*, p. 461; *Reason of Church Government*, *CPW*, I.816–17. On the medical analogy in Milton's interpretation of catharsis, see Steadman, 'Passions Well Imitated', pp. 175–207.

85 See Samuel, '*Samson Agonistes* as Tragedy', pp. 235–57; Wittreich, *Interpreting Samson Agonistes*, pp. 165–6, 221–2; and Carey, 'A Work in Praise of Terrorism?' pp. 15–16.

86 Aristotle, *Poetics*, 9, p. 1465; on *peripeteia* and *anagnorisis*, and how a tragic plot 'should be so framed that, even without seeing the things take place, he who simply hears the account of them shall be filled with horror and pity at the incidents', see *Poetics*, 14, pp. 1467–8.

87 On the 'limited vision' of Manoa and the Chorus, see Samuel, '*Samson Agonistes* as Tragedy', pp. 250–3; Bennett, *Reviving Liberty*, pp. 120–39; and Wood, *Exiled from Light*, pp. 52–9.

88 Michael Lieb, '"Our Living Dread": The God of *Samson Agonistes*', *Milton Studies*, 33 (1996), 4–5, 10, 20. Cf. Schwartz, '*Samson Agonistes*', pp. 632–48; and, on violence and the construction of the Other, Schwartz, *The Curse of Cain*, pp. 5, 19–20.

89 *Samson Agonistes*, 1746–7, 1751; *De Doctrina*, I.xxvi/*CPW*, VI.517.

90 Wittreich, *Interpreting Samson Agonistes*, p. 231; cf. Wood, *Exiled from Light*, pp. xx, 125, on the 'bondage' of 'those raised in the state of religion under the Law'. For a thoughtful critique of revisionist arguments, see Gregory, 'The Political Messages of *Samson Agonistes*', pp. 175–93.

91 Rogers, 'The Secret of *Samson Agonistes*', p. 115; Deuteronomy, 28:21, 24, 26 (King James Bible).

92 'Sinners in the Hands of an Angry God' (1741), in Edwards, *Basic Writings*, p.152.

93 Carey, 'A Work in Praise of Terrorism?', *TLS*, 6 September 2002, pp. 15–16. Carey is attacking Stanley Fish's claim that Samson's acts are 'praiseworthy' because he believes he is submitting to the divine will (Fish, *How Milton Works*, pp. 426–8). For responses to Carey, see, e.g., Feisal Mohamed, 'Confronting Religious Violence: Milton's *Samson Agonistes*', *PMLA*, 120 (2005), 327–34.

94 Lim, *John Milton, Radical Politics, and Biblical Republicanism*, pp. 150–2, 156–9; Balachandra Rajan, 'Samson Has Quit Himself like Samson', *Milton Quarterly*, 41 (2007), 1–3.

95 Schwartz, 'The Force of Justice', p. 636; Loewenstein, *Representing Revolution*, pp. 280–91.

Postscript

1 Williams, *The Bloudy Tenent* (1644), sig.a2v.

2 Williams, *The Bloudy Tenent*, pp. 172–3; *Areopagitica*, *CPW*, II.565. On Williams' strict Calvinism, including a belief that since 'the Holy Spirit would select those that were to be saved', 'the spiritual life of citizens' should be left entirely to 'the secret workings of God's determination', see Corns, 'Limits of Toleration', pp. 76–81; and Barker, *Milton and the Puritan Dilemma*, pp. 88–93.

3 See Foxley, *The Levellers*, pp. 120–2, 140. Where Overton and Walwyn held heterodox theological views similar to Milton's, Lilburne during this period was a strict Calvinist, and 'much of the Levellers' following in London was drawn from sectarian congregations with more orthodox Calvinist doctrine' (p. 140).

4 *Areopagitica*, *CPW*, II.565; Campbell and Corns, *John Milton*, p. 173; Corns, 'Limits of Toleration', pp. 72–4; According to Corns, 'since approximately the mid twentieth century, Milton's *Areopagitica* has seemed less like an iconic proclamation of the core values of western liberalism and more like a series of problems to be explained away' (p. 72).

5 Fish, *How Milton Works*, pp. 56–7, 189, 194–5. Fish's essay 'Driving from the Letter: Truth and Indeterminacy in Milton's *Areopagitica*' was originally published in *Re-Membering Milton* (1987). See also Fish's essay 'Liberalism Doesn't Exist' in *There's No Such Thing As Free Speech: and It's a Good Thing, Too*, pp. 134–40.
6 Mill, *On Liberty*, pp. 7, 18, 21.
7 Mill, *On Liberty*, p. 18.
8 *Areopagitica*, *CPW*, II.527, 543; Mill, *On Liberty*, p. 20.
9 Mill, *On Liberty*, pp. 41, 42–3. Similar statements can be found in other pamphlets of the 1640s urging freedom of inquiry, such as Robinson's *Liberty of Conscience*.
10 Mill, *On Liberty*, pp. 15–16.
11 Hobbes, *Leviathan*, Part I, chapter xiv, p. 84; Mill, *On Liberty*, p. 16.
12 Mill, *On Liberty*, pp. 38, 48. Mill comments that 'many of the persons in greatest repute with the world, both for virtues and attainments, are well known, at least to their intimates, to be unbelievers' (p. 37), and argues that it is impossible to find in the New Testament 'a complete doctrine of morals' or 'to extract from it a body of ethical doctrine' (p. 56).
13 *PL*, V.380–2; cf. 'though but feignd' in *PL*, IV.705–8. In *Tenure*, Milton says: 'That this and the rest of what hath hitherto been spok'n is most true, might be copiously made appeare through all Stories Heathen and Christian' (*CPW*, III.200–1).
14 *PR*, IV.288–91. See the discussion of the Temptation of Athens in Paradise Regained and its treatment of classical learning in Chapter 8.
15 Davis, 'Religion and the Struggle for Freedom in the English Revolution', pp. 521, 528. A similar view of an overall 'Protestant consensus' on 'the need for a godly discipline' even among those bitterly engaged in controversy – 'not in terms of discipline versus liberty, but in terms of which discipline is most effective' – can be found in Lamont, 'Pamphleteering, the Protestant Consensus, and the English Revolution', pp. 72–92.
16 Walker, *Antiformalist, Unrevolutionary, Illiberal Milton*, pp. 11, 37–8, 52.
17 Walker, *Antiformalist, Unrevolutionary, Illiberal Milton*, pp. 112–13, 127, 143.
18 Martin, *Milton Among the Puritans*, pp. 5, 15–16, 20, 50, 80.
19 *Second Defence*, *CPW*, IV.i.622, 640; *Areopagitica*, *CPW*, II.559. Cf. Woodhouse, *Puritanism and Liberty*, pp. 51–60; and Hammond, *Milton and the People*.
20 Sirluck, 'Milton's Political Thought', p. 224.
21 Foxley, 'Due Libertie and Proportiond Equalitie', p. 638.
22 See the essay by Elizabeth Skerpan Wheeler, 'Early Political Prose' in Paradise Regained *Companion*, ed. Corns: 'Classical theorists did not confront the issue of a political animal with an immortal soul in need of salvation, or a truth equated with some kind of Christian revelation. Milton clearly did … The power of *Areopagitica* comes from the irreconcilability of the two positions, and Milton's movement between the competing but equally positive values' (p. 276).

23 *Tetrachordon*, *CPW*, II.637. The allusion here is to 1 Corinthians, 13:1–3, 13, and 1 Timothy 1:5. Cf. *De Doctrina*, I.xxvii/*CPW*, VI.533, in which Milton contrasts interpreting passages from Scripture 'in a literal way' with 'a way that is in keeping with the spirit of charity': there is 'no transgression of the letter, so long as the substance of the law is, by the Spirit's guidance, preserved'.

24 Genesis, 22:1–16.

25 1 Corinthians, 13:7 (King James Bible); *PL*, III.230–1; X.960–5.

26 Walwyn, *The Power of Love*, pp. 91, 92–3. On the Gospel and the Law, see Walwyn, *The Power of Love*, pp. 87–90.

Bibliography

WORKS BY MILTON

Works by Milton are quoted from the following editions, except as noted:

Complete Shorter Poems, ed. Stella P. Revard. Oxford: Wiley-Blackwell, 2009.

Complete Prose Works (*CPW*), Don M. Wolfe, gen. ed., 8 vols. New Haven, Conn., 1963–82.

Paradise Lost (*PL*), ed. Barbara K. Lewalski. Oxford: Blackwell, 2007.

Other editions, cited in the notes, include:

De Doctrina Christiana, in *Complete Works*, vol. VIII, ed. J. Donald Cullington and John K. Hale. Oxford University Press, 2012.

Political Writings, ed. Martin Dzelzainis. Cambridge University Press, 1991.

Vernacular Regicide and Republican Writings, in *Complete Works*, vol. VI, ed. N. H. Keeble and Nicholas McDowell. Oxford University Press, 2013.

Paradise Lost, ed. Alistair Fowler, 2nd edn. London: Longman Annotated English Poets, 1998.

The Complete Shorter Poems, ed. John Carey, 2nd edn. London: Pearson Longman, 2007.

The Works of John Milton, gen. ed. F. A. Patterson, 18 vols. New York: Columbia University Press, 1931–8.

REFERENCES

Abrams, M. H., 'Five Types of *Lycidas*', in C. A. Patrides, ed., *Milton's Lycidas: The Tradition and the Poem*. Columbia: University of Missouri Press, 1983, pp. 216–35.

An Abridgement of the Late Remonstrance of the Army. London, 1648.

Achinstein, Sharon, '"A Law in This Matter to Himself": Contextualizing Milton's Divorce Tracts', in Nicholas McDowell and Nigel Smith, eds., *Oxford Handbook of Milton*. Oxford University Press, 2009, pp. 174–85.

Literature and Dissent in Milton's England. Cambridge University Press, 2003.

Achinstein, Sharon and Elizabeth Sauer, eds., *Milton and Toleration*. Oxford University Press, 2007.

Adams, Daniel R., 'The Secret Printing and Publishing Career of Richard Overton the Leveller, 1644–46', *The Library*, 11 (March 2010): 3–88.

Addison, Joseph and Richard Steele, *The Spectator*, ed. Gregory Smith, 4 vols. London: Everyman, 1979.
Alter, Robert, *The Art of Biblical Narrative*. London: George Allen & Unwin, 1971.
Aristotle, *Poetics*, in *Basic Works*, ed. Richard McKeon. New York: Random House, 1968.
The Armies Vindication. London, 1649.
Armitage, David, Armand Hiny and Quentin Skinner, eds., *Milton and Republicanism*. Cambridge University Press, 1995.
Armstrong, Brian, *Calvinism and the Amyraut Heresy*. Madison, Wisc.: University of Wisconsin Press, 1969.
Aslan, Reza, *Zealot: The Life and Times of Jesus of Nazareth*. New York: Westbourne Press, 2013.
Baillie, Robert, *A Dissuasive from the Errors of the Time*. London, 1646.
Bangs, Carl, *Arminius: A Study in the Dutch Reformation*. Nashville, Tenn.: Abingdon Press, 1971.
Barker, Arthur, *Milton and the Puritan Dilemma*. University of Toronto Press, 1964.
Barton, John and John Muddiman, eds. *The Oxford Bible Commentary*. Oxford University Press, 2001.
Bauman, Michael, *Milton's Arianism*. Frankfurt: Peter Lang, 1987.
Bennett, Joan S., *Reviving Liberty*. Cambridge, Mass.: Harvard University Press, 1989.
Blake, William, *Complete Writings*, ed. Geoffrey Keynes. London: Oxford University Press, 1966.
Bolton, Robert, *Some General Directions for a Comfortable Walking with God*. London, 1626.
Brautigan, Dwight, 'Prelates and Politics: Uses of "Puritan" 1625–40', in Laura Lunger Knoppers, ed., *Puritanism and Its Discontents*. Newark, Del.: University of Delaware Press, 2003, pp. 49–66.
Brown, Cedric C., 'Great Senates and Godly Education: Politics and Cultural Renewal in . . . Milton', in David Armitage, Armand Hiny and Quentin Skinner, eds., *Milton and Republicanism*. Cambridge University Press, 1995, pp. 43–60.
John Milton's Aristocratic Entertainments. Cambridge University Press, 1985.
Bryson, Michael, *The Tyranny of Heaven*. Newark, Del.: University of Delaware Press, 2004.
Burden, Dennis, *The Logical Epic*. London: Routledge & Kegan Paul, 1967.
Burns, Norman T., *Christian Mortalism from Tyndale to Milton*. Cambridge, Mass.: Harvard University Press, 1972.
'"Then Stood Up Phinehas": Milton's Antinomianism, and Samson's', *Milton Studies*, 33 (1996): 27–46.
Bush, Douglas, *English Literature in the Earlier Seventeenth Century*, 2nd edn. Oxford: Clarendon Press, 1962.
The Renaissance and English Humanism. University of Toronto Press, 1962.

Cable, Lana, 'Secularizing Conscience in Milton's Republican Community', in Sharon Achinstein and Elizabeth Sauer, eds., *Milton and Toleration*. Oxford University Press, 2007, pp. 268–83.

Calvin, John, *Institutes of the Christian Religion*, trans. Henry Beveridge, 2 vols. Edinburgh: Calvin Translation Society, 1863.

A Commentary upon the Prophecies of Isaiah, trans. Clement Cotton. London, 1609.

A Harmonie upon the Three Evangelists Matthew, Mark and Luke, trans. Eusebius Pagit. London, 1584.

Campbell, Gordon and Thomas N. Corns, *John Milton: Life, Work, and Thought*. Oxford University Press, 2008.

'*De Doctrina Christiana:* An England That Might Have Been', in Nicholas McDowell and Nigel Smith, eds., *Oxford Handbook of Milton*. Oxford University Press, 2009, pp. 424–35.

Campbell, Gordon, Thomas N. Corns, John K. Hale, David I. Holmes and Fiona Tweedie, 'The Provenance of *De Doctrina Christiana*', *Milton Quarterly*, 21 (1997): 61–117.

Campbell, Gordon, Thomas N. Corns, John K. Hale and Fiona Tweedie, *Milton and the Manuscript of De Doctrina Christiana*. Oxford University Press, 2007.

Carey, John, *Milton*. London: Evans Brothers, 1969.

'Milton's Satan', in *Cambridge Companion to Milton*, 2nd edn. Cambridge University Press, 1999, pp. 160–74.

'A Work in Praise of Terrorism?', *TLS*, 6 September 2002, pp. 15–16.

Chernaik, Warren, 'Linked Sweetness: Milton and Music', *The Seventeenth Century*, 26 (2011): 23–43.

Coffey, John, 'Pacifist Quietist, or Patient Militant? Milton and the Restoration', *Milton Studies*, 42 (2003): 149–74.

'Puritanism and Liberty Revisited: The Case for Toleration in the English Revolution', *The Historical Journal*, 41 (1998): 962–85.

John Goodwin and the Puritan Revolution. Woodbridge: Boydell Press, 2006.

'Quentin Skinner and the Religious Dimension of Early Modern Political Thought', in Alister Chapman, John Coffey, and Brad S. Gregory, eds., *Seeing Things Their Way*. University of Notre Dame Press, 2009, pp. 46–74.

Review of Catherine Gimelli Martin, *Milton among the Puritans, Journal of Ecclesiastical History*, 63 (2012): 827–8.

Collinson, Patrick, *The Religion of Protestants*. Oxford: Clarendon Press, 1982.

Corns, Thomas N., 'John Milton, Roger Williams, and the Limits of Toleration', in Sharon Achinstein and Elizabeth Sauer, eds., *Milton and Toleration*. Oxford University Press, 2007, pp. 72–85.

'Milton and the Characteristics of a Free Commonwealth', in David Armitage, Armand Hiny and Quentin Skinner, eds., *Milton and Republicanism*. Cambridge University Press, 1995, pp. 25–42.

'Milton before "Lycidas," ', in Graham Parry and Joad Raymond, eds., *Milton and the Forms of Liberty*. Cambridge: D. S. Brewer, 2002, pp. 23–36.

'Milton's *Observations upon the Articles of Peace*', in David Loewenstein and James Grantham Turner, eds., *Politics, Poetics, and Hermeneutics in Milton's Prose*. Cambridge University Press, 1990, pp. 123–34.

Regaining Paradise Lost. London: Longman, 1994.

Uncloistered Virtue: English Political Literature, 1640–1660. Oxford University Press, 1992.

ed., *A Companion to Milton*. Oxford: Blackwell, 2003.

Cromwell, Oliver, *Writings and Speeches*, ed. W. C. Abbott, 4 vols. New York: Russell & Russell, 1970.

Cudworth, Ralph, *The True Intellectual System of the Universe*, 3 vols. London, 1845.

Cummings, Brian, *The Literary Culture of the Reformation*. Oxford University Press, 2002.

Cunningham, Hugh, *Children and Childhood in Western Society since 1500*, 2nd edn. London: Pearson, 2005.

Curran, Stuart, 'God', in Nicholas McDowell and Nigel Smith, eds., *Oxford Handbook of Milton*. Oxford University Press, 2009, pp. 525–33.

Danielson, Dennis, *Milton's Good God*. Cambridge University Press, 1982.

'The Fall and Milton's Theodicy', in *Cambridge Companion to Milton*, 2nd edn. Cambridge University Press, 1999, pp. 144–59.

ed., *Cambridge Companion to Milton*, 2nd edn. Cambridge University Press, 1999.

Davies, Stevie, *Images of Kingship in Paradise Lost*. Columbia, Mo.: University of Missouri Press, 1983.

Davis, J. C., 'Cromwell's Religion', in John Morrill, ed., *Oliver Cromwell and the English Revolution*. London: Longman, 1995, pp. 190–208.

'Religion and the Struggle for Freedom in the English Revolution', *The Historical Journal*, 35 (1992): 507–30.

Dell, William, *The Tryal of Spirits both in Teachers & Hearers*. London, 1653.

Diekhoff, John S., *A Maske at Ludlow: Essays on Milton's Comus*. Cleveland, OH: Case Western Reserve Press, 1968.

Dobranski, Stephen and John Rumrich, eds., *Milton and Heresy*. Cambridge University Press, 1998.

Donne, John, *Complete Poems*, ed. A. J. A. Smith. Harmondsworth: Penguin, 1983.

Donnelly, Phillip, *Milton's Scriptural Reasoning*. Cambridge University Press, 2009.

Dzelzainis, Martin, 'Milton's Classical Republicanism', in David Armitage, Armand Hiny and Quentin Skinner, eds., *Milton and Republicanism*. Cambridge University Press, 1995, pp. 3–24.

'Milton's Politics', in *Cambridge Companion to Milton*, 2nd edn. Cambridge University Press, 1999, pp. 70–83.

'Republicanism', in Thomas N. Corns, *A Companion to Milton*. Oxford: Blackwell, 2003, pp. 294–308.

Edwards, Jonathan, *Basic Writings*, ed. Ola Elizabeth Winslow. New York: Signet, 1966.

Empson, William, *Milton's God*, 2nd edn. Cambridge University Press, 1981.

Escobedo, Andrew, 'The Invisible Nation: Church, State, and Schism in Milton's England', in David Loewenstein and Paul Stevens, eds., *Early Modern Nationalism and Milton's England*. University of Toronto Press, 2008, pp. 173–201.

Evans, J. Martin, '*Lycidas*', in Dennis Danielson, ed., *Cambridge Companion to Milton*, 2nd edn. Cambridge University Press, 1999, pp. 39–53.

Paradise Lost and the Genesis Tradition. Oxford: Clarendon Press, 1968.

Fallon, Robert, *Divided Empire: Milton's Political Imagery*. University Park, Pa.: Pennsylvania State University Press, 1995.

'*A Second Defence:* Milton's Critique of Cromwell?', *Milton Studies*, 29 (2000): 167–83.

'Milton in the Anarchy, 1659–1660: A Question of Consistency', *Studies in English Literature*, 21 (1991): 123–46.

Fallon, Stephen M., '"Elect Above the Rest": Theology as Self-Representation in Milton', in Stephen Dobranski and John Rumrich, eds., *Milton and Heresy*. Cambridge University Press, 1998, pp. 93–116.

Milton among the Philosophers. Ithaca, NY: Cornell University Press, 1991.

Milton's Peculiar Grace: Self-Representation and Authority. Ithaca, NY: Cornell University Press, 2007.

'"The Strangest Piece of Reason": Milton's *Tenure of Kings and Magistrates*', in Nicholas McDowell and Nigel Smith, eds., *Oxford Handbook of Milton*. Oxford University Press, 2009, pp. 241–51.

Ferne, Henry, *Conscience Satisfied: That there is no warrant for the Armes now taken up by Subjects*. Oxford, 1643.

Festa, Thomas, 'The Temptation of Athens and the Variorum *Paradise Regained*', *Huntington Library Quarterly*, 76 (spring 2013): 11–33.

Filmer, Sir Robert, *Observations on Mr Milton upon Salmasius,* in *Patriarcha and Other Writings*, ed. Johann P. Sommerville. Cambridge University Press, 1991.

Fincham, Kenneth, ed., *The Early Stuart Church*. Basingstoke: Macmillan, 1993.

Fish, Stanley, *How Milton Works*. Cambridge, Mass.: Harvard University Press, 2001.

Surprised by Sin: The Reader in Paradise Lost, 2nd edn. Basingstoke: Macmillan, 1997.

There's No Such Thing as Free Speech: And It's a Good Thing, Too. Oxford University Press, 1994.

Forsyth, Neil, 'Satan', in Louis Schwartz, ed., *Cambridge Companion to Paradise Lost*. Cambridge University Press, 2014, pp. 17–28.

The Satanic Epic. Princeton University Press, 2004.

Fowler, Alistair, 'Review of Gordon Campbell and Thomas N. Corns, *John Milton: Life, Work, and Thought*', *Milton Quarterly*, 44 (2010), 52-8.

Foxley, Rachel, '"Due Libertie and Proportiond Equalitie": Milton, Democracy and the Republican Tradition', *History of Political Thought*, 34 (winter 2013): 614–38.

The Levellers: Radical Political Thought in the English Revolution. Manchester University Press, 2013.

Friedman, Donald, '*Lycidas:* The Swain's Paideia', in C. A. Patrides, ed., *Milton's Lycidas: The Tradition and the Poem*. Columbia, Mo.: University of Missouri Press, 1983, pp. 281–302.

Gardner, Helen, *A Reading of Paradise Lost*. Oxford: Clarendon Press, 1965.

Glover, Samuel Dennis, 'The Putney Debates: Popular versus Elitist Republicanism', *Past & Present*, 164 (1999): 47–80.

Goodwin, John, *Anti-Cavalierisme; or, Truth Pleading as Well the Necessity, as the Lawfulness of this Present War* (1642), in William Haller, ed., *Tracts on Liberty in the Puritan Revolution*, 3 vols. New York: Columbia University Press, 1934, vol. II, pp. 217–69.

The Obstructors of Justice; or, A Defence of the Honourable Sentence Passed Upon the Late King. London, 1649.

Redemption Redeemed. London, 1651.

Right and Might Well Met. London, 1648.

Gossman, Ann, 'Milton's Samson as the Tragic Hero Purified by Trial', *Journal of English and Germanic Philology*, 61 (1962): 528–41.

Gregory, Tobias, 'The Political Messages of *Samson Agonistes*', *Studies in English Literature*, 50 (2010): 175–203.

Grossman, David, *Lion's Honey: The Myth of Samson*, trans. Stuart Schoffman. Edinburgh: Canongate, 2006.

Guibbory, Achsah, *Ceremony and Community from Herbert to Milton*. Cambridge University Press, 1998.

Christian Identity, Jews, and Israel in Seventeenth-Century England. Oxford University Press, 2010.

Haller, William, 'Hail Wedded Love', *ELH*, 13 (1946): 79–97.

ed., *Tracts on Liberty in the Puritan Revolution*, 3 vols. New York: Columbia University Press, 1934.

Hammond, Paul, *Milton and the People*. Oxford University Press, 2014.

Hammond, Paul and Blair Worden, eds., *John Milton: Life, Writing, Reputation*. Oxford University Press, 2010.

Harrington, James, *The Commonwealth of Oceana*, ed. J. G. A. Pocock. Cambridge University Press, 1992.

Haskin, Dayton, *Milton's Burden of Interpretation*. Philadelphia, Pa.: University of Pennsylvania Press, 1994.

Herbert, George, *Complete English Poems*, ed. John Tobin. London: Penguin, 1991.

Herman, Peter C., *Destabilizing Milton*. Basingstoke: Macmillan, 2005.

Herman, Peter C. and Elizabeth Sauer, eds., *The New Milton Criticism*. Cambridge University Press, 2012.

Hill, Christopher, 'The Definition of a Puritan', in Christopher Hill, *Society and Puritanism in Pre-revolutionary England*. London: Mercury Books, 1966, pp. 13–29.

Milton and the English Revolution. London: Faber, 1979.

Society and Puritanism in Pre-revolutionary England. London: Mercury Books, 1966.

The World Turned Upside Down. Harmondsworth: Penguin, 1972.

Hobbes, Thomas, *Behemoth; or, The Long Parliament*, ed. Paul Seaward. Oxford: Clarendon Press, 2010.

Leviathan, ed. Michael Oakeshott. Oxford: Basil Blackwell, 1960.

Howe, John, *The Reasonableness of God's Prescience of the Sins of Men*. London, 1677.

Hughes, Ann, *Gangraena and the Struggle for the English Revolution*. Oxford University Press, 2004.

Hunter, W. B., 'Milton on the Exaltation of the Son', *ELH*, 36 (1969): 215–31.

Visitation Unimplor'd: Milton and the Authorship of De Doctrina Christiana. Pittsburgh, Pa.: University of Duquesne Press, 1998.

Hunter, W. B., C. A. Patrides, and J. H. Adamson, *Bright Essence: Studies in Milton's Theology*. Salt Lake City, UT: University of Utah Press, 1971.

Johnson, Samuel, *The Lives of the Poets*, ed. Roger Lonsdale, 4 vols. Oxford: Clarendon Press, 2006.

Justa Edouardo King. Cambridge, 1638.

Kahn, Victoria, *Wayward Contracts*. Princeton University Press, 2004.

Kean, Margaret, '*Paradise Regained*', in Thomas N. Corns, *A Companion to Milton*. Oxford: Blackwell, 2003, pp. 429–43.

Keeble, N. H., 'Milton and Puritanism', in Thomas N. Corns, *A Companion to Milton*. Oxford: Blackwell, 2003, pp. 124–40.

'Milton's Christian Temper', in Paul Hammond and Blair Worden, eds., *John Milton: Life, Writings, Reputation*. Oxford University Press, 2010, pp. 107–24.

The Literary Culture of Nonconformity. Leicester University Press, 1987.

'Restoration Images of Milton and Bunyan', *Bunyan Studies*, 6 (1995–6): 6–33.

'Wilderness Exercises: Adversity, Temptation, and Trial in *Paradise Regained*', *Milton Studies*, 42 (2003): 86–105.

Kelley, Maurice, 'Milton's Debt to Wolleb's *Compendium Theologiae Christianae*', *PMLA*, 50 (1935): 156–65.

This Great Argument. Princeton University Press, 1941.

Kerrigan, William, *The Sacred Complex*. Cambridge, Mass.: Harvard University Press, 1983.

Killeen, Kevin, 'Chastising with Scorpions: Reading the Old Testament in Early Modern England', *Huntington Library Quarterly*, 73 (2010): 491–506.

'"Hanging Up Kings": The Political Bible in Early Modern England', *Journal of the History of Ideas*, 72 (2011): 549–70.

Knoppers, Laura Lunger, *Constructing Cromwell*. Cambridge University Press, 2000.

'England's Case: Contexts of the 1671 Poems', in Nicholas McDowell and Nigel Smith, eds., *Oxford Handbook of Milton*. Oxford University Press, 2009, pp. 571–88.

Historicizing Milton. Athens, Ga.: University of Georgia Press, 1994.

'Milton's *The Readie and Easie Way* and the English Jeremiad', in David Loewenstein and James Grantham Turner, eds., *Politics, Poetics, and Hermeneutics in Milton's Prose*. Cambridge University Press, 1990, pp. 211–25.

Lake, Peter, 'A Charitable Christian Hatred: The Godly and Their Enemies in the 1630s', in Christopher Durston and Jacqueline Eales, eds., *The Culture of English Puritanism*. Basingstoke: Macmillan, 1996, pp. 145–83.

'The Laudian Style: Order, Uniformity, and the Pursuit of the Beauty of Holiness', in Kenneth Fincham, ed., *The Early Stuart Church*. Basingstoke: Macmillan, 1993, pp. 161–85.

Lambe, Thomas, *The Fountaine of Free Grace Opened*. London, 1645.

Lamont, William, 'Pamphleteering, the Protestant Consensus and the English Revolution', in R. C. Richardson and G. M. Ridden, eds., *Freedom and the English Revolution*. Manchester University Press, 1986, pp. 72–92.

Lewalski, Barbara K., 'How Radical Was the Young Milton?', in Stephen Dobranski and John Rumrich, eds., *Milton and Heresy*. Cambridge University Press, 1998, pp. 49–72.

The Life of John Milton. Oxford: Blackwell, 2003.

'Milton and the *De Doctrina Christiana:* Evidences of Authorship', *Milton Studies*, 36 (1998): 203–28.

Milton's Brief Epic. London: Methuen, 1966.

Lewis, C. S., *A Preface to Paradise Lost*. New York: Oxford University Press, 1961.

Lieb, Michael, '"Our Living Dread": The God of *Samson Agonistes*', *Milton Studies*, 33 (1996): 3–25.

Theological Milton. Pittsburgh, Pa.: Duquesne University Press, 2006.

Lieb, Michael and John T. Shawcross, eds., *Achievements of the Left Hand: Essays on the Prose of John Milton*. Amherst, Mass.: University of Massachusetts Press, 1979.

Lilburne, John, *Londons Liberty in Chains Discovered*. London, 1646.

Regall Tyranny Discovered. London, 1647.

Lim, Walter, *John Milton, Radical Politics, and Biblical Republicanism*. Newark, Del.: University of Delaware Press, 2006.

Lindley, David, ed., *Court Masques*. Oxford University Press, 1998.

Loewenstein, David, *Milton and the Drama of History*. Cambridge University Press, 1990.

'Milton and the Poetics of Defense', in David Loewenstein and James Grantham Turner, eds., *Politics, Poetics, and Hermeneutics in Milton's Prose*. Cambridge University Press, 1990, pp. 171–92.

Representing Revolution in Milton and His Contemporaries. Cambridge University Press, 2001.

'Toleration and the Spectre of Heresy in Milton's England', in Sharon Achinstein and Elizabeth Sauer, eds., *Milton and Toleration*. Oxford University Press, 2007, pp. 45–71.

Loewenstein, David and Paul Stevens, eds., *Early Modern Nationalism and Milton's England*. University of Toronto Press, 2008.

Loewenstein, David and James Grantham Turner, eds., *Politics, Poetics, and Hermeneutics in Milton's Prose*. Cambridge University Press, 1990.

Ludlow, Edmund, *A Voyce from the Watch Tower, Part Five: 1660–1662*, ed. A. B. Worden. London: Royal Historical Society, 1978.

Luther, Martin, *A Commentary on the Epistle of St. Paul to the Galatians*. Edinburgh: Seeley, Burnside & Seeley, 1845.

MacCallum, Hugh, *Milton and the Sons of God*. University of Toronto Press, 1986.

McColley, Diane Kelsey, *Milton's Eve*. Urbana, Ill.: University of Illinois Press, 1983.

MacCulloch, Diarmaid, *Reformation: Europe's House Divided, 1490–1700*. London: Penguin, 2004.

McDowell, Nicholas, 'How Laudian Was the Young Milton?', *Milton Studies*, 52 (2011): 3–22.

'Ideas of Creation in the Writings of Richard Overton the Leveller and *Paradise Lost*', *Journal of the History of Ideas*, 66 (2005): 59–78.

McDowell, Nicholas and Nigel Smith, ed., *Oxford Handbook of Milton*. Oxford University Press, 2009.

McGuire, Maryann, *Milton's Puritan Masque*. Athens, Ga.: University of Georgia Press, 1983.

McLaren, Anne, 'Rethinking Republicanism: *Vindiciae, Contra Tyrannos* in Context', *Historical Journal*, 49 (2006): 23–52.

Machiavelli, Niccolò, *The Discourses*, ed. Bernard Crick. Harmondsworth: Penguin, 1979.

Mandelstam, Osip, *Selected Poems*, trans. Clarence Brown and W. S. Merwin. Harmondsworth: Penguin, 1977.

[Manley, Thomas], *Veni; Vidi. Vici: The Triumphs of the most Excellent & Illustrious, Oliver Cromwell*. London, 1652.

Marcus, Leah S., *The Politics of Mirth*. University of Chicago Press, 1989.

Martin, Catherine Gimelli, *Milton among the Puritans: The Case for Historical Revisionism*. Farnham: Ashgate, 2010.

'The Non-Puritan Ethics, Metaphysics, and Aesthetics of Milton's Spenserian Masque', *Milton Quarterly*, 37 (2003): 215–44.

ed., *Milton and Gender*. Cambridge University Press, 2004.

Martz, Louis L., *The Paradise Within*. New Haven, Conn.: Yale University Press, 1964.

Marvell, Andrew, *Poems*, ed. Nigel Smith. London: Pearson Longman, 2003.

Prose Works, ed. Annabel Patterson, Martin Dzelzainis, N. H. Keeble, and Nicholas von Maltzahn, 2 vols. New Haven, Conn.: Yale University Press, 2003.

Mercurius Politicus. 108, 24 June–July 1652.

Mill, John Stuart, *On Liberty and The Subjection of Women*, ed. Alan Ryan. London: Penguin, 2006.

Miller, Jeffrey Alan, 'Milton and the Conformable Puritanism of Richard Stock and Thomas Young', in Edward Jones, ed., *Young Milton*. Oxford University Press, 2013, pp. 72–101.

Milton, Anthony, *Catholic and Reformed*. Cambridge University Press, 1995.

Laudian and Royalist Polemic in Seventeenth-Century England. Manchester University Press, 2007.

Mohamed, Feisal, 'Confronting Religious Violence: Milton's *Samson Agonistes*', *PMLA*, 120 (2005): 327–34.

Moore, Jonathan, *English Hypothetical Universalism: John Preston and the Softening of Reformed Theology*. Grand Rapids, Mich., and Cambridge: Eerdmans, 2007.

Morrill, John, 'Cromwell and His Contemporaries', in John Morrill, ed., *Oliver Cromwell and the English Revolution*. London: Longman, 1995, pp. 259–81.

Mueller, Janel, 'Embodying Glory: The Apocalyptic Strain in Milton's *Of Reformation*', in David Loewenstein and James Grantham Turner, eds., *Politics, Poetics, and Hermeneutics in Milton's Prose*. Cambridge University Press, 1990, pp. 9–40.

Myers, Benjamin, *Milton's Theology of Freedom*. Berlin and New York: Gruyter, 2006.

'Prevenient Grace and Conversion in *Paradise Lost*', *Milton Quarterly*, 40 (2006): 20–36.

Nedham, Marchamont, *Anglia Liberata . . . an Additional Reply to All the Pretended Arguments*. London, 1651.

The Case of the Commonwealth, Stated. London, 1650.

The Excellencie of a Free-State, ed. Blair Worden. Indianapolis, Ind.: Liberty Press, 2011.

The True State of the Case of the Commonwealth. London, 1654.

Nelson, Eric, *The Hebrew Republic*. Cambridge, Mass.: Harvard University Press, 2010.

Newlyn, Lucy, *Paradise Lost and the Romanic Reader*. Oxford: Clarendon Press, 1993.

Norbrook, David, *Writing the English Republic*. Cambridge University Press, 1999.

Nuttall, Geoffrey, 'Milton's Churchmanship in 1659: His Letter to Jean de Labadie', *Milton Quarterly*, 35 (2001): 227–31.

The Holy Spirit in Puritan Faith and Experience. Oxford: Basil Blackwell, 1946.

Visible Saints. Oxford: Basil Blackwell, 1957.

Nyqist, Mary, 'The Genesis of Gendered Subjectivity in the Divorce Tracts and in *Paradise Lost*', in Mary Nyquist and Margaret W. Ferguson, eds., *Remembering Milton*. London and New York: Methuen, 1987, pp. 99–127.

Orgel, Stephen, 'The Case for Comus', *Representations*, 81 (2003): 31–45.

Overton, Richard, *An Appeale from the Degenerate Representative Body the Commons of England . . . to the Body Represented* (1647), in Don M. Wolfe, ed., *Leveller Manifestoes of the Puritan Revolution*. London and New York: Thomas Nelson, 1944, pp. 154–95.

An Arrow against All Tyrants. London, 1646.

Mans Mortalitie. 'Amsterdam', 1644.

The Hunting of the Foxes (1649), in Don M. Wolfe, ed., *Leveller Manifestoes of the Puritan Revolution*. London and New York: Thomas Nelson, 1944, pp. 355–83.

Palmer, Herbert, *The Glasse of Gods Providence toward His Faithfull Ones*. London, 1644.

Parker, William Riley, *Milton's Contemporary Reputation*. New York: Haskell House, 1971.
Parry, Graham and Joad Raymond, eds., *Milton and the Forms of Liberty*. Cambridge: D. S. Brewer, 2002.
Patrides, C. A., 'The Godhead in *Paradise Lost*: Dogma or Drama?', in W. B. Hunter, C. A. Patrides, and J. H. Adamson, *Bright Essence: Studies in Milton's Theology*. Salt Lake City, UT: University of Utah Press, 1971, pp. 71–7.
Milton and the Christian Tradition. Oxford: Clarendon Press, 1966.
ed., *Milton's Lycidas: The Tradition and the Poem*. Columbia, Mo.: University of Missouri Press, 1983.
Patterson, Annabel, *Marvell and the Civic Crown*. Princeton University Press, 1978.
'Milton, Marriage and Divorce', in Thomas N. Corns, *A Companion to Milton*. Oxford: Blackwell, 2003, pp. 279–93.
'No Meer Amatorious Novel?', in David Loewenstein and James Grantham Turner, eds., *Politics, Poetics, and Hermeneutics in Milton's Prose*. Cambridge University Press, 1990, pp. 85–101.
Perkins, William, *A Christian and Plaine Treatise of the Manner and Order of Predestination, and of the Largenes of God's Grace*. London, 1606.
Pocock, J. G. A., *Virtue, Commerce, and History*. Cambridge University Press, 1985.
Poole, William, Letter on Gordon Campbell and Thomas N. Corns, *John Milton: Life, Work, and Thought, Times Literary Supplement*, 11 March 2009, p. 6.
Milton and the Idea of the Fall. Cambridge University Press, 2005.
The Protector . . . Unvailed. London, 1655.
Quint, David, *Epic and Empire: Politics and Generic Form from Virgil to Milton*. Princeton University Press, 1993.
Radzinowicz, Mary Ann, 'How Milton Read the Bible: The Case of *Paradise Regained*', in *Cambridge Companion to Milton*, 2nd edn. Cambridge University Press, 1999, pp. 202–18.
'The Politics of *Paradise Lost*', in Kevin Sharpe and Steven N. Zwicker, eds., *Politics of Discourse*. Berkeley, Calif.: University of California Press, 1998, pp. 204–29.
Toward Samson Agonistes. Princeton University Press, 1986.
Rajan, Balachandra, 'Samson Has Quit Himself like Samson', *Milton Quarterly*, 41 (2007): 1–11.
'To Which is Added *Samson Agonistes*', in Balachandra Rajan, ed., *The Prison and the Pinnacle*. University of Toronto Press, 1973, pp. 82–110.
ed., *The Prison and the Pinnacle*. University of Toronto Press, 1973.
Revard, Stella P., 'Eve and the Doctrine of Responsibility in *Paradise Lost*', *PMLA*, 88 (1973): 69–78.
Milton and the Tangles of Neaera's Hair. Columbia, Mo.: University of Missouri Press, 1997.
The War in Heaven. Ithaca, NY: Cornell University Press, 1980.

Robins, Harry F., *If This Be Heresy: A Study of Milton and Origen*. Urbana, Ill.: University of Illinois Press, 1963.

Robinson, Henry, *Liberty of Conscience* (1644), in William Haller, ed., *Tracts on Liberty in the Puritan Revolution*, 3 vols. New York: Columbia University Press, 1934, vol. III, pp. 105–78.

Rogers, John, *The Matter of Revolution*. Ithaca, NY: Cornell University Press, 1996.

'The Political Theology of Milton's Heaven', in Peter C. Herman and Elizabeth Sauer, eds., *The New Milton Criticism*. Cambridge University Press, 2012, pp. 68–84.

'The Secret of *Samson Agonistes*', *Milton Studies*, 33 (1996): 111–32.

Rosenblatt, Jason, *Torah and Law in Paradise Lost*. Princeton University Press, 1994.

Rumrich, John P., 'Milton's Arianism: Why It Matters', in Stephen Dobranski and John Rumrich, eds., *Milton and Heresy*. Cambridge University Press, 1998, pp. 75–92.

Rutherford, Samuel, *Lex, Rex: The Law and the Prince*. London, 1644.

Samuel, Irene, 'The Dialogue in Heaven: A Reconsideration of *Paradise Lost*, III, 1–417', *PMLA*, 72 (1957): 601–11.

'Milton on Learning and Wisdom', *PMLA*, 64 (1949): 708–23.

'*Samson Agonistes* as Tragedy', in Joseph Wittreich, *Calm of Mind*. Cleveland, OH: Case Western Reserve Press, 1971, pp. 235–57.

'The Regaining of Paradise', in Balachandra Rajan, ed., *The Prison and the Pinnacle*. University of Toronto Press, 1973, pp. 111–34.

Sasek, Lawrence A., 'The Drama of *Paradise Lost*, Books XI and XII', in Arthur Barker, ed., *Milton: Modern Essays in Criticism*. New York: Oxford University Press, 1965, pp. 341–56.

Sauer, Elizabeth, *Milton, Toleration, and Nationhood*. Cambridge University Press, 2014.

Schwartz, Louis, ed., *Cambridge Companion to Paradise Lost*. Cambridge University Press, 2014.

Schwartz, Regina M., 'Milton on the Bible', in Thomas N. Corns, ed., *A Companion to Milton*. Oxford: Blackwell, 2003, pp. 37–54.

Remembering and Repeating: On Milton's Theology and Poetics. University of Chicago Press, 1993.

'*Samson Agonistes:* The Force of Justice and the Violence of Idolatry', in Nicholas McDowell and Nigel Smith, eds., *Oxford Handbook of Milton*. Oxford University Press, 2009, pp. 632–48.

The Curse of Cain: The Violent Legacy of Monotheism. University of Chicago Press, 1997.

Schwarz-Bart, André, *The Last of the Just*, trans. Stephen Becker. Harmondsworth: Penguin, 1977.

Scripture and Reason Pleaded for Defensive Armes. London, 1643.

Sedgwick, William, *A Second View of the Army Remonstrance*. London, 1649.

Serjeantson, R. W., '*Samson Agonistes* and "Single Rebellion"', in Nicholas McDowell and Nigel Smith, eds., *Oxford Handbook of Milton*. Oxford University Press, 2009, pp. 613–31.

[Sexby, Edward], *Killing Noe Murder*. London, 1657.

Shakespeare, William, *The Merchant of Venice*, ed. John Drakakis. London: Arden Shakespeare, 2010.

Much Ado about Nothing, ed. A. R. Humphreys. London: Arden Shakespeare, 1981.

Shanley, Mary Lyndon, 'Marriage Contract and Social Contract in Seventeenth-Century Political Thought', *Western Political Quarterly*, 32 (1979): 79–91.

Shelley, Percy Bysshe, *Shelley's Poetry and Prose*, ed. Donald H. Reiman and Sharon B. Powers. New York: Norton Critical Editions, 1979.

Shuger, Debora, 'Milton's Religion: The Early Years', *Milton Quarterly*, 46 (2012): 13–53.

Shullenberger, William, *Lady in the Labyrinth: Milton's Comus as Initiation*. Madison, Wis.: Fairleigh Dickinson University Press, 2008.

Simpson, Ken, *Spiritual Architecture and Paradise Regained*. Pittsburgh, Pa.: Duquesne University Press, 2007.

Sims, James H., 'Jesus and Satan as Readers of Scripture in *Paradise Regained*', *Milton Studies*, 32 (1996): 187–215.

Sirluck, Ernest, 'Milton's Political Thought: The First Cycle', *Modern Philology*, 61 (1964): 209–24.

Skinner, Quentin, 'John Milton and the Politics of Slavery', in Graham Parry and Joad Raymond, eds., *Milton and the Forms of Liberty*. Cambridge: D. S. Brewer, 2002, pp. 1–22.

Liberty before Liberalism. Cambridge University Press, 1998.

The Foundations of Modern Political Thought, 2 vols. Cambridge University Press, 1978.

Smith, Nigel, '*Areopagitica:* Voicing Contexts, 1643–44', in David Loewenstein and James Grantham Turner, eds., *Politics, Poetics, and Hermeneutics in Milton's Prose*. Cambridge University Press, 1990, pp. 103–22.

Literature and Revolution in England, 1640–1660. New Haven, Conn.: Yale University Press, 1994.

Sommerville, J. P., *Politics and Ideology in England, 1603–1640*. London: Longman, 1992.

Sophocles, *Oedipus at Colonus*, trans. Robert Fitzgerald, in *The Complete Greek Tragedies*, ed. David Grene and Richmond Lattimore, 4 vols. University of Chicago Press, 1959.

Spenser, Edmund, *The Faerie Queene*, ed. Thomas P. Roche. London: Penguin, 1987.

Spurr, John, *English Puritanism, 1603–1689*. Basingstoke: Macmillan, 1998.

Steadman, John M., '"Faithful Champion": The Theological Basis of Milton's Hero of Faith', *Anglia*, 77 (1959): 12–28.

'"Passions Well Imitated": Rhetoric and Poetics in the Preface to *Samson Agonistes*', in Joseph Wittreich, *Calm of Mind*. Cleveland, OH: Case Western Reserve Press, 1971, pp. 175–207.

Stein, Arnold, 'The War in Heaven', in *Answerable Style*. Seattle, Wash.: University of Washington Press, 1967, pp. 17–37.

Stevens, Paul, '"Leviticus Thinking" and the Rhetoric of Early Modern Colonialism', *Criticism*, 35 (1993): 441–61.

'Milton's "Renunciation" of Cromwell: The Problem of Raleigh's *Cabinet-Council*', *Modern Philology*, 98 (2001): 363–92.

'The Pre-secular Politics of *Paradise Lost*', in Louis Schwartz, ed., *Cambridge Companion to Paradise Lost*. Cambridge University Press, 2014, pp. 94–108.

Strier, Richard, 'Milton's Fetters; or, Why Eden is Better than Heaven', in Peter C. Herman and Elizabeth Sauer, eds., *The New Milton Criticism*. Cambridge University Press, 2012, pp. 20–34.

Teskey, Gordon, 'Dead Shepherd: Milton's *Lycidas*', in Richard du Rocher and Margaret Olofson Thickstun, eds., *Milton's Rival Hermeneutics*, Pittsburgh, Pa.: University of Duquesne Press, 2012, pp. 31–56.

Thomas, Keith, *Religion and the Decline of Magic*. Harmondsworth: Penguin, 1973.

Tillyard, E. M. W., *Milton*. London: Chatto & Windus, 1930.

Studies in Milton. London: Chatto & Windus, 1951.

Toland, John, *The Life of John Milton*. Amsterdam, 1698.

Tolmie, Murray, *The Triumph of the Saints*. Cambridge University Press, 1977.

Turner, James Grantham, *One Flesh*. Oxford: Clarendon Press, 1987.

'The Aesthetics of Divorce', in Catherine Gimelli Martin. ed., *Milton and Gender*. Cambridge University Press, 2004, pp. 34–52.

Tyacke, Nicholas, *Anti-Calvinists: The Rise of English Arminianism, c. 1590–1640*. Oxford: Clarendon Press, 1982.

'Puritanism, Arminianism and Counter-Revolution', in Conrad Russell, ed., *The Origins of the English Civil War*, London: Macmillan, 1973, pp. 119–43.

Vane, Sir Henry, *A Needful Corrective*. London, 1659.

Vaughan, Henry, *Works*, ed. L. C. Martin. Oxford: Clarendon Press, 1914.

Vindiciae contra Tyrannos [A Defence of Liberty against Tyrants]. London, 1648.

von Maltzahn, Nicholas, *Milton's History of Britain: Republican Historiography in the English Revolution*. Oxford: Clarendon Press, 1991.

Waddington, Raymond B., *Looking into Providences: Designs and Trials in Paradise Lost*. University of Toronto Press, 2012.

Waldock, A. J. A., *Paradise Lost and Its Critics*. Cambridge University Press, 1947.

Walker, Clement, *Anarchia Anglicana: Or the History of Independency*. The Second Part. London, 1649.

Walker, William, *Antiformalist, Unrevolutionary, Illiberal Milton*. Farnham: Ashgate, 2014.

Paradise Lost and Republican Tradition from Aristotle to Machiavelli. Turnhout,: Brepols, 2009.

Waller, Edmund, *A Panegyrick to My Lord Protector*. London, 1655.

To the King, upon His Majesties Happy Return. London, 1660.

Walsham, Alexandra, *Providence in Early Modern England*. Oxford University Press, 2001.

Walwyn, William, *The Bloody Project; or, A Discovery of the New Designe, in the Present War* (1649), in *The Writings of William Walwyn*, ed. Jack R.

McMichael and Barbara Taft. Athens, Ga.: University of Georgia Press, 1989, pp. 294–307.
The Power of Love, in *The Writings of William Walwyn*, ed. Jack R. McMichael and Barbara Taft. Athens, Ga.: University of Georgia Press, 1989, pp. 78–96.
Wase, Christopher, *Electra of Sophocles … With an Epilogue*. The Hague, 1649.
Wheeler, Elizabeth Skerpan, 'Early Political Prose', in Thomas N. Corns, *A Companion to Milton*. Oxford: Blackwell, 2003, pp. 263–78.
[Wildman, John], *A Call to all the Souldiers of the Armie*. London, 1647.
Declaration of the Free-Born People. London, 1654.
Williams, Arnold, *The Common Expositor*. Chapel Hill, NC: University of North Carolina Press, 1948.
Williams, Roger, *The Bloudy Tenent, of Persecution, for cause of Conscience*. London, 1644.
Wittreich, Joseph, *Interpreting Samson Agonistes*. Princeton University Press, 1986.
Shifting Contexts. Pittsburgh, Pa.: Duquesne University Press, 2002.
ed., *Calm of Mind*. Cleveland, OH: Case Western Reserve Press, 1971.
Wolfe, Don M., ed., *Leveller Manifestoes of the Puritan Revolution*. London and New York: Thomas Nelson, 1944.
Wood, Derek N. C., *Exiled from Light: Divine Law, Morality, and Violence in Milton's Samson Agonistes*. University of Toronto Press, 2001.
Woodhouse, A. S. P., 'The Argument of Milton's *Comus*' and '*Comus* Once More', in John S. Diekhoff, ed., *A Maske at Ludlow: Essays on Milton's Comus*. Cleveland, OH: Case Western Reserve Press, 1968, pp. 17–42, 72–7.
Puritanism and Liberty, 2nd edn. London: Dent, 1966.
Woolrych, Austin, 'Milton and Cromwell: "A Short but Scandalous Night of Interruption"', in Michael Lieb and John T. Shawcross, eds., *Achievements of the Left Hand: Essays on the Prose of John Milton*. Amherst, Mass.: University of Massachusetts Press, 1979, pp. 185–218.
Worden, Blair, *God's Instruments: Political Conduct in the England of Oliver Cromwell*. Oxford University Press, 2012.
'John Milton and Oliver Cromwell', in Ian Gentles, John Morrill and Blair Worden, eds., *Soldiers, Writers and Statesmen of the English Revolution*. Cambridge University Press, 1998, pp. 243–64.
Literature and Politics in Cromwellians England. Oxford University Press, 2007.
'Milton and Marchamont Nedham', in David Armitage, Armand Hiny and Quentin Skinner, eds., *Milton and Republicanism*. Cambridge University Press, 1995, pp. 156–80.
'Milton, *Samson Agonistes*, and the Restoration', in Gerald MacLean, ed., *Culture and Society in the Stuart Restoration*. Cambridge University Press, 1995, pp. 111–36.
'Milton's Republicanism and the Tyranny of Heaven', in Gisela Beck, Quentin Skinner and Maurizio Virioli, eds., *Machiavelli and Republicanism*. Cambridge University Press, 1990, pp. 225–45.

Index

Lightning Source UK Ltd.
Milton Keynes UK
UKHW020951200919
350124UK00022B/563/P

9 781316 607114